Understanding
ROBERT MUSIL

Understanding Modern
European and Latin American
Literature

James Hardin, *Series Editor*

volumes on

Ingeborg Bachmann
Samuel Beckett
Thomas Bernhard
Johannes Bobrowski
Heinrich Böll
Italo Calvino
Albert Camus
Elias Canetti
Camilo José Cela
Céline
Julio Cortázar
Isak Dinesen
José Donoso
Friedrich Dürrenmatt
Rainer Werner Fassbinder
Max Frisch
Federico García Lorca
Gabriel García Márquez
Juan Goytisolo
Günter Grass
Gerhart Hauptmann
Christoph Hein

Hermann Hesse
Eugène Ionesco
Uwe Johnson
Milan Kundera
Primo Levi
John McGahern
Robert Musil
Boris Pasternak
Octavio Paz
Luigi Pirandello
Graciliano Ramos
Erich Maria Remarque
Alain Robbe-Grillet
Joseph Roth
Jean-Paul Sartre
W. G. Sebald
Claude Simon
Mario Vargas Llosa
Peter Weiss
Franz Werfel
Christa Wolf

UNDERSTANDING

ROBERT
MUSIL

ALLEN THIHER

THE UNIVERSITY OF SOUTH CAROLINA PRESS

Published by the University of South Carolina Press
Columbia, South Carolina 29208

www.sc.edu/uscpress

Manufactured in the United States of America

18 17 16 15 14 13 12 11 10 09   10 9 8 7 6 5 4 3 2 1

Library of Congress Cataloging-in-Publication Data

Thiher, Allen, 1941–
    Understanding Robert Musil / Allen Thiher.
        p. cm. — (Understanding modern European and Latin American literature)
    Includes bibliographical references and index.
    ISBN 978-1-57003-836-5 (cloth : alk. paper)
    1. Musil, Robert, 1880–1942—Criticism and interpretation. I. Title.
    PT2625.U8Z927 2009
    833'.912—dc22

                                                                          2009005084

This book was printed on Glatfelter Natures, a recycled paper with 30 percent
postconsumer waste content.

To Irma

Contents

Editor's Preface

Understanding Modern European and Latin American Literature has been planned as a series of guides for undergraduate and graduate students and non-academic readers. Like the volumes in its companion series *Understanding Contemporary American Literature,* these books provide introductions to the lives and writings of prominent modern authors and explicate their most important works.

Modern literature makes special demands, and this is particularly true of foreign literature, in which the reader must contend not only with unfamiliar, often arcane artistic conventions and philosophical concepts, but also with the handicap of reading the literature in translation. It is a truism that the nuances of one language can be rendered in another only imperfectly (and this problem is especially acute in fiction), but the fact that the works of European and Latin American writers are situated in a historical and cultural setting quite different from our own can be as great a hindrance to the understanding of these works as the linguistic barrier. For this reason the *UMELL* series emphasizes the sociological and historical background of the writers treated. The philosophical and cultural traditions peculiar to a given culture may be particularly important for an understanding of certain authors, and these are taken up in the introductory chapter and also in the discussion of those works to which this information is relevant. Beyond this the books treat the specifically literary aspects of the author under discussion and attempt to explain the complexities of contemporary literature lucidly. The books are conceived as introductions to the authors covered, not as comprehensive analyses. They do not provide detailed summaries of plot because they are meant to be used in conjunction with the books they treat, not as a substitute for study of the original works. The purpose of the books is to provide information and judicious literary assessment of the major works in the most compact, readable form. It is our hope that the *UMELL* series will help increase knowledge and understanding of European and Latin American cultures and will serve to make the literature of those cultures more accessible.

J. H.

Acknowledgments

This book on Musil is the outcome of years of thinking about modern literature, science, and the relationships between the two, not to mention the connections of science and literature with politics and ethics. Several generous research leaves granted by the University of Missouri in the course of my career there have played a role in the genesis of this book, as well as a year as a scholar at Claire Hall at Cambridge University. Help from colleagues and friends, there and elsewhere, has played an essential role too, as well as the editors at the University of South Carolina Press, especially the ever-active James Hardin. Now an emeritus, I look back on this book as a capstone and hope that it can be considered as a tribute to a writer who gave himself to the institution of literature that I also hope to have served for the past forty years. In this regard my greatest debt is to all those who have helped keep Musil's work alive in the most dire times and have continued to do so.

Chronology

1880   Robert Musil is born on November 6 to the engineer Albert Musil and his wife, Hermine, née Bergauer, in the Austrian city of Klagenfurt.

1881   Family moves to Komotau (in today's Czech Republic), where Heinrich Reiter becomes a lifelong live-in friend of the family. This arrangement was presumably some kind of ménage à trois.

1882   Father takes position as director a technical school in Steyr (Upper Austria).

1891   Father takes position as professor of engineering at the Technical University in Brünn (today Brno in the Czech Republic).

1892   Musil begins study at the Militär-Unterrealschule (military secondary school) in Eisenstadt (Burgenland, Austria).

1894   Begins study at the Militär-Oberrealschule (upper-level military secondary school) at Mährisch-Weisskirchen (today Hranice in the Czech Republic). Visits prostitutes.

1897   Begins study at the Technische Militärakademie in Vienna but stops studies leading to military career after three months.

1898   Matriculates in engineering at his father's technical university in Brünn.

1901   Passes the state examination for mechanical engineering. In May submits for publication the now-lost manuscript of poems, "Paraphrasen." Begins affair with Herma Dietz. Volunteers for one year of military service.

1902   Diary entry in March suggests Musil is being treated for syphilis. Becomes assistant in October in an engineering laboratory in Stuttgart. Studies Greek and Latin to prepare for the *Reifeprufung,* or exit examination from secondary school, needed for study at a German university. Begins writing *Die Verwirrungen des Zöglings Törless* (*Young Törless*).

1903   Matriculates at Friedrich-Wilhelm University in Berlin for graduate study in psychology and philosophy. Accompanied to Berlin by Herma Dietz.

1904   In June passes secondary school exit exam. Exhausted by study, he is diagnosed with a nervous heart condition, for which rest is prescribed. Returns to graduate study in the fall semester.

1905   Finishes *Young Törless*. Continues studies.

1906   Herma Dietz has miscarriage, perhaps result of syphilis. Musil meets his future wife, Martha Marcovaldi, née Heimann. Begins doctoral dissertation and corrects proofs of *Young Törless,* which is published in October. Novel is well reviewed by the important critic Alfred Kerr in December.

1907   Herma Dietz dies in Berlin.

1908   Finishes doctoral thesis, *Beitrag zur Beurteilung der Lehren Machs* (*On Mach's Theories*). Publishes in *Hyperion* "Das Verzauberten Haus" ("The Enchanted House"), an early version of "Die Versuchung der stillen Veronika" ("The Temptation of Quiet Veronika").

1909   Musil refuses academic position at the university at Graz.

1911   Through father's intervention Musil receives position at the library of the Technical University of Vienna. First essay, "Das Unanständige und Kranke in der Kunst" ("The Obscene and Pathological in Art"), published in *Pan*. Marries Martha in April. Publishes *Vereinigungen* (*Unions*), containing "Die Vollendung der Liebe" ("The Perfecting of Love") and "The Temptation of Quiet Veronika."

1912   "Politik in Österreich" ("Politics in Austria") in *Losen Vogel.*

1913   Diagnosis of cardiac neurosis (heart palpitations) gives Musil six weeks of convalescence. "Der mathematische Mensch" ("The Mathematical Man") in *Losen Vogel.*

1914   Takes position as editor at the prestigious journal *Die Neue Rundschau* in Berlin. Called up in August after the general mobilization for war and sent to serve in South Tyrol as an officer.

1916   In Bolzano as editor of a military newspaper, *Tyroler Soldatenzeitung*. Bad health during this period.

1917   Musil's father is made a noble, making Musil Robert "Edler von Musil."

1918   Musil in Vienna as editor of the military journal *Heimat*. Discharged from military duty on December 15.

1919   Working in the press service of the Foreign Ministry. Joins a socialist society called Katakombe. Travels to Berlin in failed attempt negotiate new position with the *Neue Rundschau,* Musil will make frequent stays in Berlin until late 1933.

1920   Named "expert counselor" in the second section of the Austrian War Ministry.

1921   Publication of his play *Die Schwärmer* (*The Enthusiasts*). Begins writing theater criticism. Moves into an apartment in Vienna on Rasumofskygasse 20 (third district), where, when in Vienna, he will live until 1938. (Many of his papers were destroyed there by bombing in the Second World War.) "Grigia" published in the *Neue Merkur.*

1922   Musil an active member in the Schutzverband der deutscher Schriftsteller (Protective Association of German Writers) in Vienna. Publishes "Tonka."

1923   "Die Portugiesin" ("The Lady from Portugual") published by Rowohlt, his publisher for the next decade. His position in the War Ministry is cut. Receives the prestigious Kleist Prize for *The Enthusiasts.* First performance of his farce in three acts, *Vinzenz und die Freudin bedeutender Männer* ("Vinzenz and the Woman Friend of Important Men") in Berlin.

1924   Both of Musil's parents die in the course of the year. Publishes *Drei Frauen* (*Three Women*), containing "Grigia," "The Lady from Portugal," and "Tonka." Receives advance from Rowohlt for a novel then titled "Die Zwillingsschwester" ("The Twin Siblings"). Reads Thomas Mann's *The Magic Mountain.*

1925   In Vienna joins protest against the murder of a Jewish writer. In Berlin participates in founding the Gruppe 1925, a group of politically active writers.

1926   Publishes interview with Oskar Fontana about the work in progress. In Berlin Musil recovers from a gall-bladder operation. Publishes "Triëdere" in *Berlin Tageblatt.*

1927   Gives public lecture, "Rede zur Rilk-Feier" ("Address at the Memorial Service for Rilke"), in Berlin. Signs declaration of support for Social Democrats in the Austrian elections. Reads on the radio in Berlin from the unpublished novel, now called *Der Mann ohne Eigenschaften* (*The Man without Qualities*). Begins several months of therapy for writer's block with Dr. Hugo Lukàs (a follower of Adler).

1928   Publishes "Die Amsel" ("The Blackbird") in the *Neue Rundschau.*

1929   Over Musil's protests first performance of truncated version of *The Enthusiasts* in Berlin. Attacks of cardiac neurosis. Musil awarded the 1930 Gerhard Hauptmann Prize.

1930   Publishes the first volume of *The Man without Qualities.*

1931   Publishes "Der bedrohte Ödipus" in *Querschnitt*. For much of the next two years lives in the Pension Stern on the Kurfürstendamm in Berlin.

1932   Foundation of a benevolent Musil-Gesellschaft (Musil Association) that will last only a few months. Publishes second volume of *The Man without Qualities,* containing the incomplete part 3.

1933   Prussian Academy for the Arts gives Musil a grant on the day Hitler takes power (January 30, 1933). Musil leaves Berlin in May to return to Vienna with his Jewish wife. Opposes fascists in the split of the Austrian PEN Club into fascist and antifascist factions.

1934   Foundation of another association to assist Musil financially in Vienna. Gives lecture in Vienna, "Der Dichter in dieser Zeit" ("The Serious Writer in Our Time"), defending the rights of the individual.

1935   Gives lecture in Paris at an antifascist congress in defense of culture. Publishes *Der Nachlass zu Lebzeiten* (*Posthumous Papers of a Living Author*) with the publisher Humanitas Verlag in Zurich.

1936   Suffers stoke while swimming.

1937   Public lecture *Über die Dummheit* in Vienna. After joining the Austrian state political party, Musil is nonetheless unsuccessful with an application for a state pension.

1938   Musil is correcting proofs of twenty additional chapters of part 3 of *The Man without Qualities* when the Nazis take over Austria in March. Musil and his wife go to Zurich five months later in September. Nazis place on their list of harmful books *The Man without Qualities* and *Posthumous Papers of a Living Author.*

1939   Moves to Geneva. Helped by the Swiss pastor Robert Lejeune and the sculptor Fritz Wotruba.

1940   All Musil's works are banned by the Third Reich.

1942   Dies of a stroke on April 15 in Geneva.

Abbreviations and Editions Cited

All references to Musil's works are taken from the *Gesammelte Werke in neun Bändern,* edited by Adolf Frisé (Reinbek: Rowohlt, 1978–1981). References are made to the individual volume and to the page. Translations are my own. Other abbreviations of quoted works are as follows:

Briefe   *Briefe 1901–1942,* 2 vols., edited by Adolf Frisé with assistance of Murray G. Hall (Reinbek: Rowohlt, 1981). Musil's letters.

TB   *Tagebücher,* 2 vols., edited by Adolf Frisé (Reinbek: Rowohlt, 1983). Musil's diaries.

BzM   *Beitrag zur Beurteilung der Lehren Machs* (Reinbek: Rowolht, 1980). Reprint of 1908 edition of the doctoral dissertation.

Understanding
ROBERT MUSIL

CHAPTER 1

Life and Career

In this chapter I hope to present a short biographical guide that will allow the reader to enter directly into Musil's published work.[1] Biography can be only the beginning of understanding a writer's work, and my interpretations of Musil's work also depend on placing his life into a meaningful historical context. I will draw on his biography when it seems useful for interpretation, but my thesis in this and subsequent chapters is that Musil's work can best be understood by situating his life in the history of the culture and the literature from which the works derive. Musil's works are reactions to the major events in the history of Europe that he personally experienced, which is to say, the First World War, the decline and fall of the Austrian empire, the advent of fascism, and, more generally, the all-embracing development of modernity. This historical framework is present, implicitly and explicitly, throughout this study of Musil's fiction, plays, and essays.

Musil was a writer's writer, who drew widely on the history of European culture in his quest to create meaning in his fictional works and essays. He self-consciously saw himself as a writer who might help to give new direction to European culture at a time of permanent unresolved crisis. Musil's recurrent stance was to view the history of European culture without nostalgia as he experimented with ways by which that culture might be inflected in new directions. His works are thus intentionally complex in the way they interact with the increasingly catastrophic historical context in which he found himself. If most modernists were self-conscious about the cultural inheritance that determined their work, few were as self-conscious as Musil of being immersed in a history that they wanted to transform.

Robert Musil was born in peaceful times, on November 6, 1880, in the city of Klagenfurt in southern Austria in the province of Carinthia. He grew up knowing the bourgeois prosperity of a German-language family living in what was one of the major European powers, the Austro-Hungarian Empire. His father, Alfred, was an engineer, and his mother, Hermine, née Bergauer, came from a bourgeois family. In 1881 his family moved to Komotau in Bohemia, then a year later to Steyr in Upper Austria, where Alfred took a position as director of a technical school. Apparently Musil's mother and father began in Komotau a ménage à trois that existed throughout Musil's childhood; Hermine began a relation with another engineer, who moved in with the family. This arrangement continued even after the family moved in 1891 to Brünn in Moravia, when Musil was eleven, after his father took a position as a professor at the Deutsche Technische Hochschule, the equivalent of a university for science and engineering. The ambiguities about eroticism that play a significant role in Musil's work may well have found a first source in his early family life.

The fact that Komotau and Brünn, now Brno, are both in today's Czech Republic underscores that Musil was born into a multicultural and multilingual empire. To be sure, the German-speaking aristocracy and middle class held most of the key positions of power and authority in that part of the empire not reserved for Hungary. Shaken by the nationalist uprisings of 1848, and by its defeat by the new German Reich in 1866, Austria at the time of Musil's birth was still the center of power in an amalgamation of states and ethnic groups that, as an empire, was one of the last major repositories of traditional aristocratic and military values in Europe. In spite of the rise of a liberal middle class after 1848, aristocratic absolutism was the ideological glue that held this doddering empire together, and perhaps even more so as the nineteenth century came to an end. It was an antiquated state in which a German professor's son such as Robert Musil might consider a career as a military officer to be a crowning achievement—before deciding to become an engineer by studying at the university at which his father held a professorship. Austria was, moreover, an empire in which a professor such as Musil's father could be ennobled for his service. Military and aristocratic values were of supreme significance in the empire, even though its capital, Vienna, was the home of avant-garde modernity.

Musil was trained to become a military officer. From 1892 to 1894 he was a student at a Militär-Unterrealschule in Eisenstadt and then from 1894 to 1897 at a Miltär-Oberrealschule in Mährisch-Weisskirchen, the latter offering the equivalent of a secondary education at a military academy. The military academy provided him with the material he transformed into his first novel, *Die Verwirrungen des Zöglings Törless* (*Young Törless*), published in 1906. His experience there first gave him insight into the kind of minds that kept the empire together, and moreover, it acquainted him, without his knowing it at the time, with those who would opt for fascism in a not-so-distant future. After study at these junior and senior military academies, the seventeen-year-old Musil spent a few fall months in 1897 in the Technische Militärakademie in Vienna. The course of study at this military school, leading to a military career, was not to his taste, and he decided to return home to study engineering at Brünn in 1898.

Henceforth Musil would lead a life of intense and varied intellectual activity: preparing for engineering examinations; making his first attempts at writing; reading a wide range of authors, from Friedrich Nietzsche, Ralph Waldo Emerson, and Knut Hamsun to Maurice Maeterlinck, Gabriele D'Annunzio, and Fyodor Dostoyevsky; and engaging in sports. This list suggests what a complex young man Musil was: at once initiated into military and aristocratic values but rejecting them as a way of life, he found himself drawn to technology, science, philosophy, and, above all, literature.

Completing his engineering examinations in 1901, Musil did military service from October of that year until September 1902. It was during this year of volunteer service that he began writing *Young Törless*. He then spent the academic year 1902–3 as a laboratory assistant in mechanical engineering at the Technical University of Stuttgart, or so Musil said in a curriculum vitae published in 1908.[2] By all accounts he was unhappy with the provincialism of Stuttgart; and in 1903 Musil left for Berlin to begin a doctorate in psychology at the Friedrich-Wilhelm University. This decision may seem rather surprising after his study of engineering. However, his graduate studies in Berlin were, by contemporary standards, as much in philosophy as in the study of psychology. Moreover, they also included secondary fields in physics and mathematics, fields for which his studies in Brünn had prepared him well. However, his scientific studies in Austria had not included Greek and Latin, and he was obliged to prepare for the German secondary school exit examination so as to be able to continue his studies in Berlin. He successfully passed the examination in June 1904, but the preparation, on top of his other studies, left him exhausted. As his diaries show, he retained an interest in classical studies that seems to have grown as he got older.

Musil was convinced throughout his life that no intellectual activity that did not take science into account could be relevant to the modern world. Yet he became a writer, not a scientist, though one bent on reconciling literature with science. With his professional training in the sciences, he was equipped to understand well the difficulty involved in relating science to humanistic learning. As his career unfolded, he became increasingly convinced that it was imperative to meld literature and ethics with science in order to create some kind of meaningful whole. As *The Man without Qualities* demonstrates, this became one the major goals of Musil's writing. In retrospect it might thus appear that he had set out to educate himself precisely for this task. However, it would not be accurate to think that Musil was systematically as a young man mastering the areas of expertise necessary to understand the relationships of science, morality, and art. Rather, his was an intense but tentative process of education in which he groped about and experimented continually to find the mix that might satisfy him while he worried at the same time about how he might earn a living.

In going to Berlin in 1903 Musil had decided to pursue his intellectual and creative goals by leaving the provincialism he found in the Austro-Hungarian Empire. He wanted to pursue science and literature in what undoubtedly appeared to him to be the leading center of German modernity. Interestingly enough, most modern historians would probably accord this leading role to Vienna—but not Musil. He was far from embracing Austrian nationalism or from feeling any closeness to the parochialism he so well portrays in his fictional work and essays. However, after finishing his studies in Berlin, he found himself obliged by finances to return to Vienna in 1910. His father did not want to continue supporting Musil. Therefore, he took a position in a library that his father had arranged for him. One gets a sense of what his return to Vienna meant at the time to Musil from his diaries. Shortly after his return he described to himself his "opposition" to Austria. He writes that he walked among the people as if they were foreigners to him (*TB* 1:239). His distance from, and disdain for, Vienna—"Wittgenstein's Vienna," as it has been called in celebration of its creativity—is an aspect of Musil that one may find strange, at least until reading *The Man without Qualities*. The novel, which portrays a society hollow at the core, shows why he did not want to be considered an Austrian writer. He undoubtedly would have savored the paradox that, from our present viewpoint, he is one of the most important figures of a generation of intellectuals and writers, artists and scientists, who made Vienna a central place for the elaboration of modernity.

In 1906, still a student, Musil met his future wife, Martha Marcovaldi (who was at that time already married), and published his first novel, *Young Törless*. A little more than a year later after *Törless*'s publication, he handed in his dissertation, *Beitrag zur Beurteiling der Lehren Machs* (literally, "A Contribution to an Evaluation of Mach's Doctrines"; translated as *On Mach's Theories*). A reader accustomed to today's academic specialization may be puzzled that Musil, studying psychology, should write a dissertation claiming to be a "contribution to a judgment of Mach's theories." Ernst Mach was a leading figure in the world of physics as well as the dominant positivist epistemologist in Europe at the time. However, his epistemology, as we will see, involves claims about the nature of the psyche, which meant Mach was also considered a serious theorist on psychology. In this regard I would suggest that academic fields were not so narrowly regimented in the early twentieth century as is now the case. Musil moved from one field to another with relative ease, and thus recalls other Viennese intellectuals of the time. For example, after his study of engineering in Berlin and Manchester, Ludwig Wittgenstein turned to work in philosophy at Cambridge that also led him to investigations in psychology and mathematics; or, equally noteworthy, the Viennese physicist Erwin Schrödinger, after establishing wave mechanics as an alternative description for quantum mechanics, could later write *What Is Life?* (1944), one of the important books for the development of modern biology. Of course, this was hardly limited to Vienna: Carl Stumpf, who was the director of Musil's dissertation in Berlin, was himself a philosopher-psychologist who worked on the physics of audition.

Stumpf apparently was not happy with Musil's dissertation, and one may wonder why. Stumpf was no positivist, was quite critical of Mach, and, moreover, was instrumental in the founding of the school of Gestalt psychology that directly rejects Mach's psychological impressionism, or the doctrine that the psyche consists only in a collection of sensations. As we will see in dealing with Musil's thesis, Musil was critical of the basic axioms of Mach's theory of the nature of knowledge. Perhaps Stumpf's discontent was due to the fact that Musil was spending time writing a novel rather than a dissertation dealing with the research in perception for which Stumpf was famous.

Musil's dissertation is in fact a cogent critique of Mach's thought and of the dominant positivist doctrine that is at the heart of much scientific epistemology, then and now. The dissertation established him as an insightful philosophical thinker, and if Musil had pursued academic research, it would have opened the way to an academic career. This is not just a supposition, for in fact, after completing the dissertation, Musil was offered in early 1909 an academic position in Graz by Alexius Meinong, a leading philosopher-psychologist with an international reputation at the time—Bertrand Russell was among those who were influenced by him. However, nothing suggests that Musil ever really seriously considered entering the academic arena after finishing the dissertation. He was already busy writing short prose pieces and essays, sketching out plans for a novel, and writing some criticism and essays. The last category was partly a necessity; it provided some income for the young writer, who could not continue to depend upon his father for support.

Musil needed money, a constant problem in 1909 and for the rest of his life. Thus, to placate his father and to get a regular salary, he took a job as a librarian, an experience that, after three weeks, he described in his diaries as "Unerträglich, mörderisch"—"unbearable, murderous" (*TB* 1:236). To be sure, the time spent as a librarian was an experience he would put to use, with vengeance, in the mordant satire in *The Man without Qualities* of libraries and of the modern organization of knowledge. Writing and frequent travel around central Europe took up the time when he was not working at the library. (Interestingly, at a time when many European writers were visiting every corner of the globe, Musil seems never to have desired to leave Europe.) During these years before the First World War Musil began to write and publish criticism as well as essays centered on politics, cultural criticism, and ethics. He also began planning a series of novels, all of which today appear to be preparatory sketches for what would eventually become *The Man without Qualities*. Musil's essays are not sketches, however, and I will argue in subsequent chapters that, though not well known to nonspecialists, they are among some of the most significant political and philosophical writing of the time.

In 1911 he published his second volume of fiction, a collection of two stories, *Vereinigungen: Zwei Erzählungen* (literally, *Unions: Two Stories,* translated as part of the collection *Five Women*). In the same year he married Martha, who was divorced from her first husband. In 1913 he seems to have had a serious health crisis, the first in a series that Musil suffered in his life. Some of these illnesses may have been psychosomatic, for it is likely that he was at times on the brink of severe depression. Notably, he consulted the psychiatrist Dr. Otto Pötzl for what was called at the time severe cardiac neurosis (neurosis resulting in, if not due to, heart palpitations). The crisis in 1913 got him some much desired relief in the form of leave from the work he detested. Things seemed to be looking up when, in the catastrophic year of 1914, he got what might well have been an ideal position for him: a job as an editor in Berlin for the prestigious literary journal *Die Neue Rundschau.* However, the First World War broke out in August only a few months after he accepted this position. Musil soon found himself as the commanding officer of an infantry company on the Tyrolean front, where units of the Austro-Hungarian army faced Italian troops. Readers familiar with Hemingway's novel *A Farewell to Arms* (1929) will recall that this was a mountain front, characterized by fierce fighting and frequent artillery duels. He was not constantly involved in this combat, however. Illness compelled him to travel from the front, and in 1916 he met Max Brod and Franz Kafka in Prague. In the same year he was given a position editing an army journal, the *Tiroler Soldaten-Zeitung.* In 1918, a few months before the war's end, he was assigned to work for a new military journal, *Heimat,* apparently conceived to work against subversive influences in the army such as the growing communist movement.

The Great War was a central experience in Musil's life, as it was in the lives of millions of others. He experienced some of it on the front line, as an officer who seems to have accepted that he was defending at once the place of German culture in the world and an empire whose imperial dominion over a variety of ethnic groups was justified. After, and probably during, the war Musil recognized that the war had been an outburst of irrationality that defied understanding. However, immediately before the war he accepted, as did many German intellectuals, the belief that the war was justified as a defense, not just of the two German-language empires, but also of the very existence of German culture and, specifically, German values. His thinking was similar to notions held at the time by Thomas Mann, for example, as one sees in the essay Musil wrote for *Die Neue Rundschau* immediately after the declaration of war in 1914, "Europäertum, Krieg, Deutschtum" ("Europeanness, War, Germanness"). In quirky lines published before leaving for the front, he claimed that the German-speaking world was surrounded by enemies, indeed that a conspiracy existed whose goal was to exterminate German culture. Facing this danger, Musil felt a "new feeling" born in him as a German (8:1021). With all the panache of a departing warrior, he went on to claim that fearlessness in the face of death had become a general condition. With this declaration the reader encounters something unique in Musil's writing: an unthinking acceptance of the moment's hysteria and a century's growth of nationalism.

To say the least, the essay endorsing the war is testimony to the power of mass movements to activate in even the most critical thinkers a moment of blindness. Musil was to reflect on this experience at length, for his bellicose feelings were clearly a challenge to his own rationality. But he never questioned the need to do his duty on the Tyrolean front, which involved more than simple military duty. As editor of the army newspaper he was involved in work devoted, in part, to the task of eliminating irrendentism—the refusal of the largely Italian native populations to accept Austrian political dominance in the region. In short, throughout the war Musil remained largely and perhaps unquestioningly committed to the idea of an empire. From the viewpoint of today's postcolonial mentality, his attitude may seem suspect. However, as we shall later see, Musil's attitude was motivated largely by a belief that an empire better serves democratic values than did the nationalisms that, in fact, dictated the creation of new nation-states after the end of the war.

We can also anticipate *The Man without Qualities* and note that the novel is written from an ironic perspective presupposing the outbreak of the First World War and, with it, the undoing of all that Viennese society is doing to preserve itself in 1913. The novel's critical perspective is opposed to the enthusiastic acceptance of the war Musil expressed in 1914. His perspective on the war changed radically; as he later put it, enthusiasm for the war was like a sickness from which he later recovered. Musil's enthusiasm for the war began to wane even as he experienced it. He recognized that patriotism can be a form of homicidal psychosis and that war can take on aspects of a religious experience. This latter idea was perhaps first revealed in a crucial experience Musil underwent during the war on the front lines. One can infer this from an anecdote, found in several posthumously published fragments (*GW* 7:751–59), that is also narrated in the published story "Die Amsel" ("The Blackbird"). In these different narratives Musil recounts that he, or his fictional double, was nearly hit by a falling air dart—a *Fliegerpfeil*—a sharp-pointed sliver of metal that was dropped from airplanes on the heads of the enemy below. The narrator of one of the fragments describes the ringing sound made by the dart's approach to earth as the song of death. In his close call with the arrow and a perforated head, the narrator undergoes a kind of double negative epiphany in which the absence of God, in whom he does not believe, reveals itself. Paradoxically God is present as an absence in war. God's absence is a constant motif in Musil's writing. In the posthumous text under consideration, the narrator's ironic meditation takes the shape of a final pirouette undermining the epiphany revealing God's presence; at the end he muses with self-directed irony that he now has an idea he never had before: of God . . . or was it of astrology? Another text, "Der Gesang des Todes" ("The Song of Death"; also called "Der Singende Tod," or "The Singing Death"), seems less ironic when the quasi-fictional narrator, notably an engineer who will become a painter, notes that before the war he was an unbeliever who saw life as a bit of sunshine between two dark holes (*GW* 7:757). War, however, dissolves his intelligence, like meat from a knucklebone (7:758), which meant that he came to discover, in war, something bordering on the religious.

This experience of the closeness of death led Musil to believe that war was not a metaphor for religion but rather a form of religious experience itself. Later, shortly after the war, in mulling over his experience he states this idea quite squarely in his diaries. He means that one may understand religious experience through war, not the other way around (*TB* 1:544). But Musil also compares enthusiasm for war to a form of mental disequilibrium. He does so in a passage in the diaries in which he describes the war's beginning in Berlin. (The passage was probably written during the war, but the dating of diary passages is often uncertain.) As in the type of expressionist collage that painters such as George Grosz and Otto Dix created, in this diary passage he places in rapid juxtaposition "deracinated intellectuals," the possibility of an "inner enemy," and the jam of people trying to get the latest special edition of the news, all this while a lunatic screams in the street. In this pandemonium, Musil suggests, psychotics are in their element (*TB* 1:298–99). Indeed, this may be his most telling judgment upon his own state of mind in 1914.

In spite of the fact that Musil came to question the very basis for the war and that he had always rejected nationalism as a meaningful basis for political activity, he never in any sense repudiated his military service. On the contrary, in spite of the war's carnage he retained an aristocratic sense of duty, not unlike what the French aristocrat Henry de Montherlant called, in describing his own military service, "service inutile." With the idea of useless duty Montherlant described his own sense of the moral obligation to serve in the First World War. Moreover, Musil's pride continued to resonate some eighteen years after the war's end, as one sees in a 1936 letter describing his services to the Austrian state, written when he needed support for his request for a state pension that might alleviate his persistent financial difficulties. In his letter he described his military service, in fact, in terms that suggest he expected recompense for years of service to the state that bordered on the heroic. In this curious letter he cites his library experience in the same terms as his military activity and the medals he received while a soldier—the Order of Franz-Joseph Knightly Cross (*Ritterkreuz*) for distinguished service, the Military Service Medal with swords for bravery before the enemy, and the Emperor Charles Soldier's Cross (*Trup-penkreuz*) (*Briefe* 736). Musil goes on to cite examples of his service to the state after the war's end: as a writer in the foreign ministry and, from the fall of 1920 until 1922, as a newspaper journalist in the war ministry.

After the war Musil's life was committed to writing, though his work was interrupted at times by ill health and psychological problems. In 1921 he took an apartment in Vienna's third district, at Rasumofskygasse 20, that would be his base of operations for the next seventeen years. Revealingly, he never gave up the apartment, even after the success of *The Man without Qualities* allowed him to spend much time in Berlin in the early thirties and after he went into exile in 1938. The apartment was a point of stability in a life spent frequently traveling, often to Berlin but also to central Europe and Italy. Berlin and Vienna were the two fixed poles of his life, and Musil had friends in both cities. They were by and large writers and intellectuals, artists and professors. He had contacts with writers such as Thomas Mann, Alfred Döblin, and Bertolt Brecht. He knew Brecht, for example, in conjunction with the founding in Berlin of a political association of writers called Gruppe 1925. This group of politically committed writers included, in addition to Brecht, well-known figures such as Johannes Becher, Ernst Bloch, Max Brod, Döblin, Willy Haas, Walter Hasenclever, Ludwig Marcuse, Erwin Piscator, and Joseph Roth.[3] In Vienna from 1922 on he was active in the Schutzverband deutscher Schriftsteller in Österreich (the Protective Association of German Writers in Austria), and apparently he had some contacts with the Vienna Circle, those positivist philosophers who at the time were trying to make sense of Wittgenstein's *Tractatus.* In short, Musil knew, though it cannot be said that he was close to, many of the major German-language writers of his time.

Most notably, he became acquainted in Berlin with the poet Rainer Maria Rilke toward the end of the poet's life. In the fall of 1924 Musil wrote a letter of self-presentation to the poet who had been a major influence on him. In it Musil belittled himself in describing to Rilke what he had accomplished, saying that after *Young Törless* and *Unions,* he had written little, naming only the play *Die Schwärmer* (*The Enthusiasts*); another volume of stories, *Drei Frauen* (*Three Women*); and a farce, *Vinzenz oder die Freudin bedeutender Männer* "Vinzenz and the Woman Friend of Important Men." Musil offered to send any of these to Rilke and added that *The Enthusiasts* would probably never be performed despite its recognized literary value. The farce he had written simply for amusement, and he added that he was writing a novel that should appear in spring (*Briefe* 364). What Musil considered to be his opus in 1924—*Young Törless,* two volumes of short fiction, two plays, and a novel in progress— largely comprises the output of his entire life, though he did not in the letter mention his essays and criticism, or a number of short texts that were starting to accumulate. With the reference at the end of the letter to a novel Musil was undoubtedly talking about some early form of *The Man without Qualities,* a title would become publicly known three years later in 1927, when Musil read on Berlin radio from the work in progress. In his letter to Rilke, Musil was overly optimistic, to say the least, about when he might have something ready for publication.

This was hardly the first time Musil was wrong about when he would finish *The Man without Qualities.* He spent the rest of his life, in fact, planning to finish the novel at some predicted time, but never did so. In the letter to Rilke this prediction was in error by some six years, and that simply for the first part of the novel. Also of great interest in this letter to the greatest living German poet at the time is the deprecatory tone Musil takes vis-à-vis his own work, for he seems to think that he has not done the work that, for whatever reason, might have been expected from him. In a sense he was his own harshest critic, as is shown not only in his manic rewriting, but also in his self-condemnation for not producing books as prolifically as Mann, a comparison that distressed Musil throughout his life.

The letter to Rilke was written some three years before Musil delivered one of his most famous addresses, in Berlin in 1927, a commemorative speech in honor of Rilke after the poet's death at the end of 1926. This was the same year in which Musil also sought professional therapeutic help from Dr. Hugo Lukàs to find a remedy for the writer's block that apparently kept him from continuing the novel for some time. A passage from the "Rilke Rede," as the speech is called, may shed some light on that block, for it seems that Musil was, perhaps unwittingly, speaking indirectly of himself. It certainly can be argued that he wanted to be, in writing fiction, what he saw Rilke to be as a poet—quite simply, the greatest German writer of the time. Of Rilke Musil said that he was in a certain sense the most religious poet since Novalis, though he was not certain if Rilke had any religion at all. Rather, Musil thought Rilke had a different way of seeing: a new and inner way. And so, as Musil foresees, Rilke will have become not only a great poet, but also a great guide on a path that leads from the worldwide religious feeling of the Middle Ages and goes beyond the humanist cultural ideal, heading toward a forthcoming worldview (*GW* 8:1240). With this encominium Musil attributes to Rilke the same high stakes for writing that he had come to conceive for the novel he had described in his letter to the poet. The stakes were the creation of works facilitating the advent of a new worldview, one that in some sense would transcend the medieval religious viewpoint and humanist idealism, the beliefs that were (and perhaps still are) the mainstays of European culture. Perhaps there is little wonder that Musil experienced writers' block, for he had set for himself a probably impossibly high hurdle—to use a rather pedestrian sports metaphor that Musil himself might have employed. In honoring Rilke by describing a path of writing leading to a new worldview, Musil was talking more about himself than Rilke, for it seems unlikely that Rilke would have considered himself a leader in any sense. In any case Musil's attribution of this role to Rilke reflects back on a role that Musil had conceived for literature in its social function.

This attribution may well be a case, too, of the "anxiety of influence" that, according to Harold Bloom, leads strong writers into psychic conflict with those predecessors who influence them. For some time Musil was incapacitated as a writer by some kind of psychic conflict. He believed that the therapeutic help from Dr. Lukàs in 1927 and 1928 helped him overcome his writer's block, for he was able to publish some pieces of short fiction, essays, and criticism and then, presumably, to continue work on the novel. In 1929 he appears again to have had heart problems, this some three months before the first perform- ance, in Berlin on April 3, of a truncated version of his play *The Enthusiasts* on the stage of the Theatre in der Kommandantenstrasse. The production was not a success: the public literally jeered it. Nonetheless, Alfred Kerr, perhaps the most important critic of the time, gave it a laudatory review. In 1930 Musil published next to nothing in the way of short texts. He read much, went to the cinema, and then finally brought forth the first volume of *The Man without Qualities,* consisting of parts 1 and 2. The novel went on sale toward the end of the year and was an immediate critical success. However, this success granted no financial security to the writer, who, turning fifty in 1931, had lit- tle else to count on for income. Moreover, the novel was not a certain source of income, since his publisher, Rowohlt, who had been advancing Musil money, was having great trouble paying his debts. In late 1932 Musil handed a second volume of the novel to his publisher, this containing the first thirty- eight chapters of part 3; it too was well received by critics and other writers.

Musil's success was short-lived. The second volume of the novel was pub- lished some six weeks before the end of the Weimar Republic. Hitler took power on January 30, 1933, on the very day that the Prussian Academy of the Arts awarded Musil a subsidy. The Nazi seizure of power undoubtedly resulted in Musil's not receiving the Goethe Prize for literature that year and, more grievously, in the dissolution of a recently formed Musil-Gesellschaft, a soci- ety set up to provide financial support for him. Many of its members were of Jewish origin. Musil now felt he could not stay in Germany, for reasons of con- science, as well as for his and especially for his wife's personal safety. She had Jewish origins, and the aggressive acts of the storm troopers against Jews in Berlin showed they were already in danger there. Therefore, Musil and his wife returned to live in their apartment in Vienna, with hopes of mustering financial support so that he could continue writing his novel, which would soon be banned in Germany. Musil believed that he was healthy enough to continue writing for a long time. In fact, he had less than ten years to live when he left Berlin.

It is hard to evaluate what kind of a shock the Nazi seizure of power had upon Musil. His musings on this catastrophe show him trying to maintain mental equilibrium and emotional composure by keeping an intellectual distance with regard to the various collectivisms he saw as the dominant ide- ologies of the time. From this perspective he viewed National Socialism, fas- cism, and communism as manifestations of the same antiliberal drive that was taking over a large part of the world. It is clear that he did not believe that the reaction to these movements should be "activism" as it is ordinarily understood, however much Musil condemned totalitarian politics and however much he had given his support to liberal and social democratic causes. In this regard, with uncompromising logic he rejected any totalitarian demand that culture be submitted to politics. Minimally, this meant he was committed to noncollaboration with what he saw as an evil regime.

Specifically, to understand his personal reaction to the Nazis, one can turn to an unpublished and unfinished essay written in 1933, "Bedenken eines Langsamen" ("Ruminations of a Slow-Witted Mind"). Musil sought to understand the Nazis by trying to take seriously the premises of their "movement" (*GW* 8:1413). Facing the absurdities of the Nazi ideology, he formulated the idea that the writer must maintain autonomy of mind, or *Geist* (8:1425). He cannot endorse political activism, for the writer's allegiance is to culture. He must work with a sense of the history of that culture, which transcends politics. He further developed these thoughts in a lecture he gave in late 1934 to the Schutzverband deutscher Schriftsteller in Österreich. In this lecture, called "Der Dichter in dieser Zeit" (translated as "The Serious Writer in Our Time"), Musil proclaimed that only the individual writer could develop culture. In the era of collectivist totalitarian states, the writer must hope, as Musil put it, for a return of better times, which a proper historical perspective showed to be not unreasonable. His lecture was apparently well received in Vienna, since he was invited to give it again a year later in Basel.

By 1935 Musil had an international reputation among writers and intellectuals, and his belief that modern capitalist society might be coming to an end was not a secret. As Annette Daigger points out in her essay on Musil's political stance, Musil had in 1918 signed a fairly radical left-wing resolution of the Politische Rat geistiger Arbeiter Berlin, or the Political Council (or Soviet) of the Berlin Intellectual Workers.[4] And as mentioned earlier, though no active revolutionary, he had nonetheless been part of the group of mainly communist and socialist writers who founded the Gruppe 1925. In 1930 he had politely filled out a questionnaire for the Soviet journal *Novy Mir* in which he had expressed hope that the Russian Revolution might give intellectual or spiritual support to all those who hoped that something good might yet come of humanity (*Briefe* 472). For these reasons, not to mention the critical stance of *The Man without Qualities,* it is not surprising that in 1935 Musil was invited to Paris to participate in Le Congrès international des écrivains pour la défense de la culture. The congress was organized largely for left-wing propaganda purposes, and communist writers such as Louis Aragon, Henri Barbusse, and Brecht, as well as a number of sympathetic noncommunists, were also invited to it. The congress failed, however, to produce a show of solidarity for the Communist International. Notably, on this occasion the leading French surrealist writer André Breton broke with the movement, and other writers were unwilling to play the role of spokesmen for the Communists. In this charged atmosphere Musil read a paper that rejected almost all the tenets calling for activist political mobilization of writers in the face of Nazi Germany. Musil made enemies at this congress, with some of the participants excoriating him for his individualism.

Having left Nazi Germany to take up permanent residence in Vienna, Musil found himself relying from 1933 until 1938 on strictly Austrian resources for survival. These resources included support from another society set up to help him financially while he completed the novel. He also had some revenue from sales of his books by the publisher Bermann-Fischer, which, having set up a branch in Vienna, took over Musil's contract from Rowohlt. In his lively book on Musil, Wilfried Berghahn thinks that, all in all, Musil's financial situation was, for a year or so in Vienna, not too bad. One may doubt that Musil would have shared that opinion, for as Berghahn also points out, he expected to have a lifestyle that included the best clothes and the finest food.[5] In any case, along with some sales of *The Man without Qualities,* Musil also had a new publication with the publishing house Humanitas in Zurich, which, in 1935, brought a collection of assorted short texts called, with acerbic irony, *Nachlass zu Lebzeiten* (translated as *Posthumous Papers of a Living Author*). With this title Musil proposed that the German writer, both himself and in general, was a moribund creature.

In 1937 Musil gave in Vienna another marvelous, but difficult, lecture that can be taken as his public statement about the Nazis. Published later as a book, it is laconically called *Über die Dummheit (On Stupidity)*, a title whose concision suggests Musil's affinities with classical moral analysis. In the lecture Musil, perhaps to avoid incitement to violence, never overtly names the Nazis. Of course, there can be no doubt that in analyzing stupidity, he wanted to come to grips with a political movement that had already gained wide acceptance in Austria. *On Stupidity* is about the seemingly incomprehensible politics that had turned Germany into a land of barbarous irrationality that was now threatening Austria, which itself had become an "Austro-fascist" state in response to the Nazi threat to take it over. There have, of course, been many analyses of the roots of the Nazi movement, though perhaps none are more insightful than Musil's subtle analysis of how stupidity is at once a defect of the understanding and of the emotions. As such, stupidity is a dangerous phenomenon, having political ramifications, which can take the form of a collective movement. This lecture was probably Musil's last intervention in the public political arena.

Under pressure from Bermann-Fischer to produce some more pages of *The Man without Qualities,* in 1938 Musil gave the publisher twenty more chapters. His timing was characterized by his usual bad luck: these chapters were in galleys to be corrected virtually at the moment the Nazis annexed Austria. It appears, in fact, that the galleys were set up shortly before Hitler rode victoriously into a cheering Vienna in order to welcome his native Austria into the Third Reich. Thereupon, Gottfried Bermann-Fischer, a Jew, fled for his life; his firm was confiscated, and Musil took back his galley sheets. Then he, too, was on the road to exile. He briefly went to Italy and then took up residence in Switzerland, alleging to the Nazi authorities in Vienna that his health demanded a period of recuperation. Musil kept up this legal pretense until he died, since he wanted to get back some copies of his books while demanding a justification for their being banned. This fiction also probably eased his delicate situation vis-à-vis the Swiss authorities, who, in their position as "neutrals," wanted no trouble with the Germans, who kept sharp watch over the lists of immigrants in Switzerland trying to escape them.

Musil's correspondence documents that the last years of his life in Switzerland were not happy. He worked sporadically on his novel while worrying constantly about finishing it. He was also kept busy complying with the bureaucratic requirements to retain residency in Switzerland, first in Zurich, then in Geneva. He took some steps toward emigrating to the United States, though one may doubt that he really wanted to go to a country in which Mann, Adorno, Brecht, and other German writers might be well received but where nobody, he thought, had ever heard of Robert Musil. Although he had, through his wife, relatives in the United States, his sporadic attempts at emigration came to naught, in spite of support from various quarters, including the most famous living émigré, Albert Einstein.

In these final years Musil's foremost desire was to finish the novel, and thus he probably found it most expedient to sit tight where he was, where he had freedom to pursue this task. He seems to have feared that moving to an unknown country whose language he could not speak might mean the end of his work. After much difficulty in finding a proper work environment, he finally settled in a house in Geneva in which noise was not a major impediment to his work. However, throughout these exile years life was mean. He had little money, he virtually had to beg for support, and he lived with the constant worry that the Swiss authorities might decide not to renew the periodic permission required for residence. Psychologically and materially, conditions for work on the novel were always less than ideal, and sometimes the admittedly temperamental Musil found that his surroundings simply prevented him from thinking. It is also difficult to explain why, when he could work, he wrote and rewrote chapters multiple times in ways that do not suggest he wanted to finish the novel with any great dispatch. His writer's block may have transformed itself into a kind of self-defeating perfectionism that assured, moreover, that Musil would be able to live out his novel as he wrote it, day by day, page by page, thought by thought.

Death came unexpectedly. In the early afternoon of April 15, 1942, Martha Musil found her husband dead on the floor, victim of a stroke. Musil reportedly thought he had many years ahead to finish the novel. Of course he had health problems, but nothing made him or others suppose that he would die before reaching the age of sixty-two. His relative isolation in exile was underscored by the fact that only eight people attended his funeral on April 17. In the context of the war raging about him, his death was not a newsworthy event, and few knew that a man who would be considered one of the great writers of the twentieth century was cremated that day in Geneva.

Martha's concern with her husband and his work did not end with his death. She found a publisher in Lausanne for a third volume of *The Man without Qualities* that she patched together from manuscripts in 1943. Moreover, she managed to save thousands of pages of diaries, letters, and unfinished manuscripts, carrying them heroically from Europe to the United States and back.[6] One must salute her for her devotion in keeping Musil's work alive. She was responsible for the fact that a new edition of the novel and the first edition of unpublished writings could be undertaken, beginning in 1952, the year in which it was said that Musil was rediscovered.[7] Actually, one had to wait until 1978 for an edition of Musil's collected works, the edition that made known the scope of his oeuvre, especially the essays and criticism as well as variant sketched-out possibilities for an ending of *The Man without Qualities.* However, I doubt that we can speak of a final version of Musil's work even at the date of this writing, or that one will ever be able to do so. The fact that the thousands of pages of manuscript, many of them unpublished, are now available on CD-ROM, makes a definitive oeuvre an unlikely proposition. That a CD-ROM allows critics and readers to go through the manuscripts via a search engine seems a strange fate for these fragile testimonies to the perfectionist Musil's desire to find the ideal final formulation for his life's work. His great novel is unfinished, and I will deal with it as such. Of course, he wrote much besides *The Man without Qualities*—fiction, plays, and essays—and in the following chapters we will deal in detail first with these texts, the published texts, before concluding with the novel he didn't finish.

CHAPTER 2

Early Diaries and
Doctoral Dissertation

After a profile of Musil's life, and before dealing with his main published works, it is useful to turn to the kinds of artistic and philosophical problems the young writer engaged as he ended his engineering studies and undertook graduate work in psychology and philosophy. In this chapter I want specifically to comment on some of the early writings in what have been published as his *Tagebücher,* or diaries. Then I will consider the doctoral dissertation that Musil published in 1908. Taken together, the early diaries and the dissertation allow us to understand Musil's intellectual interests as he set about to become a creative writer. The diaries show him educating himself as he experimented with conceptual frameworks for developing his own thought. His doctoral dissertation on the physicist Ernst Mach is another key moment in this education. In this academic work Musil sets forth a critique of the positivist view of science that would occupy him throughout his life. His analysis of Mach is, moreover, a cogent and perceptive piece of philosophical analysis that is of great interest in its own right. It outlines, through opposition to Mach, the young Musil's views concerning the foundations of scientific knowledge. There is nothing definitive about the dissertation; but it does set out the terms for the debate about science that is recurrent in Musil's work, whatever the position he, or his characters, may take at any given moment.

In the confusing mass of notes composing Musil's early diaries, one immediately encounters familiar philosophical figures, notably the American essayist Ralph Waldo Emerson and Friedrich Nietzsche. Readers may be surprised to find these two thinkers linked in Musil's texts, but it is clear that they were the most important sources in helping him come to his understanding of the writer's task. Linking these two names is actually not so strange. They were often paired at the end of the nineteenth century, when Emerson enjoyed a great reputation in Germany, in part due to the praise Nietzsche gave him. Musil's early diaries, which begin around 1900, show that these two thinkers were instrumental in shaping his intellectual concerns as he finished his studies. They were determining influences in causing Musil to question the foundations of his own beliefs and values.

A caveat about Musil's diaries: in their present form they come to more than one thousand pages, written over a period of forty years; they were not intended for publication. There is much that is problematic and opaque in them, and they are perhaps best viewed as a writer's scratchpad or notebook rather than a traditional literary journal. They are nonetheless useful, especially the earliest diaries, for documenting Musil's attempts at thinking through certain types of problems, for they are a place in which he not only annotated his thoughts and feelings, but also commented on his readings and recorded quotations from works that interested him. He also wrote down sketches and drafts, some of which are first steps in the writing of works that would eventually be published. The diaries are thus a kind of writer's workshop. With this caveat in mind about their inchoate nature, we can read the early diaries to see specifically how Emerson and Nietzsche, among others, contribute to the understanding of much of what Musil was to undertake subsequently.

In brief it was in these early notebooks, published in 1983 as his *Tagebücher* and available in part in translation, that Musil really began his writing career by meditating on various thinkers and writers while sketching out creative projects. For example, on the first page of the diaries, written perhaps in 1899, Musil conceives for himself a literary persona called "Monsieur le Vivisecteur." The "vivisector" portrays himself as he sits in his room and, apparently for the first time, perceives that his room is a unitary sum of colored surfaces that are organically linked with the night outside. With this unity of perception he experiences a kind of pantheism, or a materialist view of the divine, emerging from what he calls physiological knowledge of himself. With this experience he then sets out to write his diary—his night-book, as he then calls it—and will consider his task accomplished, he says, when not a single word disturbs the beautiful unity of his present perception or sensation (*Empfindung*) (*TB* 1:1–2).

The diaries' opening pages portray Musil in effect imagining himself to be a Nietzschean philosopher. The vivisector is the image Nietzsche used to characterize the future philosopher, who, beyond good and evil, will not be afraid to cut to the quick in laying bare the moral prejudices of the present hypocritical age. The pantheistic feelings conjured up in the diary, however, reflect Emerson's religious doctrine, with Nietzschean overtones: Musil says that it is knowledge of the body that offers him a vision of the union of the writer and the cosmos. This claim also reflects directly the way Nietzsche lays great store by the body's determination of thought. Finally, it appears that the incipient psychologist in Musil is already inclined to think of perception as a totality and to seek in that totality the perspective that will allow him to interpret the world in its particulars. This holistic viewpoint of perception will later oppose him to Mach, a philosopher of knowledge for whom only individual sensations offer the material out of which one builds the analytical propositions and equations that can properly be called knowledge. According to Mach, complexes of individual sensations, not the total gestalt of perception, are the basis for knowledge. The Musil who was reading Emerson and Nietzsche will reject this atomistic viewpoint of perception most of the time for most of his life—but not always.

In the first pages of the diaries, it is clear that Emerson and Nietzsche proposed a view of knowledge that differed from what Musil encountered in his study of engineering, physics, mathematics, and later psychology. Emerson and Nietzsche had challenged the rationalist belief that science can provide a unitary vision of knowledge, and that rational inquiry should culminate in a single version of what must then be considered truth. Rather, Emerson and Nietzsche had stressed the idea that truth must be sought through the use of multiple perspectives, because no single perspective can exhaust the truth that might underlie any phenomenon. The search for multiple perspectives on the same object of knowledge became the guiding impulse behind much of Musil's writing. This "perspectivism" led him to embrace the idea that both scientific generalization and aesthetic intuition, laying hold of the unique percept, can with equal justification claim to be knowledge.

In the diaries and later in his essays, Musil used the ungainly neologisms *ratioïd* and *non-ratioïd* to delineate the Emersonian distinction between law-like generalization and the truth of the individual example (*TB* 1:159, for example). The coining of this pair of terms should not lead one to think that Musil's view of knowledge is always based on a simple binary opposition. Emerson had insisted on the necessity of the play of multiple viewpoints in the quest for truths, if not truth, and his idea informed both Nietzsche's and Musil's thought in this regard. In this light it is arguable that Musil's perspectivism is not based on polarizing dialectics. True, *ratioïd* and *non-ratioïd* sound as if they offer another way of saying that the irrational is the negation of the rational. However, Musil uses this pair of terms to set up a broad spectrum of types of truth, all of which may operate at once. This notion of spectrum is related to that of "essayism," which Musil also took over from Emerson. Writing from the essayistic viewpoint necessarily entails that the writer is always willing to entertain more perspectives on an object than one, since the writer must be ready to admit more truths than one.

The early diaries present, moreover, the beginnings of Musil's conception of literature as a totalizing project that should include science as well as philosophy in seeking new ways of conceiving the multiple truths of experience.

I say "totalizing" to stress the fact that Musil hoped in his work to encompass both the rationality and precision of science as well as the expression of values and emotions found in literature. But totalizing does not mean that Musil ever thought that all truth could be reduced to anything like a philosophical system such as German philosophers had often tried to construct. System building, designed to describe the totality of existence, was a feature of German philosophy from at least G. W. Leibniz in the seventeenth century through G. W. F. Hegel in the nineteenth. Musil was viscerally anti-Hegelian, though he seems occasionally to use Hegelian terminology—such as the idea of totality. Totality in Musil refers to the means of knowledge, not the object.

Especially important for the orientation of Musil's later work is, in the first diary notebook, his ruminating on Emerson's *The Conduct of Life*. This book is a collection of essays Emerson published in 1861. They were immediately translated into German in 1862 (which permitted Nietzsche to read them with care relatively early in life). These essays were published a generation after Emerson's more familiar earlier essays, such as found in the collection *Nature* (1836), in which he is a proponent of pantheistic transcendentalism. In *The Conduct of Life* Emerson developed themes from his pantheistic philosophy while pursuing new themes marked by a growing skepticism and, at the same time, the belief that culture owes its existence to the inventions of great individuals. Nietzsche and Musil were deeply impressed by Emerson's theory that great individuals, striving for power, are also tempered by the culture they produce in their striving, so that the pursuit of power tempers itself as it were. The Emersonian theory of culture finds resonance in Musil's abiding belief (such as he espoused in his Paris lecture in 1935) that the individual is the locus for the creation of all cultural values. Musil was at times attracted by socialist ideas, but his hope that socialism might bring about social justice did not conflict with his belief that only the individual can be a creator. To be sure, he was aware of the dangers inherent in an ideology of unbridled individualism. But, like Emerson, Musil never relinquished belief in the primacy of the individual as the creator of culture, and he never believed in collectivism as a solution to any problem.

What is striking in the first notebook of the diaries is that Musil several times writes down, in English, the title of Emerson's collection of essays *The Conduct of Life;* but then he follows the title by writing out quotations from Nietzsche, such as a passage from *The Twilight of the Idols* in which he proclaims that immoralists such as himself are ready for all kinds of understanding and acceptance: they lay their honor therein to say yes, not to deny (*TB* 1:33). Why this juxtaposition of Emerson's title and Nietzsche's writing? Most likely, it seems that Musil, in making this amalgamation, is joining Emerson and Nietzsche as writers pointing toward a future of transformations opening up new possibilities of knowledge. And perhaps he is underlining for himself the idea that the type of thought running through Emerson and Nietzsche should find its culmination in his own future writing. Emerson and Nietzsche are thinkers looking to the future, to a history yet to be written, and Musil was clearly drawn into their orbit because of their visionary way of looking at the development of a history in the making, in which they were self-conscious participants. Musil's antiromantic lack of nostalgia for the past takes on its full meaning in this context: the future is the meaningful dimension of time, for it is only in the future that some meaningful transformation of culture can occur.

To formulate this aspect of Emerson's and Nietzsche's thought most concisely, one can say that Musil was attracted to precursors who had a sharp historical sense that postromantic culture was at a turning point. He saw that, with the advent of secular modernity, thinkers such as Emerson and Nietzsche believed that something new had to emerge in Western culture. However, the future was hardly evident. Emerson hoped for a new religion, one that would transcend the parochial limitations of the Protestantism of the cultural milieu in New England in which narrow-minded Puritanism had flourished. Nietzsche actually desired much the same insofar as he scorned the evangelic faith of the German Reformation. Nietzsche mocked the moral bankruptcy involved in the creation of a German Reich that pretended to be Christian even after it had murdered God, to use Nietzsche's well-known expression. With the demise of religion and aristocratic values, however, Nietzsche believed the coming of nihilism to be inevitable. In the wake of Emerson and Nietzsche, Musil himself was to dream at times of a utopian future, accompanied by the advent of an atheistic mysticism, in which life might be transformed. The diaries make clear that, even before the First World War and the subsequent collapse of the Austro-Hungarian Empire, and well before the cultural catastrophe brought about by the rise of National Socialism and its military state, Musil believed that contemporary European culture was at a turning point. For better or worse, new cultural forms were on the horizon.

In many regards Musil's postromantic mind seems more attuned to Emerson than to Nietzsche, especially Musil's desire to find secularized mysticism that could be the basis for new forms of experience. Like Emerson, Musil had great respect for science; and, also like Emerson, he believed that meaningful thought had to account for the particular as well as formulate the generalized law that is science's domain. And what is also striking is that Emerson, though hardly well versed in mathematics, preceded Musil in an awareness that the new science of statistics seemed to confirm that the influence of the individual on society disappears as, in a given domain, the number of individual cases increases. In other words, the science of statistics as interpreted by Emerson, and then by Musil, was fated to transform the understanding of the unfolding of human enterprises. This reason for this transformation was that statistical reasoning had found laws that could be interpreted as a new form of fate ruling over the destiny of societal collectives. Statistics could formulate laws about aggregate events, determining what must occur in society with near fatal accuracy.

In his essay "Fate," Emerson meditates on the fact that the Belgium scientist Lambert Quételet (1796–1874) had transformed social science with his mathematical notion of the statistically average man. Quételet's work defined a perhaps mythical, but nonetheless mathematically real creature—homo average, a man with mathematically certain properties. Emerson interpreted statistics as a science of society that minimizes the individual's role in events involving large numbers. Seemingly, the individual is dominated by series of general facts or laws that, as Emerson puts it, preserve society's existence. From this perspective statistics sets out laws that are a new form of determinism or destiny. In surveying populations statistics may decree that great individuals are born every so many million births, but this is hardly cause for optimism: statistical laws mainly determine that average people do average things with the relentless regularity that characterizes the molecules in an enclosed gas. The diaries show that Musil read much in the way of statistics, but it was clearly in Emerson that he found the view that statistics describes fate. This view of social determinism underlies Musil's thought about the dilemma posed by the laws of social causality, defined by statistical patterns. These laws exclude consideration of individual human freedom from the calculations that predict, with undeniable accuracy, how many people will be born each year, die, catch a cold, or shoot their neighbor.

Musil knew that it is only the belief in freedom that allows individuals to transform themselves and perhaps thereby to transform history. Individual freedom can appear to be a meaningless concept when set against the statistical laws that apparently decree with causal rigor what shall occur in the aggregate social world, no matter what the individual decides to do. In *The Man without Qualities* Musil seems to have conceived of a character without determinable qualities precisely as a check on the law of averages. His protagonist, Ulrich, is, among other things, the anti-average man. In the early diaries we find the preparation for the creation of this character in Musil's meditation on freedom and the law. It takes various forms, ranging from Musil's analysis of

Aristotelian tragic fate to meditation on Edmund Husserl's phenomenology of mind. In these notebooks Musil was looking for the philosophical grounds for believing that the mind is strong enough, as he says, quoting Nietzsche, to form the matter of its own thought (*TB* 1:163). Musil recognizes that in shaping our thoughts we are dependent on unconscious conditioning, inheritance, history, and the like; but he nonetheless affirms that through feeling and fantasy the individual can have power over the "web of the mind" that these factors determine (*TB* 1:162). In fine, in the early diaries Musil pursues a series of thoughts and readings in order to formulate a justification for his belief in the power of the individual mind to shape the substance of its own thought.

If Emerson's view of fate suggested to Musil, as well as to Nietzsche, that inevitable historical change lies on the horizon, none of them believed that a historical transformation of culture would emerge from the various socialist programs propounded during the nineteenth century. Marxist historical determinism, for instance, with its view of the inevitability of socialism, did not inform their understanding of historical change. Nietzsche was especially hostile to socialism, for he viewed it as a self-deluded, secularized form of Christianity and the slave morality enshrined in it (as in *On the Genealogy of Morals,* 1887). Musil's negative view of collectivism probably found its origins in his response to the way both Emerson and Nietzsche envisaged the future as an evolutionary project depending upon the creative individual. A superior future needed the superior individual who should actively transform culture and its fundamental values.

It is not entirely clear how the creative individual can interact with the statistical laws that blindly decree that social change takes place. But one must keep this determinism in mind when reading Musil's diaries, for he conceives of the problem of the individual in society as one of *Lebenskunst*—the art of life, or life conceived as art. Around 1905 he began a fairly systematic study of the romantic writers and encountered an essay by Ellen Key, a Swedish educational reformer who, drawing upon the romantic rejection of scientific rationality, thought that art should play a fundamental role in shaping the personality (*TB* 1:152). Musil was attracted to the idea of *Lebenskunst* but did not accept Key's critique of science and reason. He embraced enthusiastically the idea that the creative mind must shape itself like a work of art in order to develop its transformative powers. In this belief is found the germ for the creation of Ulrich, the artist of life and not books. For the young Musil, the idea that the mind should be made the object of study was, as he put it, simply a form of salvation—another term to be born in mind with respect to Musil's self-directed satire in *The Man without Qualities* (*TB* 1:168).

Musil is close to Emerson in his thinking about literature, not only in linking art with self-development and historical change, but also in recognizing that literature has an epistemic role in society. In this regard he undoubtedly drew on Emerson's essay "Behavior," also found in *The Conduct of Life,* in which Emerson argued for the role literature plays in our knowledge of society. Using the metaphor that society is the stage on which manners are shown, he sets up a relationship between literature and society. However, Emerson says that it is not theater but novels that offer knowledge of these manners. He develops a rather subtle thought that Musil took to heart, especially the idea that a function of novels is to offer moral knowledge. For Emerson the manners depicted in novels are forms of ethics, and these ethics are invented by genius or love; they are not and cannot be legislated by law.[1] Throughout his career Musil sought to realize Emerson's conception of the novelist as an inventor of ethics.

Musil seems to have understood well Emerson's belief that manners are embodied by the individual but produced nonetheless through historical social development. In other words, manners are unique forms, although they function as universals, and the novel shows this functioning. Emerson thought no rules for developing culture could be given in advance. In the modern era only literature could serve as a guide in this regard. A comparable thought runs throughout the early diaries in Musil's critique of philosophy and his belief in literature as a source of learning and moral knowledge. There is nothing systematic in Musil's writing, but, influenced by Emerson, his meditations on ethics and his irritation with philosophy (*TB* 1:149) are clear bases for his desire to offer in his planned novel knowledge about the relationships between human beings (*TB* 1:148).

Thus, early on in Musil's writing we can see him planning the novel that will become *The Man without Qualities.* He is working in these notebooks to find the grounds for moral knowledge that are embodied in his novel about manners and in his man without qualities, a character who continues the author's quest. Much of *The Man without Qualities* turns on Ulrich's search for the knowledge that would grant the individual the power to invent new manners and thus new ethics, and hence a mind that might transcend the statistical average. In a nutshell, Ulrich assents to Emerson's idea that manners are forms of power springing from self-reliance.

There are to be sure more references to Nietzsche than to Emerson in the diaries. As I suggested above, there are many quotations from Nietzsche written down more or less literally. However, Musil's detailed attention to Nietzsche hardly amounts to an uncritical endorsement of the philosopher's challenge to a liberal, rationalist view of knowledge and ethics or an approval of his anti-Christian historicism. Musil may have despaired of Quételet's "average man," but even as a young man he did not entirely subscribe to Nietzsche's desire to reinstate superior cultural values that would put the democratic "herd" in its place. Musil was well aware that Nietzsche was a hostile critic of the liberal democracy of which Musil counted himself a product. Thus, his comments on Nietzsche oscillate greatly between distanced critical commentary and, sometimes, enthusiastic endorsement. In the diaries we see Musil's chafing against the constraints of rationalism as he pens reflections on Nietzsche's critique of knowledge and morality. In effect, the diaries show how he absorbed and reworked Nietzsche's thought. His reception of Nietzsche, whose writings were extremely influential among German intellectuals of the period, became the basis for Ulrich's own hesitant Nietzscheanism and, ultimately, his critique of the entire culture that had accepted the philosopher of the will to power.

Musil's ambivalence about Nietzsche stands out, for example, in a passage called "Something about Nietzsche" written between 1899 and 1906 (*TB* 1:50). In it he recognizes that many people think that Nietzsche is not a serious philosopher, since his works read as if they were witty games. He goes on to write that Nietzsche can be criticized since he never seems to carry out any of the possibilities he suggests. Moreover he offers nothing to those who need the assurance of mathematically calculated thought—such as a rationalist like Musil. So, Musil writes, it appears that Nietzsche is not of much interest as a thinker. He then reverses his own thought by concluding that Nietzsche would be of interest only if ten or so intellectual workers joined together to implement his ideas in some near future. Then, Musil writes, Nietzsche's thought might change culture for the next thousand years. Musil's use of the millennium as an image of some future historical, perhaps utopian, time appears in the diaries before Musil uses it to characterize part 3 of *The Man without Qualities*. In the diaries the millennium is linked with the idea of intellectual and ethical transformations resulting in a new culture produced by a small brigade of serious Nietzscheans.

In a sense young Musil is writing about two sides of himself when he envisions Nietzschean workers looking for future possibilities while recalling those thinkers who can accept only mathematically exact results. He identifies with both visionaries and scientists. Thus it would seem that as a young man he is already thinking about a utopia embodying the science he respects and the transformation of values that will produce the new culture Nietzsche called for. This diary passage shows that at the same time that Musil dismisses Nietzsche, he endorses the near-programmatic side of Nietzsche's writings, nothing less than the transforming of culture and values through the superior individual's creative and intellectual work.

In Emerson, before Nietzsche, belief in the possibility of the transformation of culture is accompanied by an affirmation of the role of the will to power, especially as manifested in the individual's desire for self-affirmation. Musil is not quick to accept the central role of the will to power. Rather he is more attracted by the concomitant idea that there is no stable reality, only alignments of force; and that in great individuals, there is a quest for power that results in the creation of culture. In the diaries one also sees that the young Musil was impressed by, if critical of, Nietzsche's call for the advent of an *Übermensch,* or "superman," who would be the creative agent who transforms values and hence culture. From Nietzsche's perspective the superman is a hypothetical necessity for overcoming the nihilism he saw as the likely future of European culture. The "superman" sounds rather preposterous to contemporary ears. Yet encapsulated in this idea is the central philosophical problem for anyone who takes Nietzsche seriously, for taking him seriously means accepting the challenge to find the grounds for any morality or ethical thought. His hypothesis about the *Übermensch* is a thought experiment directed against the collapse of values that Nietzsche, accurately enough, saw as the coming fate of European culture.

Under the influence of Nietzsche, Musil's development as a writer turned on his attempt to understand the collapse of the belief in values while probing regions of conscious from which new values might emerge. He wanted to become a proponent of a new morality that might fill what Patrizia C. McBride, in her study of Musil, sees as the "void of ethics" that is at the heart of his work.[2] If one reads the diaries from this perspective, one finds Musil regularly thinking about the foundations of ethics, using distinctions he derives from Emerson as well as Nietzsche. For example, in a key passage, perhaps from the early 1920s, he makes the distinction between the "moralist" and the "ethicist." These terms are notoriously subject to hairsplitting by philosophers. With Nietzsche explicitly in mind, Musil makes a clear, if eccentric, distinction. On the one hand, the moralist is the academic philosopher who categorizes moral statements as an appendage to theoretical philosophy; and on the other hand, the ethical thinker is the thinker whose work transforms of the nature of morality (*TB* 1:645). Musil's ethicist is a moral visionary who changes the content of ethical thought. His examples of ethicists are revealing: Confucius, Lao-Tzu, Christ, Nietzsche, mystics, and essayists, to which Musil later appends stoics and Epicureans (*TB* 1:645). He recognizes that his ethicists are all different, though they all are akin to poets, in that they are what he calls "teachers of humanity" (*TB* 1:645). The reference to essayists is clearly to Emerson, a poet and near prophet. The inclusion of Christ and Nietzsche in the same list of teachers might well have astonished the self-proclaimed anti-Christ Nietzsche, but Musil is casting his net wide to find historical examples of thinkers, prophets, and poets who have been able to fill the ethical void that he saw, from his youth on, endangering Europe.

Musil could extol Nietzsche as an ethical thinker comparable to Christ, but by 1920 he also recognized that Nietzsche had had a deleterious influence on the development of German culture, especially in the development of its reactionary, racist ideologies. Musil pondered in the diaries about what a nasty thing it was for fate to have caused Nietzsche and socialism to show up in the same historical epoch. Nietzsche was being used to combat social democracy. Because of his influence, Musil writes, the ideology of race, "aristocratism," and antidemocratic thought had gained philosophical respectability and a role in public political thought (*TB* 1:395). He bemoans the fact that Nietzsche's thought lent itself to supporting the antidemocratic, right-wing ideologies that opposed a democratic state. As an opponent of the very idea of race, Musil never entertained any of the racist fantasies of German nationalists (nor did Nietzsche, for that matter). And as a liberal proponent of individual freedom, he never promoted any belief in a superior type of human. However, Musil saw that with relatively little difficulty nationalists and racists could and were using Nietzsche to endorse their pseudoscientific beliefs in superior races as well as their antidemocratic beliefs directed against the Weimar Republic. In short, with little distortion Nietzsche could be cited to support their contempt for liberal democracy and democratic socialism.

Today postmodern Nietzschean thinkers (and most postmodern intellectuals have been Nietzschean) interpret Nietzsche's proposal that the will to power is the central motif of human existence to mean that he rejected belief in the existence of objective truth. The scientist and the rationalist dupe themselves with the belief they pursue objective truth, when they are actually pursuing power by framing truths that enable them to maximize their control over others. This means, as Nietzsche put it in *On the Genealogy of Morals,* that deluded scientists cannot be free spirits since they still believe in truth.[3] Musil rejects Nietzsche's belief that truth is delusion, accepting instead Emerson's belief in multiple truths. He is rather more Emersonian than Nietzschean when he argues, in the diaries and essays, that there is a truth of the individual as well as the truth of the scientific generalization. He rejects the Nietzschean viewpoint whenever it entails the denial of scientific rationality or the rejection of the belief that well-grounded knowledge is possible. Musil's diaries are at one in this regard with his doctoral dissertation and its critique of positivism: there are grounds for truth, or rather multiple grounds for multiple truths. In brief, then, in the early diaries Nietzsche's influence shows itself to be as much negative as positive, though one could also say that this is precisely what Nietzsche wanted from anyone who read him with care.

The diaries show that there is another way in which Emerson corrected Nietzsche for Musil. Preceding Nietzsche, Emerson framed the hypothesis that the quest for power is central to human character, but he saw culture to be a means of taming this quest (not unlike the way Freud saw culture as a repressive force that kept human beings from the self-destructive, unbridled pursuit of the pleasure principle). Musil seems to have meditated on Emerson's essay "Culture" (from *The Conduct of Life*), in which he states, "Whilst all the world is in pursuit of power, and of wealth as a means to power, culture corrects the theory of success. A man is the prisoner of his power" (1017). Culture's goal should be liberation—or emancipation, as one might say with Immanuel Kant and the Enlightenment values in mind. From Emerson's perspective culture is the most general set of beliefs, manners, mores, institutions, and values into which every individual is born. Individuality is not only consistent with culture and its universals, but, as Musil took to heart, the individual is the basis for the creation of culture. In this Emersonian dialectic between culture and individual existence, we find a key for what Musil meant by his recurring notion of *Geist,* or mind/spirit. In Musil's sense it is the individual mind identified as the locus for the creation of culture. Mind creates culture, while in turn the end of culture is to eliminate all extraneous elements from mind and to leave it in free control of its pure power, as Emerson put it (1015). Musil repeated this idea in various ways in the diaries. The empowered individual mind is the goal, and also the producer, of culture. The interaction of individual and society should ideally aim at the liberation of the empowered individual, who creates values that, perforce, must be generalized in society if society is to be transformed by them. Musil's reliance upon the term *Geist* shows that he wanted to avoid the suggestion that society or some social aggregate is the locus for creation, for *Geist*—with its Hegelian antecedents—suggests that the individual mind and the historically evolving space of culture can coincide even as they are different.

The tension arising from the contrast of culture and the individual mind characterizes much of Musil's work, from *Young Törless* to *The Man without Qualities*. In the diaries he frames his inquiry into this relation in a notably questioning, skeptical spirit. It seems that the kind of skepticism that Emerson praised as a necessary attitude in, say, his late essay "Providence" also informs much of what one finds in Musil's early diaries. Skepticism, claims Emerson, "counterbalances any accumulations of power" (1055). And so we can see in the diaries that skepticism is a guiding principle as the young Musil reads, writes, makes notes, and argues with himself while questioning various propositions and intellectual positions. As he writes about writing, meditates on various philosophers from Kant to Husserl, and analyzes key concepts of philosophy and psychology, Musil's diaries resemble at times a kind of laboratory for experimental skepticism, one in which the writer's will to power is kept firmly under control. Perhaps this skeptical play is what is most interesting in the musings making up the diaries: there is something tonic about encountering a mind engaged in the most serious form of play.

In sum, in these early notes, Musil skeptically meditated upon his mind's own working, questioning a vast number of ideas and beliefs, while spinning off possible writing projects. Constant is the belief that mastery of his own mind might lead to freeing it from the weight of history and social determinates. At the same time, undergirding this questioning is the recurrent question of how to bring together the exigencies of scientifically accurate thinking with the desire for a renewed culture in which ethical thought allows for the full development of human possibilities. Entertaining, but rejecting, the belief that Nietzsche's aristocratic superman could create a new culture, young Musil began to formulate for himself the utopian task of seeking the basis for an ethics and a renewal of culture that even his friends among the Viennese positivists could accept.

The Doctoral Dissertation

When young Musil left Vienna to go to Berlin in 1903, the positivists of the Vienna Circle had yet to come together. The antecedent event for their formation as a group had already occurred, however, when the Chair for Inductive Sciences at the University of Vienna was created in 1895 for the renowned physicist Ernst Mach. The next occupant of this chair, Moritz Schlick, was instrumental in founding the Vienna Circle in 1922. This was a group of thinkers, in various disciplines, whose endorsement of positivism honored Mach's work. The members of the circle first gathered to discuss not Mach, however, but Wittgenstein's *Tractatus,* perhaps the most important work of philosophy by a Viennese thinker in the early twentieth century (published in 1921 as Wittgenstein's doctoral dissertation at Cambridge but written several years earlier). In it Wittgenstein undertakes investigations into the conditions of possibility for making meaningful statements. The *Tractatus* is in part a critique of Mach's work on the nature of scientific truth, but it is a positive critique and differs radically from Musil's dissertation. I bring up these facts to point out that, in criticizing Mach, Musil's dissertation attacked a thinker whose work was at the center of some of the most important contemporary epistemological questions brought up by major minds not only in Vienna but throughout Europe. With these facts in mind, let us turn to consider what Musil did in writing his dissertation dealing with the scientific epistemology of the Viennese physicist Ernst Mach, the inspiration for Viennese positivism and, through Wittgenstein, major trends in Anglo-American philosophy.

Musil's dissertation is about the foundations of science, so a word about his education in science is in order. He was educated in an environment in which the assumptions about the nature of knowledge were in some respects different from those found in the English-speaking world around 1900. For one thing the practice of science in Germany and Austria was coupled with an interest in epistemology not usually found among English-language scientists. Though Mach's major works were translated into English, his positivistic thought was not widely embraced in the Anglo-American world. This lack of response to Mach's epistemology contrasts notably with the influence he had on European thinkers as diverse as Freud, Einstein, and Wittgenstein—as well as Nietzsche, who scoffed at Mach, and Lenin, who, as a theorist of dialectical materialism, wrote a hostile book attacking him. (Mach's influence on American thought became massive, it should be noted, when the Nazis drove the Viennese positivists to take positions in the United States in the 1930s.) Another difference between, say, English-speaking physicists and German-speaking physicists is that in 1900 physics was divided between those scientists, mainly English, who thought that the end of research in the physical sciences might be in sight and those, mainly German, who understood that, with the introduction of Max Planck's quantum theory in 1900, the very foundations of physics had to be rethought. In Austria and then in Germany Musil was thus educated in a world of science that was open to the need for radical change in both physical theory and the epistemology this theory engendered.

It may nonetheless seem unusual that a young engineer and nocturnal literary vivisector should be concerned with problems of scientific epistemology. His engineering degree undoubtedly prepared him for this concern. Musil's university education in engineering, in the European context of the time, meant that he received a firm grounding in pure science, including mathematics and theoretical physics. He was thus acquainted with theoretical considerations concerning the basis of scientific knowledge—which is the more restricted meaning the term *epistemology* usually has in Europe. One can understand the nature of an education in engineering at the time if one considers that Albert

Einstein also first studied physics and mathematics at a German-language technical university resembling the sort Musil attended. After completing his engineering studies in Brünn and spending a period of roughly a year as an engineering assistant in Stuttgart, Musil went to Berlin to pursue a doctorate in psychology, rather than physics or mathematics, while writing his first novel. His curriculum shows that he was quite serious in looking for the way that would lead him to an intellectually meaningful life.

His parallel scientific, philosophical, and literary activity at the time underscores the fact that, throughout his life, Musil wanted to bring science into literature and to use literature to bring a moral dimension to science. His understanding of this situation differed from that of many of his contemporaries in that he believed science set the model for precision that humanistic endeavors might learn from. He was not ready to jettison science in the name of postromantic irrationalities. Read in this light, his dissertation shows that the young Musil was searching for an epistemology that can offer criteria for truth, for all types of truth, including moral truth. His search for criteria should be viewed as central to his fundamental project of bringing literature and science together, so that moral thinking might possess scientific accuracy and scientific rationalism could be brought to bear on ethics. From this perhaps utopian standpoint, the moral basis of Musil's scientific dissertation is complementary to the use of science in his novel *Young Törless,* which, as we will see in the next chapter, portrays a psychological crisis born of a failure to find a grounds for knowledge.

After reading the diaries, especially the earliest notebooks, one is struck by the fact that, in his critique of Mach's positivism, Musil does not directly invoke Emerson or Nietzsche to criticize Mach. In fact he defends a theoretical position close to that of the traditional realism of empiricism. A more subtle reading of the dissertation, I add, could argue that, by putting himself in opposition to Mach's positivism—a doctrine that clearly attracted him—Musil was indeed applying what he had learned from Emerson and Nietzsche, to wit, the idea that truth can only emerge from a play of opposition and contradiction. And ultimately, Musil criticizes Mach with an Emersonian sense that truth is not an arbitrary construct, no matter how many kinds of truth one may discover. This is perhaps the most important lesson drawn from Emerson: there are many types of truth, but they are not as arbitrary in their construction as Mach would have it.

In selecting Mach and his epistemology for a dissertation topic, Musil had decided to deal with one of the three or four most important scientific thinkers in Europe at the turn of the century. In the European scientific community

Mach had the status of figures such as the French mathematician and episte-mologist Henri Poincaré, the Austrian physicist Ludwig Boltzmann (Mach's main adversary in physics), and the French physicist Pierre Duhem, who, in radically restating Mach, proposed in his *La théorie physique* of 1906 the idea that physical theories have nothing to do with reality, that they are simply an ensemble of hypotheses, expressed mathematically as laws, that may or may not be confirmed, more or less satisfactorily, by empirical testing. Poincaré had developed a comparable position in his *La Science et l'hypothèse* of 1902 with his theory that science knows nothing about things in themselves: it knows only the mathematically described relations between things. Contrasting with these ideas that foresaw no closure to scientific research—for "reality" could be described by an indefinite number of more or less satisfactory theories—was the variant of physical theory proposed by Boltzmann, who defended the atomic hypothesis against Mach. Given his epistemology claiming all knowl-edge is based on perceptible sensations, Mach logically rejected the theory of invisible atoms as a form of metaphysical belief. (And Musil must have been impressed by the fact that Boltzmann killed himself in 1906 in despair over the harassment he had received in Vienna.)

Musil knew that in his work on thermodynamics Boltzmann, the founder of classical statistical physics, had endorsed the idea that invisible particles have real existence. Their real existence seemed to account for the effective-ness of hypotheses to explain, for example, heat, energy, and entropy. In historical terms, then, Musil was writing his dissertation in the wake of an ongoing controversy in physics about the substantial reality of atoms in which many German and Austrian positivist physicists—such as Mach—rejected the belief in these particles as mere metaphysics. This dispute was taking place during the years in which the English physicist J. J. Thomson theorized in 1897 that he had found a particle, the electron, even smaller than the hydrogen atom; Planck presented his idea of the quantum in 1900; and Einstein published in 1905 his first papers on Brownian motion, light, and special relativity—the paper on Brownian movement being a substantial contribution to confirming the well-grounded nature of atomic theory. In this context, Musil had set for himself a task that was in effect concerned with central issues in European sci-ence. He was placing himself right at the center of the ongoing debate about the nature of scientific hypotheses and their relation to a putative reality.

The understated title of Musil's dissertation, "A Contribution to an Eval-uation of Mach's Doctrines" (published in English as *On Mach's Theories*), belies, however, the intense commitment with which he was devoting himself at once to science and to literature as conjoined ways to search for multiple truths. Bearing in mind what Musil learned from Emerson, one is perhaps not surprised to find in his thesis a skeptical form of defense of realist epistemology, skeptical in its critique of Mach and the positivism that allowed him to dismiss "reality" and ultimate truth as a metaphysical dream of no interest for science. Musil's reading of Nietzsche had also prepared him for his encounter with Mach, though from a different perspective. The antipositivist Nietzsche had, in his critique of science, made of science a question of relativist perspectives and arbitrarily accepted axioms, so that much of what he says about science actually parallels what Mach says: for both men scientific truth is an arbitrary formulation. For Nietzsche it is an arbitrary codification of the will to power, for Mach an arbitrary relation for which the scientist happens to find a functional description. Having doubted Nietzsche's ideas in his diaries, in his dissertation Musil was hardly ready to accept Mach's idea decreeing that scientific truth is simply a functional description of regularly recurring sense data—with the data allowing any number of possible functional descriptions.

Moreover both Nietzsche and Mach—who scorned each other—rejected the idea that there is a substantial self or mind that can entertain the objective truth of propositions. Rather, truth is what one must call, for lack of a better term in this context, a subjective phenomenon, one foisted onto the knower, by the will to power, according to Nietzsche, and by the accidents of sensation and perception, according to Mach. From Mach's perspective the belief in self is an unjustified corollary to the fact that there are sensations. For this reason Nietzsche had dismissed the Cartesian cogito and its affirmation of a self knowing itself. I will return to the question of psychology at the end of this chapter. Here I want merely to stress the parallel between the enemies Nietzsche and Mach and to point out that if Musil could not accept Mach's epistemology, he nonetheless admired the power and coherence of Mach's thought, much as he did Nietzsche's. In fact, like many others in the world of German thought, and indeed throughout the European scientific community, Musil never freed himself from Mach's influence, no more than he freed himself from Nietzsche. Arguably, there is probably no tenet in Mach's thought that Musil—personally or through the character Ulrich—did not experiment with later in life.

In his dissertation, however, it is clear that young Musil wanted to exorcise Mach's influence by showing the weaknesses of the arguments upon which his epistemology was based. This was a daunting task, and it bespeaks Musil's intellectual courage that he took on perhaps the most influential philosopher of science at the time—and this a time when it was probably not yet clear in his own mind whether he would begin an academic career or not.

Admittedly Musil's thesis director, Carl Stumpf, was quite critical of Mach, but much of the European intellectual community was more inclined to admire in very positive terms the way the aging positivist had rid science of the residues of romantic metaphysics. For example, in his early paper on special relativity of 1905, Einstein respected Mach's strictures on how the unexamined use of physical concepts such as mass, time, and space can import metaphysical notions into science. Mach's influence is directly present in the definitions Einstein used in framing the special theory of relativity. Like Einstein, Musil was drawn to a thinker who had rendered problematic any naive belief in the objective existence of truth confirmed by received concepts.

However, Mach's epistemological restrictions, used by Einstein in formulating relativity theory and later by Niels Bohr and Werner Heisenberg in their interpretation of quantum mechanics, impressed the young Musil as restrictions that limited access to knowledge bearing on human concerns. It is apparent that Musil saw no place for human concerns in the kind of restricted empiricism that Mach had imposed as the reigning physical theory, which became the basis for positivism. In other words, in framing his critique of Mach Musil was already thinking about science in terms of its import for ethics and other human concerns, and all the more so in that Mach's thought placed the human self in question. For this reason Musil wanted to find the weak points in an epistemology that declared that physical theories were only so many representations that could be replaced by other representations as functional descriptions. Looking for reliable truths, he was loath to accept Mach's view that physical theories are simply fictions that have demonstrated usefulness. In the dissertation Musil gives the impression that he was hungry for something like what metaphysicians call reality or a substantial ground for truth and self. From the perspective of the empirical realism Musil adopts in the dissertation, Mach denies the possibility of any real knowledge of a unified world, which is necessary if one is to unify accurate knowledge with moral thinking. Finally, as Hannah Hickman stresses in her insightful *Robert Musil and the Culture of Vienna,* Musil reacted strongly to Mach's view that science, though it describes facts as minutely as possible, does not offer an explanation of the world containing those facts.[4] Musil wanted knowledge that explained the world in itself, a necessity if sensation is to take on meaningful shape. Individual percepts, from Musil's viewpoint, only have meaning when placed in a total gestalt.

At the beginning of his dissertation, Musil lays out succinctly what he finds to be the six most important points for understanding Mach's epistemology. First, he sees that Mach does not believe that science explains nature. Science can only describe it, and it usually does so with mathematical symbols. Today, I note, the difference between description and explanation has become canonical for many thinkers. In the historical context of Mach's thought this distinction meant that physicists have nothing to say about phenomena that cannot be set down in functional relationships. This first point entails the second point, namely, that just as there are no explanations of any sort except in the form of descriptions, there are no causal laws. Science cannot ferret out hidden forces, for it proposes only "functional" diagrams, or charts of relationships. If this is so, then it cannot be said in any meaningful sense that one fact is the cause of another fact. A fact exists only in a calculable relationship to another fact. Third, with the dismissal of the principle of causality, Mach also dismisses the grounds for the belief in essential things or substances. The concept of substance has in fact no meaning, since the substance to which a cause would be inherent plays no role in a functional description. The concept of "thing" is simply an economical concept that allows a kind of shorthand for the attribution of sensations. But unchanging things do not exist in any meaningful sense for science. Therefore, the notion of eternally valid substances or "things" has no interest for the scientist. Fourth, since scientific laws do not describe ultimate substances, laws can best be viewed as functional auxiliaries that perform their role best when they function most economically—what is classically known as the principle of parsimony. The best law is the most economical law in that it offers, in the simplest terms, a résumé of the greatest number of cases. (A hostile critic might observe that parsimony is a trick of rhetoric and nothing intrinsic to the world.)

The fifth point that Musil underlines finds resonance in psychology, since it concerns the nature of the subject who knows scientific laws. Mach claims that the problem of the relations between the objective world and the subjective world is a pseudoproblem. The distinction of the known world and a knowing subject separate from the world is unnecessary. From the standpoint of Mach's science the distinction is nugatory, for, as Musil describes it, such a distinction is of use only for a primitively oriented world. From the point of view of Mach's economy of means the distinction of self and world is superfluous and can play no role in epistemology. There are sensations, sciences bases its descriptions upon them, and that is all. Psychology and physics study the same thing from a different perspective. Finally Musil's sixth point is that Mach believes that the basis for natural science is the study of the relationships between sensations or what he calls abstractly "elements." Colors, pressure, movements, and the like are the basis for the elements that science studies in order to frame the equations that describe their relationships. These sensations that are the basis for physical laws are also the basis of psychical life. This is another way of saying that sensations are all we perceive and ultimately all that we know. In knowing the world, we know the self, and thus, to restate Mach's point, physics and psychology have the same object in common.

Musil is well aware that Mach's epistemology is powerful in that it draws in large part upon the actual practice of science, especially the physics of mechanics. But there is one aspect of Mach's epistemology that Musil does not find in accord with scientific practice, and this is his restatement, in terms of mathematical physics, of the skeptical rejection of causality and of the belief in necessary connections in nature. Musil knows that modern skepticism about causality precedes Mach by more than a century, since it begins with the thought of Scottish philosopher David Hume in the eighteenth century. Hume was rebutted on this point by Kant in his theory of knowledge. With his rejection of causality as mere metaphysics, Mach comes down squarely on the Scottish skeptic's side, against Kant—much as Musil does at times later in his life.

Musil's relation to Hume is worth commentary, since Hume was frequently on his mind. We see this in Musil's sketch in the diaries for a critique of Husserl's interpretation of Hume (*TB* 1:123), as well as later in the diaries when Musil quotes Hume in preparation for an introduction to an edition of essays that he never finished (*TB* 1:664). Moreover, in a late passage in *The Man without Qualities* Ulrich also ponders Hume's rejection of causality when talking to his sister. She is in fact a Humean skeptic without ever having heard of the philosopher (4:1270). In brief Hume's skeptical rejection of causality was on Musil's mind all his life. If, as Dagmar Barnouw has argued in her study of Hume and Musil, Musil was actually quite close to Hume in his skepticism, it is also true that in his dissertation he seized upon Mach's reprise of Hume to criticize Mach and Hume in the name of the actual practice of science.[5]

From another perspective, I suggest that in considering Musil reading Mach reading Hume, we can see that the Enlightenment continued to inflect modernist ideas, especially modernists such as Musil who recognized that their roots were in an Enlightenment they could not fully accept. Musil was drawn to Hume precisely because he is the most unsettling of Enlightenment philosophers, the most modern of them, and his rejection of the principle of causality is as astonishing today as it was in 1739 when in *A Treatise of Human Nature* he denied that a causal power can be validly deduced from the fact that one event always follows another, as, say, when a billiard ball hits another ball and "causes" it to move. In his critique of Mach Musil obviously needs to come to grips with Hume's argument is that it is the mind that frames ideas of

36

necessity and that necessity is simply an effect of observation, as Hume puts it in the *Treatise*. If necessity is an effect of observation, then it is nothing but an internal impression of the mind, or simply a "determination to carry our thoughts from one object to another" (book 1, part 3, section 14). Hence according to Hume and later Mach, there is no natural necessity in nature. All we can say is that, when many uniform instances appear and when the same object is always followed by the same event, then we assume there to be a customary connection. Necessary connections are much like a fiction the mind contrives for its own needs.

Mach took Hume to mean that appearances are only appearances, and that there need be nothing behind them, neither causal forces nor the "thing in itself" that Kant had posited as the hidden reality behind phenomenal appearance. Thus the scientist need only to attend to what actually manifests itself in sensation, using equations as shorthand to express relationships that may or may not—but usually do—repeat themselves. In his dissertation, then, Musil questions Hume's and Mach's view that the law of causality is something of a fiction, for Musil, here a skeptic about skepticism, doubts that in reality one actually practices science with the view that laws are merely functional descriptions of relations holding among sense data. In defending an empirical realism he argues that there is a larger world beyond the limited range described by functional variables. With this argument Musil is seeking access to some reality that has no support in the Machean view that the equations establishing relations between variables are an interesting but non-necessary attribute of the perceiving mind.

Musil is hostile, in fact, to most of the implications of Mach's view that science should be conceived as functional relations or a series of relationships perceived between sensations, some of which are part of physics, some of psychology. In the dissertation Musil feels that Mach, after Hume, eliminates a real world behind appearances, be it in the observed world or in the observer of the appearances. With this type of monism, moreover, Mach rejects the Cartesian tradition separating self and world that many believe has been the basis for Western science since the scientific revolution of the seventeenth century, and the scientific ground for the metaphysics of reality. Mach was not alone in this rejection; many other scientists in the late nineteenth century also did so, though not in reaction against Descartes. One can now see that their positivism was a reaction against the preceding two generations of German scientists, for whom the quest for some nebulous ultimate reality had been considered equally as important as the search for mathematical precision. In this regard Musil could only sympathize with the positivist rejection of the romantic extravagances of the science that was called in German *Natur-philosophie*. He knew well that only by strictly limiting scientific inquiry, in mathematical terms, could one contribute much to real knowledge. The ultimate reality that romantic scientists sought was not found in chemical equations, the laws of thermodynamics, or an understanding of electromagnetic phenomena, all of which became part of lasting knowledge. By stating that scientific models are simply heuristic devices having logical but no metaphysical necessity, Mach was also part of a general movement to rid science of a great deal of nineteenth-century philosophical claptrap.

Musil also understood that, in adopting Hume's critique of causality, Mach was in effect trying to free science from philosophy. Mach's strategy was to propose that "reality" is underdetermined, which means that any number of laws or models may describe the same phenomena composing a world of arbitrary relations. There are no metaphysical absolutes. In his desire to free science from metaphysical speculation Mach was undoubtedly one of the most successful thinkers in the history of Western thought. However, he left science with a world in which, as Musil skeptically notes with irony in his thesis, one lives with some difficulty if one desires to believe in regular causal connections that allow some degree of certainty about what the future may bring.

In the conclusion of his dissertation, in fact, Musil scoffs at the idea one can live without causality. He refuses the idea that idealization is simply a matter of abstracting from sense data, according to the arbitrary connections that a scientist happens to perceive. The connections are not arbitrary, he implies, and representation is constrained by natural necessity. In his portrayal of Mach's viewpoint on causality, Musil in fact took delight in finding a large number of quotations from Mach's work in which he contradicted himself on the principle of causality, since, like most ordinary mortals, when dealing with the world of events that actually impinges upon consciousness, Mach did act as if there were objective regularities imposed by nature itself with the force of causal necessity. In his defense of epistemological realism, Musil was agreeing with thinkers such as Einstein and Poincaré, theorists who accepted Mach's notions of relativity but broke with Mach by pointing out that necessity does constrain what an observer can offer as an idealization. Musil's critique of Mach and Hume in the dissertation was not his final thought on causality. Actually he was never really convinced that Mach and Hume were wrong. The thought that one could live without causality later led him to experiment with new ways of conceiving explanations of phenomena, such as through stochastic thinking, using probability theory. And from a different viewpoint his later novella "Tonka" is an extravagant, but moving, thought experiment about how one might try to live while rejecting causality.

Musil's critique of Mach's view of causality is accompanied by his rejection of Mach's relativism, which in the historical context leads to Einstein, the great theorist of relativity. The triangulation of Mach, Einstein, and Musil sets the outlines of a central debate about scientific epistemology in the early twentieth century, which eventually came to an end with the acceptance of the revolution in physics ushered in by Einstein's relativity theory. If in his philosophical thought, Einstein, like Musil, never accepted Mach's positivist limitations on science, he did take to heart Mach's rejection of metaphysics when he framed definitions for his theory of relativity. Moreover, it is now generally accepted that Mach's thought on limited relativity enabled Einstein to think through the logical implications of total relativity. In the dissertation Musil is aware of the implications of Mach's demonstration of the relativity not only of space, but also of time. Unlike Einstein or Poincaré, Musil is simply dismayed by the thought that both space and time are relative notions. He resembled Einstein only in his critical reaction to Mach that affirms a realism accepting causal constraints as grounds for defining truth. But unlike Einstein, Musil was completely hostile toward Mach's version of relativity theory, a theory that denied absolute space and, as Einstein developed it, absolute time. In fine, young Musil was not ready to accept Mach's denial of the Newtonian and Kantian framework for defining reality. The young engineer believed that there could be an absolute measure of space and time that are the coordinates of what we call reality.

The contrast of Musil's reaction to Mach with Einstein's is illuminating. Einstein's understanding of Mach is now part of the received history of science, and Einstein himself made sure his relation to Mach would be understood when in 1918 he coined what he called, in homage to Mach after the latter's death, "Mach's principle." By Mach's principle Einstein refers to Mach's idea that all inertial masses can only be measured in a relationship of one body to another. There is no other framework by which they can be measured. Correcting Newton, as it were, Mach had said that all temporal measurements exist because one measures a relationship of change between bodies in relative motion. Therefore, there is not, as Newton believed, any absolute scale by which time exists. Thus time and space can both be defined as relative properties, which Einstein then defined, much to Mach's distaste, as relations between inertial frameworks. Time and space can thus change with regard to a given observer. The only constant in the universe is the speed of light, an idea that the aging Mach, respecting the logic of his own phenomenalism, also rejected. Einstein was a realist who showed that time and space are known in relation to frames of reference: with the exception of the speed of light, there are no final absolutes for determining reality.

Young Musil's distaste for relativity springs from his insight that Mach's relativity undermines the possibility for a "solid" definition of the real. So Musil undertook a defense of the realism threatened by Mach's rejection of absolute epistemic frameworks. Quite simply, he proposes in the dissertation that it makes sense to speak about absolute frameworks when dealing with everyday appearances. His objection to Mach's relativity aims at preserving the possibility of knowing things, specifically the identity of things in time, so he argues for the existence of constant frameworks that preserve a world possessing epistemic solidity. Musil argues that temporality and knowledge of the world are interrelated, and not simply in relativistic terms. I quote the dissertation so that the reader can judge the subtlety of Musil's argument: "It is precisely the fact that one can speak of the same spatial or temporal behavior even though one is making comparisons with different bodies (by which is meant that judgments about, for example, the time, could be made by reference to a clock, the earth's angle of rotation, a fall in temperature) which is evidence for the claim that such a behavior is independent of the bodies we resort to for purposes of comparison" (*BzM* 65).[6]

Musil is arguing that something independent can resist being dissolved into relations that have no existence other than in relative descriptions. In the dissertation relativity is conceived as inimical to realism, since relativity dissolves all properties into a question of comparative frameworks, which eliminates the possibility of defining qualities as things in themselves, in short, the possibility of an *Eigenschaftsbegriff,* or a concept of a quality or property of a thing or concept (*BzM* 54–55). This question remained of crucial importance for the novelist, who, as he matured, resisted while recognizing the strong attraction of the idea, shared by Mach and contemporaries such as Poincaré and Duhem, that knowledge can only be of relations between things, not of things or qualities in themselves. In one sense this question of how to define the properties of things became the ironic subject of his novel about a man without properties.

Mach was a relativist who refused to recognize absolute time and space precisely because "reality" is known simply in the form of bundles of sense data that cannot be absolutely constrained by any framework. For Musil, as for a contemporary scientist such as Planck, who attacked Mach, Mach's kind of relativity and his psychology dissolved the world of things and concepts into arbitrary sensations. In an insightful study of Mach's thought, Guillaume Garreta stresses this side of his work, according to which what one takes to be a "thing" is in fact only a symbol in thought representing a complex of sensations having only a "relative stability." Mach held that "there is no permanent nucleus hiding behind phenomena, the world of the thing in itself and of the transcendental is an imaginary world. Showing this, Mach took the counter-viewpoint of traditional realism, even the refined form given realism by Helmholtz, according to which sensations are not the faithful reproduction of things, but rather their symbol. For Mach, the thing is an abstraction, and its 'elements' are what is real."[7]

What one perceives—sensations or the "elements" making up percepts—is the basis for all knowledge. Since all elements are of the same type, Mach's epistemology can be characterized as a reductive monism.

The skeptical psychologist in Musil was quick to note that the very nature of sense data and perception is problematic, and in this respect Musil's critique is most insightful. In defending the view that epistemic representation aims at an invariant necessity, known by a knowing self, he thought he had found the Achilles' tendon of positivism. And in a sense he surely had. Sense data, Musil pointed out, is central to Mach's epistemology, but the concept of sense data or sensation itself is accepted a priori. It has no conceptual rigor. Musil asks what exactly a bundle of sensations is, and found no answer in Mach. He asks what a law-governed connection between sensations is, and again finds no precise answer. Obviously, Mach had not thought out the most difficult part of his epistemology and had rather assumed as given precisely that which had to be defined and demonstrated in rigorous terms (*BmZ* 121).

Thus, according to Musil, Mach offers no rigorous definition of sense data. Rather he has defined knowledge as sense data with no concrete example of such, and, in short, can be accused of making an a priori definition function to cover up what needs to be explained. In pointing out this circularity Musil's point is that, if Mach has no precise definition of sense data, then one must doubt that science offers only so many arbitrary images of relations, images painted on the observing retina-like "pictures" of the facts. Musil argues that the positivist becomes in fact an unwitting metaphysician by postulating images where it is dubious that they exist. Moreover, Musil asks, what are these images for which there is only an illusory self to entertain them? Can one rationally argue that perhaps nobody sees them?

The infatuation with the iconic or mimetic powers of propositions was not limited to Mach. His belief that perceptions are mirrored in the "idealizations" framed by science finds echoes in many Viennese modernists, especially in the Viennese group of logical positivists to which I earlier alluded. They were following the lead, not only of Mach, but also of the first work of the young Ludwig Wittgenstein. Influenced by Mach, Wittgenstein proposed in the *Tractatus* that knowledge is based on visual mimesis, though he never defines in meaningful sentences what exactly is reproduced in the representation. From Musil's perspective he is repeating the same mistake Mach made with sensations. By coincidence, then, in criticizing Mach, Musil is criticizing much of what is found in Wittgenstein's first theory of language as set forth in the *Tractatus*. Consider in this regard how Wittgenstein describes language itself as a "picture of facts" that are supposedly visualized in language in the form of *Sachverhalten*—roughly, a factual state of affairs. (This was a notion probably first proposed by Musil's doctoral adviser, Carl Stumpf.) In the *Tractatus* Wittgenstein proposes that true propositions exactly mirror the constituent parts of what they represent. Like Mach, Wittgenstein rejects the idea that these are "things." Propositions mirror the exact parts of facts, though nobody could ever point to exactly what they might be. The parallel of Wittgenstein's *Sachverhalten* with Mach's complexes of sensations seems clear, as is Wittgenstein's idea that propositions mirror logical relations. The facts visualized in meaningful language are the substance, but also the limits, of what language can say. All that can be meaningfully said is what can be mirrored in propositions in language, which means that truth is limited to a fairly narrow realm of empirical facts. And, Wittgenstein adds, the world is the collection of these facts. Virtually every one of these ideas was in fact already criticized by Musil's dissertation.

Yet we can also see commonalities between Musil and Wittgenstein. Wittgenstein's example shows that his positivism does not exclude mysticism, for his near-mystical belief in silence springs from the impossibility of describing the very pictures he attributed to language. Or alternatively Wittgenstein's belief that essential matters escape language springs from his paradoxical belief that what language can meaningfully picture is not really essential in any case. In other words Wittgenstein, like Musil, yearned for a reality beyond the limits of positivistic propositions or functional relations— even if Wittgenstein had framed in the *Tractatus* the linguistic cage in which he trapped himself. Musil never trapped himself in any such philosophical cage, though he was very hesitant to accept that any proposition could be meaningful if it does not in some sense respect the demands of reason. In subsequent chapters we will deal with the question as to whether Musil ever got further than Wittgenstein in pointing out something beyond language, in finding some "other condition," as he came to designate the object of his quest.

I do not mean to suggest that one can speak of a direct relation between Wittgenstein and Musil. Rather, they both reacted to Mach's limitation of knowledge to the realm of functional relations. It is noteworthy that Wittgenstein even developed his later philosophy in the *Philosophical Investigations*

(1951) in direct reaction against the metaphysics of the visual, after he decided that nobody ever saw a picture in language. (It has not been shown that Wittgenstein knew Musil's work, but it is possible.) In this sense Musil and the later Wittgenstein share a common interest in their critique of the mimetic idealization that positivists found in empirical linguistic propositions. In effect both make a critique aiming at the kind of positivism that believed meaningful propositions must mirror something like visual sensations. Finally, as Adolf Frisé has pointed out in his commentary of Musil's diaries, both Musil and Wittgenstein thought that aesthetics and ethics were overlapping domains (*TB* 2:562). I would suggest this belief is another aspect of their desire to transcend the limits of knowledge imposed by the dominant positivism of their youth. Both conceive of aesthetics as a "showing" of ethics, and of ethics as the realm where values are as real as any other aspect of reality.

This comparison of Wittgenstein with Musil suggests another way in which Musil was reacting critically to Mach's interpretation of scientific discourse as a mathematically organized picturing. According to Mach scientific discourse supposedly shows logical relations from which metaphysics is banned. Musil underscores this point by stressing that Mach says that the mathematical relations called scientific laws are not causal relations but the mimetic reproduction of facts in thought. Musil wants to show that Mach, like his successor positivists, placed in doubt the very existence of such solid constituents of reality as things. Musil asks what can be pictured in the equations if nothing exists but undefined complexes of sensations. He goes on to claim that Mach is contradictory in proclaiming things to be mere idealizations when in fact Mach the scientist must act as if he believes there is some permanence in things when he actually does physics. Musil is not totally against Mach in this regard, since Musil quotes almost approvingly when he notes the modern science has no use for the Kantian metaphysics proposing that there is a "thing in itself." Musil's distaste for Kant surfaces several times in the diaries and in later writings. Thus, in explaining Mach's thought, he seems almost to accept that the properties attributed to the thing are in some sense a creation of the observing mind, logical entities having a kind of ideal existence not unlike the ideal creations of geometry. This Musil admits by recognizing that the lever and plane described by mechanics have no real existence—since a million deformations and forces work upon every real lever and real plane, causing them to deviate from their ideal form. Thus they are like the ideal figures used by geometry. But, as Musil stresses, one must sometimes use some "things" such as triangles and levers and content oneself with their less than ideal status when necessary (*BmZ* 112).

Another major problem that occupied Musil for the rest of his life was the psychological theory undergirding Mach's epistemology. One should recall that Musil was, after all, writing a doctoral dissertation in psychology, and Mach had an influential theory of psychology. He had reduced, as I suggested earlier, psychology to the study of physical impressions. Since all knowledge is simply a recording of physical impressions, Mach had in effect declared physics and psychology to be simply two sides of the same coin: both deal with the relations that can be determined to exist among perceptual impressions. From Mach's positivist perspective, knowledge consists in garnering pure sensations, which science should study without worrying whether there is some other reality underlying these sensations. Mach's conflation of physics and psychology is logically derived from his theoretical position that all knowledge is simply a question of functional arrangements and descriptions of sense impressions.

Mach was not alone, moreover, in conflating physics and psychology, and his thought belongs to a tradition. Throughout the nineteenth and well into the twentieth century the lines of demarcation between physics, psychology, and philosophy were not rigid. The great German physicist-physiologist-psychologist H. L. Helmholtz (1821–1894) contributed as much to the psychology and physiology of vision and hearing as to thermodynamics and the theory of the conservation of energy. The director of Musil's thesis, Carl Stumpf, was as much at home in classical and modern philosophy as in experimental psychology and the science of acoustics: some of his work on sound and auditory phenomena was published in a journal for physics. Other examples could be cited. However, Mach was perhaps unique in his unifying psychology and physics through a reductionist positivist epistemology, notably one that Musil's mentor Stumpf did not accept.

Musil notes that Mach dismisses the reality of the knowing self by declaring it to be one more idealization. Mach's dismissal of the self as an idealization had a wide resonance in literary circles, for literary modernists before and after Musil were greatly influenced by it. Some modernists had staked much on the fact that there is indeed a substantial self that literature can explore and which is perhaps the source of literature itself. They might have felt personally attacked by Mach. Others held up his dismissal of the self as a form of emancipation from metaphysics—and this has continued to the present day. Understandably then, literary scholars have been fascinated by the idea that, to quote from a study of literary modernism, the self is just—in Mach's language—an "ideelle denkökonomische, keine reelle Einheit" (an ideal, not a real unity demanded by the economy of thought).[8] The self is at most an epistemological necessity, since the mimetic representation constituting knowledge demands that something be represented to something else. Apparently it is the need to justify mimesis that produces the belief in a self. In this regard the self as defined by Mach, a product of epistemological necessity, is also something of a fiction or an illusion, as Freud, another follower of Mach, later said in dismissing the importance of consciousness for the self. What is a self if it only exists to explain representation within a relativist framework? Skeptically taking up this question in *The Man without Qualities,* Musil was later to ask what might it mean to have a self having no properties that are really its own. Or, he asks ironically, can a self exist if it rejects the properties and sensations that oblige it to exist?

In the dissertation, however, Musil takes a different tack. He stresses that the Machean scientist lives in a world made up of complexes of sensations and points out with no little irony that the self that perceives them is an unfortunate, if seemingly necessary, presupposition. Musil's defense of the necessity of the self in his early career seems motivated by a desire, directed against Nietzsche as well as Mach, to defend a realist view of the self. It probably also derives in part from his work with Carl Stumpf, who was instrumental in the development of the Gestalt psychology that would displace Mach's kind of phenomenalism. As we saw in the diaries, Musil was fascinated by his early readings in the phenomenological philosophy of Edmund Husserl, another philosopher influenced by Stumpf. In both Stumpf and Husserl's work Musil encountered the idea that psychology must account for the integrity of perception, and thus the power of mind to define itself. Contesting the kind of analytical sensationalism that Mach proposed as the basis of knowledge, Musil found in his educational milieu theories proposing that an individual complex of sensations could make sense only when integrated into a total field.

The notion that perception must be viewed as a total field and not analytically broken down into atomistic sensations usually presupposes belief in something like a substantial self. This is not, strictly speaking, entirely a scientific question, for the desire for unity is as much aesthetic or ethical as epistemic in origin. This appeared to be the case for Musil, as we saw on the first page of his diaries with his description of the unity of the writer's perceptual field. I would thus suggest that Musil's desire for epistemic unity motivates his early critique of Mach as well as his later attempts to embody the knowing and the known self in a novel. He yearned for some kind of totality, a grounded totality revealed by, even as it reveals, an epistemic unity, one respectful of rational scientific criteria but also capable of accounting for the emotional and ethical content of perception.

Musil's reaction to Mach, in his dissertation and at times in his creative work, presents a role reversal of what one might expect from writer and scientist: the writer defends the truth of reality against the scientific epistemologist for whom the knowledge of laws or recurring functions is essentially a fiction created by autonomous scientists. The Machean scientist actually ends up looking like a novelist, which Musil suggests when he writes that Mach believes that "necessity . . . is only to be found in the relations of mutual dependence between our concepts, in the ideas we have of law and so on; but since these are gained by idealizations, necessity can only be read into nature in a fictitious fashion" (*BzM* 111–12). In the thesis Musil implies that he wants more from science than fictions. From a slightly different perspective this desire is also evident in his first novel, *Young Törless,* in which he shows he is aware that there were enough dangerous ideologies offering fictions parading as truth. Musil wanted knowledge that could grant access, beyond fiction, to some kind of epistemic certainty grounded in a self that is in contact with a real world.

Disgruntled with the reduction of knowledge to airy functional notations that seemingly hover arbitrarily over the world, Musil asks how this kind of knowledge can meet the elementary human need to know with some certainty a solid world with substantial reality. In his thesis he points out that Mach himself, as a physicist, acts as if there were causal regularities that describe an objective world that is "really" there for all scientists to deal with—however much the scientist may theorize that all laws are functional constructs that could be replaced by other constructs. By arguing that Mach must in fact agree in the end that rationality decrees that some theories fall out of competition and that others win, Musil wanted science, as well as fiction, to be responsible to the world in which humanity lives. Hypotheses must agree with facts, and not just on the basis of economy, as Musil says, but by "normal epistemological criteria" (*BzM* 54), which is to say, by conforming to some invariant objectivity. Musil wanted to show that only in its theorizing, but not in its practice, does science remove the world from our grasp.

In conclusion to these considerations of Musil's dissertation, the style and composition of the text merit an observation. A doctoral dissertation often reads like a collage of opinions dredged up from every possible source so that the doctoral candidate can give the impression that not a scrap of relevant evidence has been omitted. Musil's dissertation does not at all resemble this kind of work. Instead, he takes six major books by Mach and reads them closely. He often quotes from them at length to let Mach speak directly to the reader to make a point. Though there are numerous references to the history of science, especially that of mechanics, there is virtually no reference to a secondary source in the dissertation (and hence no bibliography other than Mach's texts). Reading the thesis is a bit like reading a novel in which Musil stages the thought of his main character, the philosopher-physicist Mach. As narrator or stage director, Musil intervenes at key moments with commentary that sometimes criticizes Mach, but at other times simply orients the reader toward a clear understanding of Mach's viewpoint. Musil gives the impression of hovering around Mach's powerful presence, with commentary, at times ironically critical but at other times almost espousing Mach's viewpoint, which in the case of direct quotation is facilitated by the fact that the reader seems to hear Mach's voice. This kind of textual play preludes to Musil's being the anti-Machean Machean he became in later life. He does not offer a fully developed ironic play of juxtaposing viewpoints; nor could he do so in a doctoral dissertation. But his admiration for, and his critique of, Mach are already engaged in a tug-of-war for which Emerson's essayism will offer the form of expression in much of his later work.

This near espousal of Mach is shown in the concluding résumé Musil makes of his critique of Mach. In it he reviews the points he has made to show the difficulties involved in living without causality as a basic principle. He states that in the course of his argument he began with the requirement of a demonstration that experience can be grasped in a scientifically satisfactory way, yet without going beyond what is perceivable. Thus he first seems to agree with Mach. Then he says that he showed that the steps leading from this point to the interpretation of functional connections as a matter of economy and calculation resulted in a denial of natural necessity. It is not altogether clear at this point that he disagrees with Mach. And from there, Musil says, he went in two different directions: to show on the one hand the role of idealization and of the process of abstraction, which, he says, could only misleadingly be held to be the foundation of idealization; and on the other hand to study the view of science as a mere economical inventory and collection of instruments, a view that follows from the denial of natural necessity (*BzM* 125). In his résumé it may appear that he is at once endorsing and rejecting Mach, and the reader may well ask if this is critique or positive exposition. What seems clear is that Musil easily takes up the gambit of playing viewpoints against viewpoints in the search for a truth. In fact, essayism is obviously held in check in the dissertation, for most of the points made against Mach might be made in his favor. This may also explain why some of Musil's commentators have actually thought that in his dissertation he is endorsing positivism.

Musil's encounter with Mach is decisive in many respects: it marks the beginning of a continuous debate about where lies the center of those things to which we are wont to attribute properties and qualities. These concerns occupied Musil until the end of his harried life. For example, in late diary entries from around 1940, Musil was still trying to reconcile particle physics with Mach's distrust of the metaphysics that he found at work in the very idea of invisible entities. In notebook 30 Musil tries to puzzle out what one can mean by *atom* in contemporary physics. He notes that *Atomon,* meaning something indivisible, belongs as a concept in the category of "thing" but that, by its basic nature, it contradicts the very notion of a thing (*TB* 1:788). The atom conceived as a thing is a contradiction, since its behavior as described by the formalisms of quantum mechanics does not coincide with what is usually meant by that word. Musil also found a contradiction in applying the concept of thingness to particles such as electrons that can be described both as particles and as waves. But at this late date in his life Musil thought that Machean epistemology itself allows one to escape the paradox he saw in the falsely unifying concept of thingness. In other words at the end of his life Musil was still thinking through scientific problems from a Machean viewpoint. Thus he could decide that the concept of the atom is not contradictory if, as according to Mach, one does not demand anything more than some kind of unambiguous linkage between concept and thing. The problem with the concept of the atom, he observes, is that one uses terms such as *projectiles,* or *divisible* and *indivisible,* to talk about it, which is an unjustified application of a model based on the notion of a thing. So Musil muses, in very Machean terms, on the idea that an atom is essentially a mathematical construct that explains certain phenomena and not the "smallest particle" (*TB* 1:788). In a very Viennese manner, Musil finds that pseudo-problems arise from the misuse of terms, since the idea of "thing" is problematic when used outside of the domain of the term's application. In this way a philosophical problem arises by the unexamined use of concepts. Quantum mechanics entails the description not of things understood as absolute solids but, as Musil puts it, of "a new relation of appearances"—"eine andere Bindung der Erscheinungen" (*TB* 2:788). This description is couched in a purely Machean formulation of how science functions with its alternative descriptions. It seems that Mach may have finally carried the day.

Finally we can state that Mach was a representative for young Musil of how modern science had unsettled the confidence one could have about the knowledge science offered about the world. This is of course one of the most widespread problems of modernism. And it is not surprising that Musil's angst about science's demolishing its own certainty lies at the heart of his first novel, *Young Törless,* published two years before the dissertation was finished. The dissertation and the novel share this common concern. The desire for certainty about truth links Musil's critique of Mach directly with his novelistic portrayal of the artist as a young scientist wanting to know what might be the foundations for knowledge of the world. In this respect *Young Törless* makes explicit the ethical and aesthetic needs motivating Musil's critique of Mach. The need for epistemic certainty as portrayed in this novel could hardly be reconciled with Mach's dismissing causality, with his presentation of space and time as relative notions with no absolute dimension, nor with his reduction of laws to conventional functional notations or pictures of sense data. Musil understood that Mach, with great theoretical elegance, had dissolved knowledge into a series of operations whose only logical requirement is economy and consistent fidelity to experience—whatever that might mean. It is precisely the question of fidelity to experience that, in the novel, Musil brings to the fore in the depiction of the boy Törless, of the boy's education, and of his needs, needs notably not fulfilled by that education.

CHAPTER 3

Young Törless

Musil's first published literary work, *Die Verwirrungen des Zöglings Törless* (first translated in 1955 as *Young Törless*), was published in 1906, two years before his doctoral thesis on scientific epistemology. Not surprisingly the question of science and its role in life is central to Musil's first novel, including his concerns with possible certainty in knowledge and the belief that knowledge is the ground for a stable self. The novel sheds light upon the fundamental project of the dissertation, since Musil's concern in fiction with psychology was a concern with understanding how the self might affirm itself. Such understanding aims at grasping the human self as a knowing, feeling, and evaluating subject. We find in the novel, as in early diaries, that knowledge is as important as emotion for the ethical subject that Musil wanted to create for himself, in life and through fiction. Going beyond anything found in the diaries or suggested by the dissertation, the novel also has great success in showing that the need for knowledge is linked with forms of psychopathology and social deviance.

An understanding of *Young Törless* requires different rhetorical skills from those required for reading a dissertation.[1] One specific skill for reading any narration, fictional or not, is the capacity to make a distinction between plot and fable, or discourse and story. By these received critical terms, I mean that one distinguishes between the narration, conceived as a chronological order proceeding from a first event to a last event, and the actual order of the narration as it is developed in a given narrative. The narrative order may well begin with any event in the story and leap back and forth in time for purposes of the aesthetic construction of a work. If one reads *Young Törless* with this distinction in mind, one sees that Musil uses some subtle shifts in a novel that, upon a cursory reading, may appear to be a fairly chronological narration beginning with Törless's arrival as a boarding student at a famous school and ending with his leaving it (more precisely, his arrival at a *Konvict,* a military academy modeled on the one Musil attended). From the point of view of narrative order, the novel relates, in approximate chronological order, a series of events set at the school, involving Törless's sexual initiations, his disarray in trying to understand science and philosophy, the sadistic cruelty of two of his comrades, who beat and sexually abuse a third student, and, after the scandal comes to light, Törless's brief flight from the school and the school's subsequent decision that it would be best for him not to remain there any longer. This brief outline of the novel's story or "fable" suggests that it is a portrayal of a youth's development, something of a bildungsroman. This is in part true, for the portrayal of an individual's education and psychological development is a central concern. However, in the representation of other students, the novel opens up onto a portrayal of ideological trends that lays bare the nature of the society in which Törless is coming to maturity.

Attention to narrative order shows certain significant deviations from a straightforward narration. One of the key deviations from the strictly linear unfolding of the narration occurs with the narrator's intervention to tell the reader what Törless will become in the years ahead. This intervention occurs notably after Törless has had a period of sexual involvement with the student Basini, a half-willing victim who has been tortured and used sexually by two other students, Beineberg and Reiting. The narrator's intervention can be likened to a prolepsis, or a view of the future that reveals what it holds for Törless as an adult. This proleptic narration is the result of the narrator's anticipation of the reader's negative reactions to Törless and is a way of countering them by assuring that the boy will turn out alright. It brings up the question of who is this narrator who anticipates what his public is thinking. He often appears to be an objective third-person narrator, something like an open camera lens focusing on the stage of action. Interestingly, however, he does refer to himself in the first person once in the early part of the novel (6:9). The narrator is thus distant, but not so distant that he does not personally comment on what is occurring in the work in order to orient directly the reader's interpretation of Törless's experience. He is obliquely present, but his few interventions show that he knows is he addressing an intelligent, indeed intellectual, middle-class audience. But he does not editorialize in the manner of the narrator found in, say, Honoré de Balzac or Charles Dickens.

Rather one might look more to Gustave Flaubert or perhaps Dostoyevsky for a parallel. The narrator allows his characters to talk, often at length, which is to say that he orchestrates a play of voices not unlike the way Dostoyevsky sets characters against each other in a counterpoint of speeches. Musil's narrator is also privy to the consciousness of his main character, Törless, but generally not to that of the other characters such as Beineberg, Reiting, and Basini. The narrative voice might be taken as the voice of Musil himself, though my description should suggest that if the narrator is largely nonjudgmental, it is precisely because Musil does not identify entirely with him.

51

The narrator's proleptic intervention occurs late in the novel, after Törless has engaged in what for the normal, bourgeois reader of the time would be scandalous and shocking behavior. In 1906 representations of this sort in fiction bordered on the unacceptable—Musil, like André Gide and James Joyce, endorsed the modernist agenda that rejected the taboos against certain subject matter in favor of explicitly representing and evaluating all aspects of human behavior. However, Musil's narrator also wants to assure the reader that the novel is not about a young man who will end up in the dregs; in fact Törless condemns his own behavior, which points up that it will not have devastating consequences. To today's readers it might appear that the novel endorses the acceptability of all forms of sexuality. This is not quite the case even though, as we shall see, the condemnation of the boys' sexual acts does come from their abuse of power, not from the form of sexual activity it took. Somewhat amused by those who saw him anticipating gay emancipation, Musil wrote in the diaries that he was not especially interested in the problems of homosexuals, though, as we shall see, he was scientifically as well as literarily interested in many forms of sexuality (*TB* 1:1217).

After the description of Törless's sexual experience, the narrator relates that later in life Törless overcame the events of his youth and became a young man with a very refined and sensitive soul (6:111).The narrator goes on to say that Törless is to be placed among the intellectual-aesthetic types for whom the observance of laws and conventional public morality offers a certain comfort, since this observance relieves them of thinking about something vulgar. The narrator sees Törless's development in rather aristocratic terms, since, when Törless is later asked to be interested in moral issues, he assumes the stance of someone combining somewhat bored insensitivity with an "ironic sense of what is correct" (6:111). The narrator says that Törless will have known a growth of the spirit and of the mind and become one of those men who are indifferent to the nature of the objects that challenge their sense of moral correctness (6:112). Moreover, he will not regret in later life the tawdry conduct of his earlier years. As the narrator directly says, Törless's later feeling when encountering a debauchee will not be to scorn him simply because the debauchee is what he is, but rather to feel scorn because such a person isn't anything better—and mainly because the debauchee is stupid and his understanding lacks any balance (6:112). Törless will later say, when asked if there was not something shameful about his experience at school, that it was obviously base but that what remained of this earlier humiliation was a little bit of poison that was necessary to keep his spirit from enjoying an all too certain and complacent health and to give it instead a finer, sharper, understanding (6:112).

The narrator's intervention has evoked adverse critical responses, some bordering on outrage, because the narrator seems to be endorsing Törless's becoming an indifferent aesthete. But such an interpretation does not really do justice to the narrator, who is situating himself and the adult Törless on a level that allows them to judge conventional ethics. The narrator neither condemns or endorses Törless's youthful homosexuality, but rather portrays the circumstance as part of the inevitable steps the young character takes on a path toward his development. Of course, the narrator's interpretation is subject to interpretation. A Nietzschean might observe that the narrator is describing a course of events leading to a modernist reevaluation of values, since no fixed values are appealed to here in evaluating Törless, only relative values derived from the possible results of his experience. And Nietzschean echoes seem clear in the narrator's aristocratic disdain for moral judgments that do not have an aesthetic component. From a different perspective a Freudian can hold that the narrator is making a claim that adolescence must unfold according to determined stages of life that cannot be subjected to a priori values.[2] These references to Nietzsche and Freud should not be taken as assertions that the narrator is a spokesman for either, but rather are intended to point up the company he is keeping: he is a modernist who demands that experience be looked at from different perspectives. His projected image of a future Törless is of the perfected modernist skeptic who knows that truth rarely lies in appearances; he will then know, as the narrator puts it in a pointed comparison, that lovers, to reach the apparent tenderness of which they are proud must go through hell (6:113).

One may also interpret the narrator's comments to be something of an apology for his own life; in that context it would appear that he is offering, somewhat like Joyce, a portrait of the artist as a young man—or perhaps more appropriately, the scientist as a young man or the scientist as artist, and in some respects this is an even more interesting proposition. The biographically inclined critic will note that, when Musil was writing this novel, it was perhaps not clear in his own mind which, scientist or artist, he himself was to become. A similar choice faces Törless, who as a young student burns his first poems while worrying about the nature of imaginary numbers. In effect the narrator's proleptic remarks work retroactively to inscribe Törless's development in an itinerary that seems destined to lead him into the world of bourgeois existence where modernist aesthetes and scientists view morality from a perspective beyond trite conventional judgments.

The novel begins with the presentation of Törless and his parents in a train station located apparently somewhere in eastern Austria, on railway tracks that go through nearly endless desolation toward the steppes of Russia. In this

Kafkaesque landscape Törless attends a famous academy located in a remote small town. His mother believes her son will be protected from the dangers of the big city there (a detail that shows how Musil used irony from the very beginning of his career). The scene at the train station is a repetition of one that took place some four years earlier when Törless first came to the school; much of the novel that follows relates through retrospective narration what has preceded this moment. The school was considered a good place for the children of the best families, and the luster of prestige had caused Törless's parents to give in to their ambitious boy's insistence to go there (6:8). The opening scene has been repeated over the four-year period, and as the narrator's initial résumé of Törless makes clear, the boy has already undergone significant changes since he first arrived. Countering the theme of development and *Bildung* that one might expect, the desolation of the setting strongly suggests that it is not the sort in which young boys can best grow to fulfill their potential. Rather than pointing to growth, the opening scene of repetition suggests that parents and students act out roles—indifferently, lifelessly, and mechanically—such that the narrator likens the scene to a puppet theater. This derisive image sets the scene for a dramatic unfolding that, as we shall see, bears much relation to a theatrical play.

Curiously it is not clear exactly how old Törless might be. Upon first arriving at the school four years earlier he had been young enough to miss his parents terribly. But now, the homesickness that had once been a source of a higher joy for him makes itself felt to him in its absence (6:10). He has a nostalgia for his past nostalgia, which is another of Musil's deflationary strategies in the novel: Törless progressively discovers there are no homelands to which one can even yearn to return. To be sure, he is vaguely discontented and is looking for something new to serve him as a "support." The metaphor of "support" is suggestive, but so open-ended as to obscure what precisely Törless's needs are. Törless himself has no idea what he might want. In this regard the narrator offers little precise psychological analysis, no more than he gives precise temporal coordinates as he continues his narration with an anecdote about an episode from "this time" that prepared the young man for "later development." The reader experiences Törless's past much as the boy presumably experiences it, outside of the strict coordinates of objective time, living in a "now" that takes on its meaning mainly by opposition to the "then" of the past. In other words neither the narrator nor the boy whose consciousness he explores peg their experience on any precise chronological or historical framework. Törless's experience takes place on the edge of adult history, in the marginal world of adolescence, and his time is the open-ended and limitless time of late childhood. The historically minded critic might add that Törless lives in the eternal present of an empire that thought it was destined to survive forever.

The principal episode that the narrator highlights in the opening flashback is Törless's getting to know a young prince from one of the oldest noble families. Musil's fascination with the aristocracy is constant, partly for negative reasons, because the aristocracy was an historical anachronism and yet a source of values that continued to permeate European culture before World War I. As the earlier diaries show, Musil was questioningly aware of the fact that many, including Nietzsche, believed the ongoing decline of the aristocracy was emblematic of European decadence. Emblematically the prince had offered Törless initiation into a world of values that no longer had any historical justification. The prince offers for a short time the experience of what the narrator calls an idyll (6:11). The contrast between Törless and the prince is especially instructive with respect to the social context in which Törless and his comrades now live. Törless has been raised in a bourgeois family that accepts the secular, rationalist values of the Enlightenment. This means that he learns from the prince things that he could not learn at home, for example, that the slightest gesture can have meaning. Through the prince's example Törless also learns the meaning of personality—presumably the idea that the aristocratic individual considers himself different from all others (6:11). But secure in his rationalism—and perhaps resentful of the superiority assumed by the young aristocrat—he cannot refrain from assaulting the prince with objections to the aristocratic beliefs that the prince unquestioningly holds, especially to his reactionary religious faith. With the rationalism Törless has learned at home, he can triumph over the medieval mentality the prince embodies, but this is a pyrrhic victory. He triumphs at the price of alienating the prince, who shortly thereafter leaves the school in which he did not feel at home; and Törless is left with the feeling that he has destroyed something very fine and full of a pleasure that he is not to find elsewhere—"etwas Feines und Genußreiches" (6:12). This episode can be taken at once as a commentary on the arrogance of rationalism and the impossibility of living an idyll in the era of post-Enlightenment rationality. The aristocrat is a living symbol of values that are fine but archaic; distinguished but meaningless; superior but without application. *The Man without Qualities* will develop these same insights from a satirical perspective.

The moment of emptiness for Törless brought about by the prince's departure is where, chronologically speaking, the narrative begins. Törless is now older, subject to the sexual urges that beset a young man entering puberty (6:12). Doubts also beset the boy, for with his feelings of emptiness Törless is coming to doubt that he has any character at all (6:13). This feeling is engendered in part by the prince's counterexample, for he had the self-assured character that is an intrinsic part of being an aristocrat; and in part by the psychological disarray caused by puberty. Törless finds himself in an environment in which peasant women offer examples of earthy sensuality, but where the only available woman is the prostitute the schoolboys visit.

After recounting the episode involving the prince, the narration comes back to the train station and the end of the visit by the boy's parents. The narrative then continues in fairly linear fashion with the unfolding of events as Törless experiences them. There are occasional flashbacks to fill in background on the other characters whose lives intersect his life, especially the three older students Basini, Reiting, and Beineberg. The young baron Beineberg steps forward at the train station when, in another moment of irony, Törless's father asks him to look after his son and to let him know should anything happen to Törless. Beineberg, however, is instrumental in introducing Törless to sadism. After the parents depart, the boys leave the railroad station and walk through the town. Musil offers a pithy and ironic view of the empire's multiculturalism as the boys walk by women who make jokes in a Slavic language and show their bodies in a display of easy sexuality. That the narrator does not even say which Slavic language they are speaking points out that the boys, future members of the German ruling class, view the women simply as non-German, without a defined identity other than their sexuality. Törless, moreover, reacts to the women's saucy provocations and is aroused by their shameless eroticism (6:17).

With Beineberg facing Törless, the narrator digresses by offering a description of Beineberg's father, whose cultivation of Indian thought is the source of the mystical viewpoint that the young baron advocates. Musil contrasts Törless's psychological state with Beineberg's in a demonstration of the power of ideology to grant identity. Beineberg is sadistically certain of his identity because of his irrational ideology, whereas Törless, with his vague rationalism, feels alone in a world that is like a great, dark house (6:24). In this mood he assents to go along with Beineberg to visit Bozena, the local prostitute. This encounter continues the contrast between the world of the local Slavic population and that of the whore's young gentlemen visitors. She is a peasant who had worked as a servant, serving women of the boys' social class, but now she leads an independent life of pleasure—with cigarettes, cheap novels, alcohol, and men—that allows her the self-assuredness to make fun of the boys while taking money from them.

The narrator stresses that of late Törless could hardly wait for these visits, though he seems quite subdued during the visit he makes with Beineberg at the novel's outset. He realizes that he needs these visits to satisfy some psychological need to abase himself, and perhaps to flee from his social world of privilege, for in anguish he recognizes that each time he really wants to step out of his favored position so as to be among common people, in fact to go beneath them and "deeper than them," as he thinks to himself (6:30). In his desire to descend into the mire, Törless gives the prostitute a silver coin he had just received from his mother, a gesture that ties together the two extremes of the feminine condition in this patriarchal monarchy—the angelic, sexless mother with the fallen whore. Törless experiences a kind of masochistic urge here to debase himself intentionally in his own eyes as if to punish himself for his own privileges. Bozena enjoys debasing the boys. She claims, perhaps falsely, to have known Beineberg's mother and tells stories about his family in which Törless feels himself personally involved. Whipping him with a mother's image, as it were, Bozena leads Törless to reflect in anguish again on the impossibility of reconciling sexual desire with the image of purity he associates with his mother. In short, princes and prostitutes bring him to experience the contradictions in his own schema of values, which are the dominant values of the patriarchal culture in which he lives.

The scene with Bozena also first presents, indirectly, Basini, another student with whom Törless has close dealings in the novel. Bozena also knows Basini, for she relates with some amusement how he conducts himself with her. Comic and noble, he drinks only wine, but he is very dumb, she says. He boasts of his knowledge of women but has no sexual contact with her while telling her what a man must do to please women. This introduction to Basini, the boy who will be tortured and sexually used by the three others, suggests that this noble lad is not quite like the others, though what is at the center of his identity—if anything—is open to interpretation. Perhaps he is a homosexual—his supposed scorn for women suggests it as well as his later sexual compliance—or perhaps he is simply egoistically vacuous. In any case Basini serves as something of a sounding board for all the characters in the novel to reveal their feelings and desires, including the peasant whore Bozena, who thinks that the fine young gentlemen are by and large a rather pathetic lot.

After the episode with Bozena, the major characters have been presented, and the main events of the plot can unfold with the rigorous workings of a nearly classical tragedy, albeit one that is dubious of the possibility of the tragic in the modern era. The narration is extremely economical, and Musil connects events with a rigorous causality that suggests a tragic plot. Basini is caught stealing. Reiting and Beineberg use this as an excuse to vent their manias on him as well as use him sexually. Törless gets caught up with Basini in a sexual relation that he cannot or does not want to resist. Reiting and

Beineberg then decide to push Basini to the limits. When the boy can no longer stand their torture and Törless does not help him, Basini turns himself in, and the scandal involving the little ring becomes known. No longing wanting to be at the school, and no longer desired there, Törless leaves. When he reunites with his mother he discovers that he enjoys the perfume emanating from her body. This final image suggests that he has perhaps made some progress in overcoming his own, and society's, contradictions.

The articulation of these events merits a more detailed examination, especially concerning how the plot unfolds. We can then look in some greater detail at what the characters represent in their participation in these events and conclude with some consideration of the major themes involved in this tightly constructed demonstration of what it was like to be an Austrian youth a generation before the Austro-Hungarian Empire ceased to exist.

Once all the background information is in place, the event that sets the main plot in motion is the revelation that Basini is a thief. It is Reiting who tells Beineberg of the thievery. The everyday setting for this revelation is important. The boys are in their usual schoolroom with whitewashed walls, a great black crucifix, and the pictures of the empire's monarchs by the side of the blackboard (6:36). A significant contrast is produced by the juxtaposition, on the one hand, of images of church and state and, on the other, adolescent boys who have little concern for the order represented symbolically about them in the display of crosses and pictures. The contrast is further developed when, to discuss the theft, the boys go up to a loft in the attic of the school where Reiting and Beineberg have set up a secret meeting place. The loft's intentional theatricality also contrasts sharply with the ordinary classroom that the boys leave. The loft is a hidden space, set up literally behind stage sets, in which they can plot, dream, and act out their fantasies subsequently by inflicting real torture. In the theatrical loft the boys can escape whatever contact they have with the puppets in power in the adult world, with its crosses and emperors, so as to enact their own performances of imagined power. Redolent of that power is a loaded revolver that hangs from the wall. From the outset Törless does not like this chamber (6:39). Listening to Reiting's excited chatter here, he feels totally detached, empty, and rather like an actor without a role, though he also feels that everything that he does is just a game—or a *Spiel,* which can signify both playacting as well as playing games.

Reiting has found out that Basini, owing him money, stole money from Beineberg's storage locker in order to pay him off. Reiting is delighted now to have power over Basini. He gloats over the fact that he has Basini promising to do anything he wants so long as Reiting does not denounce him. He has even offered to be a slave, and Reiting is excited by the very disgust that Basini's greedy anguish awakens in him (6:45). Now that he has power over Basini, sadistic power to be sure, Reiting wants the others to help decide what is to be done to their "slave." This is a moment during which all conventional expectations have been destroyed for Törless, but he is almost indifferent to what is happening. He finds everything fantastical, and can only wonder how anything at all is possible. His is the first of several cases in Musil's work where wonder about what is possible—*möglich*—contrives almost to put in question the possibility of reality itself. If from Törless's perspective the impossible is really possible, why isn't anything else possible?—or so goes the line of reasoning that results from the character's disengagement from the world. In this case it is a negative sense of possibility that overwhelms Törless. He looks at the two sadists gloating next to him and wonders if his fantasy has, like a distorting lens, produced the effects he is viewing, for he feels that he has become totally estranged from the familiar world (6:49).

Musil outlines sadism with uncanny precision as the boys contrive to torture Basini. Reiting declares to him that he has "forfeited" his existence, but rather than turn him in, they are offering him grace so that he will not be sent away. He will be informed subsequently what are the special conditions he must obey in return for the special dispensation that Reiting will oversee. Reiting invents a theatrical ritual, sadistic in nature but clearly imitating Christian ritual. This creation of ritual corresponds to those described today by adolescent psychology. Arguably, adolescent psychology could only come into existence after schools for this age group had been created that isolate adolescents from society. (Throughout much of history, most humans had usually already finished whatever secondary schooling they were going receive before they reached Reiting's and Beineberg's age—around seventeen or so.) In this sense Musil has undertaken pioneering work in showing what adolescents do when isolated in a special realm that sets them apart from society. Strikingly, they set about mimicking adult rituals in proto-theatrical terms. This does not mean that their performance of ritual is not serious; as we shall see, it is play, but with bloody consequences.

The play takes a new twist when Beineberg tells Törless that they are being deceived by Reiting. Törless is seemingly naive as to what this might mean, so Beineberg enlightens him by alluding to a great scandal that occurred in the school four years earlier, when some boys were sent away for committing sexual offenses. This was around the same time Törless arrived at the school, and the reader may deduce that as a young boy he never quite grasped what other boys might be up to in the dark. In any case Beineberg is slightly exasperated with young Törless's naïveté. But rather than talk about what Reiting may be doing with Basini, Beineberg is much more anxious to talk about his own plans for Basini, whom he wants to use and torture so that he can try out some of his own ideas. Beineberg shows himself at this point to be an adolescent fanatic, representative of the intellect gone mad. I will return presently to this point. In the context of the plot's development Beineberg is another example of the impossible possibility, and Törless does not know how to react to this demonstration of intellect unchained and pursuing a sadistic desire for power.

The discovery of Beineberg's desires leaves Törless in a state of reverie in which, the narrator says, he has trouble distinguishing between Beineberg's fantastic scheming and his own psychological malaise. Finally he had the feeling that a giant loop was been drawn evermore tightly around everything (6:61). The image of the loop or noose (*Schlinge*) in this passage is a metaphor for the constriction that the situation is creating, the constriction that the plot itself is knotting around Törless. The image of constriction recalls the metaphor used in the classic description of tragic plot development, from Aristotle through the seventeenth century. In tying together events, a plot unfolds like a rope that coils into constricting knots, and only the tragic finale can untie them—producing the "unraveling" or the denouement in which tragic recognition takes place. Musil literalizes this metaphor by using it to describe Törless's psychological reaction to the plot's unfolding. He is being choked by it.

From this point the narrator continues the exposition of what Törless sees as his psychological problem by introducing a separate but parallel line of events. These events are not directly centered on the other three students but occur at the same time as the main plot unfolds. For example, Törless goes into a park and, while lying on his back and looking at the sky, has an intuition of what the physical infinite might be. The narrator stresses that this is not the mathematical infinite that impinges upon Törless's consciousness but an infinity that might exist outside of the mathematical procedures used to calculate infinite sets. Törless knows the word *infinite* and is sufficiently versed in mathematics to understand that one can do calculations involving the infinite as a mathematical concept. The term shows up, he recalls, constantly, though until this moment of solitude he had never tried to represent anything to himself with it (6:63). But what he experiences in the park has nothing to do with calculations involving infinite sets. He has a vision of the sky, with its potentially unlimited expanses, that brings home to him the disparity between the calculations one does and the reality he views. In other words, it is not clear at all that the certainty offered by mathematical reasoning can be used to find certainty in the opening in the sky that engulfs the boy. The uncertainty about perception Törless feels when dealing with Beineberg's fantastic ideas in the loft is compounded now by the uncertainty that undermines his everyday perception in broad daylight. I will return to these considerations of mathematics in the conclusion here. In the context of the unfolding plot it is important to underscore that the it brings Törless to an early encounter with the unfathomable.

As the plot develops Musil then contrasts the day's unsettling encounter with night's fantastic darkness when the boys meet in the middle of the night in the loft with Basini. In the night their sadism is given free reign. As Basini smiles at Reiting, perhaps requesting his help, Reiting slugs Basini in the face and knocks him down. In the dark Törless makes out that the two other boys strip Basini of his clothes, beat him, and then use him sexually (6:69). Törless himself is a spectator to a scene of sexual sadism that, if it first makes him dizzy, finally excites him, too (6:70). Törless tries to reintroduce a modicum of normal thinking into the scene by suggesting to Basini that he should simply admit that he is a thief. By normal standards, confession should put an end to this ritual aping of Church conventions. But Beineberg and Reiting immediately seize upon Basini's admission to embroider upon it and pursue the ritual of sadistic torture: they immediately demand that Basini admit that he is a animal, in fact, a thieving, piggish animal (6:72). The contrast between Törless, with his brief attempt to introduce normal standards, and the two others stands out in this sadistic use of a confession. But this time Törless is drawn into their sexual sadism—it takes hold of his "scalp with fine claws" (6:71).

The scenes of sadism are not the only moments in which Musil undertakes modernist analysis of sexual behavior and affect. By "modernist" I mean analysis from the viewpoint that the values embedded in the experience are open to transformation. For example, Törless recalls being alone in bed as a child, when the world was amorphous and comfort could take on different shapes. It was at a time when he still wore little dresses, when sexual differentiation was not yet clear, and he remembers that he had an inexpressible longing to be a little girl. The desire lay not just in his heart, he recalls, but tickled his entire body and ran along his skin. There were even moments during which he felt that he was a girl, and since he knew nothing about bodily differentiation, he could not understand why everyone thought he would have to remain a boy forever (6:86). And in the night at school, feeling guilt about his sexuality, he thinks he feels something comparable again. These memories of innocence are a prelude to a dreamless sleep, as though a regress to childhood could be a sedative. Or perhaps regress might show him there is nothing shameful in pansexuality, something he experienced as an innocent child.

Plot development is thus exploited for purposes of psychological exploration and evaluation of the sort associated with modernism, in literary texts such as those of Marcel Proust, James Joyce, and Virginia Woolf, and in psychoanalytic writing. I would not argue for the direct influence on Musil of fellow Viennese modernists such as doctor-writer Arthur Schnitzler and writer-doctor Freud, but there are clearly overlapping areas of interest, theme, and concept. Vienna was undoubtedly a capital for the development of free-thinking about sexuality in the late nineteenth and early twentieth centuries, and Musil's first novel fits into this cultural environment. For example, the notion of fluid bisexuality and the ambiguity of sexual identity are themes that characterize both Musil's novel and Freudian analysis. Musil kept his distance from Freud, however, and he never tried to build a general theory of sexuality. Törless's recall of his desire to be a little girl, as well as his feeling that his sexual identity is amorphous, are part of the uncertainty of identity he experiences. In the context of the novel, they foreshadow his engaging in a sexual adventure with Basini.

Before this adventure Törless undertakes to write his own philosophy: *De natura hominum,* a theory of the nature of humanity that in effect mirrors the novel's own project of analysis. The narrator observes, with restrained irony, that the boy believes that he owes a Latin title to such a philosophical inquiry (6:88). Doubling the narrator's own attempt to show the nature of man, the boy writes to undertake self-analysis, to make inquiry into whence comes the "strange indecent feeling" he feels, using biblical terminology to express a sense of the forbidden (6:89). He finds that this feeling centers on Basini, who happens to be in the room at the moment Törless is writing. In portraying the boy as he has a pen in hand, Musil creates a strangely poetical, albeit almost comic, scene. Törless is immersed in his reflections and memories while the object of his desire sits in the room with him. This juxtaposition creates the illusion of a vision, the optical illusion that he is seeing himself in the act of seeing—which is another ironic duplication of the novel's depicting in deformed fashion its own mirroring of characters.

Törless is hardly able to write, since memories overpower him. The narrator deflates the idea that the boy has any great insight, noting that, whatever be the religious power of Törless's inspirations, he had as yet no idea about the intuitions that great artists have (6:92). Young Törless may impress himself as if he were a member of the elect, or even a saint, but his education in literature and art has been sorely deficient. Thus his self-knowledge must be deficient as well. Törless is not unaware of this lack, for even without acquaintance with major writers, his own writing appears to him to be dead letters (6:93).

Self-analysis leads to a blank: Törless's situation seems suspended as he thinks he sees, at night, Reiting and Beineberg continuing to go to Basini's bed (6:94).

Using theatrical terminology to describe the plot's "knotting" or development, we can speak at this point of its central turning point, or *peripeteia*, when the course of the interlocking events is inflected in a decisive direction. It happens during a four-day holiday when most of the boys leave the school. Remaining at school, Törless and Basini find themselves virtually alone together for the first time. This is a kind of fated accident that theatrical plots often exploit to bring about encounters in which passions, as they intensify, result in an inexorable sequence of events. Törless is moved with desire, though at a loss to know how he might satisfy it with Basini. He awakens the sleeping boy, who almost automatically leads Törless up to the loft, where a curious initiation scene takes place. Basini undresses, Törless demands to know what the others do, and Basini begs not to have to answer. To Törless's stammering question if he is their "mistress," he replies that he is their "friend" (6:101). The most peculiar moment in this scene is precisely that Basini can say nothing interesting about what he feels or does: he can only claim that he has to do what the others demand because he needs money he "borrowed" or simply because they order him. Törless wants an explanation—he wants analysis, as it were, of the nature of man—and he gets a vacuous description. Even after threatening Basini with physical torture, Törless can get nothing from him and ends up with no idea of what goes on in the other boy's mind when he steals or consents to be humiliated. The modernist quest for analysis is blunted in this moment, for no knowledge is easily available. As if to compensate, Törless loses himself in a meditation, trying to analyze what he is feeling at that moment. He feels that he is and has been in some kind of danger. However, now that the initial shock is over, now that he is no longer horrified by the banality of what he has discovered, he discovers the seeming banality of the unmentionable, and the feeling attracts him (6:105).

His initiation in homoeroticism is delayed, however, when Törless returns to bed. Shortly thereafter, he is awakened by Basini's pressing his "naked, quivering body" against him, and Törless finally gives in to his sensuality, a sensuality that takes the shape of an autonomous force in the dark that abides no questions and justifies itself, as the narrator suggests, by its simple presence (6:108). If one insists on finding a theory of sexuality in Musil—and his work does invite this project—certainly its first principle is this demonstration of Eros as a force on the other side of language. But even after Törless has stepped over the limits drawn for conduct by conventional morality, it is not clear that this is an especially significant event. Eros simply is, and perhaps little more can be said. *The Man without Qualities* will pursue this line, toying finally with the perverse pleasures found in violating the incest taboo. It is not clear that Musil succeeds even in the novel in his extraordinary essayistic attempt to find some language adequate to eros.

Törless's initiation into eros marks a slack moment in the plot's development with the beginning of an indefinite period of time during which he refrains from seeing Reiting and Beineberg. He meditates on his discovery of sensuality. Conventional morality largely mediates his sentiments: he feels disgust, for example, whenever he encounters Basini in the daytime. Conventional moral considerations lead him to wonder what his parents would think about him if they knew. Yet he feels little remorse for this ongoing sexual relation. On the contrary—he feels as if he had awakened from a long "agony" or disease that he cannot forget (6:111). The image of chastity as a disease is contrasted with an image of lust as an anonymous state. The narrator compares the rush of Törless's feelings to a round of masked women who, with their dresses tied up to expose their sexuality, intoxicate him, though he knows not one name of the dancers (6:111). This vision of desire without name is comparable to the portrayals of a Viennese orgy Arthur Schnitzler uses twenty years later in his depiction of sexual life as an anonymous encounter in his *Traumnovelle* (*Dream Novel,* adapted as the 1999 Stanley Kubrick film *Eyes Wide Shut*). Musil's analysis of the anonymity of eros, of its presence as an autonomous force, is perhaps what is most new in the modernist psychology of sex, new in that it insists upon anonymity as a condition of possibility for its existence. There is no sentimentality in Musil's portrayal, no moralizing, and, remarkably in the case of Törless, no sense that sex is power over the other. Rather, the boy is given over to feelings he cannot control and that he barely understands.

It is at this moment in the plot that the narrator makes the prolepsis to which I referred earlier: it is almost as if the narrator wants, preemptively, to keep the reader from being too judgmental toward a character who cannot judge himself at the time. The narrator perceives his function as being first to serve understanding, not judgment. Of course, the values of conventional morality intrude, for they are present in the fact that Törless knows that he has stepped over conventional boundaries. From the perspective that received morality offers, the question arises: How did it happen that Törless finds himself caught up in a sensual dilemma that conventional society would judge to be outrageous? The narrator's intervention can thus be read as a way of orienting the reader's response, for he assures the reader that the experience in conventional immorality does not harm for the boy's future development—which may lead one to question what is moral and immoral in this experience and what is indeed a matter of moral indifference.

Given the logic of the plot development, it seems almost inevitable that when, a "few days later," the three boys find themselves together again, Reiting announces that it is time to go a step further with Basini. Exceeding the limits of conventional morality is a logical extension of Reiting's need to exercise power and Beineberg's desire to trounce common sense with his wacky experiments in controlling Basini by overcoming the laws of nature (6:119). Their desires set the stage, in a quite literal sense, for the culminating moment in the plot in which Beineberg absurdly forces Basini to attempt to overcome the law of gravity. Reiting and Törless are spectators within the scene when Beineberg orders Basini to undress, aims the loaded pistol at him, and threatens to shoot him if he disobeys (admittedly with the promise to bring him back to life afterward). Beineberg orders Basini to stare at a flame and to find the point at which he is no longer sentient. (This scene may have a parodic side, inspired by the French psychiatrist Jean-Martin Charcot, who gave lectures Freud attended, at which he demonstrated publicly the suggestibility of mental patients through a form of hypnosis.) When Basini no longer answers him, Beineberg declares that the boy's spirit is no long bound by the fetters of natural law. To demonstrate that the soul has left the body and that body may float in the air, he then orders to Basini to bend forward. Basini does so until, quite expectedly, he falls flat on his face at Beineberg's feet (6:122). Beineberg begins to beat him unmercifully with a belt.

This scene can be called the culminating moment in the plot, since the pathologies unfolding in the plot's development explode here in violent absurdity. The scene underscores at once that the adolescents are at great risk destroying themselves and capable of the brutality more usually associated with the adult world. The gun Beineberg has in hand is a stage prop, but it is also loaded. Musil emphasizes the ambiguity of the notion of play that is fundamental to an understanding of the boys' psychology. Play is an attempt to transcend the limits of reality, and in this it can be extraordinarily serious business; yet, at the same time, it involves role-play and make-believe. Thus Reiting plays at being a man of power and Beineberg at being a seer and magus, while Törless looks on wondering what role should be his. It may appear that his disarray is due, for better or worse, precisely to the fact that he can find no role to play. As for Basini, the hapless victim, apparently passive homosexual, and petty thief, one is inclined to think that he plays at being victim as long as it brings him pleasure; but in this scene the game has clearly gotten out of hand. He risks getting beaten to death, if not shot.

When Basini later comes to Törless to beg for help, Törless denies that he has ever been affectionate to the suffering boy (6:123). He orders Basini to keep quiet about what has happened between them, since Basini's "disgrace" has put an end to the "dream" in which Törless has found himself (6:123). There is something heartless, even cruel, in Törless's refusing to recognize any commitment or commonality in his relation to Basini, who is at his few wits' end. To be sure, there is a heady complexity about the way Musil presents his adolescent with cruel objectivity. His narrator depicts the boy's disarray when confronting a situation for which he has, arguably, responsibility, as well as his indecisiveness in the cruelty he inflicts. On the one hand Törless agrees to spend the night with Basini since the two persecutors will be asleep, having spent the previous night torturing Basini. On the other hand he tells Basini that he can find no reason to be interested in such a debased and cowardly being. In a sense Musil gives readers freedom to react to Törless in accord with their own standards of judgment, or the standard of judgment that they are able to derive from the novel's portrayal. His narrator is in any event nonjudgmental, while the boy's own words express a confusion that springs from his lack of experience and from his uncertainty about what constitutes a moral viewpoint.

Törless finally decides to have nothing more to do with other boys. He is perhaps egged on by Reiting's extraordinarily vicious vulgarity. (He tells Törless he should observe Basini eating shit.) This break may appear to be a logical development after the culminating scene, since Törless can accept neither Reiting's bullying will to power nor the magical nonsense Beineberg offers as superior knowledge. Their pretensions appear to be rationalizations for the pleasures they take in sadistic violence, though this is not what directly motivates Törless's decision to break with them. At once ethical, aesthetic, and intellectual, his decision is motivated by a desire to maintain some integrity, coherence, and wholeness when confronting the world. Törless is not capable of articulating the nature of his desire, and as the novel unfolds, it increasingly appears that a central problem he confronts is precisely his inability to speak of his own decision-making process.

However, Törless is willing to deal with the consequences of his decision. Threatened with denunciation by Reiting, he finds that the world of conventional morality has moved to the front of the stage, for it is conventional morality that dictates what may happen to them all. Törless thinks of his parents, looking upon them as the embodiment of law and ethics in the society from which he may be expelled, and he recalls the simple advice they gave earlier after Törless had written to them about the Basini's thievery. He had been disappointed that they had given the "right-thinking, boring" ethical advice that

Basini should turn himself in (6:128). His parent's ethics may be boring and conventional, but Törless can come up with no better idea. Therefore, he writes a letter in which he counsels Basini to turn himself in. His advice is also motivated by pragmatic reasons, because, as Törless tells Basini, he may well be beaten to death if he does not turn himself in before, inevitably, the scandal finally becomes known (6:129).

One of the most powerful episodes in the novel occurs as the plot unfolds its denouement, when Beineberg and Reiting begin letting their fellow students know that Basini is a thief. Fomenting the other students against him, they begin a defensive maneuver to deflect from themselves future inquiry into their conduct. In a strange scene, Reiting mockingly reads to a group of students Basini's letters from his mother. There are biblical associations in this scene in which the mob is worked up to torture a victim, but it is also a masterly political portrayal of how people can be manipulated. The young Musil was already attuned to the kind of demagogic exercises in public power, to which he would be later an unfortunately frequent witness. The exercise in public mockery in the novel notably does not whet Reiting's and Beineberg's appetite for torture, however, and the narrator summarily concludes this scene of manipulation by noting that on that night Basini was to be beaten with rapier blades (6:130). Hardly surprisingly, the victim finally turns himself in, though it is not clear if he does so because he is following Törless's advice in ethical pragmatism or if he is simply at the limit of suffering. This distinction would undoubtedly be beyond Basini's ken.

With this denouement the basic plot comes to resolution. Törless is not suspected for having had a part in what has happened, though he is questioned as part of the school's investigation. In the context of theatrical plotting, the denouement should be followed by a recognition scene. Indeed, the rest of the novel relates Törless's coming to awareness about what kind of an experience he has undergone in these events that have come perilously close destroying the characters. In Törless's case this means he looks for language that can articulate his motivations and reasons for why he has done what he done. To this end, before his interrogation he looks at the notes he has written, recalls his recent past, and tries to make some sense of what has happened. Yet, as the narrator says, all Törless seems to know is a feeling of growth, like that of an annual tree ring, so that "wordless, overpowering feeling excused all that had happened" (6:131). The boy's feeling is wordless, and it is the narrator who articulates Törless's mental state with the metaphor likening the soul, or the mind, to a growing tree trunk. The metaphor is problematic. One wonders if it is to be taken as an intervention expressing something outside of Törless's consciousness. It seems equally plausible to say at this point that the narrator is articulating something immanent. Is the boy conscious of being excused? and by whom? or is this absolution simply the narrator's opinion? This kind of ambiguous stance characterizes Musil throughout his career. The ambiguity is pointed in Törless's case, because one inevitably asks who is excusing whom. In any case the narrative proclaims the boy's innocence as an established fact. The reader may hesitate.

From another, more theatrical perspective, one might say that Törless undergoes something like a cathartic experience in which guilt is dissipated by an emotional, but not yet intellectual, recognition of what the recent experience has meant. This emphasis on emotional knowledge, or knowledge granted by feeling, is another important aspect of Musil's work. He wants to portray the work of the emotions and feelings as concomitant parts of the subject's life, which is to say that they coexist with the intellect and the intellect's basic tool for representation, to wit, language. From this perspective the narrator's metaphor of growth expresses this work of the emotions. The boy Törless must still struggle, however, to find a language adequate to what he feels.

Thus Törless's condition of innocence, in a moral if not in a legal sense, is presupposed in the conclusion of the novel, when he faces the committee of adults before whom he must struggle to find words that they can understand and that are also commensurate with his emotions. He knows in advance that he will have difficulty. If asked why he has mistreated Basini, he knows he cannot simply answer that it was due to some process in his brain; that the process interested him at the time, but he now hardly knows anything about it; and that today it seems without importance (6:132). Apparently this dismissal of the past characterizes Törless's attitude. It must be said that the past weighs lightly upon memory throughout Musil's work: there is no nostalgia in Musil, the most antiromantic of writers in this regard.

It may also appear that, with his meditation on a process in his own brain, young scientist Törless is indulging in irony to himself. The courage required by self-irony, however, is belied by the fact that he disappears from school on the day before the interrogation. He does not go far and is brought quickly back. The flight is a curious event, for it is the one point in the novel's sequence of events from which he is briefly absent. The event creates a vacuum in the plot's focus. Most critics agree that Törless's flight is an attempt to avoid conflict in moral or psychological terms. This does not explain why, however, the narrator does not accompany him. The absence of Törless's point of view from the narration creates a kind of momentary void, as if the star actor who had been on stage permanently until this time suddenly ran into the wings of the theater.

During this brief moment the spotlight is cast upon Reiting and Beineberg, who, fearing Törless has taken their threats seriously, conspire to cast the blame for everything on Basini. They denounce him as an "unworthy, thieving" fellow who repaid all attempts to better him with more crimes (6:132). It was, as the narrator says, a well-planned comedy, staged by Reiting, in which they played at evoking all the ethical tonalities they knew would resound well in the educators' ears (6:133). The novel's portrayal of adults is never favorable, and the educators are represented again as puppets whose strings are easily manipulated. The boys know the adults' conventional values in advance and can, hence, cynically appeal to whatever may please them. The question brought up by this cynical staging is, then, whether there is a world of values *not* known in advance? Are there values that might emerge from the situation in which the players find themselves acting? These questions directly emerge from Törless's situation. He is looking for a language to express values that he only feels, but cannot describe, values that he discovers as the plot unfolds. The vocabulary to describe the search for values may sound as if it comes from the existentialism of a later generation, but these terms emerge from reading Musil's novel. Musil could be said to anticipate existentialist philosophers Jean-Paul Sartre and Simone de Beauvoir in their attempt to formulate an ethics that constantly questions itself in a concrete situation—though of course this common view of ethics also reflects the fact that all of them were working in the wake of Nietzsche's critique of values and are part of the modernist constellation seeking a new grounds for ethical thought.

The public charade Reiting stages sets the scene for Törless taking center stage in his final recognition scene. He confronts the school's director, the class leader, and two other teachers—the instructor for religion and the school's mathematician—who seek to understand what has happened. Refusing to comment upon his flight from the school, Törless feels challenged to find adequate language with which to tell the truth when asked why he concealed Basini's misconduct (6:133). Musil narrates the recognition scene using a counterpoint between what Törless says and the reactions of the adults, showing that the latter by and large do not understand him but attempt to interpret his words in terms of their preestablished convictions. The ironic effect is not unlike that of a tragic hero who confronts a doddering chorus incapable of understanding anything other than the conventional belief they uphold. When Törless says he was concerned with Basini's *Seele*—his psyche or soul—the religion teacher immediately supplies words to interpret, in biblical terms, this concern as "disgust" with the evil that must have enchanted Törless, as a snake does with its victim (6:134). The other teachers are happy with the religion teacher's conventional Christian allegory. But Törless is relentlessly honest—

or naive—for he refuses the allegory by saying he felt no disgust, he had no thought of punishment, but rather he felt a kind of "leap" each time he thought of Basini. This is beyond the teachers' ken, and the only thing the teachers and Törless can agree upon is that he is "confused" (*verwirrt*) (6:134). The notion of confusion only serves to point up that they have arrived at a vacuous agreement, ironically underscored by the fact that they all, including Törless, agree that he should not remain at the school.

Törless's thoughts are reported with little ambiguity in this recognition scene, which signifies that the narrative viewpoint and his inner world are nearly ready to coincide: "He felt himself that he had badly expressed himself, but the contradiction and the atmosphere of misunderstanding that he encountered gave him the feeling of a rather arrogant superiority over the older people who seemed to understand so little about the conditions of inner life" (6:135–36).

One can think that at a later age Törless might credit these adults with more understanding than he does in his youth, but probably not much more. He clearly sees that the educators all use facile categories—"sin" rather that "emotions," or "guilt" rather than "responsibility"—to understand extraordinarily complex things. Perhaps it is a sign of adolescent pride that Törless thus sees himself as their judge, but it may also be taken in a positive sense that Törless is about to move beyond the damaging restrictions of narrow, conventional moral thinking.

At the end of the denouement Törless speaks out in a classical recognition scene resembling a courtroom showdown. This kind of scene, familiar to every cinema fan, culminates in Törless's awareness that he has an inner life of his own that he cannot find adequate language to express: "So, just as I feel that a thought may come to life in me, so I also feel that something lives in me when I'm looking at things, when thoughts remain silent. There is something dark in me, beneath all thoughts, that I can't measure with thoughts, it's a life that can't be expressed in words and which is still my life" (6:137).

The speech is directed against his teachers and his judges who want to reduce what he says to preestablished categories. Some critics have seen here a generalized expression of a crisis about the capacity of language to express human needs.[3] Undoubtedly many Viennese around 1900 were skeptical of language, partly as a reaction against the pretensions of romantic thought and partly as a result of the ongoing crisis centered on the failure to find a political ideology adequate to historical reality. Yet Musil was less skeptical of language than many of his contemporaries. Rather Törless's speech rejects the belief that all mental life takes the shape of the language foisted upon the psychological subject immersed in a given society. Musil dramatizes in Tör-less's speech a meditation on the mind and the mind's genesis of values. He suggests the multiple dimensions of mind, which must be grasped as a whole if one is to realize the integrity of self. Neither language nor inchoate perception taken alone are constitutive of mind, and Törless's defense of his self stresses that it cannot be reduced to a single theme.

The theatrical concepts we have drawn upon to understand the novel can also be of use when we turn to the other characters in the work. The novel invites us to use theatrical analogies, not only for understanding the plot, but also to understand the two main characters who, with Törless, are actors on the novel's stage, Beineberg and Reiting. Their behavior is framed as role-playing, a notion that suggests they adapt them themselves to identities offered to them by their milieu. Thus they indulge themselves in long speeches, rather like soliloquies, that are quoted at length. Because of the direct presentation of their speech, the narrator does not often evaluate the characters directly. But it is obvious that, through these soliloquies and in the roles they choose, the two characters embody tendencies that Musil saw animating not just Austrian military academies but more generally German culture in those years during which he came to maturity. In this sense the two boys are playing roles that are emblematic of the irrational forces in culture that would determine German cultural and political history until the collapse of the Third Reich. In its portrayal of the cultivation of irrationality the novel points out the potential foundations for repressive political structures.

In quite specific terms the reader encounters in the roles Beineberg plays a foreshadowing of the irrationality of racism conceived as a pseudoscience; and in Reiting's playing with power the glorification of the kind of perverted will to power underlying militarism and aggressive colonialism. Both boys' roles embody an incipient ideology that proclaims conquest to be the ultimate justification of existence. In both are found wacky religious doctrines and "metaphysical" beliefs that were part and parcel of the swell of early-twentieth-century irrationalism, as well as a dislike of science and reason. They have selected roles that will lead them to reject political institutions that promote science and Enlightenment education. In fine, if in his dissertation Musil was critical of the reductive rationalism of positivism, in his first novel he was fearful of its contrary.

In their long speeches Reiting and Beineberg embrace most of the irrational currents prevalent at the end of the nineteenth century. In Beineberg's speeches such metaphysical entities as the transcendental ego, the unconscious self, and, implicitly, ethnic or racial identity are taken to be the basis for privileged knowledge. Serving as the basis for irrational cults as varied as theosophy and mystical nationalism, these constructs later served to justify the pure emotional appeal of fascism. In Reiting's soliloquies fewer themes are present, because he acts out the role of a single-minded, cynical proponent of power and its manipulation, undertaken in the pursuit of the joys of violence. What is exceptional about Musil's presentation of these two characters is that they are nothing exceptional. They are ordinary boys of the sort found in a military academy, variants of which could be found throughout Europe. Reiting is part of the group of Törless's boisterous new friends presented at the novel's outset, in the train station, after Törless has lost the prince's friendship. His parents are favorably impressed by this new group made up of what they see to be raw, more manly friends. They take comfort in the fact that these boys are mainly interested in ordinary activities, such as playing cards, telling tales about the teachers, and smoking the cigarettes that Törless's father had brought from home (6:14). Undoubtedly, the parents want their son to imitate these average young males for fear that he might well have other ideas about what he wants to become—a justified fear confirmed by narrative's view of a future in which Törless will not be material for the Austrian bureaucracy nor the army.

Reiting shows from the outset that he enjoys ordinary adolescent sadism when he makes cutting remarks to Törless, some two years younger than he, snickering at the "little boy" for being homesick (6:18). Törless is embarrassed, because Reiting has looked right into his mind and has known how, gratuitously, to inflict pain on him from the fairly crude macho viewpoint of which Reiting is a relentless representative. The desire to inflict pain informs Reiting's main soliloquy in the loft after he has discovered that Basini is the culprit in the theft of Beineberg's money. The narrator prefaces this moment by telling us what Törless already knows much about the roles Reiting plays, though he does not understand what he knows. For example, Reiting's greatest pleasure is to set two boys against each other, pretending to be a friend of one and then the other, in order to enjoy the hatred he can foment between them. This sadism is paralleled by the masochistic way Reiting trains his arm muscles by boxing against hard surfaces and tries to harden his hands by forming calluses on them (6:40). An adept of irrational brutality, Reiting is also clever. He is an opportunistic "tyrant" who changes his role constantly so that he appears to keep himself on the side of the majority. He apparently dreams of exercising his will to power in the kinds of war that Napoleon led a century earlier (wars that Törless believes are now a thing of the past). In short, Reiting selects roles expressing a sadomasochist mentality. A military career might offer a natural outlet for the expression of his savagery, for the role of officer can reconcile honor and brutality. The school seems ideally suited in this regard to serve him as a training ground for the pleasures of psychological warfare, if not genuinely bellicose activity.

Based on his understanding of psychopathology, Musil aims to show that rather primitive instinct animates complicated role-playing. For example, Reiting's lust for power is given detailed expression. In the oration he makes about catching Basini, he emphasizes, with obvious arrogant pleasure, how clever he has been in the capture. This egotistical role-playing is paralleled by his delight in the other's suffering, which Reiting underscores when he claims that he had seen such a suffering face as Basini's only once before, when a policeman had arrested a murderer whose face betrayed anguish at the prospect of the gallows awaiting him (6:45). Reiting wants to play at being torturer, which is revealed in the relish with which he tells how Basini began to shed tears and to beg for mercy. He exults in his power over the other boy, and the soliloquy comes to an end with the logical question as to how to continue to exercise power over the defenseless lad—logical once one accepts that making the other suffer is the supreme goal.

The loft is thus used by the boys to set up a kind of stage for their role-playing. On this stage the question about how to continue to exercise power receives a blunt answer when Reiting, having led Basini to the loft, begins the session by striking him down with a blow in the face (6:69). This is a savage form of the theater of cruelty, not a child's game, and it is with remarkable power that Musil now blurs the line between ordinary and extraordinary acting in Reiting's brutal exercise of power. Playing at a role transforms itself when the boy's identification with the role leads him to commit to acts that are real, not make-believe. The boy begins by acting out the game of power for the sake of power, which then leads him to perform on a stage that becomes the scene of the real. It does not seem hyperbole to propose that the affective hold that such theatrical enactments can have on the imagination would be the basis for the Nazi hold on power some thirty years later. Taking on the role of supermen, the Nazis began to act out the role with real acts of racist murder.

Törless also discovers in this enactment that sadism is tied up with eroticism. Both Reiting and Beineberg play at being nascent Nietzschean explorers of the irrational joy in power, though Musil shows that their irrationalism is also grounded in rationalizing sexual impulses. This is especially evident in the way Beineberg exploits the Basini sexually. He justifies his savagery with intellectual pretensions. His desire to achieve transcendence with a whip is complementary to the superiority he feels for having become an adept of

Indian philosophy and for the transcendence it grants him. Beineberg is a more subtle character than Reiting, for the role he plays allows him to lay claim to a kind of asceticism in his devotion to esoteric thought. There is also a connection to military ideals in this devotion: Beineberg's father is a military officer from whom he has inherited the ideas leading him to claim to live in world-denying fantasy. In this critique of Nietzsche, Musil calls nonetheless upon Nietzsche in his portrayal of Beineberg's role-playing. According to Nietzsche self-denial can be a ploy for the attainment of superior knowledge, which is to say, another way of pursuing power. Musil's description of the quest for revelation undertaken by Beineberg's father underscores that he and his son play at being devotees of a modern gnosis that wants to abolish all limitations on knowledge—which in context means they have a desire for unlimited power.

In practice a requisite for success in taking on the role of seer is that the adept of superior knowledge must refuse all debate about alternatives. The narrator describes Beineberg's father not simply as an adept of Indian philosophy but as a seeker for absolute truth and unquestioning certainty: "When he [the father] read, he did not want to reflect on opinions and controversies, but, at the very instant of opening the book, he wanted to enter through secret doors into the midst of elected knowledge. His had to be books whose mere possession was the sign of a secret order and the guarantee of supernatural revelations. And such books he found only in books of Indian philosophy, which to him did not seem to be simply books but revelations, something ultimately real—books for decoding reality like the alchemical and magical books of the Middle Ages" (6:19). This passage is a concise summary of the antithetical stances toward the world that Musil saw in modernity as he was working on his doctoral studies and thinking about Mach and Nietzsche. On the one hand Musil, himself educated in science, was accustomed to evaluating probable opinions and constantly changing theories, and hence saw the necessity of dealing with "opinions and controversies." On the other hand, in Vienna and Berlin he could frequently encounter the type of mind that wanted sudden revelations, without question, of "something ultimately real." In the irrational demand for absolutes Musil might ironically see a caricature of his own desire for certainty and mystical unity—but he also saw that in this demand for certainty he had encountered the need for an identity that would refuse all alternatives. The young Musil understood well that the will to power embodied in these demands for certainty entails rejection of the epistemological practices of science—which Musil could not accept. If Nietzsche scoffed at the illusions of science because of its belief in truth, Musil saw that the rejection of rational procedures for knowledge had led historically to increasingly nihilistic demands for revelation predicated upon the desire for self-affirmation. Nietzsche predicted the arrival of nihilism; it is not clear if he realized that his attack on the truth value of science promoted that nihilism. Musil clearly did.

Most notably desirous of transcendence is Beineberg, who inherited from his father the desire for revelation that mere science cannot offer. Arguably, he has also acquired a racist attitude that allows him to experiment on Basini, whose Italian-sounding name suggests that his ethnic background is different from Beineberg's. Unarguably in his quest for knowledge Beineberg's contempt for Basini is total. Thus, he feels no remorse in literally undertaking experiments on the boy, because he sees in Basini an inferior being who has no significance in comparison with the great world soul that, embodied in Beineberg, justifies his putatively superior existence. Beineberg coldly expresses his contempt for Basini as an inferior being by declaring that when a hiker encounters such a creature on the road, he perforce must consider him to be as insignificant as a worm or a rock and then decide with indifference whether to step over him or to crush him underfoot (6:56). The contempt Beineberg expresses is born of his belief that one's superiority is as much a matter of absolute gnosis as blood. It is the wordless contempt of the torturer for his victim, of the racist for the being whose destruction only serves to magnify the sadistic racist's superiority. The beating Beineberg subsequently administers to Basini is another brutal demonstration that violence is readily sanctioned by irrational belief, especially when this absurd belief is frustrated in its will to power.

In theatrical terms Törless acts as something of a foil character who confronts in fascination and disbelief the protofascist irrationalists Reiting and Beineberg as they act out their fantasies with real blows. He is not immune to the power of their acting, and their irrationality is dramatized in such a way that the reader sees the power it exercises over Törless, the spectator who becomes an actor in his turn. Thus the novel functions theatrically in dramatizing through soliloquies the nature of the two brutal boys, and functions as a novel in its portrayal through narration of Törless's inner world. At first the reader sees that Törless only knows that he does not understand what is happening around him. In curious ignorance he goes along with the two older boys in their schemes, taken in by the affective enchantment worked by the irrational. In this regard the other characters offer him extraordinary revelations, such as the seeming magical power of enchantment worked by gratuitous evil or the discovery of a sexual desire he had not known before. Their exercise of power over Basini seems briefly to confirm the power of their knowledge, for their raw cruelty seems to illuminate the darkness that surrounds Törless.

Needing to find some light in the darkness of the uncertainty that threatens to undermine his sense of self, he is fascinated but then disgusted by Reiting's and Beineberg's practice of sadism. Moreover, Törless comes to see the certainty with which they find solutions to doubts about certainty is only part of a grotesque charade staged to assuage primitive impulses.

Perhaps the most important episode for understanding Törless's disarray occurs, however, when he is alone, at moments when he undergoes a kind of fall into the darkness of uncertainty. When left to himself Törless experiences what amounts to an ongoing negative revelation. Though young, he comes to understand that, for all the light that science has shed upon the world, the cosmos has become dark with the advent of modern cosmology. In the course of the novel he learns that the illuminations and revelations promised by sadism or esoteric posturing are only sham attempts to bring light to the pervasive darkness. This recognition does not assuage his dilemma about where to find knowledge. He must contend with the fact that science, the embodiment of the light of knowledge, has seemingly been responsible for bringing darkness to the world. Doubts about science and knowledge are complementary to the perverted certainties proposed by Reiting and Beineberg.

The nature of Törless's unsettled state is illustrated, for example, by the malaise he feels when he is asked to solve equations using imaginary numbers, such as the square root of -1. Such numbers do not "really" exist, though of course they are a necessary part of modern mathematical operations. With a rare sense of the dramatic importance of the intellect and its concerns, Musil introduces mathematics to show how scientific education does not always meet the emotional as well as intellectual demands of students. Musil succeeds in demonstrating, through Törless's example, that emotion and intellect are two sides of the same coin, of the unified subject or the complete self. In this depiction the boy feels deeply about the operations of science, just as he tries to think rationally about his emotions.

Despairing about his lack of understanding about imaginary numbers, Törless goes to ask for help from his mathematics teacher. That he goes to see his teacher, and not a priest, about problems of intellectual curiosity and existential security says a great deal about the world in which the boy has grown up. However, the teacher is unable to give Törless any help. He offers him a few banalities about the world of mathematics and assures Törless that he will understand the necessity of imaginary numbers when he has studied the subject further. Meanwhile, he says, Törless must accept on faith that imaginary numbers function as they should, which, as Beineberg later scornfully points out, is what a priest would say in trying to persuade a student to accept his

76

dogma. In this regard Beineberg is not wrong. Moreover, his cynicism about modern science reflects the extent to which the Nietzschean view of the arbitrary nature of knowledge had permeated Austrian culture.

In the professor's room, however, Törless sees that the young mathematician keeps on display a book of Kant's philosophy. He is duly impressed, perhaps because the notion of "transcendental" is attached both to certain domains of mathematics and to Kant's philosophy. Törless has seen volumes of Kant enshrined in his father's library at home. The narrator offers, with irony, a résumé of Törless's naive attitude toward philosophy and literature at this point in his life, one embodying the kind of culture idolatry that Musil could not abide. Noting that Kant's name was used in Törless's presence with an expression reserved for that of a saint, the narrator says that Törless could not help but think that all the problems of philosophy had been solved by Kant, so that henceforth philosophy was a pointless activity—"indeed in the same way that he believed that after Schiller and Goethe it was not worth the effort to write any more poetry" (6:78). At this point the narrator makes another brief proleptic intervention to point out that Törless's attitude would later cause him trouble, since it prevented him from understanding what his goal in life might be, which might suggest that his goal will be to be a writer if not a scientist (6:79). And in the immediate context this attitude causes him to tear up and burn the poems he has written. Musil makes a sharp critique of education here, for education, seconded by the culture idolatry it promotes, results in the boy refusing the possibility of his own creativity even while he despairs about coming to understand what he can expect to know.

Törless is looking for grounds for having beliefs justifying what one thinks one knows. He needs reasons to justify beliefs and knowledge, so it is with irritation if not with anger that he scornfully retorts to Beineberg's provocations. He knows he is not seeking something supernatural, but precisely something natural, an understanding of what lies within the realm of nature and hence within himself. He has no need for airy speculations (6:83). Törless is endowed with a level of self-consciousness that marks him as a highly intelligent young man. Yet his intelligence is as much a problem as a help in confronting the problems of finding an orientation in a school in which little has been thought out for the student who *needs* to understand why he believes what he believes.

At this point we can now see another way in which the novel links up with Musil's dissertation. In the dissertation he wants to show that much of modern scientific epistemology is contradictory in dismissing the idea that there is some bedrock nature to which scientific knowledge conforms in its representations.

And in the novel he is showing that this bedrock is existentially as well as epistemologically necessary if there is to be a world whose invariant solidity can give the lie to our irrational fantasies. In *Young Törless* Musil set out to do more than simply deplore the loss of the unity of knower and known or of the belief in a substantial reality to which science ought to give access with reasonable certainty. This is clear in the tropes Musil uses early in the novel to portray Törless's revelation that the cosmos, once humanity's house, has become dark. This experience of dark uncertainty was not unique to Törless in turn-of-the-century Austria. For example, it stands behind the anguish one finds in the poetry of the Musil's contemporary, the poet Georg Trakl (1887–1914). Trakl concludes his hymn to the night, "Gesang zur Nacht," with a revelation that concisely describes Törless's experience of the disintegration of his self when the boy cannot ground it in secure knowledge:

> Du bist in tiefer Mitternacht
> Ein Unempfangner in süssem Schoss,
> Und nie gewesen, wesenlos! (lines 119–21)

> (You are in deep midnight
> An unreceived one in the sweet bosom
> And never have been, are beingless!)

Trakl's outcry against the dark void parallels Törless's intuitive experience of darkness. Being refused reception in one's home—"being beingless"—is a modernist description of alienation when the light of knowledge fails to provide essential illumination so that the quester for light experiences the loss of all footing.

The cosmic night impinges upon Törless's consciousness, and his experience recalls Trakl's for the way Törless skirts the insanity Trakl experienced at the end of his life. Törless wants to flee the world of adults, but he finds isolation to be a kind of confinement. Alone, the boy recalls that once earlier in isolation he underwent a negative revelation that disclosed a world plunged into darkness: "It was a world unto itself, this darkness. Like a swarm of black enemies, it had come over the earth and had slaughtered or driven away people or done whatever it took so that every trace of them was extinguished." He recalls the moment nonetheless with a strange pleasure: "The world appeared to him afterwards like an empty, dark house, and in his breast there was a shudder, as though he must now search from room to room—dark rooms about which one didn't know what their corners hid—and, while groping, step over the thresholds, which no human's foot other than his would ever touch again, into a room whose door would open before him and then shut behind him and in front of him would stand the mistress of the black horde herself" (6:24).

The memory images suggest why Törless feels, after the prince has left the school, that he has no solid framework to his self, for he is again alone, again with no "unmoving background" that would allow him to ground his self in something fixed or substantial (6:14). The ignorant prince, with the self-assurance born of unthinking tradition, had apparently suggested, for a moment, some other mode of being, but that moment is now gone, and Törless finds himself groping again for direction.

The memory of dark revelation Törless recalls foreshadows another negative epiphany he undergoes while at school. This occurs when, quite literally, he is struck by the infinite. This epiphany notably does not take place in the confines of romantic darkness that is the scene for Törless's memory image of the world as a dark house. His later waking nightmare unfolds in the harsh light of day, when the brilliance of the sun impresses upon him the literal endlessness of space. The objective power of light, the rationalist symbol of knowledge, drives, as it were, Törless into a darkness in which he sees the cosmos as an abode harboring madness. This revelation is strongly correlated with his need for science. He intuits that mathematical representation might offer some structure bringing order to the void. He tries to imagine a world order described by mathematics. He desires a world of rational certainty, but his imagination cannot conceive that order in palpable symbols. Thus mathematics becomes a source of anguish when he is overpowered by infinity's invading his world.

The pivotal scene in this revelation occurs when Törless, lying in the grass, looks at the sky and sees it to be a blue, ineffably deep hole between the clouds. There is no end to this hole. It appears to be moving always away, an unending movement that is encapsulated in the concept of the infinite—a previously empty word whose capacity to engender anguish Törless suddenly discovers nearly three centuries after the French mathematician Blaise Pascal concluded that the real, physical infinite mocks our belief that we can have certainty about knowledge. The sky is a menace for the boy who desperately needs a closed universe in which there are certainties, moral rules, and a means for knowing the inner world of others. He needs, in short, a bedrock certainty that allows one to negotiate the world with some security of judgment based on knowledge. It is in the moment of his revelation that "a kind of madness came over Törless that made him feel that things, processes, people, were all something equivocal" (6:64). Turning his eyes toward the sky, the boy feels the sky's empty silence confronting his deep solitude.

At this moment the narrator says, "Der Himmel schwieg" ("The heavens were silent"), and in this negative perception, the anguish that Pascal once felt before the silence of the infinite spaces revealed by science is renewed by Törless's perception (6:66). I stress the intertextual connection with Pascal, because it seems clear that Musil's text intentionally recalls the fearful silence that Pascal found in empty spaces. Without paradox, this silence reverberates in Törless's perception of endless emptiness. In many respects Pascal was the first modern mathematician as well as the first existentialist, and his presence is found throughout Musil's work, as first reflected in Törless's knowledge that under the unmoved, silent arch of the sky he is alone, like a little living dot, in a timeless, unspeaking world (6:66). With the intuition of a seventeenth-century mathematician Törless feels himself to be nothing more than a geometric point in the real unfolding infinite.

Perhaps as much as any later modernist writer, Raymond Queneau, Jorge Luis Borges, and Italo Calvino included, Musil conceived the epistemic possibilities of literature with the sensibility of a mathematician. This sensibility is found in Törless's intuitive grasp of the infinite, with which Musil has updated Pascal, by dramatizing that the modern schoolboy's perturbation is brought about by the very thought of the infinite. He portrays convincingly that a modern schoolboy, who has in effect mastered roughly the level of mathematics developed in the seventeenth century, could react to his scientific education in existential terms. Musil gives Törless a mathematician's intuitive understanding of the infinite. The intuitive grasp of the indefinitely large can serve as the basis for the idealization that leads to the concept of the infinite—to paraphrase mathematician Shaughan Lavine's elegant argument about how one might find the origins of the concept of the infinite in perception.[4] In the case of the Jansenist mathematician Pascal, this intuition of the actual infinite led to a desperate need to combat the revelations of mathematics and science with religion. However, Törless does not embrace religion. Momentarily he finds a surrogate for religion in the temptations of his companions' sadistic will to power. In his unsettled state he allows himself to be cajoled by Reiting and Beineberg into joining in their torture of the hapless Basini. The experience of groundlessness, of what Trakl called "unbeing," leads Törless to try out perverse surrogates for belief.

His mind nearly unhinged by the illumination of infinite darkness, nonetheless Törless remains a child of the Enlightenment. As mentioned above, when he seeks advice from an adult he does not go to the school's priest for help but rather to the mathematics teacher. He does not, and perhaps cannot, entertain the idea that religion might help him. Perhaps naively, he expects an explanation of the foundations of mathematics to help him find certainty, for his education in mathematics up to this point has undoubtedly held it up as the model of certainty (which it would lose as the new non-Euclidian geometries became known). Törless's demand for an explanation is part of his need for principles with which the boy can build a picture of the world, and this need brings us back to Musil's doctoral dissertation.

Törless's desire for a picture suggests that Musil already had in mind Mach's doctrine about the mimetic nature of epistemic propositions.[5] Mach's notions about the iconic nature of knowledge are also called into question in Musil's presentation of Törless's unsuccessful attempt to picture things with mathematical propositions. Törless wants these propositions to give him images of the world. Imaginary numbers, however, make him dizzy. He cannot picture how the calculation of things that do not exist in the real world— imaginary numbers—allows the description of things that do exist. Nor could Mach or Wittgenstein, for that matter, and Törless's disarray here is already an implicit critique of the notion that functional descriptions have a mimetic capacity. For Törless, using imaginary numbers to picture the world is like using a bridge "where only the beginning and ending piles are there, with none in the middle, and yet one crosses it just as surely and safely as if the whole thing were there" (6:74). Without quite realizing it, Törless has taken on the knottiest of epistemological dilemmas, for it is not at all clear why mathematics functions, sometimes, to describe processes in the world. Musil is not ready, however, to revert to the traditional Newtonian-Kantian belief that mathematics, especially geometry, is inherent to space. His distaste for Kantian answers to the problem is reflected in the way Törless is shunted aside by the Kantian math teacher with the feeble explanation that one must live in this world for a long time in order to feel what is necessary in it. Musil believed no less than Törless in the *Denknotwendigkeiten* or "necessities of thought" the teacher offers as an explanation of mathematics that Törless will one day understand (6:77). If these necessities of thought are conceived of as some category inherent to the mind, then they are as useless as any other form of metaphysical speculation, at least from Musil's sometimes Machean point of view.[6]

Törless's anguish also reflects Musil's doubts as to whether science offers any understanding of the world in its moral complexities. I suggested earlier that the doubts about science of this kind were already expressed by Pascal, who, in declaring that complexities are not part of science's purview, said they must be dealt with by the *esprit de finesse,* or intuition. But the doubts Musil expresses about science are not intended to promote some wisdom superior to science, not even intuition, since the alternatives to science, as seen in *Young*

Törless and Musil's other works, appear rather to be superstition, the ludicrous striving for knowledge beyond reason, and, finally, ideological aberrations. Science may be destructive of the light that once supposedly existed, but in *Young Törless* Musil leaves no doubt that the contempt for scientific rationality is ultimately part of a nihilist mentality that, in promoting the irrational, ends up embracing absurdities, if not perversions. However, at the end of the novel, the questions remains: How can science enable one to live in this world?

CHAPTER 4

Experiments in Narrative and Theater

Musil's career began with éclat: he published back to back a well-received first novel and an important doctoral dissertation. These publications marked the last time in his career, however, that he wrote creatively with ease. Henceforth, his publications of fiction were infrequent, apparently costing him much time in conception, and even more in revision, before he deemed something worthy of publication. This description certainly characterizes the two short pieces of fiction that he worked on for some two years after publishing his dissertation. His prolonged labor in writing the two stories resulted in a slender volume, published in 1911, titled *Vereinigungen* (*Unions*). In this chapter I will deal with these two experimental narratives, the only short fiction he published in book form before World War I. Then I will consider Musil's efforts at writing for the stage. The two plays he wrote can also be considered early experiments, undertaken as he set out to establish himself as a man of letters in the heady climate of the early years of the Weimar Republic.

The two stories making up *Unions* are "Die Vollendung der Liebe" ("The Perfecting of Love") and "Die Versuchung der stillen Veronika" ("The Temptation of Quiet Veronica"). A first impression of them may well be that these stories were not written by the same author who wrote *Young Törless*. In them one decidedly does not encounter the nearly classical plot development Musil used in the novel to dramatize the disclosure of meaning. Rather, one's first impression may be that both texts are nearly amorphous in the way they chart feelings and impressions and relegate the exposition of events to the background. In reading them the reader must decipher layers of impressions to find a plot. Some may find this a rewarding intellectual challenge, and agree with those critics who think the two stories are among the finest examples of experimental fiction in German literature. Others may not.

What is certain in any case is that Musil's desire to experiment with fictional form meant that he did not repeat what he had already done. It would appear that his scientific cast of mind led him to feel that once an experiment had been performed, the knowledge to be gleaned from it was available, and there was no point to repeat it. (This was an attitude he shared with James

Joyce.) The idea of experiment, in a nearly scientific sense, is useful to shed light on what Musil was about in these stories. A scientific thought experiment consists in asking what would be the case if a given hypothesis were true. For example, Einstein asked what would be the consequences if it were true that the speed of light is the limiting velocity for the transmission of information. He then deduced a relativistic universe in which clocks slow down as they approach that limiting speed and time is no longer absolutely the same for all frameworks of reference. Einstein's universe may appear to be a fiction, and, in a sense it is, for nobody will ever travel at something approaching the speed of light. So the consequences Einstein came up with are in part imagined, but not necessarily imaginary. Though the young Musil had not yet assimilated what Einstein had done, he knew well the history of thought experiments and, more crucially perhaps, the work of the scientist who had most influenced Einstein in conceiving such experiments: Mach.

Mach is a primary example of a scientist for whom thought experiments are an indisputable key to advancing knowledge. He believed in the seminal epistemological function of thought experiments at the same time he conceived of them as interesting fictions. Turning the example around, we can speculate that Musil wanted to see what would be the result if he were to use scientific speculation to generate fiction. For example, what would be the case if the psyche or self were only a concatenation of sensations, or "elements," as Mach notoriously phrased it? If the self were only a sequence of sensations, what would the representation of this self look like? Would it be a representation of a series of representations? This might seem logical if primary sensations themselves are in some sense representations to a self that happens to be the central point at which the chain of sensations can be perceived as a chain in the first place.

The narrator of "The Perfecting of Love" seems to experiment with this reasoning when he explains his heroine's feelings by saying that her present self is an affair of chance. He proposes that one's feelings live only in a long chain of other feelings holding themselves together so that the existence of something like a self depends on whether in life one point lines up with the next without a rupture—though "there are a hundred ways" for this alignment to happen (6:188). There are a hundred ways to have an ego, and apparently a hundred ways to be or not to be in love. Consequently, chance is of the essence in the construction of the fragile thing called a self or a psyche. Hypothetically, or in experimental terms, "The Perfecting of Love" aims to show the consequences of taking as axiomatic that the self is a contingent alignment and chaining together of feelings, emotions, and perceptions. If this arrangement of sensations is all an affair of chance, what would a self look like as it goes about perceiving itself? Or, perhaps in other terms, what would a Machean scientist see were he to fall in love?

There is another experimental aspect of "The Perfecting of Love": its examination of the consequences of this view of the self for ethics and the foundation of moral judgments. Continuing in this regard what he had begun in *Young Törless*, Musil appears to experiment with the framing of moral judgments. He wants to see what will be the case if moral judgments and ethical decisions are embedded in the emotional shape of the self at a given moment (cf. *TB* 1:232). Can moral experience turn out to be the opposite of conventional morality? This is suggested by the title "The Perfecting of Love." There is an irony created by the idea of the perfecting of love, since in this story the "perfecting" of what is already often considered perfect involves the heroine Claudine's consenting to adultery with a fatuous seducer when, on a trip, she is distant from her husband, whom she loves.

Perfecting love through adultery may appear to be an ironic, if not paradoxical, trope, and the moral experiment here turns on showing that the character's inner sensations can warrant the claim made by the title of the novella as well as by the title Musil selected for his volume, *Unions*. Notably, neither story in this volume illustrates unions in any conventional sense. The function of this irony is undoubtedly to underscore that these stories intend to experiment with, and perhaps challenge, the axioms underlying conventional moral expectations and idealizations. "The Perfecting of Love" begins by highlighting the question of moral questioning. At the outset of the story's narrative discourse (but not the plot, for the total story really starts with the tale of Claudine's earlier life), Claudine and her husband discuss a common acquaintance, G., who seduces young women and in so doing causes them to disgrace themselves. Claudine asks her husband if the acquaintance intends to do wrong. He answers circumspectly that maybe he does, maybe not, and finally that perhaps one shouldn't ask such questions about "such feelings" (6:157). Claudine retorts that, without meaning to refer to just this "one chance person" or to G., she believes that he means to do well. She seemingly believes that there is a disparity between the world of intentionality, embedded in feelings, and the world of events, judged usually by publicly accepted norms. In this regard she is not far from Törless.

The story's opening scene encapsulates much of the story. The husband understands that acts are a question of "such feelings," and in the rest of the story acts are basically read as feelings and feelings and perceptions are much like acts. Claudine has her own interpretive framework for acts, which at no point allows it to be said that she intends to do something bad. The rhetoric of the fiction is in the service of this experiment in which Musil poses as his initial hypothesis that morality is a question of feelings and then looks at what are the consequences for the acts that ensue. The rhetorical stance of the third-person narrator is a key to understanding this experiment, for at virtually no point does the narrator reveal anything about the fiction's world except the unfolding of Claudine's feelings and perceptions. Seen from this limited third-person perspective, evil and intentionality may appear to be mutually exclusive.

Musil is laying down a challenge for the reader. It is not unlike the challenge Socrates makes in declaring that nobody can actively desire or intend to do evil. One can only desire the good—though, as Socrates allows, one may well be ignorant as to what the good truly it is. This reference to Socratic psychology suggests the perennial nature of certain kinds of ethical thinking. Moreover the reference is also justified in the story by the way Musil alludes to the Platonic myth of the androgyne in describing how Claudine and her second husband go together like the two halves of one being, once separated, now fit back together, and whose inner being flows from one into the other (6:159). In other words there is an intertextual dimension to this experiment that opens up beyond the immediate, rather claustrophobic enclosure. Plato is the first important thinker about ethics in our tradition, and it is not surprising that Musil should, here and later, maintain a dialogue with him.

To recall again the distinction of plot and narrative order, one sees that, by beginning his story's narrative with the discussion of G. and his motivation in seducing young women, Musil shapes the reader's reaction to the narrative flashback relating Claudine's behavior in the past. The flashback centers on Claudine's past sexual conduct, before the main narrative line begins to unfold with Claudine's leaving alone on a trip. The narrator says nonjudgmentally that before her marriage she led a life of promiscuity, even when she was still married to her first husband. The first husband is not the father of the child who was born to Claudine and who is now at school in an institute in some small city (6:160). Claudine's subsequent travel to visit her child provides the motivation for the plot in the rest of the story. In the flashback, however, before continuing to describe Claudine's present impressions, the narrator offers a privileged perspective on her self-perception during the years in which she humiliated herself in degrading relationships with a series of men. Or so the narrator characterizes Claudine in saying that, seemingly with no willpower of her own, she allowed men to do to her what they wanted, to the point of self-victimization (6:160). Although the narrator says she debased herself, he also states that what she did, fundamentally, did not touch her and "had nothing essential to do with her" (6:160). If we accept that the narrator is reliable, then in these moments she experienced a split between her acts and her self. Impressions and acts are disconnected so that, according to the narrator, the stream of events rushed by her, as with any other frequently adulterous woman. In spite of her many concrete acts, all the while "she had the feeling to just be sitting motionless and lost in thought" (6:160–61).

Various theories of medical and clinical psychology can be called upon to describe how Claudine feels that what happens to her body does not happen to her. The critical literature on Musil offers numerous examples of Freudians, Lacanians, gestalt theorists, clinical psychologists, and others who use their theories to explain the story, or, more usually, the story to prove their theories. The point of Musil's experiment, however, is to offer the description of a woman who may be called masochistic, alienated, borderline psychotic, perverse, a victim of anomie, without the use of a theoretical framework. Though a doctor in psychology, Musil allows his narrator to make no use of preexisting theory. The narrator in his descriptions espouses the heroine's consciousness and limits himself to a phenomenology of what unfolds in consciousness. (The term *phenomenology,* meaning the study of how consciousness is constituted, is taken from the philosopher Husserl, another thinker influenced by Stumpf and read critically by Musil in his early years.) In a thoughtful essay on Claudine's alienation, Fred Lönker stresses that Musil was irritated by those who conflated literature and psychology. Drawing upon Musil's essay "Über Robert Musils Bücher" ("On Robert Musil's Books"), Lönker recalls that Musil remarked that psychology in art is "only a wagon in which one rides. If, of the writer's intentions, you see only psychology, then you are looking for the landscape in the wagon."[1] In other words, to continue our analogy here, Mach's concepts about the nature of consciousness can provide the hypothetical basis for the experiment, but in the experiment he wants to see concretely what kind of a psychic landscape, free of all conceptual interpretive grids, might result if the world were simply made up of a series of impressions.

To this end Musil's narrator's describes minutely the way Claudine falls back into earlier modes of feeling as she travels alone in a train to see her daughter in a small town. There Claudine is caught by a snowstorm. In the train station, upon her departure, she has unexplained feelings of disgust, against which she can find no defense (6:161–62). In the train she then feels that something suddenly has broken loose and that a "wound in her depths" has opened up (6:163). She has fantasies about music, which cause her to imagine that she could belong to another man. The narrator says that this appeared to her not as infidelity, but like a last nuptials—some place where she and the other would only be music (6:165). The text is at times ambiguous, and the syntax of the narrator's sentences espousing feeling and fantasy is distorted, but the disjointed sensation of feelings not quite fitting together is part of the representation of representations flitting by a consciousness that may be on the verge of disintegration.

The past invades the present, and Claudine's memory of her present husband wanes. In fact she starts to yearn for the life of abuse that men once inflicted upon her (6:167). The upsurge of memory is a strong leitmotif in the story, though it does not take the form of romantic nostalgia. A psychologist might speak of a regression to the past, though from the story's perspective the invasion of the present by the past operates as a form of disjunction, tearing apart the continuity of her self. Later, in her hotel room in the small town she also becomes confused about time, as if she had not left her husband, but then finds that she is "sinking back" into time (6:177). During the first night in her room, when the seducer whom she encountered earlier first knocks at her door, she falls to the floor in distress, with a "hateful feeling of self," during what may be a "fall backwards into her past" (6:190). This presence of the past is instructive. In a sense the interruptive presence of the past is a challenge to a positivist reduction of the self to a current stream of perception. The recurrence of memory shows that something can exist permanently through time, something that—whatever one may call it—can disrupt the present and transform it. The positivist may retort that images purporting to represent the past always exist in the present moment, and Musil would probably not disagree with this viewpoint. In his experiment the past can be read as an ambivalent presence. Or, alternatively, when the past disrupts the present with no firm distinction between the two, then madness is lurking nearby. And Claudine seems on the verge of a psychotic state.

The story's final lines, narrating Claudine's consent to the seduction, contain her remembrance of something happening in springtime, something that could be there "for all men and yet only for one" (6:194). These lines may summarize her desire, or the paradox of the desire she once had to belong to every man and in so doing to belong to just one. The surrealist poet Paul Eluard wrote the same thing in a poem expressing his surrealist desire that the possession of the true object of love entails the possession of every woman. For the surrealist, however, desire is a form of transcendence. Claudine's desire for every man provokes disgust in her when it takes on the form of animal lust and instinct, but her abnegation and self-abasement may lead her paradoxically to transcendence—a connection that is part of a very Christian experience.

In this story, as in "The Temptation of Quiet Veronika," Musil uses animal imagery to stress the bestial or purely biological dimension to erotic instincts, with images at once reminiscent of Kafka and Freud. For example, after her first night in the small town separated from her husband, when lust invades her consciousness, Claudine awakes to find "an animal in her breast" and a desire to be humiliated (6:173). It is a platitude to observe that conventional morality reproves those who give into their animal side, but less platitudinous is Musil's representation of the way that sexual psychodynamics involve debasing innocence in acts that transform pleasure into pain and vice versa. In other words Claudine seems to long for pain as part of the pleasure her animal body demands from her. Certainly pure bestiality underlies her attraction to the seducer encountered in the train, an anonymous stranger who is ready to pin her down into the present moment (6:169). Her sensuality is awakened by his bearded, animal appearance and by the fact he is a stranger to her. As the story unfolds she experiences various fantasies in this regard, including sodomy, in the sense of copulation with an animal. The term *sodomy* is the closest thing to a technical term used in the tale and should be read with reference to the Bible and biblical notions of transgression. As the narrator says, in sodomy lay the temptation of Claudine's love (6:180). This impression comes after she has already begun thinking of the stranger as a shaggy animal, giving off the odor of a beast (6:178). To be excited by animal odor bespeaks her desire to attach herself to something raw and carnal that will deprive her of personal identity. This desire is continued during the first night in the hotel. She wants to be nothing less than an animal herself and to "throw herself on the rug, then to kiss the disgusting prints of his feet, and like a sniffing bitch dog to excite herself on him" (6:189). This first night comes to nothing, but the seducer returns to disgust and excite her on the following day, when she finds the "perfecting" of her love.

Disgust is thus a leitmotif in this perfection. This includes disgust with self, for she does not reach full sexual excitement until she commits a betrayal she cannot abide. She denies that she loves her husband, and with this lie, she finds again the "charm of her lies" from times gone by (6:187). These were the times when she wandered in the streets like a "lost dog" and looked at people. Her lying betrayal is completed on the next day when the fatuous stranger announces to her that she loves him, though she doesn't realize it, which, he says, is "the sign of true passion" (6:193). With this he sets off another wave of disgust in her, and "then her body is filled with lust in spite of everything" (6:193). Perfection would seem to be the inversion of perfection. Her "perfection" involves the denial of conventional ideas of perfection, so she arrives at a state of abnegation that at the same time affirms conventional morality by denying it. Claudine's excited acceptance of betrayal culminates in this dialectic of opposites.

The narrative experiment here reaches its most complex moment, both in terms of perception and moral content, as Claudine reports to herself about what her body is doing when it is surrendering, if that is the word, to the bearded animal that has pursued her. Musil is asking the reader to enter the inner life of an individual caught up in a unique, though not altogether unusual, situation. Musil's understood axiom, here as elsewhere, is that every human situation is in some sense unique. If we look for universal traits in it that are amenable to generalization, Musil thinks we are undertaking the task of science and not literature. The task of literature is to strive after what he called in the diaries, with reference to *Unions,* "a certain individual truth" (*TB* 1:214). If we take Musil's lead on this question, it is clear that he believes that only after the reader has encompassed Claudine's experience of her emotions, perceptions, desires, and finally choices can she be evaluated from various perspectives, though the first perspective must be the one that the narrator gives in narrating the perceptual and moral truth of this individual case.

From this perspective Claudine appears to be a woman who chooses debasement as a form of punishment for her desires, and thus achieves a form of salvation or transcendence. It is an inverted moral choice from the point of view of conventional morality, but it is a moral choice. This may seem paradoxical; and it is certainly ironic in the simplest meaning of irony: her act signifies its opposite. And it is indeed irony that holds together the logic of triumphant moral debasement. This may be irony needing God's perspective on the world, one uniting all opposites. Something like the need for God is suggested by the story's last, rather disjointed sentence, in which, after Claudine has accepted her seducer, the narrator declares: "At a distance, in the way that children say of God, he is great, she had a representation of her love" (6:194). Claudine's understanding of her love must unite debasement and betrayal with triumphant perfection. And while Dante would have consigned her to the last circle in hell reserved for those who commit betrayal, in her own understanding betrayal has elevated her.

Musil struggled in his own understanding of his characters, as the diaries make clear, such as when he wrote that he sought the true, and not just the ethical or psychological, determinants of the behavior of Claudine and of Veronika, the main character in his second story in *Unions* (*TB* 1:232). What *true* might mean in this context is not clear, but presumably it is what can emerge from the experiment with representing the unfolding of consciousness.

He next struggled with a comparable experiment, based on paradoxical irony, in "The Temptation of Quiet Veronika." In the diary he related this story to "The Perfecting of Love." According to Musil, if one sees that in an inclination toward an animal can be found something like surrender to a priest, or if infidelity can in a deeper inner region be a form of union, then has one paraphrased the basis for Veronika and Claudine. Bestiality is at work in the transgressions of "The Perfecting of Love." It remains for "The Temptation of Quiet Veronika" to exceed this transgression by relating the animal and the priest. If animal lust and priestly sublimation set out the traditional dichotomies of a culture founded on repressing the body and elevating the spirit, then ironic understanding sees that the animal and the priest can be sometimes part of the same thing—or at least this appears to be one hypothesis underwriting "The Temptation of Quiet Veronika." Musil is experimenting with ethical dialectics in the second story, much in the same way that he portrays in the first story that infidelity and union can be aspects of the same desire. In the second story, however, he enacts a moral experiment even more explicitly conceived in terms of classical Platonic and Christian ethics. Subverting the notions of higher and lower, the final result of this experiment is to show that the moral framework Christian culture wants to impose can often produce the opposite result from what it intends.

"The Temptation of Quiet Veronika" begins quite differently from "The Perfecting of Love," for Musil does not limit the narrative voice to one espousing Veronika's consciousness. Instead the narrative opens with something like stage directions telling readers that somewhere they must hear two voices—or perhaps not—and that perhaps somewhere in the world there is a point where the voices can rise above the surrounding noise and, like two beams, set each other aflame and clasp each other (6:194). The voices are those of Johannes and Veronika, potentially a pair of lovers, though soon separated in the story when Veronika sends Johannes off to kill himself. The first voice in the text seems to be that of Johannes, a young man perhaps about to become a priest, though Veronika's inner voice and perceptions dominate the main body of the tale. The narration is again centered on the consciousness of a female protagonist, but not exclusively in this case.

The biblical allusions tied up with the two characters' names are suggestive of religious themes. Johannes is perhaps a modern version of John the prophet, or John the evangelist, a prototype for a priest. He is a character identified in some sense with God, as indeed is the name of Veronika. Veronica is the saint who supposedly wiped the dead Christ's face on a cloth upon which an image of the face remained imprinted. However, it is improbable that Musil wanted to create a direct Christian allegory by alluding to this miraculous event. Rather we can make more sense of her character by seeing that the religious aura surrounding her name parallels her attempt to create a cobbled-together world in which she can create myths that allow her to transcend her anguish. Comparably Johannes is, by his biblical name, associated with priesthood, which does not exclude that he is an alien, an animal, and at the same time a possible evangelist of truth, a figure seeking a god who does not appear in the story except perhaps in his flagrant absence—something sardonically suggested by the fact that even Veronika knows that she sees angels only when she has fever.

Johannes is about to be crucified by his relationship with this woman, for Veronika wants him to leave and kill himself for her. He is weak, vacillating, self-consciously filled with angst, and is an object of contempt. Veronika chides him, asking him if what he calls God, which he considers as a reality outside of himself, is not in fact a projection of his own inner cowardice and weakness (6:196). But Johannes believes there are things "behind the horizon of consciousness," so that he believes there are ideals that have yet to be embodied (6:196). Whatever else he may be, Johannes is an idealist, and he is starkly contrasted in this regard with the third character in the story, Demeter. In the web of allusions Demeter's name recalls the world of the Greeks, for his namesake is the goddess of agriculture. Aptly Demeter projects an animal-like existence. Veronika looks upon him as a cock or rooster and uses him to torture Johannes. For example, she taunts Johannes with memory of the time when Demeter was insulted by the fact that she had boasted to him that Johannes was better than he. In response Demeter told Johannes that he was a coward and then hit him in the face to prove his point. Johannes's reaction was to flee; and it was afterward that he told Veronika that he wanted to become a priest.

In Musil's world of reversing ethical polarities the identification with priesthood transforms Johannes into an animal. Transgressive dialectics underwrite consciousness in this story, as in "The Perfecting of Love," for upon learning of Johannes's desire for saintliness Veronika now understands that he, not Demeter, has something of an animal about him (6:198). The identification of priest with animal in Veronika's mind suggests that there is again an attraction-repulsion mechanism at work in her desires. She desires and dislikes the spiritual animal at the same time, though it is not at all clear to the reader, nor to Veronika, how she means to express or act upon this polarized feeling—except by driving the animal-priest to his death.

Even more than Claudine, Veronika verges at times on utter madness. Johannes may be the New Testament expositor of logos, but Veronika's use of logos, of that language that coexisted with God in the beginning, exceeds what Johannes can understand. She tells him, for instance, in terms that seem to have biblical overtones, that what he means by God is not what she knows to be God, who is nowhere because he is everywhere. She goes on madly: "He is an evil fat woman, who forces me to kiss her breasts, and at the same time he is me who, sometimes, when she is alone, lies down flat before a cupboard and thinks these things" (6:201). God is the master of disjunction and paradox, a personal impersonal being; something so impersonal, Veronika reasons, could only be an animal, and she begs Johannes to help her understand why her thoughts center upon bestiality (6:202).

Indefinite time flows by in the narrative, polarized between an indefinite past and another past time that is the present of narration. In this polarized time the couple has a strange relationship in which Johannes knows that Veronika can only conceive of him as an animal (6:203). It is a state in which both know that there is some form of sickness hovering over the scene of their interaction. The narrative line takes a clearer shape when it becomes certain that Johannes is going to leave. The departure begins with Veronika's hearing birds singing, whereupon she finds herself submerged in memories (6:204). Her mind is invaded by the nearly lyrical presence of animals as the past invades the narrative present. She recalls a Saint Bernard dog she once had. A kind of anguished sensuality animates her recall of lying near the animal once so that his "shaggy breath" made her want to stop breathing (6:205). This memory suggests a parallel between her present desire and a past attraction-repulsion she felt in the presence of the dog. That same sense of alarm is present to her now, years later, when Johannes, the priest-animal, stands before her. Like Claudine, she recalls the way she became disassociated from her body as life began to live itself, with her remaining a mere spectator: her body lived on, with no relations to anything, though at times a "viscous disgust" permeated the world in which her body lived (6:207).

Musil narrates this series of feelings with images conveying an intense sense of the alienation that can characterize a human being unable to merge with her own body, such merger being the relation normally linking a person to the world. Everything the world offered to Veronika is perceived as foreign, strange, alien, with the result that she feels loathing for everything, including her own body and the would-be suitor Johannes, now the emblem of otherness (6:207). Pursuing his experiment with perception, Musil narrates a world in which inner language and desire are so objectified that inner life becomes an exterior object, at least as Veronika perceives it. Moreover, past and present are mixed together and objectified, and thus perceived as separated from the person who normally would identify with objects perceived in time.

As Johannes's departure takes place, there is a moment of equilibrium. Veronika can picture herself and him as two animals, so that their "horror and expectation" dissolved and "began to circulate (*kreisen*) dumbly and blindly and slowly like a blowing blood around them" (6:211). This strange image—with the verb *kreisen* meaning to turn about or circulate—recalls the opening passage in the story, in which Johannes twice cries out "Kreisendes" (6:194), meaning roughly "something circling." Critics have found it difficult to interpret the purport of this shout. It might well mean that he is crying out for the circulation of the blood in an affirmation of the body constantly denied by Veronika, whose fascination with animals is really part of an ongoing refusal of the animal body that is her own. In any case this image of blood moving seals the departure, and perhaps not so paradoxically; since she cannot have Johannes in his real absence, Veronika is now feeling lust (6:212).

The next movement in the narration describes Veronika's night after Johannes's departure. It encompasses a kind of epiphany or ironic annunciation. Veronika imagines Johannes's progress toward the sea, where he will kill himself, or to continue the religious analogies, he will immolate himself in sacrifice (6:212–13). It seems to her that she has waited years for this evening upon which real or imagined candles flicker about her and her illuminated body rises up (6:214). In a nocturnal meditation she discovers that one can love children and the dead or, in spite of however much she dislikes them, even animals, since none of them have a soul (6:215). In this inverted schema of values she only loves the animal body or something that cannot really love in return. She oscillates between Demeter and Johannes, one an animal, the other about to die, and both appear desirable (6:215). Finally, however, even as she wishes Johannes to be dead, she is conscious that madness is investing the fabric of her perceptions (6:216). This awareness coincides with her giving in to sexual desire, vicariously at least, by undressing in the night, her body feverish as the morning comes. There is a now a dimension of self-consciousness about her consciousness, which suggests that Veronika's temptation is coming to an end. Her temptation has been to live as a detached spirit hating all that is alien to her, which has resulted in the perpetual temptation to know animal debasement. With soft lust and a sensation of closeness, she feels a secret spiritual union. That this union is a fantasy does not detract from the fact that, impermanent though it may be, it brings her to recognize that somewhere beyond herself there is another world (6:220).

She knows now that Johannes is not going to kill himself, and on the next day she receives a letter to that effect. The story ends with Veronika being cured, in that she begins in faltering fashion to have contact with others. She can look upon people, though at first she is afraid of being treated badly by them (6:221). Looking at Demeter, she perceives his knees in his riding pants; sees his lips, which look to her like a bloody little cut; and then fixes upon the tip of his beard, which appears huge (6:223). The fact that she still perceives his body in parts suggests that she has some progress to make before she can acknowledge the human whole. One wonders if she will ever be able to accept a human being with a normal body. That is an open question, but the conclusion, with almost comic irony, suggests that her attraction and repulsion continue to coexist, though perhaps in ways that will allow her to accommodate her lust to human possibilities in the world about her.

Some critics have interpreted Veronika to be a hysteric, in the late-nineteenth-century sense of the term as used by the French doctor Charcot and then by Freud and for several decades by official psychiatry. As an officially recognized syndrome, hysteria disappeared from the psychiatric handbooks later in the twentieth century, and today there is debate about the meaning of this diagnostic category. It was applied nearly always to women who suffered somatic symptoms taken to be an expression of a form of psychopathology, usually a sign of the body's reaction to the repression of sexual desires. Musil would have been quite familiar with a syndrome that features predominantly in Freud's early work as well as in clinical psychiatric medicine. It is thus cogent to interpret "The Temptation of Quiet Veronika" as a near case study in which Musil constructs from within its subject a depiction of the hysterical denial of lust. This experiment is not undertaken by Musil to offer a theory of hysteria. Rather, as David Midgley argues about the plausible use of medical psychology to understand Veronika, "what the imagery of softness and fluidity in this text suggests is that Musil is here evoking a mentality which can achieve its full realization of its own vitality and authenticity only in *opposition* to the language of rigid conceptual categorization."[2] True to his belief in the individual, Musil is not looking for a universal syndrome. One might say that, in portraying Veronika realized in her full individuality, he is writing an anti–case study. This does have implications for psychiatry. In his story Musil implies that madness can be a creation of self, an individual act that must be understood in terms of the individual dynamics underlying it. He is experimenting, then, to see if literature and madness can coincide in the creation of a deviant self, a unique moment that is fictional, both in the madness of real life and literature, in that madness entails invention, elaboration, and the suspension of disbelief.[3] This suspension results in the belief in a world that exists only in an individual self, one whose perceptions the reader is privileged to witness in reading the fiction. Musil's mad Veronika is difficult to understand precisely because she is individualized in such a radical way, one that defies any ready-made syndrome drawn from medical or philosophical thought.

Two Forays into Drama

In the years before World War I Musil got to know the theaters of Vienna and Berlin. For example he went to the Deutsches Theater in Berlin (where, in March 2007, a world premiere of a theatrical version of Musil's novel *The Man Without Qualities* took place). It was at theaters such as the Deutsches Theater that the young Musil formed many of his ideas about drama. There, for example, he saw plays produced by Max Reinhardt, who, in reacting against the naturalism that had come to dominate many European stages, created a poetical theater that drew upon the Greek classics, Friedrich Schiller and Johann Wolfgang von Goethe, William Shakespeare, and modern symbolist playwrights such as the Belgian Maurice Maeterlinck and the Austrian Hugo von Hofmannsthal. The theater criticism that Musil began to write before the First World War and continued to write for several years after the war shows that he was quite attentive, but not always favorable, to what Reinhardt brought to the stage in his attempt to make of the theater a poetical spectacle. Musil's criticism also records that he went to productions of Constantin Stanislavski's Moscow Art Theater, which arguably was the most important influence in Europe for creating a new vision of theater: a dramatic creation that, released from the realistic constraints of naturalism, might innovate in every aspect of a theatrical production to create what Musil called, in writing about Stanislavski, a theater for poets, a "Dichtertheater" (9:1528). In short, through his contact with theater companies such as these, Musil became actively interested in theater, which led to his writing drama criticism and then to his completing two plays, *Die Schwärmer (The Enthusiasts,* also called *The Visionaries*) and the untranslated *Vinzenz und die Freundin bedeutender Männer: Posse in drei Akten* ("Vinzenz and the Woman Friend of Important Men: Farce in Three Acts").

Musil did not entirely accept either Reinhardt's ideas or the vision of a stage freed from realist constraints that was exemplified by the Moscow Art Theater's production of *Hamlet* in 1912. However, several of Musil's pieces of criticism show he thought that one of Reinhardt's leading actors, the Albanian Alexander Moissi, was a great performer, and these essays speak to the positive influence Reinhardt had on Musil in spite of his reservations (9:1498 and 1509).[4] Influenced by the poetic freedom of Reinhardt's productions of Shakespeare and Maeterlinck, Musil kept his distance from a theater dominated by a director whose work, as he said about Reinhardt in 1922, represented a party to which he did not belong (9:1600). Musil's theatrical "party," much like his political party, was that of the poets, and this party he had found earlier in Stanislavski and in the "the music of voices" of the Moscow Art Theater—though the voices were speaking a language he couldn't understand (9:1477).

He also had reservations about Reinhardt because Musil retained a sense of the poetic importance of naturalism, especially as developed in the theater of the Norwegian dramatist Henrik Ibsen. Musil respected what Ibsen had done to transform theater into a force for exploring society and laying bare its corrupt moral mechanisms. This respect in apparent in a critique he wrote in 1921 of a Viennese production of Ibsen's play *Brand* in which he stated that European theater had not taken Ibsen's real lesson to heart. Musil harshly judged the theater he saw about him by comparing it to what he saw as Ibsen's fidelity to truth, which the postwar theater had rejected. Rather, he charged his contemporaries with grossly and childishly reproducing Ibsen's symbolism, "the technical means having the least expressive capacity" (9:1534). Musil saw Ibsen's realism as a means to a spiritual end, by which he meant that the end is basically ethical. He returned repeatedly to this proposition in his theatrical criticism. For, as Agatha Schwartz has pointed out about Musil's critical attitude toward Schiller, Musil wanted not just to bring humanity back to ethical standards as Schiller did, but he wanted to create new moral standards that in a sense would produce a new humanity.[5]

Musil's theater criticism shows he expected little from the state in this respect. In an essay in which Musil berates Viennese critics for misunderstanding a play by the symbolist Paul Claudel, he also chides the city administration for closing down a play by Schnitzler. And he goes on to state lucidly that the state has only one type of relationship with art, which is to create the institutional facilities that guarantee its existence. The stage is a moral institution. However, the state's only obligation is to protect it and to leave considerations of ethics and morality to the theater itself (9:1474). In these thoughts reverberate Musil's distrust of the state to regulate in the realm of morality as well as a near-utopian desire to find in art that ideal locus in which society could promote the discovery of what morality should be. This is precisely what he thought he saw in the Moscow Art Theater, a company whose performances were no mere "ballet exercise" or "tyrannical discipline" but represented the "life of a spiritual community" (9:1480).

To sum up: in his criticism Musil did not want theater to be a showcase for actors, however much he admired certain actors, or a "exercise field" for directors, however much he admired a few directors (9:1476). He believed theater to have a social and moral function, embodying the pursuit of truth in the manner Ibsen had illustrated and the communal values he found exemplified in productions by Stanislavski. This desire for ethical truth, set in a societal framework, provides a context for understanding Musil's first play, *The Enthusiasts*. Published in 1921, it immediately received a major literary prize but was not performed until 1929, and then in a truncated version that was greeted with cries of protest and outrage. Musil was not at all happy and, as the diaries show, brooded for the rest of his life over the play's relative failure. The failure was not permanent, for *The Enthusiasts* is now performed in Germany and Austria on a regular basis. Musil scholars and critics have been divided as to its literary merits, though recent criticism has been in general quite favorable to it, with some critics ranking it as one of the major plays of the twentieth century.

Musil never gave up his belief that in the play he had created something exceptional, and late in his diaries he mused on what he had done in the work, comparing it with works by classical playwrights such as Pierre Corneille and Gotthold Ephraim Lessing. It is undoubtedly in the context of classical theater that one can best situate Musil's innovative experiment, for the play presupposes familiarity with the history of drama. And considerations of Musil's own historical context may explain why he had a hard time getting the play performed during the years of the Weimar Republic. *The Enthusiasts* is a sumptuous play that likely would have found reception in the heyday of theatrical experimentation in Berlin before the First World War. After the war, in a time of political crisis, economic turbulence, and fighting in the streets, the German public was far less interested in the kind of poetical and intellectual theater Musil had created. (It is noteworthy that Reinhardt stopped working regularly in Berlin shortly after the war and preferred to participate only occasionally in productions there while devoting himself to creating a drama festival in Salzburg and working in Vienna and elsewhere.) In his later diaries Musil recognized that, after the First World War, the social conditions of German life meant that the "old theater" was finished and that *The Enthusiasts,* like the works by Stanislavski that he had earlier admired, had become utopian in their opposition to the theater of the Weimar era (*TB* 1:782).

Musil's experiment in *The Enthusiasts* uses poetical and at times densely suggestive language to transform a classical comedy of adultery into an exploration of modern ethics and psychology. Specifically, it dramatizes interactions among a series of characters, none of whom can be described as having any kind of moral equilibrium. There is an experimental side to this portrayal of unbalance, which Wilhelm Braun pointed out some years ago in commenting on the characters and their universal failure to find a stability that might grant them happiness: "We can look upon Musil's *Die Schwärmer,* his visionaries, as an experiment on the way to a new balanced man. The experiment, though of necessity a failure, has at least the merit of pointing out the direction that man's activities must take if such a balance is ever to be achieved."[6] Reflecting an earlier generation's belief that the play is somehow a failure, Braun rightly saw that, for its experimental side, the play can be compared with Musil's preceding stories in *Unions*. The play is an experimental exploration of what would be the case if something is accepted as a hypothetical axiom. The axiom here is that the characters live without a moral center. The play then shows the consequences for characters and their interrelation if there is no center that allows them equilibrium—and by this one means simply the satisfactions found in leading a life in which what one does squares with what one desires. Or, alternatively, if Nietzsche were right that our sense of values has floundered on a lack of foundations, what are the consequences of living with the ensuing nihilism?

The play's plot recalls situations often found in classical comic theater, since it turns on a seducer's success in alienating a woman from her husband, to describe succinctly the relations that the hypocritical mythomaniac Anselm has with Regine, a married woman. Anselm seduces Regine, who is married to Joseph, a powerful functionary in the educational bureaucracy. It turns out, however, that Anselm has used Regine in order to approach and seduce Maria, Regine's sister and the wife of Anselm's friend Thomas. The latter is an academic scientist who, after years of work, is about to succeed in being promoted to a full professor. For two acts the play bears resemblance to a more complicated version of *Tartuffe*, Molière's classic portrayal of a hypocrite seducer. It resembles a *Tartuffe* in which Thomas might keep his wife only if the powerful bureaucrat Joseph can, like the royal agent of the king in Molière's play, reestablish order by invoking the law and the norms that punish those who violate it. In Musil's play this does not happen. And that is the point: there are no effective norms, and Joseph's intervention to punish Anselm in the name of the law accomplishes nothing. In conclusion the play's plot deviates from the classical plot's reestablishment of order when Musil's characters go off on their own paths. Thomas's wife, Maria, leaves with his now former friend, Anselm, and the powerful Joseph seemingly loses Regine when she goes to join Thomas. Yet at the end she may run away, perhaps to commit suicide.

The comparison with Molière involves more than plot. In the intellectual comedy that Molière created, the central characters act in ways that are deviant from rational norms, and that is the measure of their comic flaw. The flaw is defined by a clear deviation from the norms for rational conduct that the enlightened seventeenth-century public held. Every rational human being knew that hypochondriacs, misers, and misanthropes, not to mention seducing hypocrites, are deviant from what normative reason prescribes, and they are thereby comic in their blindness vis-à-vis the norm. (Tartuffe may not be blind, but then, he may not be comic—it is the husband who, blindly trusting Tartuffe, plays the comic role.) Musil pays homage to this theatrical tradition of intellectual comedy by creating characters who seem to deviate from some norm, but then he experiments with seeing what happens if there is no norm that is commonly accepted. All the characters consequently appear to be emotional cripples, which is to say floundering beings with no justification for their acts. In viewing the play a psychologist might speak of neurotics and borderline psychopaths—though such talk would presuppose a norm for what mental health is, and the metaphor of mental health itself is placed in question.

This lack of norms even for mental health is pointed up when Thomas, a professor and a scientist, plays the game of psychological clinician. Underscoring the game's uselessness, he analyzes Regine for her rationalist husband. With his belief in norms, Joseph cannot fathom why his wife did not have confidence in him when she was being seduced. Thomas points out to Joseph that the categories a rationalist would use to explain her conduct are useless because they are all correct, which is the same as if none are correct: "You would have shown her moral defect, and you would have been right. She could have then gone to a doctor and he would have told her: erotomania due to a neurasthenic-hysterical condition, apparent conditions of frigidity with a pathogenic lack of inhibition, and he would have been right!" (6:398).

Medical and moral terminology barely touches the individual woman who has been, it seems, a frigid nymphomaniac, a problematic condition from a rational perspective. The uselessness of such categories is pointed out by a scientist who is also a hapless "visionary." Moreover, he no longer knows how to relate to his own wife. *Visionary* is perhaps not quite the right term for Thomas: a dreamer or fanatic lost in his own world is perhaps a better way to describe the condition of this scientist who, in the name of mutual understanding, at one point practically pushes his wife into Anselm's arms (not unlike Molière's Orgon, the pious husband who pushes his wife onto falsely pious seducer Tartuffe).

Musil's disenchantment with science is probably greater in this play than in any other of his works. This is seen not only in the way he confronts the scientist Thomas with the rationalist defender of normalcy, the bureaucrat Joseph, but especially in the creation of a comic foil character who has totally embraced science as a cause. This character is Stader, the detective hired by Joseph to gather evidence against Anselm. Stader has had many occupations in his life—including being Regine's lover some years earlier—but now he has become a scientific detective, the investigator who knows that there is no chance in the universe since everything obeys at least the laws of probability. Statistics returns as destiny here. Stader appears to be the parodistic incarnation of the scientific mind in its purest embodiment. He is the positivist who knows that the only meaningful statements are those that are confirmed as "eternal laws."

In his first confrontation with Regine, Stader dismisses their past in the name of the greater interests that occupy him, namely, uniting all the sciences together with the detective's mission, or as he explains it: "Modern science and Detectivism are continually narrowing the realm of chance, of events without order, of the supposedly personal. There is nothing that is a matter of chance. There are no individual facts. Indeed! There are only . . . scientific relations" (6:339). Mach, the theorist of scientific relations, joins Quételet the statistician in the detective, whose interest in sciences includes not only probability theory and statistics, but also, not surprisingly in this satirical context, psychoanalysis and experimental psychology. Stader is thus the man to bring some "facts" obeying statistical norms into the relationships, scientific and otherwise, that these characters have among themselves.

Musil intensifies his comedy about science in the latter part of the play when Thomas and Stader meet. It turns out that Stader has followed Thomas's career, is very impressed by his scientific work, and even offers him a position with his detective firm. Ironically, in light of Musil's early writing on science, he has Stader read to Thomas words that Thomas had written years earlier to Joseph. Thomas had proclaimed that humanity was standing on the threshold of a new era that would be led or destroyed, but in any case directed, by science. Declaring that the "old tragedies" were dying off, Thomas wrote that one could not yet know if there would be new tragedies. This is especially true for an era in which, in animal experiments, an injection could cause a male animal to take on the soul of a female. With this vision of possible transformations, Thomas had gone on to write that whoever cannot solve an integral equation or master an experimental technique should not speak about spiritual or ethical questions (6:393). The cogency of this viewpoint is all the more questionable in that the distance between the Thomas who wrote this manifesto and the hapless character standing on the stage is great. Stader affirms that he, too, once was a visionary, but now, having found the confidence in real science Thomas once had, the detective has found equilibrium. He has discovered that it is only "science that can confer peace and order" (6:393). Stader's faith in the power of statistics is parodistic, and perhaps a form of self-satire undertaken by Musil, who had seen statistical probability as a form of fate. Stader's profession of faith shows that Musil—often critically, sometimes approvingly—never stopped thinking about the way scientific law impinges upon human self-knowledge. Stader's exaggerated faith in science is, to be sure, part of the experiment that asks what would be the case if there were no norms. Can one imagine that statistical laws would take their place? The imagined results of the experiment seem in this respect to be negative.

Stader is a foil to both Thomas and Joseph, characters who embody Kantian complements: Joseph is the practical rationalist who believes in law and hence has hired a detective for future legal action, whereas Thomas has been the theorist who believes in reason. Ever the anti-Kantian Musil sets *Verstand* against *Vernunft,* or the understanding versus pure reason, in their Kantian sense. It is this opposition of reason and pragmatic understanding, moreover, that sets out the basis for much of the psychological interactions in the course of the play. Pragmatic understanding is of little help in saving Joseph's marriage; and reason has apparently killed feeling in Thomas. In his relations to his wife, in fact, reason has led Thomas to tyrannize her with rationality, or so she says.

The confrontation of Thomas and Joseph shows that another strategy for the play's experimentation is to bring each of the characters into an agonistic encounter so that their individual disequilibrium stands out. Disequilibrium is the equivalent of deviation from the classical norm, for it also presupposes a point of equilibrium that existed once in the characters' lives. In an illusive way remembrance of equilibrium survives in the patriarchal framework in which the characters find themselves. Accordingly, the male characters feel entitled to define the framework of rationality and hence irrationality in which the women pursue their lives. Ibsen's social analysis undoubtedly oriented Musil in this portrayal of society; and it should be observed that if Musil chafed under the realist presuppositions, he nonetheless by and large observed the conventions of realist theater—even if the stage directions suggest that the play's decor should resemble a subjective landscape in which the characters should seem to pursue each other almost as in a dream. Actually, Musil's characters are quite realistic representatives of the dominant European bourgeois. In this patriarchal world some men pursued bureaucratic careers while other men pursued their wives. Equilibrium had heretofore been defined by norms now lacking in foundations, and there is nothing unrealistic about Musil's positing that the foundations of patriarchal order were crumbling.

Arguably, the scientist Thomas is the play's central figure illustrating the demise of this order. In some respects he is an early version of Ulrich, the man without qualities. Like Ulrich, Thomas is committed to the reign of reason, though he has not had the variety of experience that Ulrich apparently has had before the novel begins. He has single-mindedly pursued his career by obeying the conventional norms for success, though his material success is threatened if he does not help the bureaucrat Joseph get his wife back. He is disabused from the play's beginning, for reason enables him to understand every situation and idea, as well as its opposite, and in understanding, seemingly approve of everything—such as his own wife's leaving him. There is a measure of cynicism in this capacity for capacious understanding, as when, for example, Thomas proposes that his idealism is made up of dead ideals and that his successful careerism is shameful in its very success (6:313–14). Ready to define everything by its opposite in dialectal play, Thomas shows he can play all verbal games with great facility. But seemingly meaningless dialectical play is not his alone, since it informs the way the other characters view each other. For instance, at the play's beginning Regine reproaches Thomas with being too strong to understand weakness (6:316). This is a woman's viewpoint concerning the rationalist male, though Joseph's later evaluation of Thomas as a weak being is the opposite. From the juxtaposition of viewpoints emerges a portrait of Thomas as a vacillating strongman, an irrational rationalist, and, in any case, an unstable man who doesn't know what he wants. He is, in short, an academic Hamlet.

The characters also define themselves in large part by their attitudes toward love and eroticism and the norms that once governed sexual relations. Thomas has an ironically deprecatory toward attitude them. Marital love, he proclaims, is a state in which one goes about on four feet, which always makes for double breathing. His savage description of conjugal love reduces it to a bondage in which one finds oneself lying wrapped up in flesh (6:321). His disabused cynicism indicates that any religious or moral norm for marriage has disappeared. This modern motif is set off from the play's beginning by an opposing development when Thomas proposes to Regine that they must be brother and sister now. (Regine is his sister-in-law, though he also calls her cousin.) His erotic interest in his so-called sister has an uncanny resonance with the idea that sibling incest would be a superior form of love, an idea first broached in 1923 in Musil's poem "Isis und Osiris" and later suggested in *The Man without Qualities*. The union of sibling opposites suggests a mythic norm that finds parallels in the Platonic myth of love as union with the lost other, though it also suggests the destruction of all societal norms. Perhaps Thomas thinks this sibling union, involving the thrill of transgression, would be superior to one involving simply animal attraction. Such is the attraction he feels for Maria, who, as Regine describes her, is like a cat that arches her back whenever she is rubbed (6:321). Animals are never far away in Musil's early work.

The destruction of norms gives rise to the sense of homelessness that these characters know. This feeling lies behind their yearning for a realm of self-realization that does not seem to exist. As Thomas puts it, he knows homesickness without having a home. Superimposed on this essentially romantic theme of desire for the impossible, or nostalgia for the ineffable, is Musil's favored motif that the lucid human knows that whatever exists could be radically different from what it is. The lucid human knows that reality is lived as antithetical to possibility. In this regard from youth on Thomas has lived his life as a fall from what could have been, as a constant fall into what simply is (6:330). What is is notoriously less bountiful or fulfilling than what could be. Again like Ulrich, Thomas is the man who seeks existence beyond the conventionally real. Perhaps every authentic scientist is driven to a certain extent by a rejection of received ideas and theories about existence. But there is a negative side to this compulsion to frame new theories; and when accused of living with theories, Thomas recognizes the truth of the charge. But he is not without justification; and he defends himself with the retort that there is nothing in normal, boring human reality, with its vices and virtues, that can compare for a sense of the adventure suggested by an elliptic integral or an airplane. In short there is nothing in everyday reality as exciting as the precision of science, the adventure of invention, and the joy of new discovery in the realm of the possible (6:330). Musil draws upon recent history for his metonymies illustrating the scientist's adventures in the realm of the possible: elliptic functions had been the object of much advanced work in nineteenth-century mathematics, and the airplane was a recent emblem for the scope of invention at the beginning of the twentieth century. Musil is defending the joys of the sciences at the same time he is satirizing their abuse.

The romantic roots of the spirit of scientific inquiry come to the fore when Thomas, in his defense of "theoretical man," shows himself to be a kindred spirit of the earlier romantic who could not stand the destructive boredom of daily normal existence. Through the character Thomas, Musil overturns the received idea that science kills the moral spirit. It is the conventional mind that endangers the spirit of possibility expressed in the relentless questioning undertaken by science. Science's unending invention of theory originates in its praise of the possible. But this praise does not constitute an unconditional approval of the overturning of reality. The play's development points up the contrary as it works out the consequences of, say, Thomas's being a singularly rational human being.

In spite of Thomas's assessment of himself, the other characters are more or less in agreement that he is without feeling. Anselm thinks that he is a monster capable of living without others, accusing him of living only by that power of reason that dominates the world today. Though a hypocrite, Anselm praises powers Thomas does not value, those powers found, as Anselm says, emanating from human faces or those between swallows in autumn, or the indemonstrable powers, as well as the truths, that arise and flare up like a spark between two beings (6:333). The power of these singular truths does not impress the scientist Thomas, or so Anselm argues persuasively in his role as the poet of the unique. And in their confrontation Musil conjoins the two sides of truth as he understands it, letting the mad rationalist and the conniving seducer each have his share of it, for the little good that it will do either.

This portrait of Thomas as a man who refuses the truth of the singular is modified when he appears in the second act. The man of reason comes on stage in a scene in which Anselm is with Maria in the dark. Finding them together, Thomas claims to have a pistol in hand and threatens to blow out Anselm's brains (6:359). His errant behavior shows minimally that Thomas has another side, and all the more so when it turns out that he has no pistol in hand when the lights come on. His feigned or perhaps real readiness to commit murder may be taken as a nod toward the truth of tragedy, the truth of an individual crushed by his flaw or deviance. But it is only a nod. In the spirit of a bedroom farce by Georges Feydeau, Anselm runs scrambling out of the room. It must be said that at times there is as much bedroom farce as intellectual comedy at work in *The Enthusiasts*. Farce offers, in fact, another model or set of norms for understanding this play in which husbands, wives, and a would-be seducer run in and out of the dark, not to mention flit through the window, with a gusto that belies any reductive interpretation.

When confronting his nemesis, Joseph, however, Thomas changes his viewpoint and refuses to believe that Anselm can intend evil. To this extent he plays the role of a rational Platonist, but it is only a role. It is apparent that Thomas is really irrationally intransigent, because he does not want to give in to Joseph, the man of pragmatic power, who is quite ready to have Anselm arrested. Rather pigheadedly Thomas refuses to recognize the power of this academic bureaucrat who embodies the negation of Thomas's life devoted to possibilities. The theoretical man Thomas, but not for theoretical reasons, does not want to give in to Joseph, the man of adamant practical reason. Thus Thomas is even ready to help his own wife run away with Anselm, whom Joseph is ready to destroy. In short Musil uses these encounters—such as between Thomas and Anselm or Thomas and Joseph—to point up the inconsistent character of these players without norms, without a fixed center, without any consistent set of values.

Thomas is aware that he is unable to assent to anything because he sees the truth of every viewpoint, and hence any viewpoint. He explains his view of truth to Maria by saying that finding one truth always involves a trick, such as when you solve an equation having several undetermined variables: you suppose that one of them is constant so that you can manipulate the others. According to Thomas this strategy is analogous to positing an arbitrary first principle, such as a supreme truth, or values, or a constant ground for truth, or an ideology, so that one can be religious or modern, pacifist or militarist, adopting whatever "the intellectual marketplace" is offering on that day for spiritual needs (6:385). Thomas's description of the arbitrary nature of the multiple truths one finds in the marketplace is the most Nietzschean moment in *The Enthusiasts*. And Thomas, not to mention Musil, would probably be receptive to the viewpoint that this is at once a portrayal of intellectual bankruptcy and of intellectual freedom. With this viewpoint one can conclude that Thomas is characterized by a thorough Nietzschean cynicism. These are among the many consequences resulting from the hypothesis that the foundations of truth no longer exist.

The play culminates in the moment when the man of theory Thomas, giving up on his career, goes on the attack to show that practical Joseph's supposedly rational attitudes are full of contradictions. He points out, for instance, that Joseph is willing to allow widows to get married again while declaring that love is eternal; or that he subscribes to the biblical command to love one's neighbor while he also endorses the ideology of life as a struggle; and that he proclaims that one must be ready to die for the highest values while presupposing in actuality that nobody will live even an hour in accord with these putative values (6:399). Faithful to his position as a representative of practical reason, Joseph is not convinced by Thomas's display of rhetorical fireworks. Joseph demands to know if Thomas finds him either too demanding or the opposite. Logic demands that every situation be characterized by A or $-A$. Since Thomas can no longer accept the logic of either/or, Joseph concludes, using his fundamentally normative sense of logic, that Thomas is sick in the head.

The ambivalent status of Thomas's mental well-being is suggested by the norms that Joseph still respects, at least verbally. And to return to an earlier point, the uncertainty about sanity suggests parallels with the Shakespearean ambiguity characterizing Hamlet. The parallel with Hamlet is directly suggested in the play when the self-proclaimed sane Joseph says that among the sick present in the play, Thomas is an *Angekränkelter*—another sickly person (6:400). The German word has precise intertextual resonances, since in the best-known German translation of *Hamlet,* that by August Wilhelm Schlegel, the Danish prince sees in his most famous monologue that he is irresolute precisely because his thought is *angekränkelt:* "Der angebornen Farbe der Entschliessung / Wird des Gedankens Blässe angekränkelt" ("And thus the native hue of resolution / Is sicklied o'er with the pale cast of thought") (3.3.85–86).

There is some strong intertextual irony in the way Thomas is a modern Hamlet figure, since he is at times a comic one. The intertextual dimension also suggests, with regard to the play's other hesitating characters, that "conscience does make cowards of" them all.

The three principal male characters can in the course of the play resolve little, except to affirm and deny their vacillating principles. They are indeed cowards. For example, the embodiment of the practical reality principle, the bureaucrat Joseph, brings the charge of insanity against Thomas. Joseph then throws up his hands and flees when he cannot encompass or fears to understand, what Thomas's vacillations really entail. He flees rather than deal with Thomas's position, one that leads to the complete dereliction of all duty and action. For Thomas is reduced to the sullen contemplation of pure possibilities. His cowardly vacillation leads to a renunciation of the belief in any form of progress or meaningful commitment to action. Without some form of positive belief, Thomas's "pale cast of thought" means that he no longer finds value even in the scientific activity to which he has dedicated his life and which he is still, sometimes, willing to defend. In short Joseph does not want to understand that Thomas's critique of science and engineering is a critique of the Enlightenment values Joseph is trying to hang onto. But Thomas believes that modernity has not held its promise, and he drives the practical Joseph from the scene by throwing in his face the derisive fact that centuries of progress—culminating in inventors and scientists flying in the air, drilling through mountains, and traveling underwater—is only a derisive parable for a new humanity that has never shown up in history (6:400).

In the play's concluding scenes Thomas is with Regine, and the intertexual resonance with *Hamlet* is again strong. Vacillating to the end, Thomas desires a sisterly relation that apparently includes kissing, though the kiss the couple shares seals nothing. Thomas is playing with possibilities, and Regine, like Ophelia with her half-mad lover, cannot count upon his help, for with Hamlet-like derision he designates their kiss to be part of an "anti-love scene" (6:404). Though—or only—half-sane, Regine shares in Thomas's contempt for conventional life. Nonetheless, she implores him to help her find a reason to survive. But Thomas is the rationalist unto the end and is incapable of recognizing that Regine might do something destructive. Dismissing her threats as hyperbole, he indulges in ironic pirouettes with his pointless lucidity. He tortures her with a reductive vision of the materiality of everything, including her future dead self: "Suppose a person could afterwards stand by her own corpse, then she'd be ashamed of her rashness. Since with no respect at all the gnats and mosquitoes would on this beautiful summer day still sting you, one would be as much moved by a shudder at the prospect of infinity as by scratching" (6:407). Calling him a heartless man of reason—she is at least partially right—she rushes out, leaving Thomas to wonder if she might not kill herself after all.

The question of the nature of norms runs throughout the play. For example, set in agonistic opposite to Thomas, Joseph serves as a foil to point up Thomas's deviation from a norm, even if that norm is no longer accepted or perhaps exists only in imagined memory. Joseph is the play's one character who believes that a norm permitting evaluation exists, and with some apparent circularity, this norm is the normal. The concept of the normal is also one that Musil interrogates throughout his work, for it is not at all clear that the normal is in any way an acceptable norm. Musil's interrogation coincides in this regard with the modernist project of questioning the grounds for any norm and a fortiori the concept of the normal that might be buttressed by it.

Freud is a key figure in this questioning, since the Viennese doctor's work placed in question the possibility of defining normal sexuality when all "normal" psychological development entails neurosis and perverse desires. The normal is the abnormal, and it is not clear how one can find a grip on a desirable norm in these considerations. Historically this questioning of psychological norms appears to be an outgrowth of nineteenth-century medical research, for example, the work of physiologist Claude Bernard (1813–1878). Bernard showed how problematic, in describing pathology, is the very idea of the normal, since every pathological process, supposedly deviating from the norm of health, unfolds according to the normal laws of physics and chemistry.[7] Any deviation or pathology involves normal processes when viewed from a scientific perspective. That Musil himself adapted this viewpoint is clear in one of his aphorisms, which concisely states that the pathological is not the abnormal. As a social observer, and not only as a psychologist, he saw that analysis of such events as the success of the Nazis suggested the pathological might be the normal (7:833). Like Freud, though owing relatively little to him, Musil explored the conventionally perverse and pathological with a sense that deviation from one perspective is a normal process from another. The sense of the relativity of norms underwrites the irony of *Unions* and underlies the play's confrontation between Thomas and Joseph.

Joseph embodies the normal state of having a norm, so to speak, and is quite willing to judge by it. After all, a social or ethical norm is also a performative notion, which demands that one act according to it. But Regine confounds Joseph's normative viewpoint about the normal with her combination of lascivious and frigid conduct, as well as with insane games she plays in honoring an earlier husband, now deceased, whom she may have driven to suicide. Discomfited, Joseph applies his notions of normality and concludes that she is the most senseless of humans (6:363). In fact, he is willing to characterize as sick not only Regine and the Hamlet-like Thomas, but also the other characters about whom Joseph decides that they are not involved in love stories, but in "sick confusion"—or "krankhafte Verwirrung"—recalling the same term Musil used to describe Törless's state. A man of action, Joseph declares he would like to set up, against the other characters, a "league of the mentally healthy" (6:377). Joseph embodies not only the psychiatric spirit that believes there are easily discernible syndromes characterizing mental illness, but also the mind based on practical understanding, which holds that there are visible rules pointing to the line over which one must not step if one is to remain in the realm of acceptable conduct. He alone holds this belief, though it is unlikely that he can continue to do so.

The seducer Anselm stands in antagonistic contrast with Joseph. He is not only a loser, or at least he has never been a success by conventional norms; but he is also a blatant psychopath by Joseph's standards. He is also a liar by all standards, though an appealing figure to both women. He has seduced Regine and convinces Maria to leave with him. Unlike Thomas, he engages in no ironic display of intellectual superiority, and unlike Joseph, he does not stand upon his self-assured sense of right and rationality. He displays his fears, masochistically burns himself with a cigarette, hides, runs away, comes back, sounds like a parody of a lover, flatters, and engages in disruptive conduct that neither Thomas nor Joseph approve of. Perhaps the women, in the subordinate position they are obliged to maintain in this patriarchal order, identify with Anselm, since he is a male reproved, like them, by male norms. For example, Regine tells Thomas at the play's outset that he is too strong to understand the weak. This is an ambiguous judgment that by implication characterizes Anselm and the women; and perhaps it applies even to Thomas's lack of understanding of his own weakness (6:316). By contrast Anselm is weak enough to understand the weak. He is also, as mentioned above, the poet of the unique truth and an anti-intellectual proponent of the necessity of lies. One is not surprised to learn that he has read Nietzsche. In a parodistic twist on the thought of the philosopher with a hammer, Anselm believes that "all thoughts are false" and for that very reason must be believed (6:330). The necessity of falsehood is the basis for Anselm's existence now, and the lies he tells enchant, perhaps even because, as Nietzsche might have observed, they are in the service of life, at least of a life more varied than that of a conventional bureaucrat or a neurotic scientist. Neither of the latter, for example, would fake a suicide such as Anselm does, nor do they believe that eroticism is more than animal lust or conjugal duty.

Maria leaves with Anselm. The play's development can be said to be in large part motivated by her decision to leave Thomas. Against the backdrop of the other themes developed in the play, her decision to leave with Anselm may hardly seem momentous, but it is central. Consider how the play unfolds after Maria realizes that she has forced into a position of psychological inferiority by her husband. First feeling abandoned by Thomas, she then realizes that she wants Anselm because of Thomas, and finally leaves after Thomas does nothing more than make ironic gestures in the face of her demand for love. This process of the deflation of love begins in the first act when Maria feels that love is at an end, for she can make no other sense of Thomas's paradoxical jubilating over the beginning of his love precisely because it is at an end. He proclaims that he has in *brotherly* fashion watched her awaken to this ending (6:322). In a perverse fashion this jubilation may be Thomas's expression of his need, but Maria can hardly understand him. It is in her need that Maria seems to embody a certain norm, and nothing in the play really undoes this norm based on need, despite Thomas's antiromantic sarcasm. In the second act she gives eloquent voice to her needs, saying that Anselm has valued her more than Thomas has, that Thomas has used her for childish recreation when he was tired of thinking, and, finally, that she is, among other things, a human being needing music, not a reminder that music consists in dried catgut being scratched (6:369). Musil seems to endorse a minimal norm of need in creating this remarkable scene in which Maria expresses her needs and cries out for those needs to be met by the man whom she once loved, but who is now wrapped entirely up in his theoretical rejection of need. Thus in the third act, in recognizing that she is afraid of Thomas, she states that she is ready to leave, but she feels more as though she is being sent away; and she is partly right. She recognizes that Anselm is a loser and that, moreover, she will never forgive him for taking her away from her husband, but that solution is nonetheless better than anything she can find with Thomas (6:384–85). Her lucidity is full of pathos, tragicomic, and bordering on unbearable paradox.

Maria accepts the paradoxical nature of her desire and need, but through her acceptance she seems to embrace in a straightforward way the need of something other than paradox, even if paradox is the best she can find. By contrast

Regine is a vibrant neurotic, full of contradictions that neither the ironic theorist Thomas nor her husband, the pedestrian Joseph, can begin to master. She might be likened to Claudine in "The Perfecting of Love," who at first seeks the perfecting of love in abjection. The comparison with Claudine is all the more compelling when at the play's end Regine tells Thomas that she wishes to throw herself down upon the carpet and lie amid the flowers there (6:402), just as Claudine submissively threw herself upon the carpet of her hotel room while waiting for the perfecting of love. Regine finds no receptive response in turgid Thomas. The scientist is unable to find a meaning in her desires or in her openness to him. Thus she rushes from the scene, with Thomas wondering haplessly what she may do.

Regine is an extraordinarily interesting character. In her Musil straightforwardly created a character who is a victim of her era's conventions. She is also the truly disenchanted character in the play, to use a term frequently used by students of modernity. *Disenchanted* was used by the German sociologist Max Weber (1864–1920) to describe what he found to be the quintessential condition of modern life: a general disaffection with institutions and values, which constitutes the essence of the modern condition. Regine is an example of disenchantment lived out to its extreme consequences. At once victim of collapsing patriarchy and of her personal failure to find something to endow life with meaning, enchantment, or value, she is another borderline case. She is a rather sublime one, and it is not for nothing that she is "Regina," or queen in Latin, and is also called Potiphar by Joseph, recalling the Egyptian queen who wanted to seduce the Old Testament Joseph (6:317).

Regine is a disinherited queen from the play's outset, suffering from mental disequilibrium. Notably, she has been claiming to see her dead husband. Regine may be playing psychological games, for in claiming to have special powers she consciously makes a protest against the strict either/or logic her husband uses. She wants to find the "third possibility" that would escape the excluded middle of conventional logic (6:311). She plays at being mad with a disabused lucidity that makes her a figurative sister to the Danish prince who may have played the same game, admittedly well before disenchantment become the modern condition. She knows she creates scenes in order to overcome the powerlessness of her speech. This is one sense of what she means in telling Thomas, when he asks about the dead husband, that unlike normal people who help themselves by speaking, she will not speak; since in her situation something is true only so long as she remains silent (6:314). However, in spite of her lack of belief in her speech, Regine does talk. She says with great articulation that while the other characters all feel authentically with false feelings, she by contrast is able to have true feelings for a dead man whom she does not take seriously. Regine's speech embodies a paradoxical vision of disenchantment. She points out that it is mainly false feelings that moderns take seriously, though the chiasmatic opposition suggested by having real feelings that one doesn't take seriously means that all emotional resources cancel each other. Such is the emotional vacuity of disenchantment portrayed by the play through Regine.

Regine is also another of Musil's characters who, like Törless and Claudine, disassociate their outer actions and their inner feelings. For instance, at the end of the first act she confronts the detective who has gathered proof of her adultery; she is indifferent and tells him to turn over to her husband all the evidence he has gathered. His institute for scientific detection will never understand, she says, that in one's inner life one can be as holy as the sun god's horses and at the same time be on the outside the guilty person described by the detective's damning evidence (6:343). Her comic comparison of herself with the sun god—or with his horses—suggests Regine's wacky sense of her regal position and also her capacity to be above all that happens around her, even if she spends a good part of the second act offstage enacting an hysterical crisis.

She returns to the stage toward the end of the second act, accompanied by Joseph, who has been trying to convince her that a stay in a "sanatorium" would not be the same as confinement in an insane asylum (6:372). She is lucid again, for she knows exactly what has been happening. When Anselm fakes a suicide, she bites his hand to make him stop playing that role and then, without apparent irony, declares that she has become a reasonable person (6:379). I say without apparent irony, though in the context of the play's ongoing development it is quite possible to argue that nobody is reasonable, nor ever totally untouched by irony. At this moment in the second act Regine seems to be in possession of herself and ready to face a future without Anselm or Joseph. She does not seem to be playing a role, although it is also true that Musil's psychological theories indicate that all at any moment are playing roles, whether they are aware of it or not. Regine and Thomas are largely aware of it.

The third act opens and closes with Regine's confrontation with Thomas. He plays various games with her, at once acting jealous, being affectionate, and ironically destroying any belief in the possibility of mutual feelings. With cruel lucidity Regine sees the utterly animal nature of the human body, and in her disenchantment with the beast attached to her, in the form of her own body, she finds suicide an attractive remedy. She is even disgusted by the morning sunshine and asks Thomas to accompany her in finding purity in abjection. This will be done by walking barefoot in the mud, which will confound the investigators who come to find them later, lying there, enigmatically barefoot suicides (6:382). Claudine's search for perfection in abjection is undoubtedly analogous to Regine's desire for transcendence in the mud. But Thomas does not take this possibility seriously. After Maria's departure with Anselm, he is nonetheless willing to listen to Regine recall memories of their common childhood, even though he knows that she wants to go beyond all limits. She has always had this desire, she says, for she started life with ideals and desires, though different from his. She wanted to transform existence. She tells him several examples: as a schoolchild she wanted to adopt a small boy secretly and raise him as a prince; she wanted to marry their old governess to rescue her from loneliness; she invented a magic formula for happiness and sang it for hours while she pinched and struck the gardener's daughter, who only cried instead of becoming more beautiful. Somewhat like a child version of the sadistic mystic Beineberg, she wanted to overcome the laws of reality, and when she discovered she could not, she decided one could not love humanity (6:386). In her powerfully concise soliloquy, Regine expresses her personal manifesto of unhappiness—or disenchantment—though she has in front of her the wrong listener.

Regine returns at the end of the third act to conclude the play with a bravura dialogue with Thomas, both acting roles, masking and unmasking themselves, until it is unlikely that either is sure which roles they are playing. What is clear is that Musil is ending his experiment with a duet performance spinning out the negative results. Regine comically complains that Anselm had proposed to her a flight into unreality, but now he has left with Maria on a cowardly flight into reality (6:401). Regine is Thomas's equal in making ironic reversals, and he tries to be her match in elaborating fantasies, for he begins to emote about a memory provided to him by a recent dream. Regine and he were hiding in a wardrobe, and this privileged enclosure appears to propose an image for some kind of union they might now find. She counters with another parable of disenchantment, remembering how she once put a beetle in her mouth, but no amount of counting her pulse turned the little beast into a prince; this, she says, has been the image of her life ever since that moment (6:403). Not beetles, but worms, are their four lips, says Thomas, in giving her a kiss designed to seal their mutual alienation with a vibrant affirmation of the body's grotesquery.

One might see another version of Musil's ironic "unions" in this final scene between Regine and Thomas. In their disabused role-playing, playing at union, however, it is dubious that Regine takes Thomas's brotherly overtures seriously, for the scene culminates in a powerful exposition of the impossibility of playing roles of lucid disenchantment with any consistency. Not even theatrical conduct can counter disequilibrium. "Pale thought" endows their playing at unions with paralyzing self-consciousness, or, if one prefers to use later existentialist notions, one can say that Regine and Thomas are actors or players who in different ways know that no matter what they do, they will be conscious of playing a role that could have been utterly different. This, for example, is the purport of Thomas's comment after Regine says that she does not understand how the others manage to fill up the empty hours of their life. He replies that "naturally they are swindlers, they have a profession, a goal, a character, acquaintances, manners, axioms, clothes," which all serve to set up a barrier to keep them from "falling a million meters into the depths of space" (6:405). With this rejection of all conventional roles, the play concludes with Thomas's assertion that he and Regine are dreamers who go through life looking at the people who feel at home in existence, knowing that they are unaware of what the dreamers know: that at each moment they sink without going under (6:407). This image of floundering without drowning is a powerful depiction of the existential players who know that there is no ground or foundation for whatever role they take on or whatever feelings they may ironically entertain. As Regine and Thomas express it, when they find that all they really possess is an animal body that does not fully characterize their being, their discovery of their utterly contingent state leaves them open to feelings of visceral disgust. Such is the sense of Regine's cry for help at the end of the play when she begs Thomas to do something, since otherwise her willpower will be reduced to a "pulp of disgust" (6:407).

Regine's encounter with disgust occurred almost a generation before Sartre made nausea a key emotion in the discovery that when stripped of its universal categories, the palpable body ties a person to an amorphous overflowing of being. Musil's Regine and Thomas discover in their wormlike bodies the existential anguish of contingency that accompanies the necessity of role-playing in a disenchanted world. It is a world in which the only alternative to role-playing is the bad faith involved in believing that one has an existence that is justified and grounded in some sense or the other. From Thomas's viewpoint Joseph is a prime example of the convinced swindler who does not know that he swindles, though one could say as much about Stader, the ambitious detective who has found a faith in the scientific method. Anselm, on the other hand, is the self-conscious actor who apparently outdoes either Regine or Thomas in his willful creation of roles to play: scientist, monk, husband, seducer, suicide. Anselm is an actor who creates roles on the spur of the moment.

With these thoughts in mind, I suggest that *Die Schwärmer* might be better translated as *The Dreamers* or even *The Actors* rather than *The Enthusiasts* or *The Visionaries*. For one thing readers familiar with the history of English literature are immediately inclined to think of those "enthusiasts" or Protestant dissidents, possessed of the spirit, that Jonathan Swift famously lampooned in his "Tale of the Tub." Nor is enthusiasm in any modern sense at issue in the play, at least not when we see the characters on stage, except for Stader. Maria, Regine, Thomas, and even Joseph have all lost their youthful visions—enthusiasms, if you will—and now live in an adult realm characterized mainly by disappointment. They are no longer visionaries, if they ever really were. Their world is characterized by modernity's disenchantment with everything for which a believer might once have had enthusiasm. And to those who are skeptical about the idea of disenchantment—for one can argue that an era without disenchantment never existed—it can be said that, whatever the modern condition, the play's drama calls upon both classical theatrical conventions and existentialist premises imposed by an era in which values have no foundation. Undoubtedly, every era has had its unjustified believers and its actors, its conventional patriarchs believing in their justified existence, as well as those who find that nothing really justifies anything. And part of the power the play is that it treads a path between the classical and the modern. In short the tension between convention and anguished doubt endows *The Enthusiasts* with traits that recall the conventions of classical comedy as well as the Shakespearean antecedent of crippling doubt found in *Hamlet*. Future directors of the play should feel empowered to use all the theatrical resources at their command, for this is not just a play to be read in an armchair. It is play for actors who can perform while maintaining contact with a social world of referential reality. That is, as Musil knew well, no small challenge.

Musil's theatrical experimentation did not come to a close with *The Enthusiasts,* for he published one more play, *Vinzenz und die Freundin bedeutender Männer: Posse in drei Akten*. The play was performed in 1923, then published in 1924, but it has not been translated. It has been performed a number of times since. Most of Musil's critics have paid little attention to it, though some have made claims for it as another major theatrical work that can be understood only if one overcomes the prejudice that theater should be naturalist in mode.[8] There is undoubtedly some truth in this contention. The fact that Musil wrote the play quickly is not a reason not to take it seriously, nor is the fact that it is a farce. It is a farce in which Musil experiments with a number of antitheatrical devices in order to create a work that is self-consciously a play, a play denouncing itself as theater. I refer especially to the characters' staging scenes as theater within theater or a play within the play. This inner mirroring of a play within the play creates a self-referential dimension by which the play asserts that what is represented as reality is really theater. This is not something new, of course, since there is a venerable tradition in Western literature proclaiming that the world is a stage. From Shakespeare and Pedro Calderón de la Barca to Luigi Pirandello and Samuel Beckett, many notable playwrights have been drawn to this self-fulfilling metaphor.

Musil's farce also illuminates a certain face of the Weimar Republic, for it reflects comically many of the themes characteristic of works of that era of anger and despair: the fluctuating nature of sexuality, the power of money to buy everything, the generally uncertain nature of identity. If Grosz and Dix, to name two satirical artists whose works embody these themes, do not immediately come to mind on reading or seeing the play, then it may be because the play is also something of a parody of the boulevard comedy and the Viennese kitsch by which Musil was appalled in theater after the war. The Viennese and the Berlin perspectives focus on different readings of the play, and both are valid: *Vinzenz* is at once a farce playing with the themes of disintegration that characterize the art of the Weimar Republic and a tramp through the clichés of conventional commercial theatrical production.

In the play's first act, a prewar vamp, the liberated woman Alpha, comes home with a lover, the millionaire businessman Bärli, who threatens to shoot her and commit suicide if she does not marry him. He ties her up and waves a pistol around, only to be interrupted in his violent courtship when the would-be hero, Vinzenz, shows up, apparently keeping a date he made with Alpha fifteen years earlier. It turns out that Alpha has already been married for years; her insecure husband makes an entrance, followed by a retinue of her admirers, each equipped with a key to her apartment, who come to shower gifts upon her for her name day. Her husband receives the gifts, all of them items of women's attire, which allow him to dress as a woman and put on a drag show.

The second act opens with Alpha explaining to her woman friend, a lesbian-inclined nymphomaniac, that Vinzenz is a mathematician who studies the laws of statistics that allow insurance companies to make money by calculating the odds of dying. Pursuing Musil's favored theme of probability, Vinzenz enters saying he has found the statistical law that will allow him to break the bank at every casino, so that they will now be fabulously rich and can do whatever they want. It turns out that this is only one of several hoaxes. Bärli again appears, pistol in hand, and takes shots at Alpha and then himself.

This violence is all a comedy that Vinzenz has staged—for money he received from Bärli—and the act ends in discord between Vinzenz and Alpha. The goal of these fireworks could be described as a parody of the catharsis that Aristotle described as the goal of tragedy: Bärli seems properly purged.

The third act is the liveliest in that the preceding spoofing sets the stage for Vinzenz to engage in an epistemological argument against reality. Apparently he has recently digested relativity theory, since he claims that the frame of reference for truth is a matter of choice. Alpha finds that her swindler, as she now calls him, is irresistible and wants to marry him. The admirers enter, enacting a parody of a Greek chorus, and tell Alpha that she must get married—although she already is—and that Bärli with his money would be the right and rational choice of a spouse. The female friend returns; it appears she has slept with Vinzenz; and a fight ensues between her and Alpha. But this, too, has probably been staged, or perhaps the claim that it was staged is itself staged. In any case Alpha's husband returns, which gives occasion for a debate as to whether Vinzenz is a swindler. He solves the matter, with a paradox typical of Musil, claiming that he is a swindler only because he is not one (6:450). This seems to imply that all the others in the chorus of notables—businessman, politician, professor, musician, and the like—are swindlers in confirmation of Vinzenz's proposition that everyone inevitably swindles. Alpha ends the farce by deciding to marry an ugly, sickly dwarf, a certain Baron Ur auf Usedom. Musil's humor is a bit abstruse: the German island of Usedom has prehistoric ruins, and this may be his comment on the nature of the decrepit Austrian aristocracy (perhaps made more ironic by the fact that Soviet writer Maksim Gorky took a vacation on the island in 1922). The sickly dwarf would be at home in any case in a Weimar parade of freaks.

With actors who are willing to push the play to its campy limits, *Vinzenz* is a farce that could yield an evening of tawdry delights for its parody of theatrical conventions as well as social norms. The culture of the Weimar Republic anticipated in many ways that of the New York of Andy Warhol, and Americans should be at home with Musil's protocamp farce playing on bourgeois convention and sexual identity. For an era of sexual liberation, the chorus of enlightened bourgeois notables who do not want Alpha to be free offers an image of the ironically grotesque. The same campy grotesque also characterizes the free-floating sexual identities. Alpha's husband and Vinzenz are both tempted to play feminine roles, and Alpha is feminine in her masculinity, or perhaps vice versa. In more general terms Musil's farce is a work experimenting with some of the boundaries delimiting what theater can be. I would not claim that Musil is terribly innovative in this regard—surrealist experiments in France after Alfred Jarry's *Ubu roi* (*King Ubu*) and Guillaume Apollinaire's *Les mamelles de Tirésias* (*Tiresias with Tits*), not to mention Dada happenings in Paris and Berlin, went much further in this respect—but *Vinzenz* is not negligible. Musil, like his character Alpha, admired the anarchistic freedom that lies at the heart of farce, which turns on the controlled destruction of conventions and norms while affirming the freedom to entertain all possibilities, even and especially the most absurd. This appeal to unlimited possibility is probably why farce appealed to Musil, for it confirmed his belief that freedom is inevitably truncated when possibilities are limited. As Musil's contemporary theater theorist the madman and genius Antonin Artaud knew, farce can embody metaphysical propositions. However, after *Vinzenz* Musil did not return to pure farce in theatrical form, and perhaps it is a pity. That he published nothing more in this domain seems to be in accord, however, with what now appears to be his desire never to repeat an experiment.

CHAPTER 5

Three Women

In 1923 Musil published a short volume, *Drei Frauen* (*Three Women,* included in the collection *Five Women*), containing the stories "Grigia," "Die Portugiesin," and "Tonka." Comparable to the two stories in *Unions,* each of the stories in *Three Women* is centered on a woman protagonist, though more importance is given in them to her dealings with a male character. Less experimental than the earlier two narratives, the stories in *Three Women* cover a greater range of experience.[1] Perhaps this is because the tales in *Three Women* reflect Musil's experience of the Great War. They do not depict the war directly; rather their themes and situations reflect aspects of the experience undergone by Musil and millions of others during the years of senseless combat. Musil's diaries show that they were largely conceived during the war, though one hardly needs to consult the diaries to see a relation between these stories and Musil's experience of the war. It is fairly obvious that the atmosphere of a military camp is re-created in the miner's camp in "Grigia." Moreover, the male character's separation from his wife recalls the separation and sexual temptations that many a soldier knew during the war, including Musil himself. A tale of nearly unending warfare is at the center of "The Lady from Portugal," though it is set in the Middle Ages and narrates the story of a medieval aristocrat who spends years in battle with the bishop of Trent. Finally, the plot in the third story, "Tonka," represents directly no military experience per se, but it turns on a situation analogous to one all too familiar to many soldiers during and immediately after the war: that of the soldier whose pregnant wife is bearing a child that could not have been fathered by the husband who was at the front. The war is hardly the only context for situating these stories, but it is a useful starting point, for it situates them in the concrete historicity of Musil's experience of separation and doubt.

Musil's contemporary situation is useful as an exterior framework in which to read the story. But historical understanding also demands that one grasp contexts immanent to a story. For example, "Grigia" contains multiple allusions to the earlier literary period of romanticism and to romanticism's desire to invent an antirational history. "The Lady from Portugal" is set in the

Middle Ages, and so the reader is invited to cross the historical gap to see that Musil is juxtaposing his own rationalist sensibility with the medieval sense of the marvelous and the miraculous. Finally, "Tonka" juxtaposes the contemporary context, in which knowledge is validated by scientific procedures, with an implicit appeal to some earlier time of faith, in which belief could supposedly overcome reason and find miraculous explanations.

The historicity in these stories may be summarized by one general notion. They are motivated, in a broad sense, by Musil's encounter with romanticism and certain favored motifs characterizing romantic sensibility. These motifs include historicism itself, often involved in the romantic attempt to recover the past truth of myths and folktales. The rationalist Musil was also drawn to the romantic revolt against the strict limits imposed on knowledge by rationalist philosophy and science. Musil probably first encountered in Emerson, and then in the romantic writer Novalis, the desire to use the irrational to break through the limits imposed on knowledge by the rational empiricism that Kantian thought had bequeathed to European science. The stories are not, however, uniform explorations of romantic themes, for each offers a different version of Musil's encounter with romanticism. Nonetheless, there is also a constant meditation on romanticism at work in these three tales, with their homage to nineteenth-century writers such as Novalis, E. T. A. Hoffmann, Ludwig Tieck, and others whom Musil took quite seriously in his manner, which is to say, he treated them with deep irony and respectful parody. Musil's rhetoric in these stories owes much to the concept of irony that these romantics developed: his irony, like theirs, is often based on a vision of a decentered world that seemingly allows any statement and its opposite. Like Thomas in *The Enthusiasts,* the romantic ironist cannot find a center from which to make truth claims resisting ironic reversal. In claiming that these stories are ironic, often in parody and with great humor, I am thus proposing that they are tributary to these German romantics who knew that the world's absurdity was a starting axiom for an endless quest for something that by definition escaped all definition.

The first story in *Three Women* is "Grigia," a title whose meaning is steeped in romantic ambiguity and self-canceling ironies. The word means at once "gray" in Italian, but is used by a German peasant woman to name her cow. The woman in turn is called Grigia by her geologist lover, so that she is in turn associated with an animal, with Italy, and, more generally, with the blurring of distinctions between black and white. The geologist lover is named Homo, evoking the phrase *Ecce homo* ("Behold the man") used to designate Christ on the verge of his crucifixion and, by extension, recalls Nietzsche's parody with the book *Ecce homo*—by which he meant himself among others.

Lumped together, Nietzsche and Jesus suggest the ironic dichotomies Musil is laying out here. Homo is also a scientist, in fact, a geologist like the poet Novalis. His name is a reminder of the species, *Homo sapiens,* of which Homo is an exemplar, the *sapiens* indicating that he is a hominid that knows something. The reference could be, however, an ironic sign of the hubris of scientists who believe they can master any situation, as Homo does.

Homo the geologist explores at least one cave in the story, presumably his last one, since he appears to die in it when Grigia's husband seals him in it after discovering the scientist in a tryst there with his wife. Again there is an ironic comparison to Jesus' resurrection from his tomb, since Homo does not escape from his cave. The geologist also evokes Novalis's well-known fictional character Heinrich von Ofterdingen, who in dreaming finds the ultimate object of his romantic quest for meaning in a cave: the blue flower that can symbolize some ineffable goal or meaning beyond existence. In *Heinrich von Ofterdingen* a secondary narration tells of the consummation of blissful erotic love that also takes place in a cave. In short, much of "Grigia" reflects an homage to, and parody of, the romantic notion that meaning is to be found in caves. As the earliest home of *Homo sapiens,* the cave is a place where primitive mentalities may or may not keep alive some superior way of life dating to premodern times.

This portrayal of the landscape in "Grigia" clearly belongs to a romantic worldview. When summer comes Homo finds himself separated from his family in the midst of a romantic paradise. He runs through meadows that are "white and violet, green and brown." There he finds that a "fairy-tale woods of old larch trunks, hairy with dark green, stood on emerald slopes." In this fairy tale, "under the moss might live violet and white crystals." A brook runs through the middle of the woods, and—shades of Novalis—"there was a large scarlet-colored flower, it was to be found in no other man's world, only in his, thus had God ordered it, a great miracle" (6:240). Having discovered in this landscape some of the secrets of nature, Homo stops writing to his wife. Logic no longer binds his mind, which Musil shows by narrating juxtaposed associations that evoke the contrary of what they affirm. Things are disassociated, Homo's mind becomes unsettled, and nature overwhelms him in its guise of a romantic dream. The borrowing from romanticism is apparent in the images of living crystals and emerald slopes, but so is Musil's ironic distance from romanticism. Homo is coming apart in a landscape in which his finding singular miracles is a sign of unbalance in a scientist, for the not-blue flower's color, scarlet, portends passion and death, not fulfillment.

This meadow scene contrasts notably with the reader's first impression of Homo, who is so representative of modern man as to be almost banal. He is generic, with his wife, one child, and career. Until he leaves to work in the mountains, he has never been separated from his wife, though he allows her to leave him when their child needs medical care. However, this is not for altruistic reasons: he simply does not desire to be with them. The tale's beginning gives way to play with romantic irony when Homo then decides, almost capriciously, to join a mining expedition organized by a Mr. Mozart Amadeo Hoffingott, a comic name that underscores Musil's play with motifs from the romantics. The name recalls that the composer Amadeus Mozart was so admired by the romantic writer Hoffmann that the latter changed his name, adding Amadeus to it as a form of homage to the Austrian musician. Musil outdoes Hoffmann by coupling *ama-deus,* or "love-god," with *Hoffingott,* or "hope-in-god." This humorous doubling expresses an ironic admiration of the harmonies of the Enlightenment world of Mozart while it parodies the name of Hoffmann. This parody in turn references the romantic self-reflexivity of Hoffmann, whose tales of madness and magic are a supreme romantic achievement in contesting rationalism. However, the modern capitalist entrepreneur Hoffingott is neither musician nor writer. He is a scavenger wanting to ferret out the gold that may remain in abandoned mines lying somewhere in the south, that is, on the margins of time and modern organization. Instead of the rich allegorical mines that the romantic Novalis could exploit, the modern entrepreneur who shows up a century later finds nature ravaged. The metaphor of an overworked mine might be taken as a form of self-critique by a modernist looking back upon the creativity of the romantics.

Musil spent his war years in the mountains on the Italian front. That locale is filtered in "Grigia" through distorting lenses that produce an image of dissolution and decline set in a region that has no fixed identity. In the streets of the mountain village where the expedition sets up its base, "snow and the south" are mixed together in the month of May (6:235). This conjoining of opposites parallels the way Musil mixes realist and mythic motifs in his description of the mountain region. The peasant women are turned into beasts of burden to work for the mining enterprise (6:237). This inhuman image seems at once to reflect a fairy-tale enchantment, a literal description of the practices of human animals, and an indictment of the savagery of capitalist practices. The landscape is also invested with an easy eroticism, emanating from the women, and with signs of death. When narrator describes a peasant standing with his sickle against the sky, for example, the grim reaper is so obviously present that one can hardly avoid a smile at the heavy irony with which Musil creates his romantic landscape pervaded with sex and death. Eros and Thanatos are also the most classical of juxtapositions.

Time is subject to distortions mixing past and present. History lives on into the present so that one may lose a sense as to where exactly one is. A recurrent motif in Musil is that the past can make itself felt in the present, although there is no way to reach back from the present to grasp the past authentically. For example, the peasants' household goods include cheap manu-factured items and dishes that go back to the time of the Reformation, the period during which their ancestors immigrated to the region. The peasants' language today seems to be a mixture of modern German dialect and terms accumulated along the way, such as French from some distant past when the French were in the region. And the mines themselves speak of some lost time when the region knew something other than the decline and stagnation that now characterize it. In this world in which the past lives into the present, Homo is tempted to believe he is in a space in which time does not exist.

Homo's sense of time is parodied after he undergoes his near epiphany in the mountain meadow where he encounters the red flower. He discovers that he had heretofore been living a miracle in the form of the love he had known with his wife. In this landscape he thinks he is illuminated by encountering a "word surrounded with youth"—the word is *Wiedervereinigung,* or "reunion." The word gives him contact with eternity, as the narrator says, and in turn allows him to see that "all the little blemishes, which the years had inflicted upon the beloved, were taken away from her, it was eternally the first day." With this discovery Homo realizes that he cannot be unfaithful to her, "since nobody would sacrifice eternity for a few minutes of frivolity, and he experi-enced for the first time that without doubt love is a heavenly sacrament" (6:241).

After the two stories in *Unions,* Homo's recognition of the sacred nature of fidelity must strike the reader more as pathology or ironic self-delusion. It appears that Homo, the skeptic, has accepted the Christian vision of love and salvation. He has, moreover, accepted love as the romantic fulfillment of exis-tence in a world in which nothing else can grant fulfillment. Homo is looking for some kind of salvation, but which kind? Is he Christ who arose from the cave or Nietzsche, who went mad? In his confusion of time and roles, Homo will in any case appear to be another unbalanced rationalist who then com-pletes his union, or reunion, by performing sacred acts of degradation, not unlike Claudine and Veronika. Or he may be simply an adulterer with preten-sions.

His revelation notwithstanding, Homo meets the woman who will cause him to sacrifice eternity for a few minutes of frivolity, for some time spent lit-erally rolling in the hay. She is Grigia, the bovine lover whose German dialect may include French from years past and who, in supine position, recalls Michelangelo's sculpture in the Florentine Medici Chapel (presumably the voluptuous Dawn matched with Twilight). The low and the sublime are condensed into her name, Lene Maria Lenzi, a name redolent with suggestions in German of springtime and rebirth, as well as the Virgin Mary. When she pronounces her name, the narrator notes, it sounds like Malga Mendana, or a deformed doublet suggesting the opposite of the Virgin, Mary Magdalene, the putative prostitute who found salvation at the cross (6:461). Following the epiphany in which he discovers a "reunion" that seemed to be a pledge of renewal of the love he bears his wife, Homo's breaking of the sacrament appears, minimally, to be part of a sardonic portrayal of the modern human being's incapacity to remain attached to any viewpoint. Or, as I suggested, Homo must commit the inevitable transgression that Musil sees occurring whenever anything is affirmed as sacred.

The sardonic viewpoint is reinforced in the scenes in which Musil portrays the mining camp, and especially the men gathered there to exploit whatever remains of the mine's natural resources. These scenes depict the various types of men of the mining enterprise. In them Musil offers a satirical portrayal of European modernity, as underscored by the narrator's declaration that in the mining camp there was one general measure of mind, it was the mind of Europe (6:244). Just as Homo is Europe's universal man, so is modern European culture the standard of measurement, the *Einheitmasse,* by which these gold-seekers measure everything they encounter. The result is not flattering for the European mind. In fact it is often hard to find mind at all in the narrator's series of anecdotes, in which there appears to be little difference between the men and animals, for a common measure applies to a tortured thief, frightened horses, or a slaughtered pig (6:241–43). All species of animals—*Homo sapiens* included—behave in comparable ways, which is to say that all animals are just animals, usually fearful beasts at that. This is Darwinian reductionism taken to the limit.

The entirely male camp mixes representative classes and types who have come from all over Europe. They socialize in a vicarage that has been converted into a casino. This is Musil's sardonic image of how the sacred and the profane are not separated in modern Europe. A modern gramophone provides music while a teacher, a business entrepreneur, a former prison inspector, a mining engineer, and a retired major try to find a subject of conversation in a "cloud of sadness and dance" (6:243). They speak what the narrator calls an animal language centered upon nostalgia and sex, family and dirty jokes, and occasionally lust for a famous opera singer whose voice now comes to them by means of recorded sound. Musil masterfully juxtaposes emergent traits of European culture and modernity from the early twentieth century. It is a culture selling identity through eroticism in various forms of media; it finally promotes the disintegration of everything into a heterogeneous collection of objects onto which lust is projected. All this takes place while the miners exchange murderous blows, display jealousy, undertake business, and talk about automobile racing (6:244). These juxtapositions convey a sense of a culture about which one would say that it has fallen apart if one had any sense that there was a time when it was different. It has no central identity, and can apparently no longer offer a reason for these men not to kill each other. Like the dogs in the town that the men have gathered together for their own protection, they quarrel ferociously for little reason and refrain from murder only because of an overriding sense of basic self-interest.

The juxtaposition of vicarage and casino offers a concrete synecdoche for Nietzsche's thesis that the churches are God's tomb. Nietzsche's presence is heavy here. The churches and their appendages are close to being bordellos, and the men within resemble the nihilists whom Nietzsche saw as the forthcoming generation. Musil had more actual experience with nihilism than did Nietzsche, and one detects echoes of this wartime experience, in which competing European armies murdered each other in defense of their values or lack thereof, in his portrayal of the camp full of nihilistic Europeans. This miscellany of types has come to this backward region for one reason: profit. With American financing they ransack the countryside in the hopes of huge returns and turn the locals into servants, if not wage slaves. With this depiction of the interior colonization of a European region by a "globalizing" firm, Musil is stressing, with pointed irony, the fact that the developments in European culture that eventuated in the Great War were part of a total historical development.

This development shows that the European *Homo* is as talented at self-destruction as at economic development. And his hubris is that he calls himself *Homo sapiens.* The idea of *Homo sapiens* stresses that we are animals and thus part of nature and its universal order. Yet, at the same time, the species part of the name implies an order that is not universal, since human beings believe they are somehow not entirely included in it. They are "knowing" animals and hence more than animals, or so it might appear from much European thought on the matter. Musil plays with the ironies of what a "homo" might mean while showing that the animal who thinks he is not quite part of nature is subject to it nonetheless.

Homo, the character as well as representative European animal, brings about his own destruction. Illustrating a nihilist viewpoint, perhaps in the end he desires his own demise. In any case the narrator says that, presciently, Homo feels that he will soon die. This feeling begins during his liaison with Grigia, a love affair that, Homo claims to himself, makes his love for his wife even stronger (6:248). He begins this sexual relation with the feeling that he is perhaps contravening what he once took to be the natural order of things, but he refutes his own thought by arguing that "nothing is less natural than nature" (6:245). The lines of demarcation between nature and non-nature become increasingly blurred, however. He discovers that in his relation with the "natural" woman Grigia he has stepped out of what he took to be the nature of things. Through her he discovers that where humans have not imposed their force upon nature, nature is "earthy, sharp, poisonous, and inhuman" (6:245). This is hardly the romantic vision of nature that Homo the geologist encounters in discovering the "earth." One recalls that Nietzsche adjured his reader to remain faithful to the earth, which Homo does by being unfaithful to his wife with this woman of the earth. But is she really a woman of the earth if she is, as Homo experiences, an animal whose kisses are compared to slurping from a beer mug (6:246)? The magic of her love is simple, for in quality it resembles what Homo sees in "the horses, the cows, and the dead pig" (6:247). In short, it is an example of odorous animal instinct. Musil is surely pointing out that the idea of nature plays a contradictory role in much European thought, not to mention erotic life.

Homo lives out the paradoxes he encounters with no bad conscience. In this regard he seems to be a prime example of the species of European man who wants his Christian romanticism and his biological bestiality at the same time. An interpretation underlining his paradoxes allows one to understand such a remarkable idea as the following description of their lovemaking: "when he kissed it [her mouth], he never knew if he loved this woman, or if a miracle was being shown him and Grigia was part of a revelation that tied him even more with his beloved in eternity" (6:247). Homo's belief that his adultery ties him in transcendence to his wife contrasts vividly with the following passage about copulating in the hay: "The hay would hold you up in all positions. You could stand in it up to your calves, at once uncertain and gripped too securely. You could lie down in it as in God's hand, were you to want to roll about like a doggy or a piglet in God's hand. You could lie in it obliquely, or vertically, like a saint that was traveling to heaven in a green cloud" (6:249).

In short, Homo is a pig looking for eternity. The humor evinced by these passages shows that Musil has moved beyond the deadpan concern with abnegation and masochistic self-destruction found in "The Perfecting of Love." There is more than a little satire in this ironic grotesquery, which is due to the ironic distance Musil maintains between this novella and the romanticism that inspired it. Yet, parody or satire notwithstanding, Musil was an experimentalist, and he is also imagining an experiment to see if one can conceive how infidelity might lead to greater love. This is very much a modernist experiment in transforming values. Homo's example, however, does not point to a successful experiment, for even readers of slight scientific inclination will probably reckon that dying in a cave as a result of one's infidelity is a negative result.

Death in a cave is a negation of Novalis and his attempt to imagine a locus of revelation and salvation on earth, indeed, in the earth. Musil appears to have Novalis's example explicitly in mind for the conclusion of "Grigia" with its setting in a cave. To get there Homo refuses to accept Grigia's refusal to make love and forcefully persuades her to go up into the mountain in search of a place for trysting. Not without dark forebodings and premonitory signs—all romantic emblems—Homo forges ahead with his reluctant paramour. They find a cave, an abandoned mine shaft, enter, and immediately copulate. Homo does not even bother to see if the ground is clean. Little of the bliss found in the comparable scene in Novalis's novel accompanies Homo's lying on the ground with Grigia, who has up to this point rather stoically accepted what is apparently the inevitable. Her husband finds them and seals the cave opening with a heavy rock. This rock is not to be rolled back. Screaming, Grigia proclaims her innocence to her husband and promises better behavior in the future. After some indefinite period of time, she finds an opening somewhere in the cave and escapes, but Homo does not follow her. He is too weak to return to life or did not want to, or perhaps had lost consciousness (6:252). At this very moment, as Homo is giving up, Hoffingott gives the order to stop all further work since, as the narrator reports, the mining enterprise has failed.

Offering uncertain hypotheses about what might have been Homo's state before his death, the narrator then withdraws without further commentary. This final narrative pirouette is comparable to the kind of ironies Kafka uses in order to open up hermeneutic possibilities. Readers are obliged to invent an explanation, to build their own hypotheses, and begin anew an interpretation of the entire story in order to account for the demise of man. It is clear that, whatever the various motivations one can find for his demise, Homo does not get out of the cave, and "Hoffingott" has been a vain enterprise. Another comparison with Kafka is also useful at this point. Just as Kafka often uses distorted religious images that tease the reader into reading, and then rejecting, theological interpretations of his work, so Musil proposes a near-expressionistic image of Christ's failure, which annuls itself once one realizes that if there had been a Christ, there could be no failure. Followers of the philosopher Heidegger would call this procedure a way of reading signs placed under erasure: the signs of Christian allegory and romantic hermeneutics are still visible even after we have scratched them out because we think they no longer function in our modern intellectual economy. But the signs show through the erasure nonetheless: Ecce homo.

"The Lady from Portugal," the second story in *Three Women,* is surprising. In terms of genre it is different from anything else Musil published. Using the idea of experiment to frame our reading of it, one can say that the story is an experiment in writing a romantic fairy tale, set in the Middle Ages, for a modern audience. The overcoming of historical distance involves, moreover, another form of writing under erasure, for Musil appropriates the categories of medieval thought and aesthetics to write a story for moderns who presumably no longer believe in miracles and magic, though both appear in the text. The moderns have erased these types of events from their texts, but they understand them nonetheless. And from Musil's rationalist viewpoint, it may appear that moderns sometimes do believe in miracles and magic, especially to the extent that Christianity continues to inform their worldview or to the extent that they believe in the miracles that war is supposed to produce. Musil implicitly makes this point by situating the story precisely at the geographical location where, in the Great War, he was expected to be a modern warrior and in a sense enact a reprise of a medieval epic. The tale's setting is a southern region where German and Italian cultures overlap, a region where cultural identities are not always clearly delimited and history has fluid contours.

"The Lady from Portugal" is a tale about love and the strategies of love, love and religion, love and the mystical, as well as love during the omnipresence of war. Narrating these themes with conventions taken from medieval and romantic literature, Musil allows himself a great deal of whimsical leeway in another ironic disquisition into the ways of love and romance. At the beginning the narrator assumes a conventional medieval stance, relating not what he has seen but what he has found in *Urkunden,* documents from earlier times. In these documents the hero's family is sometimes called von Ketten, sometimes delle Catene—the German and Italian terms for chains, preceded by the appropriate particle designating nobility. This ambivalence about language reflects a cultural space in which identify fluctuates. It is also a procedure used by a romantic writer such as Hoffmann, who playfully offers Italian and German doublets of the same character to show that the character is not to be pinned down to a single identify (such as Coppola/Coppelius in "The Sandman"). This indirect homage to Hoffmann shows the kind of refractory nature of the allusions in Musil's text; it is a reflection of, and meditation upon, nineteenth-century romantic fairy tales that in their rebellion against rationalism call upon the conventions of medieval fantasy. A romantic writer such as Tieck would be at home here.[2]

The fantasy is underscored by the location of the von Ketten castle. It stands, like some Walt Disney creation, upon a prominence five hundred feet above a roaring river whose roar creates a sound barrier around the castle. However, if no sound "penetrated from outside, through the overhanging mat of savage noise, into the castle of delle Catene," it is remarkable that "an eye that could oppose the roar could go without obstacle through this resistance to fall reeling and astonished into the rotund depths offered by the sight" (6:253). The castle resembles a magical space into which only gifted sight can penetrate. It is thus something of a synecdoche representing the tale itself, or perhaps fantastic and religious tales in general. One must have gifted vision to enter the tale and its castle. The castle sits above the world, impenetrable, a world unto itself in which the reigning order of reality may well be suspended—unless vision can penetrate it.

In this region of magic, modernity is recalled with a parody of modern anthropological description. Like an anthropologist, the narrator describes the exogamy that the von Ketten family practices in its marriages. They go extraordinary distances to find brides to bring back to their castle, so that it is part of the family ritual practice that the current lord of the castle has gone to Portugal to find a bride and, after riding for years, is bringing her back to his home. Anthropology is not the only science on the horizon of the narration. Musil also makes a pointed biological analogy to describe the rapid flow of time for the newly married couple: time had flown by like a nuptial flight of insects, a *Hochzeitsflug* (6:253). The comparison of the wedding party and cortege with the pageantry and mating rituals of insects sets the stage for the role animals again play in what one might call Musil's bestiary. The line of demarcation between humans and animals is never clear, which foreshadows the fact the line between God and animals can also be blurred. If Musil is drawing upon scientific categories to show that most humans in most cultures do not think like modern scientists, he also suggests that, from the viewpoint of the ironical anthropologist, Christian concepts such as the Incarnation lead to ironic views of the relations of humans, animals, and God. These views may seem either satirical or blasphemous. In any case they are quite humorous.[3]

However, "The Lady from Portugal" is more than just a respectful parody of literary form and of religious myths. It also gives direct expression not only to the rage that war produces, but also to the unrelenting devotion required by war and the unending sense of duty it inculcates in those smitten with the passion for victory. This passion is seen in the following strange events. Upon arriving at his castle, von Ketten wants his wife to return home. No explication is given, though it appears it is because he suddenly feels the need to carry on war against the family enemy, the bishop of Trent. He might feel his wife to be a hindrance to his military madness, though that is an assumption. Causal connections between events are not spelled out in the story. In fact Musil uses a nearly medieval form of parataxis to narrate events. Parataxis, such as in medieval epics, means that one event is simply juxtaposed with another sequentially as the events take place, without causal connection. In this case von Ketten arrives at his castle and immediately wants the Portuguese wife to go back. She does not want to leave until she knows the reason why. Subsequently the reader learns that the bishop of Trent is an enemy that von Ketten must fight. His acceptance of military duty means that an uncertain battle of years' duration stands before von Ketten (6:254).

With regard to the theme of war there is a useful comparison to be made with Rainer Maria Rilke's work, and especially with his depiction of duty in *The Lay of the Love and Death of Cornet Christoph Rilke* (1906). In this work, which many a German soldier carried in his knapsack in the First World War, Rilke portrays the unending ride of a soldier going to war to stop the Turks in their siege of Vienna. In "The Lady from Portugal" Musil draws not only on his personal experience of war, but also, I believe, on Rilke's image of the seemingly unending warrior's mission in evoking the fate that awaits von Ketten. I evoke Rilke's work at this point not merely as a question of literary influences, but also because in Musil, as in Rilke's work, is found one of the last evocations of the *honor* involved in military service. After the debacle of the First World War it became virtually impossible to evoke war—any war—without a sense of anguish or a smirk of disbelief before its absurdity, at least among modernist writers. This is true of novelists as diverse as Ernest Hemingway, Jaroslav Hašek, Erich Maria Remarque, and Louis-Ferdinand Céline. By contrast, there is nothing ironic or satirical in Musil's evocation of the soldier's task in "The Lady from Portugal." He had fulfilled his duty with a sense of honor, even if he came to view it as senseless, and he does not intend to disparage those who have also done so. By following Rilke's example in displacing the vision of the soldier's life in a distant past, Musil granted himself the distance necessary to create a vision of war with irony but without anger, even about its meaninglessness. The saddled days of the knight's saga evoke an era in which warriors fought as warriors and not as frightened animals hunched down in trenches scattered from Greece and Serbia to Russia, Italy, and France.

On a first reading the narration of war may appear to be a pastiche of medieval epics, though a second reading should convince one that in this fairy tale Musil is working out, almost therapeutically, his generation's traumatic relation to the years of warfare in which, from an Austrian viewpoint at least, nothing was accomplished—except the fulfillment of duty and the destruction of an empire. In this sense the fulfillment of a moral imperative meant a commitment to the void of pure heroism.

Rilke's influence can also be sensed in Musil's creation of the medieval marvelous that awaits the Portuguese bride. Musil was not by instinct a writer of the fantastic in the way that Rilke was. Rilke could enter into the mind of a medieval monk and re-create his worldview in which the marvelous accompanies the quotidian. But borrowing a few images from Rilke, as well as the German romantics, Musil sets forth in his tale an enchanted world with a castle that von Ketten's bride does not want to leave, however ugly she may find it at first. In the woods near the castle live all manner of animals, including the unicorn; in the underground gorges are found the lairs of dragons; and high upon the mountain is found the realm of spirits and demons, a place that no Christian would frequent (6:255).

This world of fantastic beings contrasts strongly with the war von Ketten undertakes for some eleven years. In contrast with fantasy, the world of warfare offers direct contact with reality. By this one should understand that warfare is the unfolding of the absolute power that settles all arguments about reality. Echoing Machiavelli and Nietzsche, the narrator affirms that this is von Ketten's viewpoint, for he believes that power defines what is and that the ultimate act of power is war. In war there are no doubts: "To command is clear, shining bright; certain is this life; the thrust of a spear under a throat-plate pushed aside is so simple, as when one can point with the finger and say, this is that" (6:259). But von Ketten begins to desire something different. He yearns for something beyond the order of the real as defined by the thrust of a sword. Taking no joy in order, household affairs, and his increasing wealth, he looks beyond power and the real—beyond the "reality principle," as Freudians say—searching for a region that might be some "other condition." We will see that Musil frequently meditated on another condition throughout his life. In the context of "The Lady from Portugal" the other condition would be a state transcending the bloodily truncated but eminently knowable form of reality found in war. And thus von Ketten takes less and less pleasure in saddling up; and, as time passes, the evening repose from killing finds him yearning increasingly for an ineffable lying beyond the solid certainties of the battlefield and the unremitting exercise of power.

Having reached this moment of saturation with reality, so to speak, the narration takes a turn back toward the world of fairy tales. The realm of the real recedes, and animals step forward to play an important role in the narration. These are not the humanized animals of children's fairy tales, such as the wolf in "Little Red Riding Hood," or their Hollywood descendants in cartoons. Rather, Musil's animals are beings that human beings resemble; humans may even be transformed into these animals, for the animals are embodiments of forces and symbols that are part of a mixed world of humans, gods, and animal spirits. Most of Musil's stories contain identification with, and metaphorical exchanges between, the human and the animal, and, as we have seen, the ironies derived from this play of narrative and trope are complex. There is probably no general rule describing Musil's use of animals and animal imagery, the mixing of human and animal categories with nods toward biological theory. To be sure it often has a deflationary purpose, though this is not necessarily the case in "The Lady from Portugal." For example, a wolf enters the story when the Portuguese queen observes that her two sons seem to resemble young wolves; when a young wolf is brought to her from the woods, she raises it. The wolf somehow embodies the absent husband. Its "silent wildness and the strength of its eyes" remind her of von Ketten (6:260). The appearance of the wolf marks, almost magically, the end of the warfare, since the bishop dies and von Ketten seizes the moment to gather a new army and to lay claim to victory. In effect, he is the victor. Human pretensions are not deflated here by these associations with animals. Rather, the opposite seems case, as if these animals might have totemic associations and grant powers to the humans who identify with them. The relationship of the wolf and von Ketten also resembles straightforward allegory on another level. He has been the wolf harassing the bishop, until by dint of persistence he has carried off the victory, like a patient predator, harassing his prey until at last it falls.

Nonetheless the relation between wolf and human is obscure, though it clearly seems to presage the introduction of themes of malevolence and magic. Joy in victory is cut short when von Ketten falls ill after being bitten by a poisonous fly. Perhaps the cessation of war entails near death for the wolfish aristocrat that must exist as a constant predator. Thus, he falls prey himself to an insect when his combat ceases. Von Ketten returns home in a wretched state, and his Portuguese lady reveals herself to be something of a witch. She places secret signs around the door of his room and his bed (6:261). The warrior's fever subsides but, significantly, does not go away. He is held in submission by animals and by a woman.

Lying in illness, von Ketten is drawn to his wife, but his "moon-night magician," as she is called, has drawn away from him (6:262). He is not totally abandoned, however. He lies weak in bed—an apparent victim of magic—and it seems that "all lay in a giant, kind hand that was as gentle as a cradle and at the same time weighed everything" (6:262). Musil uses this image of lying in the hand of God in "Grigia," though the adulterous context makes it seem quite ironic. In "The Lady from Portugal" the image of God as the all-embracing hand, holding all things that move, is one that Rilke might have created in recasting the medieval mind in his poems. Comparably, Musil expresses in this story a moment of religious fullness, without irony. It is a moment in which the medieval warrior waits upon something, something beyond the real, opening onto another realm. It is not clear that there is any such opening. But his waiting can be likened to a pivotal point in the narration, in which von Ketten hopes to move on to another realm where love exists with the plenitude of a deity. This is perhaps one way of understanding Musil's constant preoccupation with a condition that is found in a world other than the particular world one happens to be in and in which love is not always a perfect union.

In narrating this postbellum world in which the sick von Ketten may be cradled in the hand of God, Musil finally creates an almost humorous allegory, re-creating the medieval view of the moral relations between gods, humans, and animals. Von Ketten awakens to find his wife's wolf looking at him in the face. He tries to arm his crossbow; but, too weak to do so, he has a servant shoot the wolf and hang up its coat for all to see. Von Ketten has killed his double. Thereby he has transgressed a basic moral law of self-preservation as well as a totemic taboo. In outrage at his immorality, his wife vows to carry out vengeance, saying that she will make a hood of the coat and then suck out von Ketten's blood. Her threat to become a werewolf underscores her union with the animal world. The world of totemic spirits will be avenged, just as, in accord with the medieval concept of justice, the immoral act will inevitably be punished by retribution. And this is indeed the case. Von Ketten's head shrinks so that his fur cap falls down upon his ears. From a modern perspective this is a rather comic image; but it is also one that is also consonant with the medieval belief that the body can be physically marked by divine retribution. The poisonous fly takes on another meaning in this regard, marking correspondences between the venom it injects and the sins of omission and commission that von Ketten has done. Having killed the wolf, he is reduced to the status of a dog and lies in humiliated submission when the Portuguese lady receives a male friend she had known in earlier days.

A triangle now forms that may place the married couple's love in danger or that, from Musil's experimental perspective, may affirm it. Musil represents the moral ambiguities of the threesome in perplexing ways. In a certain sense von Ketten is now forced to do penitence for neglecting his wife. His penitence is made in the seductive presence of a handsome and decently clad foreigner who makes von Ketten's miserable state, complete with his shrinking head, stand out all the more. He is a passive witness to his own cuckolding. His suffering is all the more bitter in that it proceeds from the physical misery characteristic of medieval hagiography, in which the penitent is often reduced to covering his emaciated body with lice-filled rags. Von Ketten's suffering is now something like that of a martyr. And it is necessary for him to accomplish some act, or receive the grace, that will transform suffering into victory and transfiguration.

Grace, if that is the term, comes with the arrival of a small cat at the castle door. Like temptation and downfall, grace comes from the animal world. The quasi-human cat stands before the wall but does not leap over it. Rather, it requests entrance in a human way and arches its back as a sign of welcome, rubbing up against the boots and clothing of those present (6:265). A cat conducting itself like a small child may have a mission, manifesting the strange machinations of the divine, though of course in folklore it may also be a devil. The magician queen takes the kitten in care, and a name is found for it in a fairy-tale book—though, teasingly, the name is not revealed (6:266). All possible magical and totemic feline associations are held open, since all that is certain is that the cat is a visitor from elsewhere. This minimally suggests that the little beast is from that another realm, perhaps one unlimited by rational notions of reality.

The cat begins to grow sick. This illness suggests another totemic identification with von Ketten, for it would appear that the cat begins to undergo the same martyrdom he has undergone. It is hard to say at this point whether Musil is drawing more on medieval folktales or the anthropological literature about totemic animals, or perhaps he is simply parodying all these associations. In any case the cat is transformed into an ironic bearer of penitence and a double of von Ketten. With all appropriate irony, "Ecce homo" applies to both man and cat as imitators of a suffering god. This means apparently that the god who undergoes incarnation in the flesh in this case becomes a cat. This explains perhaps why the cat appears to take on von Ketten's sins. The feline sufferer gets sicker and sicker and is chased off, but, like any totemic animal, it returns to the castle, only to collapse before von Ketten, his wife, and her lover. They feel, as the narrator says, that the cat's dwindling away was as if it were becoming human—it is a *Menschwerdung* (becoming human)—so that they looked at it almost with reverence: "None of these three people was, in their individual situations, spared the thought that this was their own destiny" (6:267). In fine the cat-god becomes man and apparently takes on the destiny of all who observe it.

At least two sets of tripartite relations are unfolding here: young lover, wife, and sick husband; and sick warrior, cat, and God. Musil is writing something like an anticipatory satire of structuralism; or from the perspective of the 1920s, he is parodying the desire of anthropological science to arrange neat categories of explanation for primitive or antique cultures. Recall that at the outset the kitten appears to be a rather unremarkable animal. It gets sick and vomits; threatens, perhaps through pollution, the social order in the castle; and hence is sent to live with peasants who apparently are not so concerned with having cat vomit around. This level of daily banality is juxtaposed with allusions to the divine, both within the story and through interpretive frameworks imposed by the reader from without, that turn the cat into a god or totem figure. It is this juxtaposition that creates the parody, bordering on satire, of anthropological attempts to turn myth into scientifically ordered schemas.

A servant finally takes the cat and disposes of it. The narrator observes that all the characters feel guilt, as if a great crime had been perpetrated (6:268). The dogs in the courtyard show signs of distress (though notably, in their innocence, children think it perfectly appropriate that a dirty old cat should be gotten rid of). Von Ketten and his wife encounter each other, look at the dogs, and find no words, for, as the narrator, asks, "The sign had been there, but how was it to be interpreted, and what was to happen?" (6:268). Postmodern readers brought up on Kafka will find this question to be eminently self-referential, since the entire story seems to culminate in this question about the meaning of what has been going on. With this question the story interrogates itself as to whether it has any meaning. But in posing questions about what can be the meaning of experience, the story also broaches the most typical of medieval questions, for medieval romances often turn precisely on the hermeneutic game of making sense of the senseless. Who has ever figured out, for example, the meaning of the Holy Grail that Perceval sees, or if he has even seen it? In this regard Musil uses both the medieval sense of hermeneutics and the anthropological belief that meaning is to be found everywhere in order to construct both a parody of myth and a parody of making sense of myth.

Yet it is a respectful form of parody, as is evident in the bravura ending in which von Ketten decides that, if he is to get well, he must undertake an exploit during which he feels he will undergo the judgment of God. He decides to scale the rock cliff upon which the castle sits. In this knight's mind, this feat means imitating the cat, since he feels that it is not he but the "little cat from the other world" that will show the way. Yet, like any Christian imitating the Christian God, he is not free of doubts as to what might be the meaning of his quest, for, as we have suggested, success could possibly mean that the devil has accomplished the task (6:269). As every medieval monk or saint knew, hermeneutics is fraught with perils. Nonetheless, with all the skill of a contemporary rock climber forgoing rappeling tools, von Ketten scales the rock, recovers his health, and plops down in his wife's chamber. Miracles come quickly, for she is not there, but the handsome friend is not there either. Moreover, it appears that miracles restore chastity. From a medieval perspective it might be argued that fidelity is a spiritual question, such as is illustrated by medieval romances such as that of the fated lovers Tristan and Isolde. Isolde can swear her fidelity to King Mark and escape eventual judgment for adultery, since in her language, if not in bed, she speaks the truth when she swears that the king and the beggar who carried her piggyback across a river are the only men to have ever been between her legs—the beggar happening to be Tristan in disguise. Harking back to this medieval sense of the logic of forms, Musil suggests a different form of morality for erotic love, one more capacious and perhaps more inclusive than the bourgeois morality for which the evidence of the bed trumps the truth of language and legal formula.

At the end of "The Lady from Portugal" the narrator refers to the aristocrat by the Italian form of his name, delle Catene, which may be Musil's way of underscoring that there is a bit of Jesuitical, or at least what an Austrian might view as Italianate, rationalization in the story's miraculous ending. This impression is strengthened by the Portuguese wife's explanation of the wonders they have seen. She assures her husband that "if God could become a human being, He can also become a cat" (6:272). Von Ketten may for a moment feel that this is blasphemy. But he is not fearful, for they both know that no sound can pierce the sound barrier produced by their roaring river. They are safely hidden, isolated, and locked into the sounds that they produce themselves, which surely can be read as another self-referential statement about the nature of myth, at least as Musil portrays it here. Their mythic world is the hermetic world in which meanings are worked out by those within, and perhaps from without, by the happy few whose vision can pierce the wall and see the vertiginous vision that lies on the other side.

The Portuguese wife's statement about God's power to become a cat is to my mind one of the funniest lines in Musil. It is a nearly pure example of "carnivalesque" parody. By *carnivalesque* I mean that this parody effects a total inversion of the most serious myths and reduces them to a gag. As the great Russian scholar Mikhail Bakhtin (1895–1975) demonstrated in his study of carnival, this kind of parody renders homage to its object while at the same time it destroys the ossifying spirit of seriousness associated with sacred myths.[4] The function of carnivalesque parody is precisely to grant the freedom to live with the seriousness that, without comedy, would make high culture and morality unlivable. The inversion of higher and lower spheres produced by parody is also part of the spirit of medieval piety that animates Musil's tale of war and salvation, for, as Bakhtin showed, carnival laughter was a central feature of medieval literature and festivity. Moreover, the spirit of carnival parody is also an ingredient of Musil's rationalism. It is a rationalism that can on more than one count be compared with the thinking found in Bakhtin's work, a near contemporary of Musil whose historical studies of rhetoric are among the great achievements of modern scholarship. Both Musil and Bakhtin wrote to defend freedom of mind against stultifying dogma and illiberal totalitarianism. Irony and paradox, satire and humor, these are all a means of defense.

Parody blends into satire when the inversion, distortion, and hyperbole employed by the writer cease to be a form of homage and become a negative critique. Musil can be a satirist, but I do not think he engages in strong satire in "The Lady from Portugal," except insofar as he may mock, in anticipation, any interpretive enterprise that would try to turn his tale into some arch allegory of supposedly scientific methods. This question is more complex than it may first appear. Musil knew well that interpreters would look both to see if they can prove he had used scientific theories to create his story and to prove that his text can illustrate theories that the interpreters wish to use. Through anticipatory satire, then, I suggest that the story sets out, with hyperbole, schemas that invite the would-be interpreter to trip up by applying and deriving theories that the text is already derisively setting forth. Musil is a great critic not only of science, but also of the desire to use science where it is not especially applicable. This strategy will now occupy us from a different perspective in the collection's third story, "Tonka." The story obliges us to consider a reverse perspective, which to say, of not believing in science when science is irrefutable.

"Tonka" is the story that has received the most critical commentary of all of Musil's short fiction. This attention is quite understandable. It is a concise masterwork in its exploration of how narration can encompass memory and how memory can make sense of the past. Some of Musil's motivation in undertaking this experiment in narration clearly came from his interest in the psychological understanding of mental images, especially the psychological theory concerning the difference between the nature of pure thought and the nature of the images that constitute memory experience. To be sure, part of the story also found impetus in Musil's own experiences with a young woman whose death left him with a state of undetermined feelings. And both of these sources seem to have been conditioned by Musil's reading of Dostoyevsky's

1876 novella "Krotkaya" (translated variously as "The Gentle Soul," "A Gentle Spirit," "A Gentle Creature," or *Une femme douce,* the latter being Robert Bresson's well-known film version of Dostoyevsky's story.) Musil read Dostoyevsky throughout his life, and it is hardly surprising to find formal resemblances between "Tonka" and "Krotkaya." Musil builds on Dostoyevsky's form in homage to his Russian precursor but also because he found in this form an approach for the experiment he undertook to see if he could come to grips in narrative form with the pure subjectivity of memory.

Dostoyevsky's novella is narrated in the first person by a nearly hysterical middle-aged man who, after his young wife's suicide, begins to write an autobiographical report in order to understand what may have led this "gentle soul" to throw herself out of the window. In the course of the story the narrator narrates things that are clear signs of his wife's infidelity. He obviously does not realize that sometime in the past, out of contempt for him, she has been unfaithful. Her disdain for him appears to have been justified. After having been a contemptuous husband desirous of "conquering" his wife in order to make up for the humiliations he has known in life, the husband becomes a nearly demented adorer, wanting nothing more than to kiss the ground upon which his battered wife walks. This change reflects the fact that the narrator, once a military officer who refused to offer a duel when honor called for it, has fallen into the miserable ranks of the lowest form of petite bourgeoisie: he is a pawnbroker and something of a social derelict. In his blindness, the husband fails to explain her act to himself, though for his reader his narration succeeds admirably.

Musil narrates "Tonka" in the third person, though arguably this is a third person in which the pronoun *I* has simply been changed to *he.* Most of the time the third person can be rewritten in the first person with no essential change of meaning. However, this is not simply a rhetorical trick. Musil's unnamed narrator has greater distance from himself when he writes in the third person, taking on the persona of an unnamed protagonist. Musil did not use Dostoyevsky's type of first-person narration. He preferred to create the illusion of temporal distance between the moment of the act of narration, in some undetermined present time, and past events, when his protagonist meets, pursues, and then begins to live with the young woman named Tonka. Dostoyevsky's narrator is manically narrating right after his wife's suicide, with a corpse in the room. His narration reflects the disequilibrium of the nearly berserk narrator. Musil's narrator recalls the dead woman with greater distance, but nonetheless with a sense of wonder about what motivated her.

Like Dostoyevsky's pawnbroker, Musil's character has also been a military officer. He was doing his required service when he met Tonka. His personal itinerary is different from that of Dostoyevsky's narrator. Musil's unnamed protagonist is beginning to know success as a chemist, precisely when it appears certain that Tonka has been unfaithful to him, since she is pregnant and has venereal disease—so that unlike Dostoyevsky's narrator, Musil's chemist has some fairly clear signs about his companion's conduct. All circumstances, including the chemist's own clean bill of health, preclude his being the child's father or the carrier of the disease. From a scientific point of view, the odds that Tonka must have been unfaithful seem as near to certainty as medical science can offer.

Tonka, like Dostoyevsky's gentle soul of whom she is a less-gifted double, is dead when Musil's narrator begins to examine memory images, beginning with the recall of the past in the first lines of the narration. However, it is not clear where Musil's narrator is situated during the act of narration, nor will the reader know at the end. The act of narration begins after Tonka's death, and it is motivated by the need to shape the narrator's memory and to make sense of her death, which is to say, to shape a narrative in which things fit together cogently. This is not an easy task, as the narrator knows, for memory is illusive, and it often calls forth floating images that have no immediate coherence. The narrator gives himself the task to make sense of the fragments of narratives that memory offers, in language that may or may not have some relation to those visual images of the past.

Readers are obliged to ask how much confidence they can have in the narrator when he is so uncertain himself. This uncertainty characterizes the narrative from the beginning. Consider the first lines of the first of the fifteen chapters that make up the novella: "By a fence. A bird sang. The sun was already somewhere behind the bushes. The bird grew quiet. It was evening. The peasant girls came singing over the fields. What a lot of details! Is it trivial if so many details stick to a person? Like burs!? That was Tonka. Infinity flows along sometimes in drops" (6:270).

Strictly speaking, there is almost no narration in these lines, simply a list of animated memory images, though, according to the narrator, the images may be composed of an indefinite, if not infinite, number of details. The narrator sees images present in memory, with no relation to anything in particular, having only the commonality of being past. He is ironically amused by the magnitude of his task and by its banality, which causes him to compare the details present in the images to burs from the field that stick to one's clothes and to the drops of a stream for which there can be no reckoning. Tonka is nonetheless at the center of the images. To know her means the unending task of weighing the plethora of details taken from the indefinite images that memory can convey. He must stick them together to find meaning.

The next paragraph in the chapter is just as capricious, for example, when it arbitrarily finds that a red-dappled horse somehow belongs to the memory image. Arbitrary associations cause the narrator's train of thought to shift from Tonka to the protagonist, which is to say, to himself as a remembered character. He remembers that he was doing his military service and that at no time in life is a man more "laid bare" than during this time. Then, in the third paragraph, the narrator turns to himself in the present as narrator, to ask if that was the way it really was (which resonates ironically as a mocking paraphrase of the goal of positivist historiography: to grasp reality and to tell it as it was). No, the narrator decides, that was not the way it was, since he "thought all that out later" (6:270), after the fact of the image itself. Finally he finds himself confronting on the one hand the images, or what he calls fairy-tale elements— *das Märchen* (fairytale), the individual elements of time past; and on the other hand what he knows intellectually to be *Wahrheit* (truth) or what exists in truth. Truth relies not on images, since it is made up of those fragments of narratives that have been told and retold, in language exchanged between various parties, to make up social intercourse. The narrator observes that the narrated truth tells that Tonka was living with her aunt when he got to know her and that her cousin Julie, a prostitute, was tolerated at the family diner table. Truth characterizes a whole series of relationships in which Tonka is embedded and that are known because they have been told, not because they have been experienced by the narrator or can be seen in an image. The narrator has no image of, but only knowledge about, the jailed prostitutes who helped Tonka's grandmother with the wash and who, helping male convicts build a new correctional facility, started getting pregnant by them. He knows it is true that Tonka lived in a milieu with whores and pimps and that her background might explain much about her, although he draws no conclusions. The reader notes, to be sure, that the narrator is dwelling upon themes associated with his problems in understanding Tonka, especially how or why she might get pregnant by somebody else. Memory images are selectively dredged up by his present obsession with this question. (The reader may read around and through the tale Musil's distraught narrator tells, indeed not so differently as in the case of Dostoyevsky's hapless husband.)

"But where do such thoughts lead?" the narrator then asks, contrasting implicitly all the truth he claims to know with the present mental images of the fence, the field, the village, and the clothes Tonka wore—images of the past in his present moment (6:272). What can he make of the image of a fellow officer, a friend with whom is associated the narrator's memory of saying that he would like to have Tonka though she was "dangerous." This image in turn is contrasted with what the narrator considers the truth, which are the beginnings of a narrative based on other narratives, to wit, that the protagonist and Tonka met for the first time on the Ring Road in Vienna. And thus proceeds the narrative, fluctuating between the present instance of narration, the moment of memory with its images of the past in the present, and the correction of memory with the truth, the narrated truth, for instance, that Tonka worked with many other young women in a fabric store in which the owner seemed to have complete control over them. The reader must wonder if Tonka was sexually exploited there, though the narrator does not directly ask the question.

Adverbs designating time are a key to understanding the narrative. Each narrative utterance dealing with the past is situated as a past "now"—*jetzt* or *nun*—and by contrast utterances usually designated as *damals* or "at that time" are narrated in past-perfect tense to fill in with events from the past before the past "now" under consideration. This basic narrative schema is complicated further by the blurring of fantasy and real images. The first chapter concludes, for example, with the presentation of more images, but one must distinguish fantasy images, having the power to act as memory images, from "real" images. As in a fog the image of a smile comes to the narrator's mind, the smile of his mother, at once compassionate and full of contempt for his naïveté, since the smile tells him that "everybody knows what goes on in that store!" But where does this maternal smile come from, suggesting to him that Tonka was used for sex like every other girl working in this firm? The images are not clear, for they are mixed with other images of uncertain provenance: "But, although Tonka was still a virgin when he had known her, this smile had arisen, hiding or disguised, in many torturing dreams. Perhaps it had never taken place as a single smile, that in itself wasn't certain. And then there are bridal nights in which one can't be entirely sure, so called physiological ambiguity, where nature herself offers no clear conclusion, and in the same moment in which that stood before his memory, he knew that heaven itself was against Tonka" (6:273).

The loss of logical connectives here point up the narrator's epistemological dilemma. His mind contemplates the image of the mother's condemning smile—perhaps a fantasy—and cannot be certain whether the image condenses many occasions of condemnation or if one image offers many condemnations. And this order of uncertainty is of the same type as that which surrounds the question concerning what memory might say about whether Tonka had been a virgin or not when he got to know her. Relying upon his own mind, what can he count as evidence? What in memory can make sense? How can he evaluate evidence that exists almost entirely in his own mind?

It is more difficult to make a distinction between narrative plot and the order of the discourse in "Tonka" than in, say, *Young Törless*. The narrative discourse is frequently interrogating its own workings in establishing what might even be the plot, so that one can say that the goal of the discourse is to discover a plot. This interrogation is part of the meaning of this quintessentially modernist novella, for it asks what are the criteria for the construction of a meaningful narrative when the materials for that project are found in the subjectivity of the questing narrator. However, the plot, or at least a probable plot, is relatively simple, and can be sketched out so as to bring a maximum of clarity to further discussion. Following the narrator's attempt to recall the past, the reader shapes something like the following story. While doing his military service, the narrator meets a working-class girl, Tonka, who is an extraordinarily passive creature, hardly capable of speaking. He gets her work helping his grandmother so that she no longer works in the fabric store whose employees are, it seems, sexually exploited. After his grandmother's death and his finishing his studies in chemistry, he takes Tonka with him to a "big city," where they live together for several years. She works while he pursues, first in poverty, later with increasing success, a career in science. One day she discovers she is pregnant, and the timing of the event is such that the protagonist cannot be the father. She also has a venereal disease, and he is healthy. She refuses to admit she had done anything amiss and tells him to send her away if he does not believe her. He continues to live with her, ceaselessly seeking some explanation for her condition. She goes to the hospital without admitting any fault, and there she dies. At some time after her death, the narrator turns to this past to make sense of these years of life together with a woman whom he did not understand. This is the event presupposed by the novella's first image in the first line: a fence.

Underlying this quest for narrative are epistemological, psychological, moral, and indeed theological questions that Musil treats with both rigor and irony. No answers to these questions can be given unless the narrator in some sense recovers his past and makes sense of Tonka's conduct. Thus the questions he asks presuppose his quest as the necessary condition for finding an answer to them. These questions include: Can it be said that in some sense he believed her? If so, what was the nature of this belief? Is there any reason for him to have believed her? Does he have any moral responsibility for what has happened to him and especially to Tonka? The questions are interrelated, and any one of them seems to anticipate the others, which shows the holistic way Musil conceived the relation of knowledge and ethics, aesthetics and truth. But the first question the narrator must ask, if he is to deal with any of the others, is how he knows what he knows, if he knows anything.

My discussion of the first chapter in "Tonka" has shown that the novella begins as an epistemological quest. This quest informs the rest of its narrative structure. This may appear to be another way of saying that the narrator wants to know whether Tonka was unfaithful or not; and that all other questions about knowledge take on their full resonance as reflections of this question. In a sense this is true, but it is equally true that, for the narrator to know the truth about Tonka, he must come to grips with the question as to how anybody can know anything about the past. The answer to this question logically and existentially precedes the one concerning what he actually knew in the past, which is to say, what he thought he knew when he was living with Tonka. Moreover, if he "knew" something about her then, did he believe it? For the narrator knows well that knowledge can be in conflict with belief. The criteria that knowledge demands for validation can be opposed to belief.

Nothing is more ephemeral than the knowledge that claims a unique incident for its validation. However, Musil was committed to the idea that the unique can be characterized by or as truth. For example, what did the narrator know about Tonka when they made love for the first time? Knowledge of that necessarily unique event exists only as a memory attached to incongruous images, the strongest image being the clothes she placed on a chair (6:287). He also remembers that, once he was beside her in bed, her eyes were full of tears. Interestingly this image contradicts an earlier statement the narrator made according to which Tonka did not cry at his grandmother's funeral because she was incapable of shedding tears. Then, he recalls, there was her anguish, but this seems contradicted by his last memory of their making love. He recalls the "cleverness," as the narrator quite ambiguously says, with which Tonka had previously thought out how to possess all that she had admired in him. Then, as he strains to remember their first lovemaking, the spotlight of memory illuminating the past simply goes out, for "later he no longer remembered how it had happened" (6:287). With no knowledge really as to whether she was a virgin or not on the first night, he has little basis for latter suppositions about her, for example, about whether she might have been a sexually experienced woman inclined to adventures.

Musil recognized that most knowledge of truth is of a probabilistic nature, especially, though not exclusively, scientific truth. In this regard it is with no little irony that his scientist protagonist goes to many doctors to learn repeatedly that with a probability approaching certainty Tonka was guilty of a "common earthy fault"; the other possibility being that some "mystical event" has occurred to explain her pregnancy (6:288). Science offers the chemist a certainty of understanding based on regular causal relations and laws. But the chemist's knowledge of the regularity of the universe and its irrefutable processes is confronted by another direct presence. His knowledge of the usual way of getting pregnant and venereal disease must account for Tonka's face: contemplating the "directness" of her face, "one is far from all truth, one is in a world that does not know the concept of truth," since "Tonka had moved into the proximity of a deep fairy tale (*Märchen*)" (6:289). Her face is a concrete particular that challenges the truth of generality, or so the narrator feels. It may not validate the realm of general truth, but Tonka will die if science does not attend to her case—the narrator himself says this. The narrator, understandably, desires Tonka to be a case that no scientific law can account for, but it is all too true that such is not the case. With masterful irony Musil is at once making a case for the idea that there are two realms of knowledge—the true and the unique—and making a critique of the usefulness of the same idea.

In some respects Musil's anguished narrator is a reduced version of the narrator who, in Marcel Proust's *Remembrance of Things Past,* could spend hundreds of pages interpreting signs in an effort to know whether his girlfriend, Albertine, was unfaithful or not. Musil's protagonist spends far less time on signs that are far more certain, but, finally, certainty is not a thing of this world for him. All interpretation seems to encounter ambiguity, especially the interpretation of past images. For example, if he calls up an image showing Tonka to be as dependent on him as a dog, then that is not necessarily a proof in favor of her loyalty, for the image could simply mean she would follow off after any master (6:296). Interpretation can undermine the meaning of every memory image.

The narrator finds that the images he calls up, without necessarily being dream images, can take on a dreamlike quality that accentuates their ambiguity, such as his mother's contemptuous smile. Of course, images might well be dream images, or even images the devil puts in his mind. The ontology of images can be a narrative problem. For example, what criteria distinguish recalled dream images from recalled images of "real" perception? The philosopher René Descartes famously thought there are none, for he could find no way of distinguishing whether mental images are produced by dreams, madness, evil demons, or, occasionally, the perception of reality. Musil's narrator dwells especially on dream images. They can be a source of strange knowledge of a world of anguish in which the narrator's projected fears realize themselves as mental images. He finds that "these real dreams lay at a deeper level than his waking consciousness." They were warm like "low colorful little rooms," and in them Tonka was "heartlessly scolded because she didn't cry at grandmother's funeral," or more threateningly, an ugly man "was recognized to be the father of Tonka's child and she, when questioningly looked at, for the first time did not deny, but rather stood motionless there with an unending smile" (6:299). Separated from Tonka when she is in the hospital, the narrator finds that dreams become as important as waking moments. The recurrent torture that they inflict upon him appears to take on the weight of evidence. He especially recalls images in which a girl tells him that her lover has run away and then goes on to assure him that Tonka is a liar, for however nice she may be, one cannot believe her, since she always wanted to be a lady of pleasure (6:303). Nothing that the narrator has said to this point in the story suggests that modest Tonka had any ideas about pleasure or high living. Nonetheless the memory of dream images forces itself upon him as evidence in his quest for knowledge. One wonders if this is because dream can displace memory or if the memory of dream images has the same, if not greater, weight than memory of putative reality. The narrator has no easy answer.

One might think that Musil grants dreams a major role in the story because psychoanalysis grants it a major role in psychic life. There is undoubtedly some truth to this, though arguably he also does so in order to show that psychoanalysis is defective in privileging dreams when it cannot distinguish dream images from memory images. There is also for a more specific reason for the presence of dreams in "Tonka." Musil knows that his own epistemology, granting the unique event truth value, founders if he does not show that there is value, if not truth, in the unique moment of experience that takes shape in dreams. Unlike Freud, he does not take dreams to be universal allegories expressing unrealized, usually sexual desires. On the contrary dreams can be perhaps the most unique of unique moments in subjective life. Hence he grants dreams a role that makes them appear to be anything but arbitrary. They, too, are moments of the presence of some kind of truth, but not the truth of a general law. I stress this aspect of the novella, because it can explain in part why Musil was not receptive to Freudian psychology and its theory that dreams illustrate the general laws of the mind's working. (The Freudian allegory of the tripartite self is always found at work in dreams, at least in coded dreams that overcome the work of censorship.) Musil's representation of dreams in "Tonka" suggests that he saw them illustrating a specificity of psychic life, which could not be reduced to a general law. Thus dreams can only be understood as part of a holistic world in which the self is enmeshed in both waking and sleeping.

Musil's narrator distinguishes later in the novella "real dreams," as in the preceding example of the narrator's dream. "Real dream" is a curious notion, and one can well ask what would be an unreal dream. The notion of the "real" appears several times in the story, as if the narrator were seeking precisely some way to grant substantial meaning to what might otherwise appear to be arbitrary mental images, conjured up from uncertain sources. Yet it is not clear how the narrator can justify this use of "real." It is a category that stands in opposition to uncertain nebulous images his memory may try to impose upon him. One can doubt, however, if the narrator is entitled to use the word *real* without giving some criteria for its use. A "real" dream should have a different status from an imagined dream, but from the perspective of recalled memories one wonders what this status could be. The narrator does not eliminate the Cartesian dilemma about the criteria for knowing the status of mental images.

It is noteworthy that the narrator makes his most explicit use of the notion of reality in recalling how Tonka's body began to change as the fetus within developed. In the midst of the ambiguities about how he might interpret Tonka, he observed her body change as "her pregnancy progressed and showed what is reality (*Wirklichkeit*)" (6:301). Reality is exemplified by Tonka's awkward body, with breasts becoming udders as the stomach is distended and covered with visible red and blue blood vessels. Physiology seemingly allows no rebuttals, for the body is a kind of absolute. In a certain sense Freud and Musil would minimally agree upon this aspect of a reality principle. The principle admits of generalizations that impose on all objective observers the same conclusions about what is real. Tonka is really pregnant, and nobody can deny it, whomever or whatever be the cause. Tonka's stomach is, for the narrator, a less ambiguous piece of evidence than her face.

From another perspective it appears that Musil slips the notion of reality into the narration to oblige the reader to judge whether the narrator is logically consistent with himself. The axiom that there is a minimum level of reality, within the purview of every observer, stands in conflict with the view that truth could emerge from the solitary narrator entertaining his own images. This suggests that Musil's experiment here turns on the question as to what will be the case if we accept both the axiom that there is reality and the belief in the truth of the unique. It demands that one ask if, once reality has been accepted, can one doubt it in the name of other truth values? Or equally interesting, one wonders if the narrator can remain sane if he persists in denying the real. Musil has sharply focused on this aspect of the epistemological dilemma, for, as we have seen in earlier work, he had no little interest in insanity.

Perhaps the greatest likeness between "Tonka" and Dostoyevsky's "Krotkaya" is found in the fact that both explore the narrator's sanity. To this end Musil uses the rhetoric of fiction as part of an experiment with the possibilities of representing in the novella the play of perception by which the subject perceives his world. A few examples suffice to show that throughout the story the central issue, for knowing the world or, indeed, for saying that there is a world, is the perspective the narrator has on the world. It is this perspective that enables the subject to find consistent meaning in the world and for the reader to judge whether the narrator is coming close to being lost in madness or not.

The second chapter is devoted to this question of psychological perspective. It demonstrates that the narrator has great trouble in maintaining a unified perspective. He offers examples of memories that he first interpreted in one sense, but which, from the perspective granted by memory, have acquired a different sense. Taken together, these memories suggested his trouble in focusing on the world. In this chapter he saw "clearly" and "in the light" that Tonka really only liked children. Then he recalls interrogating her about whether she likes her work for the grandmother. This interview ends up with her laconically saying that she has to earn money. He remembers another time when, after the narrator tried to get her to talk, she began to sing, first operetta, then folk songs, or *Volkslieder*. These folk songs, in their simplicity, made him as sad, he says, as cabbage moths in sunshine (6:276). And on another occasion they sat in the edge of the woods, a brown moth alighted before them upon a flower that quivered and then became still like a "conversation broken off." The narrator recalls that if Tonka had thought like her companion, she would have seen that nature is composed of inconspicuous things, like the wasp that crawls on her foot. This detail recalls in turn an anecdote that Tonka told him about what the shopgirls said about love, which brings his perception back to his own shoe, in the woods, looking ugly, like every other detail about him. Yet he thinks that happiness can only be found in the totality of things (6:277). All of this points up that the narrator can only perceive details, absurdly salient things, that actually refuse a totality. He perceives insects, but not nature. And so it appears that, to endow Tonka with a quality he lacks, he projects upon her the idea that she did not speak the usual language, but rather a language of the totality or of wholeness—"eine Sprache des Ganzen" (6:276). Finally, facing his disjointed perspective, he comes up with the strange but perhaps warranted conclusion that all the details of his perception are ugly, for only when they are taken "together is there happiness" (6:277).

The chapter ends with the narrator's recognition that his perspective on the world had first given rise to meanings that now have exactly the opposite significance of what they had then. For some reason, only Tonka does not change, perhaps because "she was so simple and transparent," that on seeing her "one could think that one had an hallucination" (6:278). Tonka's opaque simplicity allows any interpretation with a simple change of perspective. But with the change of perspective the world itself loses it solid contours and insects can appear to be monsters. Moreover, with the passage of time and Tonka's becoming pregnant, the narrator's perspective is (or became) fragmented and seems borderline with regard to sanity. There is no totality to his vision, only perspectives. It is broken down into fragments that suggest near mental dissolution.

The experimental side to Musil's narration here lies in the way he takes the doctrine of perspectivism and uses it to see what might happen if a narrator needing truth were capable of only viewing from varied perspectives. There is a negative critique implicit in the results, which culminates in chapter 10 in what is really a brief essay on the fluctuating uncertainty of perception. After recalling examples of his mother and her conduct with her probable lover, the narrator concludes this chapter-cum-essay with philosophical analysis of his own perception. In an introspective self-description he sounds lucid, much like a would-be phenomenologist. He discovers that if the world is not present as the framework for his perceptions, if the world is not already present, then there is no world to be constructed by simply looking at the disparate things that surround him. For they are then only meaningless single things, individual elements, that are as sadly separated from each other as the stars in the night (6:298). The anti-Machean Musil has surfaced again here.

It can be argued that at no point in the novella does the narrator ever see a world in its totality, at least before the end. At the end, however, he perceives that Tonka, in her absence, unites the disparate things of his life into a whole. And one might be tempted to argue that the novella is a tale of how the narrator comes to perceive a total world. But before that moment—and perhaps not even then—the narrator has had no unified world in any meaningful sense. He is an observer of partial perspectives, meaningless insects and shoes, who realizes in the tenth chapter that a unifying world is what is lacking to his perception. He thinks that this is the reason that what he views and interprets at one moment can change its meaning at some subsequent time. Did Tonka like children because she was a decent human being? Or must he interpret her attraction to infants as a sign of her desire to sleep with everybody? Tonka may be an opaque figure, but the first problem the narrator has with interpreting the narrator's world is the narrator himself. This is not because he is mute like Tonka, but because he can interpret every thing in different ways, or so he claims.

In the tenth chapter the narrator discovers that, in his perception of the world, it breaks down into mere meaningless detached objects, since one world can be substituted for another when he merely looks out the window. Hence, he discovers that "volition, knowledge, and feeling are tangled together like a ball of yarn" (6:298). He wonders if one can go through the world other than "at the end of the thread of truth," which seems to mean that he wonders if one can really live without truth. Or, perhaps not unlike the Platonist, who believes one cannot do something one knows is wrong, the narrator is wondering if it is possible to believe in what one knows to be false. In such moments, "when a veneer of coldness" separated him from everything, Tonka suddenly appears to be more than something from a fairy tale, she has become a "mission" for him. Ethics and truth confront each other as antagonists in the narrator's confrontation of his own needs.

Recognizing his own near pathology, the narrator now interprets his relation to Tonka in moral terms, for she brings him something like an ethical goal. Reevaluating ethics was, to be sure, one of Musil's own goals as a writer. In earlier work he experimented with the idea that a higher morality might emerge from acts and attitudes judged immoral in conventional terms. In this regard Tonka herself, proclaiming her dubious fidelity, lines up with previous characters. However, in the passage alluded to above, it is the narrator who claims to have found a moral dimension in his relation with her. Given his near-pathological state, one wonders what kind of a mission he finds for himself. Moreover, if he is bound to the truth as to a thread, it seems he is tempted to snap the thread in order to accord Tonka her "truth"—though that would be an act severing self and rationality.

To pursue the metaphor of the thread, another thread of truth in the novella is the received truth of conventional morality, represented by the mother's narrator. She has had a disappointing marriage, and she wants her son to compensate for her lack of success in life. The narrator understands that "the essence of her being was duty" (6:282). This duty does not prevent her from carrying on with the writer "Uncle Hyazinth," nor does it keep her from demanding that her son dump his pregnant companion, after an appropriate payment of money to soothe his conscience. She scorns Tonka as an improper match for her son, and hence as an obstacle to her social ambitions for him. Such was the nature of conventional morality in central Europe in the early twentieth century. The narrator rejects a morality that willfully ignores its contradictions, for he leaves his family as soon as he is able. In this sense he has already snapped the thread that bound him to his mother's truth. But he has done little else, and if the narrator portrays himself as reading the poet Novalis, he also recognizes that he selects science as a course of study so as not to have to deal with unclear and multisided questions. As a young man, he says, he was against poetry, goodness, virtue, and simplicity. This means that he actually distrusts received truth about what is good and simple, though he is also wary of any complexity (6:283). In his own way the narrator is as contradictory as his mother, preferring the simple truths of chemistry to the simple truths of bourgeois morality, to wit, a nice young man simply does not marry that kind of a girl.

The narrator's rejection of conventional morality suggests that he entertains a higher idea of ethics. What is not clear is why Tonka might be considered a mission, or how any person could be a mission for another person. An answer to this question will depend largely on how one interprets the narrator as a reliable or unreliable representative of the novella's aesthetic intent. The narrator may be taken as a near-pathological case with regard to the perceptions he has. Yet his shattered state does not exclude his recognizing his need of a moral dimension. This dimension is necessary for him to have what he lacks: a world in which he can integrate feelings, knowledge, and values. This lack emerges from the analysis he undertakes of his own perceptions, so he cannot be totally benighted. Tonka becomes a mission for him since she allows him, or perhaps forces him, to find an ethical stance. Or from a cynical Nietzschean perspective, he decides to perceive himself as a moral being so as to value the feelings that he cannot help having.

The difficult problem Musil brings up throughout his work turns on ethics. His work points out that it is one thing to criticize the contradictions of conventional morality and to second Nietzsche in proclaiming the need for a transformation of values, but it is quite another thing actually to propose a meaningful alternative to conventional morality. Through his experiments Musil constantly sought new ways of conceiving the foundations for ethics and hence new ways of thinking through ethical problems. At the same time he made a critique of his attempt, which often leaves the reader with the perplexing feeling that ambiguity is the essence of Musil's sense of ethics.

One of the most challenging notions about morality in "Tonka" is the proposal that ethics is concerned as much with states as with acts. With appropriate ambiguity, this perspective is explored positively and negatively. Negatively, the narrator states that as a student he was against goodness, by which he must mean that he had contempt for bourgeois morality that conceived of ethics as a question of one's status. From this received perspective the "good" would characterize whatever a bourgeois character—such as the mother—does, because status confers goodness upon acts. This bourgeois belief is opposed to the positive idea that a character's moral status derives from the quality of the acts he or she performs. Conditioned by the bourgeois viewpoint, the narrator considers that Tonka's status might confer goodness upon whatever she does. However, her goodness emanates not from any bourgeois status, which she does not have; but from her belonging to the realm of dreams and fairy tales. (Musil is quite sarcastic in contrasting this realm of fantasy with Kant's hypothetical realm of universal reason, in which all subjects obey the same laws given by their rational self.)

In his disarray, in the fourteenth chapter, the narrator takes up the idea that ethical obligation originates in dreams. In dreams he can grasp things according to a logic grounded in feeling. For example the narrator understands that, since all hope for Tonka is gone, she believes she has rights upon him. This irrational belief is justified simply with the thought "because he was good, he belonged to her" (6:305). And in turn since she was good, there must be somewhere a "palace of goodness" in which they should live joined in mutual obligation and never leave each other. This is ethics founded not in acts, not even in being, but by "a glimmer, as when a travel coat opens" (6:306). Goodness can thus be dreamed of as beyond acts and status, in that realm of sentiment attached to the absolute particular about which no general truths can be enunciated. Goodness lies beyond reality, a beckoning call toward something else, like the siren call of travel and change. If this view of goodness is utopian, it is a utopia found in fairy tales. In fine, in his confusions the narrator is attracted by a kitsch fairy tale that every schoolgirl knows in her silent dreams. Musil makes both a form of social criticism—not least of all concerning the condition of schoolgirls—and an ironic critique of implications of his own thought about the ethics of particulars.

The story asks, moreover, if the ultimate ethical utopia might be that of the world of faith. At the story's end Musil obliges the reader to interpret the narrator's desire to believe in Tonka by analogy with the Christian notion of faith. The tale asks what are the criteria for the validity of faith. And lest one should seek a biblical parallel here, it should be stressed that the representation of faith in "Tonka" is not a simpleminded allegory: the narrator is not Joseph, and Tonka is not Mary, however much the tale may come close to parody in this regard. The illustration of faith is central to the text insofar as the narrator, challenged to believe the absurd, is called upon to be a "knight of faith." This is the term coined by the Danish philosopher Søren Kierkegaard (1813–1855) to name the true Christian believer in his defense of the absurdity of Christian belief.[5] Musil knew Kierkegaard as well as he knew the Pauline epistles. He knew well that Paul, as Erasmus reminds us in praise of folly, wrote that in the eyes of the world faith is madness. With no parody at all, Musil placed his narrator in the company of those early Christians and later Danes who had faith precisely because it was absurd or mad to do so. He seems to be destined to share company with the church father Tertullian, who affirmed famously that the Christian believes precisely because his belief is absurd.

The narrator knows that to have faith in the sense that he believes Tonka's assertions and denies the laws of nature is to be absurd or mad. The "law," both natural and conventional, condemns her, but, as we know, Paul put faith above the law, for the "righteousness of God without the law is manifested" (Romans 3:20). Faith is higher than the law for the believer, so the question is whether the narrator can accept that "faith is the substance of things hoped for, the evidence of things not seen" (Hebrews 11:1). After science and medicine refuse him any comfort, the narrator tries to reshape the world so that he can have faith. He does so in rather crude ways. He becomes grossly superstitious for a while, gambling to find signs and looking for omens that might assuage him. The question of faith, rather than the practice of superstition, finally takes shape toward the end of the novella when the narrator recognizes that only the strongest form of religious faith might resolve his dilemma. It is with a medieval sense of the possibility of faith that he envisages Tonka, thinks about the possibility of a secret connection to her, and affirms that he only needs to believe truly in her in order to become sick with the disease whose absence in him is evidence that she has lied (6:304). Despite this affirmation, however, he cannot truly say to her that he believes her, and he never does.

His faith is that of the believer who wants very much to believe, but cannot move mountains because that ultimate affirmation is lacking—or so the true believer would say. Neither medieval faith nor the Kierkegaardian leap of faith is possible for the narrator, nor can he miraculously catch a venereal disease. Musil is offering a sharp critique of the role of belief in modern life. One believes what one wants to believe, up to a point, but reality also, sometimes, coexists and may be in contradiction with the need to believe, at least so long as one is relatively sane. The narrator cannot produce a disease in himself by faith, nor does he finally go totally insane, however much he appears to live in a fragmented world bordering on disintegration. He is left with only the absurdity of his belief.

In conclusion he recognizes that, whatever the now-dead Tonka may have done, he owes her much. There is something very satisfying about this conclusion, for if the narrator appears at times to have used Tonka, and if Tonka may appear in retrospect to have been mendacious or calculating in the extreme, beyond these all-too-human faults the reader senses that the couple lived in some way for each other, and that in this "union" Musil may have expressed something utopian that is found in reality as well as in fairy tales. This is the sense of the final epiphany, in a minor chord, in which the scales drop from the narrator's eyes and he knows Tonka in the sense that he sees what she has meant to him: "then memory screamed out in him: Tonka! Tonka! He felt her from the earth right to his head and her entire life. Everything that he had never known stood in this moment before him, the bindings of blindness seemed to have fallen down from his eyes, for a moment, since in the next one something seemed to have occurred to him very quickly. And much occurred to him since then, which made him somewhat better than others, because a small warm shadow lay across his shining life" (6:306).

I translate as literally as possible to stress the images Musil uses to give a résumé of what the narrator knows in his acceptance of the shadow cast upon the light of knowledge. In his acceptance of the necessity of light and darkness for vision, the narrator now knows that in not knowing before what this woman meant to him, the torments of doubt that this relation inflicted upon him have actually enriched him. He is a better person for that.

CHAPTER 6

Epistemology and Politics in the Essays

Robert Musil is one of the major essay writers of the twentieth century, though this is probably the most neglected aspect of his work.[1] Therefore, the next two chapters will focus on these essays in the hope of showing that in them Musil produced some of his most interesting work. I will also consider some parables and short fictions. These are short pieces mainly written before he began devoting virtually all his energy to *The Man without Qualities*. Most of the essays were published in journals, before and after the First World War, whereas the other texts considered here were gathered together several years after their completion and published in 1936 as *Nachlass zu Lebzeiten* (*Posthumous Papers of a Living Author*). Taken together, these essays and parables cover a wide range of related intellectual interests, though they do not present anything like a systematic philosophy. This is hardly surprising. Musil's favored essayists, Emerson and Nietzsche, would have scoffed at the very idea of philosophy as a system. Rather than elaborating a system, Musil's essays, later parables, and short fictions turn on a number of intellectual and artistic issues to which he frequently returned. Treating these focal points from different perspectives, Musil was as much concerned with elaborating a way of thinking as he was in proposing a body of thought. One finds in these works thematic configurations whose recurrence organizes, like nodal points, his essayistic exploration of ideas and values that concern him. These recurrent issues organize the following two chapters, the first centering on essays and Musil's use of them to make a critique of knowledge and of ideology. In the following chapter the focus is on his cultural critique with considerations of his views of education, aesthetics, and ethics as expressed in essays and in the texts he published in *Posthumous Papers of a Living Author*.

If Musil, like Emerson and Nietzsche, scoffed at the desire to create a system, he hardly rejected the idea that there are central ideas and values that any sensitive writer, not to mention concerned citizen, must confront. In his essays before the First World War he sensed that a crisis was engulfing Europe; and after the war he saw that the crisis had hardly abated because of the war. A disabused pessimist, Musil saw nothing in the ongoing development of German culture that pointed to a way out of the crisis in values and ideology. A basic cause for the crisis, he believed, was that the Enlightenment had failed. In considering the failure of the Enlightenment Musil did not think that its values of freedom, rationality, and free inquiry were in some sense erroneous. Rather, he understood this failure to mean that his contemporaries had lost the Enlightenment belief in the capacity of reason to promote the ongoing improvement of the human condition. Though not an enthusiastic admirer of Kant, Musil certainly agreed with the philosopher who saw the essential nature of Enlightenment to be the release of humanity from the tutelage of all forces except its own power of reason. However, he despaired that, as he put it in the harsh words of his 1922 essay "Helpless Europe," the final decades of the eighteenth century were the last time anybody believed in reason and in such attendant concepts as "natural religion," "natural morality," or "natural education" (8:1082).

In essays, critical writing, short fictions, and parables, Musil took a position that endorsed the Enlightenment project, often with questioning irony, at the same time it deplored its failure. This is perhaps the key idea to grasp in order to understand the paradoxical way he seems to be a hostile defender of those Enlightenment values—such as liberty, rationality, objectivity—that were questioned by the successive ideological groups, from antirationalist romantics and traditionalist reactionaries in the nineteenth century to the later pan-German nationalists and the Nazis. Musil accepted the fact of the crisis, indeed of the near disappearance, of Enlightenment values; but he did not think that any subsequent ideology in the nineteenth or twentieth centuries had found a way to deal adequately with the crisis engulfing Europe. Arguably the history of German culture during Musil's lifetime bears him out. Suffice it to say that the Enlightenment culture, in whose elaboration in the eighteenth century Germans writers and thinkers had played major roles, failed to be a source of renewal for German culture in the first half of the twentieth. Musil saw that the crisis in German liberalism and democratic ideology demanded a renewal of individual and social values that, accepting science and reason, could enlighten and liberate humanity in beneficent ways. Quite simply, this is the fundamental political and ideological problem Musil confronted.

In his essays Musil examines different ideological positions: he flirts with socialism and indicts capitalism, and even at one point says that he once was a conservative anarchist (8:1011). If one wants a label for him, he was undoubtedly a liberal by default, though some Germans seem to think this makes him a conservative.[2] Facing the ideological confusions of an era in which the Enlightenment's understanding of liberalism as the rational pursuit of freedom had virtually disappeared, Musil's skeptical stance may well appear conservative for the intellectual distance it maintains. In any case, like the skeptical liberal Emerson, Musil thought that an honest thinker, looking for new forms of thought, could best exploit the essay for their elaboration. It is the literary form best suited for confronting ideologies pretending to be a total explanation of society and the cosmos. The essay's demand for multiple viewpoints obliges writers to avoid the temptations of unitary and totalizing explanation, for the form itself results from writers' mapping out the contrarieties they find within themselves. The essay form results when writers follow the mind in its own questing movement in the pursuit of truth.

The essay as a form of self-exploration is not really frequent in Western literature, and an historical commentary is appropriate to elucidate what Musil thought he was about. The French writer Michel de Montaigne coined the term during the sixteenth century to describe the writing he did at a moment when European culture was undergoing the crisis produced by the Reformation. One can cogently argue that this historical event had analogies with the crisis Musil experienced insofar as hopes for reform were concerned. The second half of the sixteenth century witnessed the wars of religion in France, which brought to an end the hopes of rational religious and social reform that the European evangelical moment had held earlier in the century. The hopes of Erasmus and Rabelais were ended with the decades of strife that pitted Catholics and Protestants against each other in mutual massacres. The religious underpinnings of European medieval culture no longer held sway, but it was hardly obvious that the Renaissance critique of medieval belief had had positive results. Montaigne's reaction was to retreat into his chateau's library and, figuratively, into himself. In his writing he came to "assay" or to weigh the foundations of European and classical culture that he found in himself, which formed the basis for his identity. Montaigne's essays in the sense of assays are collectively a meditation on self, identity, and culture undertaken in the midst of chaos.

Musil's essays and parables often offer a comparable performance in weighing out ideas and beliefs. His writing often resembles a kind of psychic theater in which the writer pursues, either in deadpan or in sharp irony, the ideas that are nestled within his consciousness as a German-language writer who also happens to be a European scientist-engineer with a sharp sense of the history of his culture. He is especially attentive to the turmoil it has undergone since the French Revolution led to the application of Enlightenment ideals to political reality. Like Montaigne, Musil takes his psychological distance from the turmoil and bloodshed. He seeks a way of thinking that might be adequate to circumstances for which there is little historical precedent.

In a 1918 essay on Franz Blei, Musil defines what he saw as the essential trait of an essayist. Ostensibly writing about his friend and fellow writer, Musil in fact describes himself and his project in writing his essays. Situating the essayist between, on the one hand, the scientist and the scholar and, on the other hand, the poet, he knows that to the rigorous thinker the essayist will appear to be a "cream puff" deriving his material from the droppings of the scholar's table; whereas to the poet the essayist appears to offer compromises that refract the poet's "shining essence in the murkiness of common rationality" (8:1024). Finding himself situated between the scientist and the poet, the essayist aims at the "articulation of feeling through the understanding" and the "turning aside of understanding from the arbitrary goals of science for the tasks of feeling" (8:1024). This task is not realized without rigor, however. As Musil put it in an unpublished essay written before the war, the essay form is a "knotting together of thoughts" and hence a logical conjunction of thoughts "proceeding from facts that, like science, it places together in relation to each other" (8:1335). But as Montaigne knew well, the essayist proposes no immediately attainable goal or statements that are demonstrably false (Musil says that the latter is the task of the philosopher). In brief the essay shows the work of the mind—*Geist*—taking place in a different intellectual economy from that of science. The criteria for the successful essay derive from the essayist's own work as he weighs ideas and beliefs, values and acts, in what often resembles a performative act.

Many of Musil's essays are concerned with the claims to knowledge that ideologies make. His reflections on the nature of knowledge are a precondition for making cultural criticism and understanding political ideas. A theory of knowledge is in effect presupposed by any discussion of politics, as well as ethics and aesthetics, for one should have some criteria for claiming to know what these fields encompass. Turning from issues of knowledge, Musil's cultural criticism deals with politics, but in a much broader sense than what Anglo-Americans usually mean by politics. This is not surprising. History obliged him to deal with much more fundamental political issues than those involved, for example, in deciding which political party to vote for. Politics for Musil entailed deciding what kind of political state one should struggle for; or, in the case of Austria, if one's nation should be a state at all.

To understand Musil's approach to political questions, one must thus bear in mind the historical context in which he dealt with politics. In his lifetime he lived in Germany and Austria under several different types of political regimes. In his first essays he addresses himself to politics in the framework of a quasi-feudal state. Until 1918 Austria was a monarchy, in which, after the victories of liberalism in 1867, liberals largely failed to develop a successful liberal democratic state. The liberal parties lost their majority in the Reichsrat in 1879, and by 1893, at the end of the ministry of a multiethnic coalition, "the German liberals, once Austria's party of government, had been reduced to being one interest group among many."[3] After the fall of the Austro-Hungarian and the German empires at the end of the First World War, Musil then lived in the new German and Austrian republics. Both were struggling for survival amid antidemocratic ideologies. Whether the Austrian Republic should even exist is a topic in his essays after the war—Musil was not a nationalist. He was also skeptical about collectivist solutions to social problems, and the failure of communist movements in Germany to make the kind of revolution that the Soviets had made in Russia undoubtedly confirmed his skepticism. The failure of the Austrian social democrats to stay in power was also hardly encouraging for a writer who had supported these democratic socialists. In any case his essays after the war focus on the intellectual life and ideological strife of the stumbling democracy of the Weimar Republic. His essays offer many insights into the conditions that allowed the Nazis to take power. We will also see that even before the First World War he was aware that the conditions were present for the rise of irrational totalitarianism in Germany. Many of his essays concern his reaction to the nationalism driving this historical development. He tried to make sense of the fact that, in both empires and in both republics, strident nationalism, antiliberalism, and violent anti-Semitism were as much a part of the political landscape as were the social democratic parties that, in 1918 in Austria, had opposed the left-wing splinter groups who had tried to make revolution. In a sense, then, as in Montaigne's essays, the intellectual distance granted by essay writing was used by Musil to confront the turbulent political landscape in which thinking about politics had become an ethical imperative.

The scope of Musil's thought ranges widely. In confronting the political irrationalities of his time, his skepticism is constant. Musil is quite conscious that his essayistic skepticism, entertaining every idea and its opposite, harbors within it the possibility of going astray. This risk does not stop him from wanting to rethink the grounds of virtually everything that undergirds political and ethical thinking. From Musil's viewpoint the risk of questioning is justified by the unquestionable success of science's constant skepticism. In fact he often comes to the task of questioning with the perspective of the scientist who never stops asking what the grounds are for affirming knowledge of anything. A common premise tying together Musil's diverse thoughts is the scientist's axiomatic refusal to believe there are final truths. Applying skepticism to the entirety of human culture, Musil knew well that he created the conditions of possibility for a situation in which he, like Hamlet, could never stop pondering if one knows anything at all that might allow one to act. The nemesis of the true believer, Musil thought that skeptical rationalism offered the only hope to unite politics, aesthetics, and ethics in a common project that might conceivably renew the Enlightenment critique of values.

Epistemological inquiry necessarily takes pointers from science, for it can be argued, and Musil did argue, that science, after the end of the Enlightenment, had been the only successful epistemological enterprise Europe had known. And it is the only enterprise in which allegiance to rationality has remained unchallenged (a true statement if one does not take into account such aberrations such as Aryan physics or Stalinist genetics). However, the limitation of the use of reason to scientific pursuits meant, as Musil saw it, that the Enlightenment belief in reason had been severely truncated. Accordingly scientific pragmatism had replaced a belief in universal reason. As Musil argues, pragmatism offers criteria only for forms of rational understanding largely limited to the sciences and technology. His recurrent question is, then, what can be a guide to understanding in all those domains in which pragmatism can play no role? Can one find a new role for reason? In his essays he broached these questions in a desire to elaborate thoughts, consonant with the demands of science, that at the same time go beyond science by seeking knowledge about those domains for which scientific pragmatism is inappropriate. The stakes involved were high, especially at a time when irrational ideologies were ready to proclaim the superiority of knowledge literally based on blood, race, and nation.

It is noteworthy that familiarity with Musil's critique of Mach does not necessarily prepare one to read his essays. In the essays he is not undertaking a logical critique of the coherence of a well-defined philosophical position. The commonality linking the dissertation to the essays is Musil's attempt to come to truth or truths by defining some criteria for whatever one affirms as truth. Unlike many contemporaries, then and now, Musil did not easily relinquish the notion of the truth. If he often finds himself taking up relativistic positions, he does not rejoice in them. Yet some critics want to see in him a precursor of postmodern relativists. Rather than with postmodernists who are largely ignorant of science, I propose that it is more fruitful to compare Musil to the first major thinker who doubted that rationalist science can provide the criteria for the truth of most humanistic or moral propositions. As I suggested with regard to *Young Törless,* it is more appropriate to compare Musil to Pascal, who invented probability theory while theorizing the limits of physics.[4] Musil's thought overlaps in important ways with the epistemology of this seventeenth-century mathematician who first recognized that the mathematical mind can provide certain knowledge in the limited domain of its application, but that, unfortunately, most questions of human interest are not subject to the axiomatic thinking used by the scientist. Thus Pascal coined the expression *esprit de finesse* to describe the mind relying on intuition in dealing with complex issues that cannot be reduced to axiomatic reasoning. Science, understood as knowledge codified by axiomatic procedures, offers knowledge of well-defined areas of reality; but, as Musil demonstrates, the complexity of most problems faced by human beings is such that science cannot be used to deal with them.

Moreover, as Musil frequently stressed, science in its quest for laws uses generalizations that are true but frequently do not deal with the concrete particulars that human beings face in their complex undertakings. This Pascalian motif is a central theme in *The Enthusiasts*. However, unlike many of his contemporaries in Germany, Musil did not find in complexity a reason to become an irrationalist. In spite of his malaise about the foundations of mathematics and of scientific propositions, he did not renounce his allegiance to mathematics as a model for thought and knowledge. Like his mathematician hero, Ulrich, in *The Man without Qualities,* he saw no alternative to the rationalism the scientific mind embraced, at least in those domains in which science can be applied. And Musil asked throughout his work if the workings of the scientific mind offered a possible model for those domains to which it could not be directly applied.

The question of dealing with the rapidly evolving world of science in the early twentieth century, with its unceasing production of new theories, is taken up frequently in the essays. Musil the epistemologist did not remain riveted to the ideas found in his dissertation. For one thing, after the dissertation he had to come to grips with the radical changes that non-Euclidian geometry and relativity theory had introduced into the scientific world. In the dissertation not only did he not accept the implications of relativity in Mach's work, but he showed no awareness of the existence of the new geometries. That Musil was modifying the ideas he had expressed in his dissertation is evident, a few years after writing it, in his 1913 essay with the Pascalian title "Der mathematischer Mensch" ("The Mathematical Man"). In this essay, published in the wake of work by mathematicians such as Poincaré arguing for the conventional nature of mathematical explanation, Musil accepts that the foundations of mathematics are no longer a source of certainty.[5] He also acknowledges, with distanced irony, that in a world given over to modern technology, the machines designed with the use of calculus run quite well—whatever be the status of their mathematical bases. Hence, according to Musil, the mathematically minded are now burdened with an intellectual scandal: modern scientists live in what he called an intellectual house standing in midair (8:1006).

By 1913, a year before the outbreak of World War I, Musil considered that this lack of foundations was no more a scandal than the fact that mathematical physicists in recent years had seemingly denied the existence of space and time—and for reasons that rose up, as he put it, as palpably as an automobile and thus are quite credible (8:1007). From these remarks and others in the essay, one infers that by 1913 Musil was inclined to accept Einstein's theory of special relativity of 1905 and the description of space-time that the mathematician Hermann Minkowski derived from it in 1907. His statement about credibility suggests that he had meditated on the development of non-Euclidian geometry and that by 1913 he had accepted the fact that the development of these geometries means that mathematics is no longer grounded in some form of universal reason. He understood that space and geometry are not commensurate. On the contrary, he accepted that our understanding of mathematics, once vouchsafing certain knowledge in the Newtonian-Kantian world in which Euclidian geometry was identical with space, had been totally transformed. The foundation of mathematics could now be viewed as a question of operational procedures that mathematicians follow according to the logic of the procedures themselves. And after Einstein's theory of relativity, spacetime is a notion ridding the world of any absolute framework of reference, either temporal or spatial.

Living with the relativity of temporal and spatial frameworks, Musil's mathematical *Mensch* was learning to live with paradoxes of reason derived from mathematical thought. Or, as Musil went on to say in this key essay, acceptance of modern science requires a certain rationalist courage that we lost once we ceased believing in Enlightenment values. Musil's indictment of one side of romanticism is clear in the following: "After the Enlightenment most of us lost courage. A minor failure was enough to turn us away from reason, and we allowed every barren enthusiast to inveigh against the intentions of a d'Alembert or a Diderot as mere rationalism. We beat the drums for feeling against intellect and forgot that without intellect . . . feeling is as dense as a blockhead (*dick wie ein Mops ist*)" (8:1007).

Coming down hard on anti-intellectualism, Musil offered a challenge to it by claiming that it is the mathematicians who exemplify ethical courage in the face of postromantic irrationalism. With this challenge the essay pinpoints a moment when dilemmas about rationality and morality, in which Musil remained caught up in for the next thirty years, were taking definite shape in his mind. The essay shows a moment when Musil's thought crystallized around the problem of relating scientific precision, for which mathematics is the model, to the messy world that literature represents in all its fallen glory— a world that in its less glorious moments was soon to give Musil a world war and then fascistic nationalisms to worry about. Like Pascal, he remained the mathematician who was all too aware that the procedures of mathematical science could not encompass the complexity of real decision making. This limitation does not discredit science in those domains in which it works. In brief, the interface of science and complexity, one of the central themes of *The Man without Qualities,* was emerging as Musil meditated on the epistemological foundations of science.

Musil's epistemological thought took on a somewhat different cast after the war, for example, in his "Skizze der Erkenntnis des Dichters" ("Sketch of a Poet's Knowledge") of 1918, which outlines a view of scientific knowledge contrasted with the knowledge propounded by poets. Musil says he can describe the poet's knowledge by first describing its opposite, that of a rational human dealing with a "ratioïd domain" (8:1026). Musil coins the term *ratioïd* to characterize the realm of scientific knowledge by contrast with the ephemeral world of unique occurrences constituting the poet's domain or, indeed, the domain of everyday knowledge. In addition to this neologism Musil spins out a web of metaphors to contrast these domains, for he clearly wants to delimit them, even if at other times he wants the apparently antagonistic domains of science and poetry to be mutually reinforcing. His essayistic attitude in this regard is highly labile. The nonpoetic, which is to say, ratioïd, domain encompasses all that can be systematized and is subject to laws and rules, which means mainly physical nature. This is Pascal's realm of geometry or axiomatic algorithms, which, as Musil says, is characterized by a certain "monotony of facts" that repeat themselves and can be subsumed under other groups of laws, rules, and concepts (8:1027). Facts in this domain can be described univocally and hence communicated. Any secondary quality—or what Musil calls any subjective aspect of their representation, that of color, weight, or velocity—is incidental to the essential fact that they can be communicated. Whereas, Musil notes parenthetically, the simplest statement in the non-ratioïd domain can entail an unending number of explanations in order to have a determinate representation. It is the domain of infinite complexity. The comparison with Pascal is especially illuminating in this regard, for it shows that Musil's polar epistemology is the outcome of an historical development in which the issue of complexity is central. Mathematical physics offers highly probable knowledge because it is simple in the number of coordinates it involves, whereas knowing if somebody has cause to be jealous may entail an indefinite number of hypotheses and arguments—as Musil demonstrated in "Tonka."

Musil's spatial metaphor in this essay on the poet's knowledge suggests the "fixed" nature of scientific knowledge. It should not be taken as a hostile critique of science, since Musil himself knows that the metaphor is not especially apt. But he frames it with something else in mind: he wants to show that any ethical knowledge that relies upon a fixed scaffolding of concepts, deductions, and laws is trying to imitate scientific knowledge (8:1028). Here is the real center of his critique: ethical knowledge that tries to find an axiomatic system for itself has made a fundamental error. It has, to paraphrase Pascal, mistakenly taken the geometric mind as the model for thinking about human concerns. According to Musil, the logical scaffolding of rigidly defined concepts results in a falsification of moral thinking. Deducing categories creates a moral system, not ethical vision, and as such is ultimately inimical to moral insight. I will return to Musil's thoughts about ethics in the next chapter, but here it should be stressed that, according to him, scientific epistemology is not a direct source for thinking about moral reform. Rather, science sets the rational limits for humanist and ethical thinking; but it cannot entertain the complexity that ethics demands.

There may be one exception to this statement about complexity, offered by statistical models with their reduction of complexity to probabilistic laws. After Emerson Musil constantly wondered if human behavior could be explained by the kind of model that charted the general movement of molecules with near certainty, although it can make no predictions with regard to any given molecule. (We saw that he parodies himself on this issue in *The Enthusiasts*.) But statistical mechanics is only one model among others that Musil considers. Starting with the early essays, he draws frequent comparisons in which science, ethics, aesthetics, and politics meet and hopefully illuminate each other by contrast. Because Musil often contrasts the rational procedures of science with other areas of human inquiry, many critics have drawn up a dichotomous picture of his writing in which reason and nonreason stand in polar opposition. But this is a misreading of Musil's understanding of the complexity of human knowledge. He may start with science as a model, but this is to stress that there are numerous and complex areas about which science has little or nothing to say. Nonreason does not necessarily stand in rigid opposition to reason, nor does Musil ever endorse the binary oppositions that some critics impose upon him—perhaps under the influence of the kind of structuralist thought that finds that binary oppositions define all areas of experience.

Many things can be defined in contrast to science, but difference and contrast are not the same as "opposition."

If we resist the temptation to see oppositions in Musil, then we can see that he often plays with dichotomies in his turns of phrase. Yet these oppositions undo themselves, as, for example, when Musil writes in 1913 in "Politisches Bekenntnis eines jungen Mannes" ("Political Confessions of a Young Man"), "There is a type of thinking that creates truth; clear like a sewing machine it sets down stitch after stitch. And there is a type of thinking that makes one happy" (4:1009). It would be an error to reduce this felicitous witticism to a dichotomous description of poetry and science, for Musil goes on to show that happiness encompasses a myriad of thoughts, and that no simple contrast can possibly encompass this mental state. The latter opens up, in fact, on the mountain to be scaled by the mind that refuses the certainties of science, a mind in this case taking pleasure in its own nearness to madness. Or, to recall Pascal, the mind in its nongeometrical workings, deals with infinite complication, not with neat dichotomies.

In fact in the 1913 essay "Moralische Fruchtbarkeit" ("Moral Fruitfulness") Musil is quite clear about his view of oppositions. Here he analyzes some of the semantic games played by those who make concepts into polar opposites. The creation of opposites offers the illusion that one has grasped substantial entities categorizing the world of real behavior—such as good and evil or hate and love—when in fact the appearances that might qualify as, say, good or evil or both can lend themselves to a gamut of interpretations that are in no way in opposition. Rather, one confronts "parallel appearances" (8:1002) that must be analyzed in their individuality. This essay shows Mach's influence, in a nuanced way, in that Musil refuses simply to accept definitions but rather insists that appearances and concepts often do not correspond in any exact manner. In this regard he plainly states that the desire to order everything in terms of dichotomies "corresponds to an earlier mode of thinking" that is hardly scientific (8:1003). Good and evil, for example, are ways of saying that something should be combated or something should be encouraged—which in itself may be a true contrast, he adds. In this essay Musil aims at showing the falsification of experience that thinking imposes upon experience when it uses a priori dichotomous concepts. From Musil's viewpoint the mind must learn to view what is the case in its specific complexity.

This caveat about dichotomies clarifies an earlier point made with regard to "Sketch of a Poet's Knowledge." Here Musil says that a description of science, or the "ratioïd" domain, offers the best starting point in order to understand the "non-ratioïd" areas of human experience. The contrast of the two domains does not open up onto a simple dichotomous opposition of poetic and scientific knowledge but rather points out that in contrast to science stands the multifarious world of experience whose complexity cannot be reduced to what can be expressed by an algorithm. Musil seems to draw again on the Pascalian notion of complexity when he maintains that one cannot have an adequate representation of even a simple sentence such as "He wanted it" without an infinite number of supplementary phrases to make sense of it (8:1027). Complexity here is not a semantic question such as postmodern deconstruction defines it by pointing out that everything can be defined by everything else. Musil does not have the dictionary in mind. Rather, his view of complexity is based on the way every experience is embedded in other unique experiences that maintain endless relations with other experiences. Science—at least some sciences—enjoys the security of a fixed point from which it proceeds to order repeating experiences. All other domains of knowledge float without that fixed point; they are multifarious and fluctuating and thus, according to Musil, are the subject of essayistic inquiries in which the mind knows that it is pursuing an individual quest among an indefinite number of competing possibilities.

What Musil deplores in his essays is that, in his experience, scientific knowledge no longer had any contact with other forms of thinking, and especially with ethics and evaluation. This separation of science from other domains of thought has often been accompanied by the reduction of reason to mere "economic reason," or what we earlier saw as pragmatism. In the 1912 essay "Das Geistliche, der Modernismus und die Metaphysik" ("The Religious Spirit, Modernism, and Metaphysics") Musil indicted modernity for its separation of reason from all areas of inquiry except its instrumental role of determining narrow truths. With the demise of the Enlightenment belief in the universal power of reason, he believed that reason had become an instrumental tool limited to judging reality and truth. One no longer asks if the truth reason perceives is desirable or not. One does not ask if its truth should be promoted. This critique of reason recalls Nietzsche's belief that truth should be in the service of life and, hence, truth can be judged on other grounds than its correspondence to reality. I am not sure that Musil is as Nietzschean as this formulation suggests, for his anger is directed specifically against the belief that the market economy is the determining locus of value and truth. In this sense he is in fact indignant that the value of a truth, other than economic, has become an almost incomprehensible idea for modern humanity.

In this essay on modernism and metaphysics Musil sets out the type of cultural criticism that he develops throughout his subsequent work. The answer to the demise of scientific reason is not, as many of his contemporaries believed, to promote more "feeling" in cultural life, however true it may be that the lack of feeling has transformed modern European culture, in its "free time," into something resembling a fairground—a *Rummelplatz* (8:989). Or, to offer another choice metaphor, the cultivation of the excess of feeling turns culture into a formless "jelly" that, though sweet, offers little nourishment (8:989). Musil's ironic indignation is directed against the reduction of culture to clichés, which is to say, culture has become the reproduction of stereotyped feelings. The result is the reign of universal kitsch for which he has nothing but contempt. Already in 1912 Musil's unfettered irony resonates with the disgust he felt for the trends of a culture in which he finds that scientific culture offers not only the only reliable knowledge, but also the only worthy activity. Otherwise he finds little in his culture but the exaltation of feeling. This exaltation has ended up, as Musil puts it sardonically, promoting a superficial religiosity that in the best of cases creates an "oversoul that reads the newspaper and announces it has a certain understanding for social questions" (8:989).

In this prewar essay on the religious spirit and modernism, Musil is quite pessimistic about what one can expect from European culture. Science is successful within its domain but has renounced its Enlightenment expectations. All that remains is metaphysics—such as monism, spiritualism, idealism—and with this Musil summarily dismisses transcendental thinking, especially Kantian metaphysics, as simply boring (8:991). He finds that metaphysics is false, science is too limited, and the church now endorses crass bourgeois values that have undermined whatever value it may once have had. Such is modernity for Musil in 1912. His dismissal of metaphysics has a positivist ring to it, though he was never committed to the Viennese positivist idea that the only meaning of a statement consists in showing the procedure for its verification. But however disgruntled his skeptical distrust of metaphysics had made him, it had for Musil, as for the Viennese positivists around him, felicitous political consequences: after the First World War they all rejected the nationalist abstractions that became the mainstay of political discourse in Germany.

After the war Musil's cultural criticism took as its main target the misleading generalizations about the nature of culture and society that were creating the ideological chaos in which nationalist reactionaries could eventually triumph over communist revolutionaries, not to mention liberals and social democrats. This cultural criticism is well illustrated by Musil's essay of 1921 on the well-known historian Oswald Spengler. The essay, titled "Geist und Erfahrung" ("Mind and Experience"), has the ironic subtitle "Anmerkungen für Leser, welche dem Untergang des Abendlandes entronnen sind"—or roughly, "Notes for Readers Who Have Escaped the Decline of the West." The title itself is sufficient to point up Musil's dismissal of Spengler's pessimistic and "deterministic" reading of Occidental culture in its decadence. From Musil's perspective Spengler sets forth, in his pretense at science, an exemplary misuse of axiomatic thinking to try to understand human complexity while promoting the right-wing nationalist ideology that was coming to dominate much of German intellectual life. Spengler's supposed use of science to prove the decline of the West was largely sham. As Jeffrey Herf has observed in his insightful study of reactionary modernism in Germany, Spengler was an irrationalist who actually believed that science killed the understanding and wanted to promote the idea that there was an "unbridgeable chasm" between reason and feeling.[6] In spite of his pretensions to scientific rigor, Spengler was an anti-Enlightenment thinker who, in actually promoting myth, devalued liberal democratic values by affirming the supreme values of "blood and instinct."[7] In short Spengler represented everything Musil could not abide.

In his critique of Spengler's misunderstanding of science, Musil describes different confusions made because of misleading ways of thinking. To make his point about Spengler's misleading analogies, he draws upon his prewar essays, especially the distinction of "ratioïd" and "non-ratioïd." Notably, he turns to the question of empiricism, for, according to him, it is obvious that Spengler does not want to let any empirical evidence get in the way of his thesis that the West is undergoing decline. The Anglo-American reader, if educated in science, may take it as a matter of course that all meaningful knowledge must in some sense respect empirical experience. And so does Musil, for he duly notes that no serious philosophy can make a claim for knowledge that contradicts experience (8:1047). In the German context he makes this assertion in order to contend with the widespread idea that empiricism is somehow an impoverished form of philosophy—an idea entertained by Ulrich later in *The Man without Qualities*. Behind the German critique of empiricism lies the idea that it does not recognize the active role that mind or "spirit" plays in formulating knowledge—a notion nourished by both Kantian and Hegelian views of mind.

Musil is not always a strict empiricist. At time he formulates the idea that mind or *Geist* occupies a mediating position. Mind mediates between the belief that only atomic facts constitute knowledge and the viewpoint according to which only syntheses created by the autonomous mind are meaningful. As defined in "Mind and Experience," mind does not stand in opposition to experience, nor does it, as many German thinkers held, operate beyond experience. Musil posits that the mind should be able to find both general laws and values in sensations and feelings that derive from individual experience. Hence, they are true to experience. He now appears to be endorsing Mach as well as the skeptical empiricist philosopher David Hume. This reversal of his position in his dissertation points toward Musil's ongoing search for a satisfactory way to define mind. He wants to account for it as the active agent that probes experience and relies on experience, while maintaining skepticism about the mind's capacity to reach absolute certainty. As Dagmar Barnouw has pointed out in the illuminating essay on Hume and Musil I referred to earlier, the approval of Hume is not surprising: Hume sets out in his own writing a model of the essayistic form suitable for promoting a skeptical science of human beings that does not fall prey to abstract a priori constructs. Against all German metaphysicians before and after him, Hume believed that by positing the human subject as a purely rational subject, epistemology becomes "abstruse" and devoid of concrete substance.[8] In other words, after his negative reaction to Hume in his dissertation, Musil was ready to use his skepticism about metaphysics in his reaction to Spengler's irrationalism.

Musil's essay on Spengler also makes clear that Musil rejects the use of dichotomous thinking and a priori binary oppositions that are often the basis for metaphysics. In Spengler's vision of decadence the notions of rise and fall offer an example of an a priori binary opposition. Rising and falling is a metaphysical construct used for describing the course of human history. Binary oppositions construct fictions, which Musil also explicitly criticizes in the use of the opposition of rational and antirational. Simplifying polarities are simply inadequate for describing the complex ways by which the mind finds knowledge (8:1050). Musil's view of writers and their relation to knowledge is especially interesting. If scientific writers can more or less be grouped together for their rational methodology, nonscientific writers such as historians, poets, and essayists cannot be easily classified under one rubric, because their work is not strictly speaking based upon *Erkenntnis,* or knowledge, in the scientific sense (8:1049). Citing writers as diverse as Hippolyte Taine, Thomas Babington Macaulay, Novalis, Emerson, and Nietzsche, Musil claims that the individual nature of their work is what is primary. These historians, poets, and essayists offer a unique specificity that he sees as the essence of literary or humanistic knowledge. They propose "representations that have not the firm foundation of sense perception or of pure rationality" but rather "are founded upon feelings and impressions that can only with difficulty be repeated" (8:1049). This domain of the nonrecurrent impression is what he again called the "non-ratioïd" —a term so ungainly that one suspects he coined it with a certain ironic intent. As suggested by the essay on Spengler, the term is intended to break the hold on our mind operated by the simple binary opposition of rational and antirational or irrational. Beyond this opposition Musil aims at undoing the opposition of Enlightenment rationality and romantic irrationality in order to suggest that mind is more capacious that either party may have thought and that one side of the opposition need not annul the other.

Musil wants to undo the unthinking power of what I call "ping-pong concepts," or concepts that in discussions of the most varied domains one inevitably bounces like a ball from one side to the other of the semantic playing field. Simple semantic movement acquires explanatory power as one side bounces off of the other. Nature and culture are such a pair of ping-pong opposites, for each means everything that the other does not. Musil points out that Spengler conflates these terms by saying nature is a product of culture, from which it then follows that everything, from time and space to mathematics, is a cultural construct. Musil mocks this vacuous idea, since it is transparent to him that many things do not depend upon human culture for their existence, including the objects of most of the sciences. (The sociobiologist today reverses the movement by claiming culture is a product of nature.) In pointing out Spengler's semantic games Musil underscores the way misleading analogies lead to absurd conclusions. His irony in this regard was never sharper. For instance, ridiculing Spengler's comparisons, he laconically argues that if both certain species of insects and the Chinese may be described as yellow, there is nonetheless an important difference to be noted in that the Chinese, and not butterflies, invented gunpowder. Not all comparisons are significant; few are, in fact, since anything can be compared with anything else.

Musil's skeptical critique shows that misleading analogies are the stuff of political ideology and the metaphysics underwriting it. In his demonstration, moreover, he wants his reader to see that his strictures on epistemology do not simply derive from abstract lessons in the theory of knowledge but from a rational attempt to think coherently about important human concerns such as ideology and politics. Some of Musil's critics have failed to grasp the nature of his attempt to think without preconceptions, especially those who come to their task with a ready-made ideology themselves. They fail to understand that Musil, as an intellectual committed to critique as a mode of thought, believed the writer must maintain distance vis-à-vis the object of analysis, however much outside his writing he may be committed to the object of his inquiry, such as democracy and democratic ideals.

As a thinker, the politically liberal Musil was, for most of his life, a conservative by temperament but also a utopian who looked upon society with a view to what it should be, not to what it unfortunately was. In fine there were no sacred cows for him. Guntram Vogt has made this point in his study of Musil and democracy, recalling that it was precisely because Musil "measured democracies according to their possibilities that he could not be satisfied with their reality."[9] Therefore, if skeptical Musil criticized democratic societies along with totalitarian ideologies, it was because he was not only a democrat but also an intellectual committed to his task.

In his first essays Musil makes another connection between politics and epistemology, which is suggested by the common historical development of European democracy and science. He examines this theme in "Political Confessions of a Young Man." He starts with the idea, or perhaps axiom in this context, that politics derives from culture (8:993). From this premise it may be argued that science and scientific epistemology have developed as consequences of the development of the culture of democracy. Democracy as a political activity necessarily demands an open public forum in which truth values can be debated by all. (This, I note, is an idea promoted by modern thinkers from Karl Popper to Jürgen Habermas.) This openness to debate has in turn promoted the rise of debate in all areas of culture, leading to the recognition that open debate is the foundation of the pursuit of truth in all its forms. In this way, Musil proposes, scientific culture originated in democratic culture. Moreover, it can be argued that in the course of history the necessity of open debate for scientific culture then contributed in turn to the ongoing development of democratic politics. This latter statement is not so much a deduction as an empirical observation, for it appears that the development of democratic societies has almost everywhere been accompanied by demands that society respect something like scientific epistemology, even as the development of scientific epistemology then seems historically to accompany the demand for democratically open societies. The operation of an open public forum is in fact the description of operational objectivity from a scientific point of view. Therefore, it is a presupposition for democratic government. In fine Musil comes to democracy from a commitment to science.

This point suggests, however, that Musil was not at first a democrat of the heart, as he puts it himself. He says he was certainly not convinced by the beliefs of the philosopher of democratic brotherhood, Jean-Jacques Rousseau. Musil is skeptical of Rousseau and notes that he does not find democracy to originate in the ideal that all men are brothers—a belief that in 1913 he finds to be a sentimental exaggeration. Rather he is a democrat of the intellect who finds that science is a result of democracy and that, under the influence of science, democracy has opened up society so that more and more people have come to work together in common ways, against all aristocratic prejudice, in recognition of individual talent (8:1011). It is in this regard that Musil the individualist recognizes that he himself is a product of democracy—"ein Geschöpf der Democratie" (8:1011).

Since it is true that not everybody could have or would have made this claim in the Austro-Hungarian Empire of 1913, one may wonder how Musil thought it came about that he was a democrat. Of course, many of the empire's civil servants, such as Musil's family, were committed to the liberal ideals of the Enlightenment, and one might think that it was by being born into the liberal bourgeoisie that he could situate himself as a man molded by democratic institutions. But he takes a different tack to explain how he became a democrat. He begins this confessional essay of 1913 with a splendidly ironic presentation of himself as a young man who is born into a world in which at first he more or less accepts the monarchist ideology of his environment. As he puts it, he accepted the status quo in which the government was supposed to function much like the servants that serve you: they do it badly, but they do it without question. The monarchist worldview was entertaining, moreover, for it provided him with a constant spectacle of disparities between reality and pretense; between, on the one hand, the image of the rich who can find no spiritually meaningful way to use their wealth and, on the other hand, the image that the rich project of themselves as comic insects that make much noise but only produce it because they have a hairy little air sac. In comparable fashion he enjoyed the disparity between the image of a church nobody believed in and the image of a state based on a religion that nobody wanted to get rid of. Less amusingly the empire also provided an image that aroused Musil's sense of social justice, for he saw around him the poor suffering in impoverished silence. He describes them as part of a vertical chain of beings that goes from Musil, situated at the apex, downward to the beasts, "and actually from the animals even farther down, since no species of animal lives in such un-animal conditions as the inhuman conditions in which many humans live" (8:1010). In brief the social conditions of the monarchy made Musil aware of social injustice in his youth. We might say, then, that he also became a democrat by reaction to the concrete conditions around him.

"Political Confessions of a Young Man" gives the impression that the young Musil was not at first inclined to think about politics, and we may well imagine that it was ethics, not inclination, that obliged him to confront the topic. Ulrich faces a comparable dilemma. However, the fact that this confessional essay was written several years after *Young Törless,* and its savage portrait of psychological forces at work in the empire, suggests that Musil is creating a foil character in his essay portraying contraries. He offers as a foil to the democrat the portrait of a dilettantish bourgeois young man coming to awareness that he lives in a society in which not only are the aristocratic rich ridiculous in their uselessness, and the poor intolerably miserable, but also the general conditions of culture do not promote the welfare of anybody, not even a well-off bourgeois. In other words the conditions are so bad that even the young bourgeois could be shocked into awareness, though I frankly doubt that Musil himself was so aloof from social conditions.

The impression that Musil creates a foil in "Political Confessions of a Young Man" is reinforced when one compares it to an essay he wrote the preceding year. In "Politik in Österreich" ("Politics in Austria"), he deals with the political predicament of the multicultural Austrian empire. The essay does not suggest that he was just beginning to understand Austria's problems—on the contrary. In "Politics in Austria" he deplores, in measured but ironic terms, that the empire has no human purpose, only an "Austrian goal" (8:993), which is the preservation of a state that does not have a middle class or *Bürgertum* that can create a meaningful political life (8:995). The word *Bürgertum* is tricky in this context, for it can mean both the liberal middle class or bourgeoisie embodying Enlightenment values and the general class of citizens capable of participating in political life, something like the enlightened citizenry. The Enlightenment bourgeoisie saw itself as a class embodying universal values. Once accepted and put into practice, these values made of every enlightened individual a member of the citizenry who could participate in politics. With the idea of *Bürgertum* Musil may be alluding to this class as a precondition for democratic politics. Democracy demands citizens possessing enlightenment to be democrats, which is something of a necessary tautology to describe how a democracy can function only if its citizens are capable of performing their civic tasks.

By contrast Musil goes on to say that Austria, with its waning feudal regime and isolated liberal circles, offers a far different example of political life than one based on enlightenment. It is a state in which "one lives his political life like a Serbian heroic epic, because heroism is the most impersonal form of action" (8:995). Musil alludes here to the strange mixture of clan mentality and feudal theatricality characterizing public life that could be found throughout an empire embracing eighteen different provinces from today's Ukraine and Poland to parts of Italy and Croatia. No unifying idea based on reason or tradition tied this collection of provinces and ethnic groups together; and Musil found no reason for the empire's existence. He notes parenthetically that the empire might have been justified as an experiment in the creation of an international state—but Musil also knew that this was an idea that was ahead of its time (8:993). With lucidity he foresees the disappearance of the empire even as he muses on a multinational union that might transcend dubious national ideologies that are bent on destroying it.

The Austrian Republic, declared in November 1918, was a republic in which apparently most German-speaking Austrians, including Musil, wanted to be annexed by Germany. Musil's pessimism about Austria's chances of becoming a political democracy was deep, for he saw no political class capable of creating a democratic culture. This viewpoint is expressed, for example, in the 1919 essay "Buridans Österreicher" ("Buridan's Austrian"), the title of which proposes the ironic image of an Austrian who, wanting to choose between belonging to Germany or to a Danube federation, is like Buridan's ass of philosophic fame, an animal that risks starving to death when placed between two equally attractive piles of hay, since the power of attraction is equally strong in each direction. This is Musil's view of the situation created by imposing a specifically Austrian political and cultural existence upon a population that had until then regarded itself as somehow above mere national politics. Vienna had been an international capital—indeed, the inheritor of the Holy Roman Empire during the early reign of the Hapsburgs. And that, according to Musil, did not create such a thing as an Austrian national culture. He goes on to argue that one cannot meaningfully speak of an Austrian culture that is somehow different from German culture. (Certainly Musil thought of himself as a German, not an Austrian, writer.) Whatever is significant in Austrian culture is, for Musil, either international by nature or encoded in the German language. Both these aspects of culture—roughly categorized by the poles of science and literature—depend upon the material culture that assures the production of cultural goods. And Musil roundly deplores the lack of material culture in his native land.

By *culture* Musil ultimately means those products a society produces to assure intellectual and spiritual life. He strongly believes that Austria does not offer much of anything in this regard, especially when compared with Germany, with its universities, scientific institutions, libraries, publishers, and the like. Musil may not be entirely fair in this regard, though one cannot fail to be impressed by the passion with which he doubts that Austria can exist as a political state, based on a supposedly unique culture. Since a political state for Musil has no purpose except to promote human welfare, which is to say, justice and culture, Austria has little point in existing as a political entity. Having thus dismissed the idea that it can be a meaningful political state—for it has no culture that might justify its existence—Musil finds, with superb irony, that perhaps the best thing to do with little Austria would be to make a big nature park out of it.

Vienna had been for several decades a center for European modernism; and one may well ask why Musil did not think that the achievements of Austrian artists and thinkers resulted in the creation of an Austrian culture. The answer is that Viennese modernist achievements were part of European culture. For Musil, if there were such a thing as Austrian culture, it was encapsulated in Viennese kitsch and *Heimatliteratur*—novels about peasants living in the Alps. Though polemical, Musil was not eccentric nor alone, then or now, in his doubts about the existence of a sui generis Austrian culture. Historian Steven Beller claims that the belief in the creation of a national culture never flourished in Vienna, as it did in Prague, Budapest, and Kraków, cities in the empire that were inflamed with the passions of nationalism and an accompanying belief in cultural revival. As Beller puts it, the attempt to create an Austrian culture "never carried much conviction," especially among the many intellectuals, scientists, and artists in Vienna who were of a cosmopolitan Jewish background.[10] The lack of nationalism in the center of the empire, a center of modernism, prevented anyone creative from indulging in the idea that there could be something desirable about creating a specifically Austrian culture. Musil, in complete self-awareness, is as good example of this refusal of the provincialism called nationalism as are Freud, Kafka, Rilke, Arthur Schnitzler, Adolf Loos, or dozens of thinkers and writers who were fundamental in the elaboration of modern science, mathematics, philosophy, literature, music, and art.

What Musil shares with many Viennese modernists is his cultural internationalism, which underlies his strong belief that the creation of something larger than the nationalist state should be the goal of political activity. Only this international state can correspond to the cosmopolitanism that makes for meaningful culture, such as Musil himself embodies it. Culture should be a goal of politics, even as politics derives from culture. Culture is a tricky concept, misleading in nearly any language, and I think the problem that the concept poses explains why Musil tried to develop a parallel concept, especially after the war, to enlarge the sphere of what one means by culture, the source of politics.

In this regard he returned frequently to the concept of *Geist* for its philosophical overtones, which, I have suggested, Musil used to mean at once mind and spirit, or reason endowed with emotion and emotion informed by thought. All of the notions meld into something like what he took to be the goal of epistemology: a theory of mind knowing itself. Inevitably, this goal sounds Hegelian, in spite of Musil or of Kant, for the term *Geist* carries with it a suggestion, in many German thinkers, of a dynamic faculty capable of shaping the

174

human understanding of reality. Influenced by anthropology, however, Musil used the term to mean something like "collective mind," the collection of basic beliefs and perceptions that inform the way a given society perceives and deals with reality. *Geist,* then, sounds much like a synonym for culture. This is all made more complex by the fact that Musil, ever the moral sociologist, at times uses the *Geist* descriptively—to describe what mind actually is—but perhaps more often he uses it prescriptively, to suggest what mind or culture should be.

Consider in this light the essay of 1918 on the writer Franz Blei, in which Musil posits that all spiritual movements, be they religious or expressionist, are the displacement of something in the world's *Geist.* This is an awkward formulation, and Musil is quite aware that he sounds as if he were endorsing a Hegelian position according to which history is the necessary development of absolute spirit or mind (translations of Hegel's *Geist* vary). But he is not endorsing Hegel, even if he speaks approvingly of the "Hegelian synthesis." His examples show that he is talking about the complex makeup of culture in its historical development, without the causal metaphysics motivating the necessary development of Hegelian history.[11] It is true that Musil recognizes that mind has an historical dimension, since it includes forms of understanding that change in time. Musil is willing to argue that understanding has made progress in its history going from, say, ancient Greek thinker Thales to modern physicist Einstein. But if the mind's faculty of understanding undergoes historical development, as Musil says, other aspects of mind do not. These aspects are the incalculable, nondevelopmental, contradictory "fundamental feelings" that nonetheless endow the mind with the quality of being historically alive or dead (8:1023). In using a historical schema to characterize partially the development of mind, Musil wants to account for the fact that there is an historical interplay between intellect and feelings, and this interplay means that we accept certain ideas and values and not others at specific historical times. (Thales accepted slavery, for example, but Einstein did not.) For this purpose terms such as *mind, culture,* or *Geist* are not important in themselves, at least according to this 1918 essay on Blei, in which Musil admits that *Geist* could be replaced by another term, such as *soul, culture, feeling-disposition,* or *domain of values* (8:1023). The important thing is that it be a designation for the product of historical development of intellect and feeling, concepts and value. In fine *Geist*—and I prefer *mind* as a translation—is an all-embracing, dynamic historical concept that Musil the essayist can describe because he finds it in himself. Mind lives in Musil, so to speak, and thus he experiences it directly as a living presence that it is his task as essayist to articulate so that understanding serves feeling for purposes of human happiness—for "menschlichen Seligkeit" (8:1024).

From this perspective one can thus understand that Musil wishes to exclude from mind the irrational caprices of nationalist ideologies as well as the dead sediments of beliefs and feelings that are no longer tenable.

In his provocative essay of 1919, "Der Anschluss an Deutschland" ("Anschluss with Germany"), Musil argued in favor melding Austria with Germany, and he did so through another critique of the idea of *Geist*. He critically confronts the idea that in the collective mind is found the expression of the essence of a nation. That a nation exists as a determining locus for culture is a stock metaphysical idea that has animated nationalist movements for the past two centuries, but Musil does not directly take up this viewpoint in his critique. Rather, weighing this idea, he concedes that it not inaccurate to speak at times of the *Geist* of the German, Austrian, or French state, just as it is not inaccurate to speak of an esprit de corps, or the spirit of belonging to a collectivity, say, an army regiment. And he further concedes that the "spirit" of a state or a regiment is something more than the "mind" of an individual in the social group (8:1034). But, he goes on to argue, this collective spirit is of less importance than the individual mind, since the spirit of the social collective is almost always running at a distance behind the minds of the most creative individuals in that collective. The mind of the collective group does not, therefore, include the minds of all of the individuals in that collective. The lack of coincidence is illustrated by the way that creative individuals are often condemned by the collective morality or the laws of a social group—such as Dostoyevsky in Russia, Flaubert in France, and Oscar Wilde in England, to cite several of Musil's pointedly international examples—showing the conflict between the national spirit and the individual mind. It is a conflict born of the fact that the collective spirit is often historically retrograde, which means it cannot include every mind in it. Hence it is a general concept of limited usefulness.

From his essayistic perspective Musil is not unmindful of those who argue that the individual is incapable of shaping the development of culture because he or she is shaped by that very culture. In various essays on nation and culture he examines this idea, weighs it, and finally counters it in order to loosen up the hold it has on the mind. There is something a bit vertiginous about examining a theory of mind to free the mind from it, to free the mind from limiting itself. This task is part of his essayistic approach to abstraction in general. And one inevitably recalls Mach when one sees that his essays parallel the work positivism did in undermining belief in metaphysical absolutes—which can include such abstractions as culture, nation, and state. Musil examines what one can mean by these abstract notions in order to argue that moral and political progress is possible only if we refuse to be blocked by metaphysical absolutes. There is no transcendental metaphysical construct called the Austrian state nor, by implication, Austrian culture, and thus Austrians, like anybody else, should feel free to entertain the possibility of new ideas, political and cultural, and to determine the shape of their political life.

Musil returns consistently in his writings to the position that the individual is the only ultimate reality in discussions of society. No state, culture, or any other social group can exist without concrete individuals. It is in the context of his thought about the individual that we can cast additional light on why he was fascinated by statistical mechanics, especially when he thought about it in a positive way. The comments he makes on individual activity, within the confines of a collective group, implicitly echoes what a physicist such as Boltzmann said about a closed system such as an enclosed gas. The gas does not exist as an abstract entity, anymore than a society, for it exists as a group of individual moving molecules. No single individual is subject to determinism, though the gas as a whole obeys probabilistic laws. This example, ever present in Musil's mind, allows him to frame mental experiments in which the model might be applied to social questions to describe the way in which a million individual decisions result in "single" historical events. The model of statistical probability, he implies, can mediate between the abstract idea of a collective human configuration and the reality of multitudes of free or undetermined individuals. In thinking about social collectives in terms of statistical mechanics, Musil carried on what mathematical physicists had done before him, but by reversing the perspective. The earlier physicists had adapted Quételet's statistical work on social phenomena to purely physical phenomena. In other words physicists such as James Clerk Maxwell and Boltzmann used Quételet's invention of population statistics and his notion of the average man as a model for finding the statistical laws governing the conduct of the average molecule in their studies of the physics of gases.[12]

To return to our considerations of Musil's essay arguing for the merging of Austria with Germany, we should note the intellectual freedom with which he examines the notion of nation and argues that the Austrian example provides an example of what a nation is not. With bemused irony he points out that the region of the two monarchies unofficially called Austria but officially called Zisleithanien (in English, "Cisleithania," from the name of the river Leitha that separates lower Austria from Hungary) from 1867 until 1918 was neither a nation nor a state, nor could *Geist* be attributed to it. Musil mockingly uses the official name for the Austrian part of the Austro-Hungarian Empire, which was the only name that could be employed legally. It was a name virtually nobody used, and probably few knew. Composed of fifteen regions, this composite empire pointed up by its very existence the arbitrary nature of political entities, often imposed by optical perspectives, as it were (8:1039), underscoring how arbitrary was the idea of an Austrian state and, consequently, that of a national culture. In short, history shows that the idea of a political state is often an arbitrary construct—like the comic-opera construct of Cistleithania.

In concluding the essay on *Anschluss,* Musil makes a distinction between two ways of speaking of culture: the culture of mind (*geistiger Kultur*) and the culture of life-forms (8:1041). In the culture of mind he includes the means of the production of intellectual, scientific, and artistic life that promote the spiritual life of the mind. By the culture of life-forms he means something like lifestyle. He sees, at least in Austria, that the two realms are separated and that spiritual or "authentic" culture does not merge with the average cultural style found in Austria. Musil as physicist and mathematician is quick to recognize that the notion of "average" is not always useful, since it has little to do with what individuals—people or molecules—actually are or do. But his point about two cultures has apparently offended some critics who are ideologically committed to postmodern cultural egalitarianism. He views the culture of mind as authentic culture, which can also be called "high culture." Musil's affirmation of authentic culture is part of his critique of the erosion of cultural values produced by modernity. He does not believe that every lifestyle or material culture is equal. Quite simply, the chaos he sees produced by modernity's leveling has not produced a culture in which needs are fulfilled. Musil suggests that only through the promotion of mind, in its authentic manifestations, does the human community have a chance to find the means to think through the dilemmas it faces in the wake of the Enlightenment's demise.

Moreover, Musil's critique of the abstract idea of the state entails the rejection of the belief that it is the supreme embodiment of mind. This critique was, and is, destined to offend all the sides of the ideological spectrum. Marxists derived a version of this belief from Hegel in their promotion of the proletariat as the supreme embodiment of the future stateless state. Hegel can also be viewed as the progenitor of the fascists and Nazis who exalted a violent caricature of the idea of the supremacy of the state. (Of course, Hegel was no protofascist, any more than was Nietzsche, but ideas do have consequences.) Weighing the idea that the state is the supreme embodiment of mind, Musil's essayistic strategy is to put forth the counteridea that the state cannot really do much to promote mind. Hence the state can do little to promote the authentic culture that might result from the development of mind. Neither the Left nor the Right could applaud this counterdemonstration. But Musil's proposition is empirically grounded, for he can find no examples of how a state ever actually embodied mind or culture. He stresses this in the conclusion of his essay arguing for Austria's *Anschluss;* he affirms that the culture of a state does not arise from the average culture and cultural capacities of its inhabitants. Against this point he concedes that the social structure, as well as many other material factors, can play a role in the creation of culture: "It [culture] does not consist in the production of spiritual values because of the state, but in the creation of facilities that enable their production by individual people and secure the real possibility of new spiritual values" (8:1042). Musil skeptically observes that the state can be a facilitator, but that is rather much the limit of what it can accomplish. Since Germany had shown that the state can do much materially, Austria would do well to become part of a political union with a state that actually has promoted the material conditions conducive to the individual mind and culture.

Musil is dealing in the essay on the *Anschluss* with the most basic political question, which is to say, how to form the political state that will promote human values and culture. Attendant upon this question in the climate of nationalism after the war is the question of what is a nation, and how does a nation give shape to a political state and a culture—terms used interchangeably, then and now, in many political discourses. However, Musil knows that, in spite of two centuries of nationalist rhetoric, there is nothing self-evident about what constitutes a nation or why a nation—if such a thing even exists— and a political state should coincide. In "Anschluss with Germany" he looks for a working definition of a nation, since the merging of Austrian and German might create a new nation or perhaps simply recognize an old nation. In seeking to shed light on what a nation might be, Musil rejects the mystical idea that attracted many nationalists among Germans who thought that their Teutonic soul might be the basis for a state. In fact, says Musil, the nation appears to have no intrinsic rapport with an ethnic group. This is because a nation does not really have any kind of unity that can be perceived from outside its own self-perceived boundaries. I think Musil's point is that the community exists when it perceives itself to exist. In making this subtle point he uses both *Gesellschaft* and *Gemeinde* to speak of a community (8:1035). By using two emotion-charged terms for society and community to suggest that both mean rather much the same thing, it seems he wants to defuse ideologically loaded terms. Clearly, he is not using any single sociological or ideological theory in his analysis of community (though Johann Gottfried von Herder's distant influence is inevitable). Basically, in his examination of concepts Musil wants to find the lowest common denominator for any meaningful usage of the concept of nation, he says, one that can be accepted by humanists or communists (8:1035).

If a nation exists only when it perceives itself to exist, this means that it does not coincide with any piece of landscape (which deflates all claims to natural boundaries). By default, for an observer exterior to the community a common language might be the key to what a nation is. Perhaps by *nation* one can mean an organized community based on language. Nationalist minorities had pressed this point, before the war, in a world in which national boundaries often coincided with multilingual empires. However, after the Great War the victorious Allies divided up the German and Austro-Hungarian empires in order to create nation-states, based on a common language, where a year earlier there was an international community. Musil judges this not to have been a successful enterprise. To him it is obvious that France and England carved up the empires in pursuit of their own interest, creating nations to maintain what these victors saw as the balance of power in their favor. Languages and nations did not coincide in many cases, and it was probably impossible that they do so.

Musil's reflections on the relations of nation, culture, and the mind culminate in his major essay of 1921, "Die Nation als Ideal und als Wirklichkeit" ("Nation as Ideal and as Reality"). The idea—or ideal—of the nation has a relatively short but homicidal history. It is worth recalling that Musil himself had been caught up in the temporary psychosis that belief in a national ideal can cause and that he later recognized that belief in the defense of the nation could also be a rationalization for the desire to escape from the limits of society in a violent conflation. By 1921 he had psychological distance from the murderous manifestation of nationalism that Europe had recently experienced. Like somebody awakening from slumber, Musil thus begins "Nation as Ideal and as Reality" by weighing the idea that in some important sense the nation has a reality. It is not a fiction as some think; or if it is, it is a fiction having real consequences, such as the recent war. Thus it behooves one to ask who caused the war: was it a nation? The answer is not difficult, Musil observes, in observing that many in Germany are willing to place the responsibility for the war on the kaiser, the generals, or the diplomats. However, consonant with his belief that society behaves as its individual members behave, he asks who undertook the war, and he answers, "Naturally we did it, we let it happen, it happened without being stopped by us. On our side as on the other" (8:1062). Accepting this responsibility, Musil then considers how it came about that masses of individuals let a massacre that demanded a great deal of collective effort happen. He answers himself with the following idea: "A people is the sum of its individuals plus their organization" (8:1063). Beyond the sphere of individuals, their organization can take on a life of its own so that collective enterprises such as war take place. Organization, in the form of the political state, has a material reality. This totality of a people plus its organization can explain the fact that the will of the collective is not the same as the sum of the will of its individuals, for in addition to the people therein one must account for the state bureaucracy, the media, economic institutions and forces, and a host of other institutional powers that inflect the expression of will of what one commonly calls a nation or a people.

Musil then turns to examine what is the nature of the "people" in question. He prefers the term *nation* to *people—Volk—*for good reasons, since right-wing nationalists were already monopolizing *Volk* to express the idea that the German nation is a mystical unity based on "blood." And precisely this appeal to blood, which is to say, to race, in order to define the nation obliges Musil then to ask whether a nation and a race are the same thing.

By 1921 the question of racism in Europe had become rather complex. Given the misunderstandings the notion of racism can give rise to, I want to make a brief excursus to clarify what Musil is talking about when he deals with race in this essay, and later in *The Man without Qualities*. He is quite aware that race is a modern concept. Only after the eighteenth century was it supposedly defined by biological criteria. Biological definitions were largely invented to buttress pseudoscientific claims that some races are superior, and races were conveniently discerned to justify white European colonization and enslavement of non-European peoples. Thus racism in this modern sense is not involved in the traditional Christian hatred of Jews, nor was it traditionally used to justify slavery (slavery existed throughout human history with no concern for the race of slave or master). Race is a recent concept developed after the invention of the idea of a nation, though it has a close relationship to the idea of a nation conceived as an ethnic entity usually corresponding to a linguistic group. In Germany the philosopher Johann Gottlieb Fichte, in calling upon the Germans to resist the French occupiers, may be credited with the idea that nation coincides with an ethnic group that, through its genealogy, remains true to its culture and language. Race is the founding notion here for the idea of nation, though it is veiled by the idea that the racial group finds its existence bequeathed to it by history. The scientific development of racist thinking occurred therefore slightly later, with the development of European imperialism. The French writer Arthur de Gobineau (1816–1882) is usually granted the founding role in scientific racism, with its glorification of the white race, though his grasp of science was much shakier than some of its later proponents. The scientific racism developed later by the discipline called eugenics claimed that there are biological markers corresponding to perceived character differences among races—which were explained by genes only after that concept of gene was introduced in the early twentieth century. For example, the eugenics developed in London held that Anglo-Saxons have well-developed genes for virile activity, the Chinese for slothfulness, and Africans for sexual drive—as one can repeatedly read in the European and American anthropological and eugenics literature of the time. Germans, Americans, and Scandinavians all warmly endorsed eugenics and passed laws to promote improvement of the race.

Jews were recognized as a race in the nineteenth century for much the same pseudoscientific reasons Africans and the Chinese were. Admittedly the inferiority of Jewish genes was paradoxical, since they also had genes that made some of them successful. Musil's Austrian compatriots apparently had genes that made them quite envious of the new generation of Viennese Jews with money. Traditional anti-Semitism, rooted in religious intolerance, took on a new twist when racists made of the Jew a scapegoat, in effect, for gentile problems. Thus, the prevalence of racist anti-Semitism in modern Europe is due to at least three factors: a long Christian tradition of intolerance; European imperialism claiming genetic superiority for white (or in Germany Aryan) Europeans as they extended their colonial power over other lands; and intolerance generated by psychological resentment. The latter factor was especially true of the right-wing Christian milieu in Musil's Austria—which was also Hitler's native land.

Musil's discussion of racism in "Nation as an Ideal and as Reality" is one of the earliest I know to subject it to a negative critique. It was not until 1940 that the anthropologist Franz Boas published his *Race, Language, and Culture,* a timely book demolishing the racist basis of much European anthropology. The identification of the nation-state with a supposedly racially defined group had become a leitmotif of right-wing nationalist ideologies. Musil's rejection of the concept of race, during a period of virulent racism, logically derives from his rejection of metaphysical abstractions as well as from his defense of the individual. In this defense he anticipates the foundations of modern genetics, for which there are no abstract species, only individuals living in breeding populations made up of individuals with their different genomes. In a homey example making this point, Musil notes that there is no abstract concept "rain" that has any meaning apart from the innumerable drops of water that fall, obeying their various trajectories (8:1064). The analogy he draws between nation or race and rain is directed against the widespread belief that something abstract such as race determines national character and conduct. With his example he is making biological as well as philosophical sense. Musil observes that rain does not produce raindrops any more than forests grow trees. Rain, like society or gas or even race, may be a useful concept; but after due exami-nation, he grants the concept of race only what it can deliver. From a biological point of view it delivers little. It only points up that metaphysical generaliza-tions found in general concepts cannot be used as causal agents. At best these concepts are useful fictions with discernibly limited ranges of application.

In his essay on the nation as ideal, Musil is frankly puzzled by the appeal of the idea of race. Everyone knows, he remarks, that every nation is a mixture of many races. Nonetheless, he finds that racism is largely accepted by the edu-cated, who should know that it is a vacuous notion. The charm of stupidity notwithstanding—and Musil was an expert in discerning forms of stupidity—it is with distaste that he feels obliged to consider the question of race in order to see why people want to speak of it as the basis for a nation. Racism is now an everyday cliché, Musil notes, and nearly all Germans are willing to say that the individual is formed by his or her race (8:1064). In brief racism is rampant and omnipresent, both as conventional wisdom and supposed scientific doc-trine. With regard to science Musil has only ironic contempt for the "kitchen Latin" with which contemporary racist anthropology tries to deck out the "disease of thinking" that he sees to be the basis for much so-called national idealism (8:1064). Buttressing its racism with shabby pseudoscience, racist "idealism" serves a purpose, for it allows individuals to look to their race to guarantee them that they possess desirable traits. Anti-Semitism is simply a screen that hides what Musil sees as the regressive nature of racism. Or as he observes with his usual unparalleled sense of comic lucidity, to the Germans racism offers "offenbar ein moralisches Schlaraffenland, unser glückliches Deutschland, wo die gebratenen Tugenden ins Maul fliegen!"—"obviously a moral land of milk and honey, our happy Germany, where roast virtues fly up into our mouth!" (8:1065) Inveighing against the abdication of intelligence that racism produces, he argues that there are simply no valid criteria for race. There are only individuals. However much racism may flatter its proponents, it is also clear that it is undermining Germans, since it is a form of self-destruction—*Sebstbeschädigung* (8:1065). Musil wrote nothing more prescient.

Having shown the irrationality of racism, Musil can conclude that race cannot be the basis for a nation in any meaningful sense. He then weighs other grounds for defining a nation. He finds that, of all the "garments for the outer dressing" of the nation that ideology proposes, the political state is the most compelling. The state is like the body of the nation and unfortunately, he says, almost its soul. Both the old German Reich and new Soviet Union confirm this view of the power of the state, the latter resembling a "proliferating protective capsule" (8:1066). Clearly, the protective exterior risks stifling the masses the state should protect. Musil suggests that the combination of a mass of individuals *plus* a state generate the "destructive oppositions" that are discharged in war (8:1066). But the material state that can engage in war is not the same thing as a nation. There is no "general will" motivating the decisions a state undertakes, such as found in the metaphysical contract Rousseau described when he made the "general will" into the deciding instance of what is a nation-state. Dismissing Rousseau's contract, Musil finds that the material state is composed of a series of "organs" that feel, think, and decide for individuals.

These organs—one might also say institutions—are the material organization of the state and are the key to whatever it may be. If it is to be a democratic organization, then it must have an organization serving the people, or as Musil says with some due sarcasm, the *demos*. There is nothing metaphysical involved in the state's material organization and its various organs or agencies, and they are not to be identified with the mass of people over whom they hold sway. Moreover, Musil does not find that these organs are in any way intrinsic to a "nation." When one actually looks at a modern state such as Germany, England, or France, as Musil does, all one sees are great masses of people. In these states by and large the individuals simply allow things to happen. With this idea of the passivity of the masses, Musil describes the concrete manifestation of the modern industrial state as he knew it in Berlin and Vienna: the industrial state has produced an individual who is reduced to acting in a passive sphere of private existence and who can perform acts in the state only by undertaking the role of a functionary and serving in an institution. In short, the state—that incarnation of right that Hegel saw in the emergent Prussia—has become the organizational manager of the masses, and this depiction largely covers a description of the social reality of the state.

In this new historical context as Musil describes it, the nation is found neither in a fictional race nor in the existing state. He briefly entertains the notion that the nation might be found in *Geist,* but the heterogeneity of modern society causes him to renounce this idea, for, he asks, what form of *Geist* can be common to both a prison and a university—well-developed institutions that are both held to be pillars of the modern state? In his essayistic questioning of the idea of the nation, Musil also wants to criticize the belief that the state is the supreme justification or embodiment of all things, such as nation, culture, even the individual. He finds the desire to affirm the supremacy of the state is everywhere at work: the deification of the state is common to both those nationalist reactionaries who would resurrect absolute monarchy and to the modern socialists who, he caustically observes, have taken over their ideas of the state from the German Reich (8:1067). Musil is again presciently sketching out historical developments. In weighing what he finds in contemporary culture, he plainly sees what is in the cards: the coming of the unitary state and the metaphysical nation rolled up into one, first in Italy in the form of the fascists that took power a year after he wrote this essay on the nation; subsequently in Germany's Third Reich, uniting German nation and corporate state; and finally in the Austro-fascist state proclaimed to keep Nazi Germany at bay. He was not unaware that a comparable identification of state, nation, and Communist Party was developing in Russia even as he wrote. The nation is undoubtedly a product of the imagination, though, as Musil says, history shows the imagination is to be taken seriously (8:1071).

In an interesting aside, Musil observes that only rebels and heretics—marginal bohemians, for example, or the artistic avant-garde—can bring a "Luciferian corrective" to what has become the "imperfect god, the State" (8:1069). The rebel who stands out against the masses is a defender of individualism that is rarely found in Musil's state. In the essay on the nation as ideal, praise of the rebel is set against a description of the state in which the organization of masses had promoted the desire for war. For war is the explosion in which one denies bourgeois life and its order and seeks release in disorder, or as Musil pithily concludes, "War is flight from peace" (8:1071). From this perspective the nation is a fiction that normally does not play much of a role in the life of the masses. They are motivated by fictions such as the nation or race that satisfy them as suggestive, releasing them from duress or exciting them. However you look at them, he says, they are fictions, products of the imagination, and not very satisfactory ones. The nation is an ideal in the name of which one celebrates holidays and mobilizes armies; or, to quote Musil's final deflationary irony, the nation is something like a house in which one sleeps on leap-year Pentecost days, while sleeping the rest of the time outdoors in a swampy field (8:1071).

If the nation has no physical reality, biological markers, or characteristic state institutions, if it really cannot be identified with a pure genealogy or with the culture of mind (are Goethe and Hitler products of the same *Geist*?), then, at best, a defender of the belief in the nation might retort that it is an ideal that demands realization in some future time. Musil introduces this objection precisely because it allows him to show that ideals in the contemporary world actually function regressively, not progressively, for racists and nationalists hold up an ideal to which the present social reality will conform in the future only if it returns to ideals held in the past. The truly ideal state of affairs for the racist and nationalist has only existed in the past, when the race was pure and the nation united—so that their politics must aim at a future recovery of it. Future politics aims at a return to a mythical past. Racism offers a flagrant example of what Musil has in mind. "Pure" Germans existed in the past before their culture was threatened or their pure blood diluted or infiltrated by foreign elements. The task of racist politics is to promote policies designed to recover that past ideal ethnic type. For nonracist nationalists—if there can be such a thing as a nationalist who must not ultimately appeal to some notion of an ideal ethnos—the nation, too, has an essence whose historical purity existed in some past moment. Deluged with these mythic ideals—at the time, I note, when in Germany literally hundreds of racist and nationalist journals poured forth claims for "Germanicity" and so-called Aryan values—Musil opines that one begins to believe that the real is the ideal and vice versa. The political consequences are that individuals begin to believe that the present must be tailored to fit a metaphysical ideal embodied in the past. The result is that ethics is reduced a patchwork (8:1072).

His essayistic demolition of essentialist thinking is one of Musil's major contributions to political analysis. By this I mean that he continually shows the illusory nature of the a priori ideals to which nationalist politics aspires. He lays bare the lack of foundation for conduct aiming at the future realization of these political goals. Essentialist ideology turns on using history to create an imaginary ideal that, presupposed to have once existed in the past, can then be used as a guide for the future. In real terms this guide means that political and ethical thinking then imposes injunctions to eliminate deviation from a supposed past ideal. This nationalist thinking revives the totalitarian side of Platonism, for its pure a priori ideals ultimately exist in some kind of metaphysical heaven not found on this earth; while it promotes atavistic irrationalism through self-serving taboos and self-aggrandizement (8:1072). Nietzsche would have had little difficulty finding the will to power expressed in one of its shabbiest guises.

Ethics and politics are intertwined for Musil. He draws upon recent political history and the experience of war for what he hopes is a realistic point of departure for new political and ethical possibilities. In the essay on the nation he bluntly says that the horrors of history since 1914 has shown that humans are, ethically speaking, something nearly "without form" or without a clearly definable nature. The war demonstrated that human beings have an unexpected plasticity (8:1072). They are capable of anything—heroism and murder in equal proportions, as Musil concisely opines. Good and evil are present in them as equal possibilities. Humanity knows no a priori constraints as to what it may do, no intrinsic qualities that define what constitutes human possibility, for the worst imaginable coexists with the best—though the war might suggest to the skeptical reader that the worst is more likely to be expressed.

However, it is not always clear what the worst is, or even if the best and the worst can be clearly defined: what is good in one context may be evil in another. We have seen that Musil explored this motif before the First World War in fictional works in which conventional good and evil entertain rather ambiguous relations. For example, Törless confronts torture and experiments with sex but comes up with no clear sense of what the ethical standards are that should govern his conduct. And Pauline's adultery in order to perfect love suggests that self-abasement might be experienced as a positive value. Consequently the war only deepened Musil's belief that there are no a priori foundations for ethical thought in the modern world.

After the observation of four years of the suicidal heroism undertaken in the name of national ideals, in 1921 Musil made the unequivocal assertion that there is no moral thought or ethical belief adequate to the historical situation. Politics has no real foundation. In the essay on the nation he looks to the East to observe the Russian Revolution, the stated desire of which was to overthrow the nation-state throughout the world. Making no moral judgment, Musil simply says that this project will require much violence. He concedes that violence may be necessary to achieve a "form of life appropriate to the era" (8:1074). However, his sympathies do not lie with violent revolution. Rather he hopes that contemporary Europe can find some kind of "world political goal," in which the "people" will find their way out of the "dead end of imperial nationalism" (8:1075). For Musil, in short, the European nation-state with its attendant nationalism was at a impasse. The historical crisis continues.

The dead end Musil observed in 1921 underlies the choice of the title "Helpless Europe" for his next major essay, published in 1922. I referred to it earlier for its description of the European crisis in values that Musil attributed to the demise of belief in the Enlightenment and the concomitant reduction of science to a form of pragmatic reason. The essay is also notable for the portrait Musil makes of the chaos of the modern mind in which the most discordant oppositions coexist. He was not alone, of course, in his disarray in trying to describe the chaos of modernity. The same sense of chaos could be found on the other side of the Rhine in the work of the well-known French poet and essayist Paul Valéry, who wrote, at approximately the same time, his widely quoted essay on the "crisis of mind" ("La crise de l'esprit," 1919). Valéry described how the modern era is a period of disorder characterized by the "free coexistence in all cultivated minds of the most dissimilar ideas" and of the "most opposed principles of life and knowledge."[13] He found that the disorder blinds the modern European observer in the same way as if the observer were looking at the disorder of a system brought to incandescent heat. Maximum entropy means maximum disorder.

In his essay on helpless Europe Musil's image for Europe's disorder is less scientific than Valéry's and, by contrast with the French poet, shows the influence of the rhetoric of German expressionism on him rather than science. According to Musil the disorder can be compared to a "Babylonian madhouse" out of whose "thousand windows scream at once, to the passer-by, a thousand different voices, thoughts, musical forms, whereby it is clear that the individual has become the playground of anarchistic motives, and that morality, along with *Geist,* are torn apart" (8:1088). Musil's image of the playground—*Tummelplatz*—also suggests the fairground—*Rummelplatz*—with which we began this chapter on science, knowledge, and cultural criticism. In either place he finds the disorder of the urban street and carnival grounds and, in them, images of the cultural disorder that threatens the mind. By contrast Valéry sees ideas themselves blinding the observer due to the intensity of the heat, whereas Musil finds that it is the surrounding disorder impinging upon the mind that threatens it with destruction. In short he is not so rigorously intellectual in his description as is his French contemporary. Rather his images portray in this disorder the domination of the culture of kitsch and a kind of insane disorder produced by children who have no self-consciousness about the chaos they joyfully create. With no awareness of the dangers they may face, children need education. Without education there can be no culture and no morality. In short there is a didactic side to Musil's essayism; and Musil's thoughts on education will be a good starting point for the following chapter on his essayistic treatment of culture, ethics, and art.

CHAPTER 7

Ethics and Aesthetics

It is not usual to consider Musil as an educator, though he could hardly have been concerned with moral beliefs without consideration of what transmits them. Transmission of moral beliefs is, or once was, an essential part of education. The root meaning of *education,* deriving from the Latin *educare,* is to raise the young "up," to elevate them so that they learn and perhaps practice manners, mores, and moral beliefs. Musil was well aware that there are many sources for education in moral values: the family, pedagogical institutions, religion, the state, tribal traditions and clan values, peer interactions, today's commercial publicity, and so forth. These all shape the mind so that it is receptive to values, and Musil's essays touch upon all these aspects. Of course, for the writer Musil a central question is the way that art and literature play a role in education. It was not clear to him and other writers concerned with ethics to what extent art and literature formulate, and are informed by, a culture's ethical and aesthetic values. To determine whether literature formulates or is informed by values is made difficult by the simple anthropological fact that values are omnipresent in any culture, and it is not clear how they arise and how they are changed, which, as Musil argued, they indubitably do in the course of history. He did not formulate the question of education in exactly this way, though it is implicit in much of his writing. His point of departure is that art and literature can transform values, which perforce suggests that literature can, or should, play a role in education.

In the course of the preceding chapters we have already seen some of the historical context for understanding the arguments about art and education that Musil encountered as he wrote his essays. First in his Austrian homeland and then in Berlin of the Weimar era, he encountered nationalist and racist groups calling for a return to so-called true German values—a satire of which the reader finds in the character of Hans Sepp in *The Man without Qualities.* On the other hand, Musil observed, and occasionally participated in, groups wanting the creation of a new society in which new and truly democratic values would be realized. At their extremes both groups wanted to impose their values through political revolution. Musil was not drawn to the idea of revolution.

Having come to believe, after Emerson and Nietzsche, that literature might play a role in transforming values, in his essays he thus felt obliged to take a stand in defense of a literature that perhaps had not yet been created—at least from his harshly critical and at the same time often utopian perspective.

There is little dealing specifically with the content of education in the published essays, though an illuminating examination of the question is found in a dense 1924 essay "Der 'Untergang' des Theaters" ("The 'Demise' of the Theater"). This posthumously published essay offers an interesting perspective on Musil's view of literature and the social role it plays. In it he links the decline of theater with a crisis in education (*Bildung*). This essay, like several others, documents that he understood well the affirmative educational function that literature played in earlier centuries. However, Musil, like most modernist writers, did not believe that literature could affirm received values in the same way classical writers did.[1] His critical essays and fiction illustrate that a defining trait of Musil's modernism is that it does not affirm the dominant values of European culture. Rather, most modernist fiction proposes to show that the values do not function and, through this demonstration, proposes a critique of values and in some instances a revision of them. In the case of the values embodied in official education in Weimar, Musil says that they are irrelevant to the society in which they are taught.

Musil made the charge, in his essay on the theater's decline, that the classical affirmation of literature as an education in culture had been derisively reduced in modern Germany to hollow pedagogical platitudes. Espousing the modernist desire to transform cultural values, he notes that this critical attitude first took shape in the Enlightenment. Thus he implies that education must capture again the critical spirit of the Enlightenment if it is to overcome its current decadent state. Also understood in this critique is the idea that the modernist writer must counter the influence of certain forms of romanticism, for they had resulted in aberrations according to which values for education were to be found in the Middle Ages or in earlier, happier times. For many educators and their intellectual spokesmen, the romantic rejection of rationalism meant precisely that the goal of education should be a return to the putative values of a German nation or *Volk*. Thus, to recall Musil's critique of the idea of the nation, the rejection of nationalism entails a rejection of educational programs that wanted to effect a return to a mythic past with its all-too-present ideology.

In "The 'Demise' of the Theater," Musil endorses the idea that the ideals of German education first took shape in the Enlightenment represented by Kant, Schiller, and Goethe, and he outlines their ideas in this regard. Drawing

190

on the educational theory of the major sociologist Leopold von Wiese (1876–1969), he sees Enlightenment education culminating in Herder's idea that education consists in direct imitation of the great models provided by antiquity (8:1123). That Musil thought education to be linked to classical theater is not surprising, for classical aesthetics had long considered one of the primary functions of theater to be education. The Enlightenment considered theater to be a superior literary genre precisely because it might further rational education in its task of producing the unfettered mind that Kant believed to be the essence of Enlightenment. Thus, in his essay on the demise of the theater, Musil reflects upon education in order to illuminate the crisis in theater in Europe, which in turn illuminates the crisis in education and culture in general.

In the first pages of the essay Musil recalls that theater has, according to a long tradition going back at least to Horace, conceived its task to be to offer a moral education as well as pleasure. So if there is a crisis in the theater, there may well be a crisis in the public's capacity for pleasure, which parallels a crisis in education—a *Bildungskrisis*. Musil pursues these interrelating themes as a way of approaching what he considers to thus be a conjoined crisis in aesthetics and ethics. Pursuing the ethical side of the coin, he states that to understand the development of theater one must understand the normative education that has traditionally been attributed to theater. This education had been based on the ethical ideal held by the dominant classes in European culture. Specifically during the Enlightenment, the conceptual basis for education was informed by a belief in the trinity of nature, reason, and freedom. Musil argues that the faith in reason was lost, again in the wake of romanticism, and was replaced by the nineteenth-century bourgeois faith in science, which considerably reduced the scope of reason. Nonetheless, he claims, this trinity has remained officially intact, at least until recently. By Musil's time, he says, a great disparity has arisen between beliefs actually held in society and the Enlightenment principles still affirmed platitudinously by educators but held in regard by few.

Musil wants to offer an historical overview in this essay that grants the necessary perspective to understand the crisis he views in Germany. The Enlightenment belief in classical education, and the theater that promoted it, is to be situated at the end of a long European development that began with the medieval clerical ideal, which was in turn replaced by the French aristocratic ideal, dominated by courtly values (such as found in the seventeenth-century playwrights Corneille and Molière), and this in turn was replaced in Germany by the bourgeois "Hellenistic-humanistic ideal" (8:1124). In noting the demise of this ideal in Germany, Musil asserts, ironically perhaps, that an education in

German classics no longer has social prestige, though not "because of the political emancipation of the working class" (8:1124). By this comment I think he makes the point that classical humanistic education and its values, supposedly promoted by elite education, do not correspond to the needs of the masses then proliferating in the industrial centers of the Weimar Republic—whatever be the pleasure the upper classes may derive from their education.[2] The urban working masses had achieved some political power, but, or so Musil seems to suggest, what is remarkable is that in this new situation no new educational ideal has come forth to replace what he calls the now "fragmented" classical ideal. Thus in his description of then current thinking about education, there "piles up an enormous quantity of badly, or not at all, thought-out ideas, so that the simplifying dominating ideas [about education] we do have at our disposition (which in general are just crumbling bits of eighteenth-century ideology that have been replaced by nothing else) do not amount to anything when compared with the ideas we previously had" (8:1125).

Newspapers have become more important than schoolbooks in the new mass society, though apparently neither the press nor Kant offered much education in fundamental values for the new masses. Nietzsche's earlier thought about the advent of nihilism is undoubtedly in the background of Musil's analysis. Of course, he did not need Nietzsche to believe that the Greek tragedy Herder and Goethe had placed at the heart of education was no longer a source of values for most modern Europeans. In this regard Musil differs from some modernist writers who, either in nostalgia or with a genuine sense of the continuity of European culture, turned to the world of antiquity in a desire to renew ethical and aesthetic values. By contrast in this regard, examples ranging from Jean Cocteau and Eugene O'Neill to Hugo von Hofmannsthal and Hermann Broch point up Musil's lack of nostalgia about the past; or if one prefers, his lucidity in his interpretation of the crisis of European culture. He had no belief that much could be derived from idolatry of the values that tradition had enshrined, though he also wanted to renew his culture's commitment to reason and freedom. But his nearly cynical recognition of the vacuity of the modern did not cause him to call for a recycling of ancient models. From his perspective that would be meaningless.

It is important to recognize for a general understanding of Musil's work that his desire for a radical evaluation and renewal of cultural values does not stem from the kind of intense revulsion that characterized many European writers and artists immediately after the horrors of the First World War. He is not motivated by the total condemnation of European values that led Dadaism to make a derisive mockery of everything once held to be of value; nor did he really embrace something like the surrealist utopian belief that the conditions of existence could and should be transformed by the liberation of Eros—albeit Musil shares some of the attitudes of both the Dadaists and the surrealists. Sympathetic to the needs of the working class and contemptuous of the empty culture of kitsch he saw consumer capitalism producing, he did not believe that socialism or revolution had any ready answer to the crisis he perceived. His skepticism about socialism as expressed in his essay on the theater's demise is a rather opaque judgment. He opines that the socialism of the Weimar era carries within its cultural enterprises the "stigma of the present" for its failure to unite the "mechanical and the spiritual" to transform culture (8:1127)

In the context of the Weimar debate about values, with this statement Musil is drawing upon an idea that was then becoming a cliché: the term *mechanical* characterized, often for reactionary thinkers, all that was wrong with the organization of contemporary capitalist society; the term *spiritual* referred to a negation of the mechanical found in some transcendental domain that existed perhaps in the past, perhaps in the future, according to one's ideological perspective.[3] Musil does not necessarily disagree with this analysis. The terms he uses here to describe socialism's stigma suggest that for him the way out of society's crisis would be through a transcendence of the present moment in some kind of synthesis. This is what he seems to mean by the desirability of uniting the mechanical and the spiritual in some kind of synthesis. Mechanical and spiritual are vague antitheses, but by using the idea of synthesis, he has in mind, I think, the reconciliation of reason and feeling, and through this a way of assuaging the present discourse of discontent that was undermining German society left and right—hence the idea of a synthesis transcending the insufficiencies of the present moment. Perhaps he did not publish this essay on the theater's decline because of the infelicities attached to the ideas of mechanical and spiritual. However, to formulate what exactly that synthesis might be is the task he set for himself for the rest of his life, notably in the unfinished *The Man without Qualities.*

The idea of a transcending synthesis may not seem to mesh with the fact that the essays refuse to invoke ethics and values in a systematic way. Indeed Musil's refusal of systemic thought seems somewhat antithetical to the idea of synthesis with its connotations linking it to German idealist philosophy, especially the writings of Hegel. One wonders what opposing elements could enter into an essayistic synthesis triumphing over the stigma of the present. It seems likely Musil never really came up with any idea as to what this synthesis might be, and perhaps reproached his ideological opponents with their lack of a synthesis mainly to point up the incoherence of their positions. He personally was not inconsistent if, without embracing any system, he demanded consistency in thought. And if Musil is consistent in anything, in contradistinction to his opponents on the right and the left, it is in his refusal to lift ethics out of the domain of individual experience.

Musil's essay on the demise of theater, with its concern for the demise of education, demonstrates his social concern with ethics. Let us now pursue the topic of ethics and the individual by turning back two years earlier to the 1922 essay "Hilflose Europa." In this essay Musil presents to the public the distinction between the ethical and the moral that we considered earlier in the diaries. He repeats here that moral thinking is part of philosophy, a branch of rational inquiry. The demands of rationality means that moral philosophy uses univocal thinking with concepts whose purchase on meaning demands that they that can be repeatedly used. This kind of moral thinking is analogous to scientific discourse in that it proposes recurrence as part of its criteria for verification and hence is a product of the understanding (8:1093). However, for Musil real ethical thinking does not share these properties, since it is part of the "non-ratioïd" domain of knowledge. It shares with love, meditation (*Einkehr*), and humbleness (*Demut*) the quality of being personal and almost unsocial. To illustrate this thought Musil adds a quotation from his favored mystic, Meister Eckhart, to the effect that Christ himself was possessed of two personalities, one belonging to an inner and the other to an outer man. And in Christ the inner man stood in "constant seclusion." If true ethics is an ineffable interiority, the reader may wonder if Christ ever managed to cross the divide between the inner ethical being and the outer social individual. Musil's thought on ethics in this essay flirts with the near paradoxes that will be the stuff of Ulrich's meditations.

It is revealing that in the considerations of ethics in his essay on "helpless Europe," unlike in the diaries, Musil does not include Nietzsche in his list of ethical thinkers sharing the stage with Christ. In addition to Christ he evokes a lineage of essayists from Confucius to Emerson to illustrate the difference between moral philosophy and the uniqueness of ethical thinking. Musil thinks that little in the way of the ethical thinking that springs from the vision of prophets and poets is occurring in Europe at the moment he is writing the essay, or at best, as he muses, whatever may be happening in the ethical realm at that moment "lives very inaccessibly in art, in essayistic writing, and in the chaos of private feelings" (8:1093). By essayistic writing one may presume that Musil has his own writing in mind as an example of the ethical, though that is not certain. What is striking is his pessimistic feeling that the realm of ethical seclusion, which Christ's nature supposedly illustrates, seems hardly accessible today. In short Musil gives the impression that there is something in the historical condition of the Weimar Republic that makes profound ethical feeling and thinking difficult, if not impossible. Such is the stigma of the era.

Musil was perhaps overwhelmed by the ideological confusions of the time, and it is difficult to imagine what the liberal rationalist could propose in a time of the triumph of irrational antiliberalism. Living in helpless Europe may have meant that Musil, with his own feeling of helplessness, had to content himself with pointing out that much of what passed for ethical thought was truly irrational, if not profoundly evil: nationalism, racism, antidemocratic desires for a strong state and racially pure culture. So Musil finds little in his contemporary culture that can illustrate his belief that great art is ethical in his sense of proposing moral vision.

For those of us who also find much to admire in the creativity of the brief Weimar era, Musil's attitude sets out a challenge: Was there really so little in the painting, music, and literature, especially expressionist art and poetry, that was ethically positive? Or was Musil right to maintain that the Weimar arts, music, painting, and poetry, were simply a "fermenting mass" on whose surface "the same clumpy pieces keeping appearing" without "the chemist" showing up to settle them out (8:1093)? His chemical metaphor is troubling, for it suggests that he saw nothing but chaos about him in the fermenting mass, and troubling too is the suggestion that there might be some chemist who could produce the unified brew Musil seems to have in mind. It sounds as if he was hoping for a prophet more than a scientist. And from another perspective, this metaphor expressing Musil's hostility toward Weimar culture resembles an expressionist image, one that shows he was at times more a product of that culture than he might have willingly recognized.

I stress this passage from "Helpless Europe," with its image of then-contemporary German culture devoid of ethical dimensions, because I think it sets out the framework in which much of Musil's subsequent thinking about ethics takes place. Turning from Weimar to Vienna, we can again compare Musil to his near contemporary Ludwig Wittgenstein. Like Wittgenstein Musil came to believe that true ethical thinking or feeling is scarcely amenable of the kind of rational demonstration that philosophers often undertake when systematically setting out the principles of morality. A system of ethics is impossible, since, according to Musil, the thinking and feeling necessary for ethics cannot be separated. "The chaos of private feelings" seemingly precludes a system. So feeling and thinking are conjoined in the domain he designates with the term *ethical,* and which, for Musil, is also the aesthetic domain in the broadest sense. Thinking, feeling, perception, perspective—these concepts are all part of what Musil believes in ethics is a kind of unique experience in which one encounters an individual moment that cannot be directly mediated simply by abstract concepts. It is unique, and hence it is the task of authentic art to reveal the truth of this unique experience. This is the experience found in the ethical prophets and essayists he refers to; and presumably it can be found in art.

Musil began to use the expression the "other condition" to talk about the unique domain in which this aesthetic experience of the ethical occurs. Most elaborately, this condition is discussed as a central issue in an essay of 1925, "Ansätze zu neuer Ästhetik: Bemerkungen über eine Dramaturgie des Films" ("Toward a New Aesthetic: Comments on a Dramaturgy of Film"). The essay begins as a review of the influential book of film theory by Béla Balázs, *Der sichtbare Mensch (The Visible Man)*, though Musil goes on in his review to express far more than his own views about the fact that cinema has become the dominant form of expression of "folk culture." In the essay he elaborates his own theory of how art functions, especially in its ethical role. The essay begins with a quotation from Balázs to the effect that no great discovery has been made without an erroneous hypothesis preceding it, which ironically implies that no great art has been created without theory. Putting this idea up front, Musil is indulging in self-directed irony. For he wants very much to formulate a theory—or perhaps an erroneous hypothesis—that will empower him to make his own discovery, perhaps a theory of ethics that might shape the long novel he was writing at that moment.

Musil begins "Toward a New Aesthetic" with a quotation ironically dismissing theory, and he concludes it by proposing his ethical theory with an hypothesis about the "other condition." Obliged to confront the pervasive anti-intellectualism developing in the Weimar Republic, he begins by noting that many complain that thought kills life by emptying it of content. There are echoes here of the right-wing cliché that intellect—a French or Jewish invention according to German nationalists—kills life and the soul, apparently Germanic properties. Musil ingenuously observes that the same critique made of intellect can be made of feeling. Once feeling is emptied of real content, the shell left behind becomes kitsch or meaningless emotion. Sterile intellectual performance resembles the same kind of vacuous activity found in the empty imitation of the forms of genuine emotion—namely in kitsch.

Musil then enunciates with great emphasis that both empty intellect and emotion are the enemy of the saint as well as the artist, the scientist as well as the lawgiver (8:1152). Musil unites these four figures for their common quest for knowledge linked to, and relying upon, feeling. These figures seek knowledge found in the sphere of genuine discovery and not simply in the repetition of formal religiosity, kitsch art forms, sterile intellectual game playing, or, in the case of the lawgiver, the mere compilation of an abstract collection of the laws of the state. When emptied of genuine content, their activities involve mere forms or formulas to be imitated by a given group. The activities then stand in opposition to the individual, inner experience that Musil sees grounding ethical thought and feeling.

The opposition of individual experience and formula to describe the nature of these central human experiences does not exhaust a description of them. In this essay on aesthetics Musil presents a complementary category, or dimension of experience, that he calls "reine Zuständlichkeit" or "pure conditionality" (8:1052). He uses a rather erudite word, found for instance in discussions of psychology and art history, to designate a dominant condition. (The word will not be found in most dictionaries.) With this term Musil wants to evoke a type of experience in which considerations of concepts, or the impossibility of concepts, do not come into play. *Zuständlichkeit* describes a condition characterized by a nonconceptual relation between the person experiencing something and the experience itself. Musil does not want this relation to be characterized as just ineffable overflowing. He wants to give it a precise, near-mathematical description by characterizing it as a sign, a vector, and a direction, all of which are dimensionless; to which he adds, moreover, that each moment of pure *Zuständlichkeit* is without relation to any other, for upon entering into a relation it loses its character of pure conditionality. In more prosaic terms, if that is possible, one might say that it is condition of absolute attention, or concentration, in which, as attention moves toward its object, experience is self-sufficing. Having described this pure condition, Musil admits, with shades of Mach, that the condition is an "abstract fiction" (8:1153). It is a fiction that exists, however, once it is described, and that moreover offers a useful hypothesis. The experience of art, for example, shows that upon entering into this "condition," we experience pleasure, recreation, relaxation, so that all that we associate with the experience of art can be described as an interruption of normal conditions of existence (8:1153). In this other condition we believe that we have found parts of a higher totality, which seems to presuppose we can arrive at "another interiority, a world without words, an incomprehensible culture and spirit" (8:1153).

In "Toward a New Aesthetic" Musil's demonstration of the other condition is the basis for his contention that in the ethical domain there is also a hostile difference, or conflict, between the creative source of ethics found in the other condition and the normalization of ethics found in the usual moral thinking, just as there is a conflict between religious experience and the necessity of institutionalized true belief (*Rechtgläubigkeit*). Only one domain can satisfy the need for a pure state of ethics, religion, or interiority: it is the other condition lying beyond "the borders of two worlds" (8:1153). Translation of these terms is terribly difficult, not least of all because Musil appears to be seduced by the meaning of terms that in German suggest different realms but in English do not exist. To wit, he argues that the experience, or *Erlebnis,* of the other condition shows that it has nothing in common with experience, or *Erfahrung.* The English speaker is a bit perplexed by this contention. Connotations of the German terms suggest the opposition of immediacy and intellectually mediated experience; and one can draw an inference from Musil's example of the way normal experience can destroy meditation. It seems he wants to describe a state of pure innerness that may either be like a mystic's state or may be like an experience of art in which art replaces temporarily the everyday world. With regard to the latter idea, it seems Musil believes that literary fictions create the conditions of possibility for their own existence, so that briefly, at least, they become part of the readers' mental space and change their fundamental being in the world. This is a fiction, but one that can be experienced. Perhaps it is the basis for the utopia Musil wants to describe in *The Man without Qualities.*

The theory he is pursuing in "Toward a New Aesthetic" is also part of his attempt to account for the way literature, and perhaps all cultural forms, can transform themselves and in so doing, transform culture. Musil accepts that the history of culture is an history of forms, formulas, and norms that are constantly changing through their interaction. It is a history of evolving individual parts that force the totality to change to accommodate them. It is thus a history "of the abnormal becoming the new norm" and, thereby, is a process of perturbing and destructive forms being transformed such that culture reaches a new spiritual or mental equilibrium (8:1140). The transforming powers of ethics, understood in a broad sense, is found in the creative, which is to say, destructive work of the writers, mystics, and essayists who in effect destroy the norm and the received forms through their individual experience. To explain this process Musil brings forth the notion of the convulsive force of new forms. With regard to literature he uses, for instance, the word *Sprengung* (explosion) to describe its effect: authentic literature "blows up" the "normal total experience" of those who experience it and opens them up for transformative experience (8:1145). This can happen when readers are able to entertain the moral worth of a reprobate such as Raskolnikov in Dostoyevsky's *Crime and Punishment,* to cite a favored example. Perhaps it occurs when one discovers the perfecting of love in Claudine's adultery.

With this rhetoric of destruction in "Toward a New Aesthetic," Musil suggests a way by which the "other condition" may enter into the social arena by motivating the creation of new forms. Seen in this light, his hypothesis about the other condition was not so distant from the ideas of other writers and artists who wanted to address the spiritual needs of the Weimar era. In Musil's case the other condition was conceived as a counter to the religious and ideological irrationalism cultivated in the name of instinct, life forces, and racial consciousness. With his hypothetical fiction, the basis for a materialist, rationalist, and atheistic mysticism, he undoubtedly hoped to be on the way to reconciling the human need for a redeeming belief with the acceptance of scientific rationalism. A greater coherence can be discerned in Musil's thought when, with these goals in mind, one sees that he elaborated a general theory of the historical nature of art and cultural change to account for the emergence of values. This theory is predicated on the role of the individual, which is also shown by the important role he assigns to prophets and religious leaders, who by their life as much as by their thought work like artists in centering culture upon new values and cultural forms.

His theory of culture in "Toward a New Aesthetic" describes the displacement of old aesthetic and moral forms through the corrosive work of ethics, which is to say, new kinds of interiority. But the exterior forms are essential, too. They are necessary if ethics or belief are to have public existence, just as they are necessary if aesthetic values can have palpable existence—which must eventually be transformed. Thus he describes the history of art and ethics as a history of the constant transformation of forms. New forms show up that reach out to the totality of existing forms and transform culture. They must be instituted by an act of destruction, not only in art but also in music, morals, and religion. If there is a radical side to the view of transformation, there is a profoundly conservative side to the belief that all cultural life depends upon mediating exterior forms: "Even so little does mystical experience without a rational scaffolding of religious dogma [exist], or music without its building scaffold" (8:1147). Musil subscribes thus to a historical theory that, if it does not endorse the idea of progress, does find change to be a necessity. Accepting the necessity of change, Musil asserts that forms are transformed by being dynamited from within by the freedom of the artist, who thus offers access to unique truth: "every artwork offers not only a direct, but precisely a never entirely repeatable, nor fixable, individual, indeed anarchistic experience" (8:1151). This historical theory culminates in the claim that the task of art (and in a sense of science) is the unceasing reshaping and renewal of our picture of the world and our relation to it by art's "blowing up," with its experience, the fixed formulas codifying our knowledge and experience, or *Erfahrung* in this context (8:1152).

199

If we step back for a moment to make a résumé of this argument, we see that Musil is drawing from his studies in psychology as much as from the self-consciously historical modernist aesthetics of his time. He conceives of cultural experience as a domain mediated by fixed forms or "formulas" that allow perception of wholes, of the gestalt, that make up the daily reality of the normal condition. These perceptual forms change. They may not change for the better, and what Musil sees about him in the Weimar Republic suggests a regression to primitive irrational beliefs that could and did result in cultural catastrophe. So he is concerned about finding a locus for change that might somehow operate outside the irrational destruction that German ideologues were proposing at the time. And in accord with Musil's liberal individualism, the locus for change is the individual artist or prophet in his or her experience of a condition beyond that accepted by the dominant culture: Jesus, Emerson, Dostoyevsky are a few examples he returns to frequently.

With regard to modernist aesthetics, I would also argue that Musil proposes his own version of the modernist belief that the function of art is to renew perception. I do not want to speak of influences in this regard, because it is difficult to speak meaningfully of influences when an entire era begins to rethink its basic axioms. Suffice it to say that a dominant theme of early-twentieth-century modernism was that art can renew a culture's vision of the world by changing its fixed perceptual patterns. In this regard Musil's ideas are close to those of theorists such as the Russian formalists as well as such modernist writers as Proust, Virginia Woolf, and Joyce. A brief comparison of Musil with Victor Shklovsky, a leading theorist of the Russian formalists, can illustrate this point. Shklovsky wrote a seminal essay, "Art as Technique," in 1917 (which was later published in book form in *The Theory of Prose* in 1925, the same year Musil wrote the essay describing the other condition). In this essay Shklovsky, like Proust, saw most perception to be conditioned by habit. Habit causes the perceiver to become anaesthetized to experience, which means no longer perceiving the habitual as well as being incapable of perceiving the new. Habit entails living experience without actually having an experience of it. Directed against habit, Shklovsky theorizes that technique in art serves to "defamiliarize" objects—which is perhaps a less dramatic way of saying, as Musil does, that art blows up received perceptual forms. But in claiming that art releases objects from the automatisms of perception, he proposes a function for art comparable to what Musil describes. There is a difference in that Shklovsky modestly proposes that artistic forms themselves perform the task of defamiliarization. Musil has a more complicated agenda in that forms are at once necessary for the artist's ethical or mystical interiority to be mediated and become part of received, publicly held conventions, and at the same time they must be blown up to allow interiority to exist anew.

From this perspective the rationalist Musil appears to be closer to the Dadaists or an avant-garde poet such as Antonin Artaud, the insane theorist of the theater, who wanted artistic forms to perform like the revelation brought about by the plague: the function of art is to submit stagnating cultural forms to an assault that would produce a conflagration that, according to Artaud, would liberate spectators for new, undreamed-of possibilities. The comparison with Artaud implies that there is a surrealist side lurking in Musil, suggested by *Unions* as well as his theory of ecstatic singularity. Finally, it is useful to recall again the ideas of the slightly younger Russian theorist Mikhail Bakhtin (1895–1975), whom I mentioned in regard to "The Lady from Portugal." More generally, Bakhtin, in his book on Rabelais and in other works, demonstrated that the destruction of ossified cultural forms through carnivalesque farce was, and is, a necessary function of art—if one is not to be stifled by these forms. Similarities between Musil's and Bakhtin's theories are perhaps not surprising if one considers that Musil developed his theory as right-wing ideology was about to strangle German cultural life and that Bakhtin developed his as Communism was destroying free cultural life in the Soviet Union.

Situating Musil in terms of European modernism is not to detract from his originality, nor to suggest that his insights have value only in relation to a specific historical period. A concept such as modernism has only limited use with a writer such as Musil, and perhaps any other major writer, serving simply to underscore that they shared common concerns and some common responses. Musil is also an original thinker: he combines the sensitivity of a scientific rationalist with the recognition that culture is changed by transformations of value and feeling, and by the value of feelings, for which there is no easy accounting. I know of no other thinker, including Wittgenstein, who stressed with such lucidity that ethical thinking and art are interrelated in their "breaking the vessels," to use an expression from the Kabbalah and the Jewish mystic tradition referring to the incapacity of the original vessels of creation to contain the light emanating from God's being. Musil's theory of the destruction of forms also suggests, by analogy, that the vessels must continually be broken so that the light may be propagated—but there must also be vessels so that it can be contained. The destruction of the forms of received thought and perception is a necessary process, which gives access to a new condition beyond received values and their rationality. Going beyond the concept of the renewal of perception used by modernist writers and aestheticians, Musil extends the use of the concept of renewal to describe ethics. Quite simply, he wants to describe why culture has a history or, more precisely, culture is history. He also wants this knowledge to be a springboard for looking beyond the present moment, which, understandably, became for him an increasingly desperate imperative.

Perhaps we can see another reason why Musil proposes no new ethical system, for that would mean looking backward at received moral knowledge; and why by ethics he means the creation of new values that cannot be known in any sense in the present since this would presuppose already knowing them and hence make them into objects of knowledge about the past. There may well be a logical dilemma here of which Musil was aware. It is one he faced again in *The Man without Qualities*. However, historical change may well have little to do with logic and its dilemmas. What is empirically clear is that ethics and values do change. Consider, for example, the values humanity has come to embrace in the past century or so, values such as the equality of all sexes and peoples, the condemnation of imperialism and racism, the belief in human dignity and human rights. These beliefs may well have seemed illogical throughout most of history. Musil knew this and knew that what one takes as axiomatic for values today does not determine what one may come to believe in the future; and he skeptically knew that uncertainty is no guarantee of moral progress.

"Toward a New Aesthetic" is a culmination of more than a decade of grappling with basic ideas in order to formulate concerns with aesthetics and ethics. From this perspective one can then argue that, from the earliest essays before the war to those of the mid-twenties, Musil sought through his essays to formulate a new way of relating art and ethics. The unity of this pursuit seems clear when we turn back to his first essay of 1911, "Das Unanständige und Kranke in der Kunst" ("The Obscene and the Pathological in Art"), in which he angrily attacks the decision of Berlin authorities to censor the publication of some drawings done by the French novelist Gustave Flaubert. Entering the realm of morals at the outset of his career, Musil presses the claim that art has the same right as science to represent the indecent and the sick. In this first essay we find now familiar ideas: Musil differentiates art from science in that art represents the specific or individual and not the general case. Nonetheless, like science, art is knowledge, it is involved in weighing where the normal and the abnormal overlap by showing "things that few have yet seen" (8:981). It does this by redrawing the lines of demarcation that set off the perverse from the normal, the sick from the healthy, the moral from the immoral. The perverse can legitimately be represented: it consists of so many normal components in a new configuration that it is art's task to represent. And in true art the obscene is no more obscene that the same representation would be in a medical textbook. Already underlying this essay is the idea that art should effect ethical adjustments through historical change aiming at future improvements, and not by recuperating the past, which Musil sardonically expresses by saying that one should reform historically forward and not backward; for, in his caustic words, "social diseases, revolutions, are, through conserving stupidity, blocked forms of evolution" (8:983). This affirmation of evolution points up, moreover, that politics, ethics, and art are interrelated in Musil's mind from the outset. His equating art with science buttresses his sarcastic refusal of state control of artistic representation, for his liberalism demands the complete freedom to pursue knowledge wherever the quest may lead.

In "The Obscene and the Pathological in Art" Musil shares the modernist refusal of moral and psychological absolutes. He is calling upon the developments in modern physiology and medicine that had blurred the distinction of the normal and abnormal to which I alluded briefly with regard to *Unions*. In the essay, in fact, Musil is explicitly using the medical questioning of the norm, which originated in the fact that medical research finds that every pathological process obeys the normal laws of physics and chemistry. I take this to be the sense of his assertion above that the pathological is the arrangement of so many normal components. In psychology the same question was on the modernist agenda: what is abnormal about the normal pathologies that make up the neuroses that characterize all humanity? In "The Obscene and the Pathological in Art" Musil thus puts in the foreground the type of interrogation of the norm that he was drawn to in his early narratives and plays and justifies the nonevaluative stance found in works that abound in what once was considered the pathological and the perverse. This interrogation is also found in a brief essay of 1912, "Penthesileiade," in which he ponders the possibility that new forms of eroticism might arise in history. There is a radical side to Musil.

But there is also a conservative side, and I conclude these remarks on the essays by calling attention to some of the last essayistic commentary he made, in 1926, in remarks gathered under the title "Bücher und Literatur" ("Books and Literature"). Musil called for the creation of a literary criticism that self-consciously knew itself to be a necessary part of the institution of literature. I call this notion conservative, because he saw that for literature to exist as more than a mere aggregate of books, it had to be endowed with a discourse that turned these books into a whole having historical existence. The function of criticism, as he describes it, is to conserve literature; it is to create a historical whole possessing the same sense of its necessity and its contingency as any other human enterprise. Musil's vision of the historical existence of literature means that literary criticism should interpret the works of literature, and in so doing interpret life, knowing that life in turn would overturn its judgments, for this overturning is part of historical development and necessary for the creation of new forms of literature and criticism. As Musil puts it, the situation of criticism is no more difficult than that of ethics (8:1169). With this witticism, however, he also suggests that the ethical side of aesthetics, the moral dimension of literature, also needs criticism to come to the light of day. Rejecting both the rule-governed criticism of classical aesthetics and the search for emotion he finds to be the motivation of impressionistic and expressionist schools of criticism, Musil wants criticism to be an interpretive enterprise that can, partially at least, translate the irrational moment of literary uniqueness into the mediating language of rationality that makes literature accessible. These thoughts, penned as he was hoping to complete *The Man without Qualities,* point up the fact that Musil was one of the most acute thinkers about literature in the twentieth century.

At the same time he was writing essays, Musil wrote a number of texts he left unpublished until, pressed to publish something, he assembled them for book publication in 1936 as *Posthumous Papers of a Living Author.* As he himself points out in his introduction to the book, they were written mainly in the twenties. In this sense they are complementary to the purely essayistic texts. However, published in 1936, after Musil had left Berlin for good, they acquire another sense in that he sardonically qualifies them as posthumous and goes on to say in his introduction that the death alluded to by the title characterizes the German writer. The German writer has outlived himself at the time when National Socialism has brought about conditions in which writers—liberal humanist or social democrat—found themselves dead as far as German culture was concerned. The historical conditions that have brought about the writer's death are more than just a political event, however. Musil maintains that the same era that has brought forth mass-produced shoes and the ready-made suit in individual sizes has brought forth the writer who can be mass-produced by sticking together "inner and outer parts" (7:473). His spleen about mass culture thus aims at more than just the writers then busy for the Third Reich's propaganda machine. Like the mass production of garments, the mass production of culture, with its destruction of uniqueness, also causes Musil to observe that the writer has outlived his time.

Having fled Hitler, and living in an Austrian state now imitating Mussolini for its Austro-fascism, Musil indulges in bitter irony in the introduction to his book not simply because of his personal discomfort, but also because of his belief that the institution of literature, as he called for in his remarks on criticism, is in danger of disappearing. Thus he says that the texts he is publishing are forms of speech about "shadows, about a life, that no longer exists" (7:474). Nonetheless, drawing upon Goethe—the Goethe whom ten years earlier he had found enshrined as a source for meaningless education—Musil hopes that ironic lessons may be found in his short texts. To this end he quotes Goethe to conclude that "in the individual thing in which something is done badly one may see a parable for everything that is done badly" (7:475). In interpreting Goethe for the present Musil himself performs an act of ironic criticism by which Goethe as writer continues to live in a present in which writers are dead. Musil shows that Goethe's remarks still have meaning, even if the critic of "little faults" must adjust them to encompass things incomparably worse that what Goethe could have had in mind (7:475).

Musil prefaces these texts with commentary suggesting that they are parables of inadequacy and failure. Undoubtedly these themes were pressing themselves upon him in the thirties, at a time when his writing then appeared, to him at least, to be of no consequence for the development of German culture. However, these texts were all written in a more felicitous time than that of their publication, and it is instructive to look upon them as something like pages from a logbook in Musil's ongoing experimentation, beginning before World War I and continuing into the twenties. To facilitate their interpretation Musil invites the reader to read the texts from the perspective of common aesthetic intentions. He does so by grouping them in four sections. Each of the four sections has a suggestive title: "Bilder" ("Pictures"), "Unfreundliche Betrachtungen" ("Ill-Tempered Observations"), "Geschichten, die keine sind" ("Unstorylike Stories"), and finally, a single narration called "Die Amsel," or "The Blackbird" (the common European blackbird is found in nearly every European city park). The texts in the first group of "pictures" are prose descriptions largely devoid of narrative content. "Ill-Tempered Observations" could also be translated as "Unfriendly Meditations" to suggest an essayistic intent, redolent of the title of one of Nietzsche's early books, *Untimely Meditations*. Whether the stories in the third section of "Unstorylike Stories" are storylike or not is not entirely clear, since they do contain some narration in the form of sharp satirical sketches. The narration about the blackbird that gives the title to the fourth section is among the most experimental of Musil's writings. All in all these texts represent a varied palette of forms, ranging from some of Musil's best irony and satire to some rather quirky pieces in which he is trying to extend his range in ways that are not always immediately comprehensible.

The first section presents "Pictures": the title stresses that this section offers different perspectives in viewing things—essentially still-life prose descriptions. These descriptive texts are largely illustrative of Musil's view that the goal of literature is to renew perception by "blowing up" conventions. To this end he seeks rhetorical strategies allowing him to renew the received vision of things as various as flies, apes, horses, and, on occasion, people. From this perspective the subject matter of "Pictures" may appear to be of secondary importance. Rather it is the angle of vision that is of primary interest. Implicitly, the texts ask, how does one look at things and from what perspective, and consequently, how does the perspective create the perception?

The first text in "Pictures" is "Das Fliegenpapier" ("Flypaper"). Twenty-first-century readers may not have recently encountered flypaper, the long curly strips of paper, covered with a sticky substance, that once hung from ceilings in summer, at times offering the fairly disgusting spectacle of dozens of flies stuck together as they dangled in the air like some macabre decorative motif. Musil's text focuses on the slow death an individual fly undergoes once it is trapped by the flypaper's viscous surface. He was clearly fascinated by this mass-produced technique of killing flies. Flypaper was another ready-made product about which he may have had some ironic doubts, for it seems to have fascinated him precisely because it was a ready-made allegory for technology designed to destroy the individual. Musil's fascination with a vision of a dying fly is found elsewhere in his work. He uses it in the comparison of character formation with the fixing of a dying fly in *The Man without Qualities* (1:131). With greater development the image also shows up with the flypaper in "Grigia" when, in the European miners' camp, the protagonist, Homo, watches a fly die on one of the many strips that are hanging about. Listening to the babble around him, Homo wonders about how they "kill, yet perceive God, perceive God, and yet kill" (6:244). And so Homo flicks the fly into a nearby major's eye, which sets off a day of strife. There is of course something derisive about the way Homo meditates, Christlike, on the contradiction he perceives between the religion these Europeans profess and the readiness with which they kill all of God's creatures, themselves as well as the lowly fly that tortures them in the camp.

Homo's fascination with a dying fly may be an expression of his disgust with the culture that the camp has generated, but in *Posthumous Papers of a Living Author* the perspective on the fly seems at first bereft of symbolism. The picture begins as a detailed description of the dimensions of the paper and the stages in the fly's hopeless struggle. The narrator mentions that the flypaper, coming from Canada, is called "Tangle-foot," which seems to imply, with impish irony, that the fly is the victim of the same globalizing mishmash of modern culture that one finds represented in the miners' camp in "Grigia." From this perspective every line in the picture takes on ironic resonances despite the deadpan character of a description depicting with exactitude how a fly is killed by putatively modern methods. The fly just sits down in the glue, obeying what the narrator calls social conventions, since so many of its fellow flies are already sitting there. And then it is done for. Musil uses a series of comparisons projected from a reverse perspective by which the human world is brought down to a fly's level. The flies resemble those sick with tuberculosis; they are bow-legged like old military men; their heads are brown and hairy, like those of anthropoid African idols; they are more tragic than workers overburdened with weight they have to carry; and finally—for German classicists —they are more truly expressive of athletic struggle than the Greek hero Laocoön. Musil is deadpan, but the irony is humorous with the suggestion that flies offer an image of class struggle. They even surpass the classic icon that once stood at the center of German classical aesthetics, to wit, the Hellenistic statue of Laocoön that either expresses classical repose or anguish and frenzy, according to one's critical perspective. And so it finally appears that struggling flies may take on different metaphorical values.

The flies relent for a moment, but then begin again their apparently Darwinian "struggle for their life," but this struggle is in vain. In their role as representatives of social Darwinism, they resemble "women who in vain try to twist their hands from a man's fist" (7:477). At the end they are like "crashed airplanes with one wing sticking up in the air," or dying horses or even people gesturing in infinite despair (7:477). Finally their movements escape the naked eye. A magnifying glass could reveal their demise, but, one feels, that would begin a new image or picture, one granted by science beyond the not-so-innocent vision of the eye armed with metaphors. This point is made in fact in the text "Triadere" ("Binoculars"), found in "Ill-Tempered Observations," in which Musil offers the description of what a optical magnification can do to enlarge and change reality as the narrator equipped with a pair of binoculars looks out his window. In fact, a number of Musil's pictures function as metaphorical telescopes that, as the narrator says, dissolve "the usual relations" between things and, in magnification, change the perspective to reveal new and more intimate relations (7:522).

The bravura text on flypaper is as much a demonstration of the power of semantic connections to generate vision as it is a picture, though it is that, too, in a metaphorical sense. In these texts Musil is actively creating visual relations in a demonstration of writing's capacity to create analogies that patently do not obviously exist in the simple nature of things. Thus one can say that pure vision is not the only goal in these "pictures" that are at times rhetorical feasts. For example the rhetoric of allegory underlies the picture offered by the second text, "Die Affeninsel" ("Monkey Island"). Musil wrote this description of social relations among monkeys in 1919, and it may seem politically prescient (at least to those attentive to the fact that Mussolini formed his Fascist Party in that year). The text gives a perspective on the power determining social relations, albeit among apes. It describes three families of apes and monkeys living on an island in the park of the Villa Borghese in Rome. The apes are described as separated from the "kingdom of Italy" by a concrete ditch. In the middle of their metaphorical kingdom stands a dead tree on which live one family of apes, the size of four-year-old children, grouped in couples. At the base lives a more powerful ape family, made up of a king, his queen, and their little, rather misshapen prince. Finally, hiding largely out of sight is a group of many small simians that dare not show themselves to the others. The powerful king ape takes walks on the branches of the dead tree and, without seeming to notice the less powerful beings in front of him, drives them from the branches by his mere presence. He walks in such a way that, as the narrator puts it, one cannot determine if he is doing his royal duty or taking a therapeutic walk that forces the inferiors to pay homage to him by making way (7:478).

Musil himself treads a space between animal ethnology and political allegory in this description of the kingdom of the three almost Italian families. As we have seen, he was consistently interested in parallels between animal and human behavior.[4] In the case of the ape king and his gratuitous exercise in power, Musil has extended scientific study of alpha males to make suggestions about parallels with human culture. This parallel is suggested by the relations between the second family of apes and the numerous little simians who dare not get their food so long as any of the more powerful animals are in sight. Sometimes, like a god falling upon them from above, a member of the second family drops down upon the little monkeys, sending them running into the ditch in terror. The description takes on biblical resonances when the little simians, as if in a late medieval painting about the Last Judgment, hold up their arms with their hands extended as they try to avoid the damning look from above that seems to seek out a guilty party upon which to fix its attention. Finally, the more powerful ape picks out, apparently quite arbitrarily, one of the smaller simians, glares at it in condemnation, and the guilty one is then tortured. The little ones then let loose their emotions: they are united in hatred, and "with a freed scream they rage away from each other, along the ditch, and flicker without light through each other like the possessed souls in purgatory" (7:479). Psychology gives way to theology, or perhaps to theological politics with an Italian resonance at the end. In conclusion Musil makes an analogy taken from Dante's vision of purgatory in which the souls are transparent to light, though the trench the monkeys inhabit resembles not so much purgatory as a circle from Dante's Hell in which the damned simian souls float about, condemned from above, for no reason they can comprehend.

As in "Grigia," animal images offer perspectives on human behavior. In "Monkey Island" one finds analogies with human mythmaking as well as the propensity to punish oneself for arbitrary sins visited upon people rather much by their own devising. From a different perspective the picture of apes reads as the description of the irrational way power imposes itself through arbitrary judgment. If the description has links with politics, it seems to be showing that the essence of power is the capacity for sadistic violence. This perspective suggests a sharp critique of the Nietzschean infatuation with power and offers a good example of exploding received ideas from within (and many of Nietzsche's ideas had become something like received ideas by the mid-1920s in Germany). In fine, ethnology, political allegory, and theological insight are knitted together, though one's interpretation ultimately depends on the perspective one takes on Musil's blend of objective description and metaphorical inflection.

Three other texts are set in Rome: "Schafe, anders gesehen" ("Sheep, as Seen in Another Light"), "Sarkophagdeckel" ("Sarcophagus Cover"), and "Pension Nimmermehr" ("Boardinghouse Nevermore"). "Sheep, as Seen in Another Light," sets out a rather comic perspective renewing one's vision of familiar things seen around early-twentieth-century Rome, namely, sheep. Of course, for Christians, in Rome and elsewhere, the lamb of God is a familiar analogy drawn from the animal realm, though Musil reverses the terms in his picture: it is not the holy who are likened to lambs but sheep who suggest human religious behavior. As the narrator wryly puts it, they are the most ancient catholic animal, leaving the readers to draw whatever conclusion they may from this vision of sheep in the Holy See (7:485).

"Sarcophagus Cover" is less concerned with semantic reversals; rather it reverses one's perspective on time as it uses a powerful thought experiment to explore the nature of art. The text meditates on past things found in the present, asking the reader to forget that a funeral representation from an ancient sarcophagus is two thousand years old. The text asks that "you" look at the human figures represented on a sarcophagus cover found lying in the garden of the Villa Borghese, as if they had awakened to a pleasure outing, by chance dressed as they had been two thousand years ago. Musil uses the second-person form of direct address to suggest that "you" can encounter the other's look if you accept that the look is present in the work, whatever shape it may be in. "You look away," but the figures carved in stone continue to be present, not as stone but existing through the look emanating from their eyes. This gaze capturing your look is the essential quality of humanity embodied in the art-work, for it meets your eyes and you are called into the basic human relation of sharing the other's presence. The extraordinary power of art is concentrated in the shared gaze, one that can in a meaningful sense bring the past into the present. Such is the picture portrayed in this picture.

The mystery of the other person resonates in the descriptions of people encountered in "Boardinghouse Nevermore," set in a typical boarding estab-lishment for foreigners spending time in Rome. Musil describes encounters with different nationalities, with French, Swiss, and Italian, but the last char-acter described, a Miss Frazer, differs from all the others in that she does not open herself to them; she remains closed in upon herself. She crochets, plays solitaire, reads, and goes to bed early without contact with anyone. Musil may be paying homage with this character to the French writer Guy de Maupassant and his creation Miss Harriet, a stern Englishwoman who, for reasons that are opaque to Maupassant's libertine narrator, prefers to die without tasting the bliss of passion. Musil's more restrained narrator opines simply that his English puritan may have found pleasure simply in being there (7:500). In her simplicity she remains a mystery. The description of the other characters in this boardinghouse offers by contrast access to an identifiably human world through their simple interests. However, historically, it is a world that has dis-appeared as completely as the world represented on the sarcophagus.

The brief text "Fischer an der Ostsee" ("Fishermen on the Baltic") also offers a perspective on a simple world of average human occupations. It pres-ents a description of fishermen putting worms on their hooks, though it ends with a curious analogy when it says that during lovely weather the dark blue sky forms a vault over the scene, and "the seagulls circle high above the land like white swallows" (7:480). One wonders why gulls should be likened to swallows in order to suggest the bucolic serenity of the scene. Musil perhaps wanted to suggest a familiar perspective to landlocked readers for whom pas-toral assurance could only be communicated by swallows, birds familiar in both myth and urban landscapes. The urban landscape is invoked in the text "Inflation," with its depiction of the merry-go-round of yesteryear. But the for-mer times of wooden horses are over, and the narrator adds, seemingly with an allusion the Baltic fishermen, "today the young fishermen drink champagne with cognac." Musil's juxtaposition of disparate images of then and now reflects his desire to change the reader's perception of modernity. This desire is further illustrated by the way the narrator depicts a then-contemporary mechanized Austrian merry-go-round. He concludes that the same people come to the park day in and day out to this new, mechanized form of pleasure in order simply to be swung around by the machine's operator—which may shed some light on what Musil means by the mechanization of modern life. The picture conveyed by "Inflation," with its description of the intoxications of cheap modern pleasure, seems intentionally juxtaposed with the quiet dignity of the text describing the Baltic fishermen, the two texts being united by the line describing the pleasures young fishermen seek now. Musil's critical evaluation of two worlds is embodied in the juxtaposition of perspectives, and it would be a mistake to read these texts as an illustration of a totally value-free, neutral vision.

Juxtaposition of perceptions plays a key role in a strangely powerful text about death, "Slowenishes Dorfbegräbnis" ("Slovenian Village Funeral"), a text having a narrator who is a character in the story. The narrator takes up quarters in a Slovenian village in a house that stinks because of the presence of dead mice, not to mention the considerable amount of garbage that has been dumped in it. After moving in to this sad place, the narrator witnesses a village funeral in which an old woman is buried during winter. The coffin is drawn on a small sled whose motion suggests something mechanical about it all. But the ceremony is changed by the accompanying music into something the narrator calls supernatural, and he is depressed to the point of tears. But then he spies a dog, indifferent to it all, playing with his master's hand, and the master plays with the dog even while his face remains stonily fixed in respect. The juxtaposition of death and play, of ceremony and spontaneity, lifts the narrator out of depression, for he has perceived, and through him the reader has also seen, a reconfiguration of the experience. The change of perspective allows one, minimally, to make something of unhappiness, which, as the narrator says with understatement, is "to bring people closer to each other, or something like that" (7:492). And so "something like" a moral value emerges from the picture.

In general, then, the renewal of perception, often brought about by a change of perspective, is at work in virtually all the pieces in "Pictures." The sections' remaining texts bear out this interpretation. In "Der Erweckte" ("Awakening") the narrator is awakened in the dark at six in the morning: he sees a different world in which chimneys are his brothers, the geometry of the city is changed, and he is projected into the night—to end up finally no longer

211

desirous to think about the astonishing change worked on his vision by the early hour. In "Hellhörigkeit" (translated as "Clearhearing," though sensitive hearing is implied) the narrator lies in bed sick, but his ill health means that he is subjected to an unbearable noisy racket as his companion, probably his wife, prepares to go to bed, though she is merely engaging in normal routine of changing clothes and washing. Perspective changes sound as well as vision.

Animals also play a role in other "Pictures." In "Hasenkatastrophe" ("Rabbit Catastrophe") the narrator watches as a fox terrier destroys the equilibrium among hotel guests when the dog kills a young rabbit; suddenly the world appears different, for as the first-person narrator observes, out of the depths surge up a powerful desire to commit aggression against people who allow such frightful things to happen (7:488). The text called "Die Maus" ("The Mouse") shows that Musil, like Saint Francis, has no preferences among the animals. Situated at the Italian front during the war, the text describes a system of tunnels a mouse has built next to a bench, situated on a mountain on the front. For incomprehensible reasons artillery shells do not hit the bench. When the tunnel-building mouse appears, its small eye looks at the narrator and produces disorientation in him, so "that one really didn't really know if this small living black eye turned about or if the gigantic immobility of the mountain moved . . . if it was struggle or if eternity ruled" (7:489). The difference between viewing a mouse's lair and perceiving eternity is abolished. Again, like Saint Francis, Musil seems to have been capable of such perception, and rather convincingly so in this text in which the survival of the mouse in its tunnels is no less miraculous than any other survival on the front.

A final aspect of these "pictures" deserves mention: the juxtapositions and reversals making up Musil's strategy for renewing perception are often quite amusing. His comic juxtapositions are part of his strategy for undermining received conventions for perception and evaluation. They are often extremely effective. Consider in this regard the comic reversal of perspective in "Mädchen und Helden" ("Maidens and Heroes"), which is narrated from a dog's perspective. The dog narrator addresses himself directly to the girls who take dogs on walks. The girls are more concerned with attracting the attention of the opposite sex than tending to the dogs' needs, especially the need to mark their territory by frequent urination. So the girls drag the dogs along, the dogs following on three feet with one leg raised in hopeless anticipation, too proud to protest their treatment in any other manner. The girls are not heartless; they simply do not realize, says the dog, what inner dog-illnesses they are causing, what "despairing neurasthenic complexes" are caused by the treatment they inflict (7:493). The existence of "complexes" in a dog not allowed to urinate suggests analogies with the neurotic who, according to Freudian psychoanalysis, represses gratification of desire. In this satirical juxtaposition, Musil changes one's perspective on the conventions of psychoanalysis, for the contrast presents, on the one hand, the claims of psychoanalytical theory and its all-encompassing theories about human, if not canine, behavior; and on the other hand, a real world of unhappiness in which questionable theory is usually misapplied.

Musil makes an explicitly satirical depiction of Freudian theory in the last meditation of the second section, "Ill-Tempered Observations," called "Der bedrohte Ödipus" ("Threatened Oedipus"). This text is also a good introduction to the ill-tempered or unfriendly considerations with which Musil pursues his cultural criticism. In this text he anticipates Freudian rebuttals of his criticism, since he appositely observes that any critique of Freud is explained away, immediately and circularly, by Freudians using Freudian terms, so that a negative critique of the theory can always be used to confirm it. This circular argumentation, Musil suggests, is the equivalent of a boy who, lacking imagination, replies to obscene insults directed at him with "You, too." Or as Musil observes with near sarcasm, such scientific methods may be acquired before puberty (7:529).

In his satirical critique of Freudian theory Musil emphasizes the way psychoanalysis is bound up with historical phenomena. To make this point he first feigns a certain ironic naïveté. At the outset he praises psychoanalysis for the historical regression it practices, since, at a time like the present when everyone is too busy for idle chatter, it has brought back the good old days when one could stretch out and gossip at leisure about whatever happens to go through one's head. In an era such as the present when the individual has lost all importance, psychoanalysis takes him by the hand and says not to worry: the suffering patient needs only a little courage and gonads in order to exist. Thus the "layperson," who Musil claims to be, wishes good luck to psychoanalysis, though he doubts that the theory will continue to last long. Turning from the past, Musil looks at the future, noting that the heart of psychoanalysis is the Oedipus complex. To have such a complex the infant must be attracted to the mother's *Schoss*—a term that means, as Musil explains, not just the lap or bosom but the entire desirable body of a plump Viennese mother of 1880. How can the Oedipus complex continue to exist, he asks, with the "new woman" who lacks the layers of fat and reassuring softness of the Freudian mother (7:530)? The alluring *Schoss* has disappeared because women now swim and ski, with the result that the father's *Schoss* may soon be just as attractive as that of the plump mother of Freud's youth. In conclusion he asks, with not entirely benevolent irony, if an Orestes complex will replace the Oedipal complex.

213

The feigned benevolence is an effective strategy for pointing up at once the pseudoscientific nature of the Freudian enterprise while allowing Musil to make comments on the historically transitory nature of concepts dealing with what are essentially cultural, not biological, issues. Much of what he includes in his "Ill-Tempered Observations" deals with the confusions of modernity, which from his perspective includes the easy acceptance of Freudian doctrines as well as nearly every other form of belief, all accompanied by the triumphant omnipresence of kitsch art forms. Musil wants to understand the proliferation and dissemination of modernity's confusions in belief and ideology. To that end in the essay "Unter lauter Dichtern und Denkern" ("Surrounded by Poets and Thinkers") he points out that in Germany immediately after the war more than a thousand new journals were started, and in an average year more than thirty thousand books were published. This explosion of publications was not necessarily a good thing, Musil suggests, if it is a sign of the proliferation of near-psychopathic beliefs. With sarcasm he suggests that true paranoiacs can no longer defend themselves against the competition presented by the omnipresent amateur maniacs with their idée fixe (7:514). The success of innumerable lunatic and fringe journals in the Weimar era was not a subject for rejoicing.

With essayistic probes in these "Ill-Tempered Observations," Musil explores a gamut of cultural phenomena ranging from kitsch to delusions induced by the proliferation of new cultural forms. Kitsch was of special importance for Musil, as it has been for many later writers, from Adorno to Milan Kundera. Omnipresent today, somewhere in the nineteenth century kitsch represented a new phenomenon in the history of European culture. It originated in the development of precast artistic and ideological messages created for the new mass audiences. To many kitsch appears designed largely to recycle a kind of degenerate romanticism. From Musil's viewpoint it became dominant as a cultural form when mass-produced art replaced authentic artistic values. He confronted kitsch, moreover, not simply as a question of good taste or authenticity in a market economy; for the use of kitsch by totalitarian regimes on the left and on the right demonstrated that it could be used to promote the collective ideological goals and values of totalitarian movements. Thus Musil's analysis of kitsch aims not only at the regimentation of art by consumerism, but is also part of his critique of the right-wing ideology that had become omnipresent in Germany. His criticism is directed at the uninhibited kitsch that was promoting "life" as a value opposed to rationality and "soul" as superior to a critical mind. This criticism is implicit in the title of the first of "Ill-Tempered Observations," "Schwarze Magie" ("Black Magic"), a title that is redolent of the right-wing political belief that magic is inherent in the essence of true German being. In his exercise in "black magic" Musil asserts that art stands in opposition to kitsch insofar as authentic or effective art scours life of kitsch, which entails that the more abstract art is, the more it helps life resist kitsch. This use of the concept of abstraction may seem curious. However, it takes its full resonance when one recalls the then-current nationalist notions according to which abstraction was a foreign product of the enemy French intellect or the perverted Jewish mind. By *abstraction* in this context Musil means something like the intellectual scope that, for a rationalist such as himself, is the goal of intellectual activity. He does not mean metaphysical abstraction; he means rigorous thinking.

In this text on black magic, Musil asks what is kitsch. His idea in this essay is simple and, I believe, remarkably insightful. He says that kitsch transforms feelings into concepts. Original feelings in art, based upon lived experience, are transformed into imitative concepts derived from previous art forms (7:502). Kitsch is something like art to the second degree, or even imitations of imitations. Kitsch concepts, too, are sheer abstractions, though incapable of the critical function and the intellectual scope of abstraction found in authentic art. This view of kitsch, and the received artistic forms it trades in, is another aspect of Musil's view that culture, in time, becomes ossified in fixed concepts that must be transformed if art is to remain in contact with living experience. Kitsch is the opposite of lived experience; and in its abstraction, as Musil phrases it, feelings are transformed into layers of concepts that, in much of what passes for modern art, are stacked upon on each other. Of course, the view that art defends life obliges one to ask what is meant by life in this context.

"Life," as suggested above, was another loaded ideological concept, especially in right-wing circles, for to evoke life was to use a kind of kitsch shorthand to designate all the irrationality that nationalists and racists wished to promote. For example, foreign rationalism is notorious for killing life, whereas right-wing ideologues claimed to stand valiantly for the forces of life in their opposition to the hordes of enemies threatening Germany, with its life-endowing will to power and its racially unique life-forms. With this rhetoric in the background, Musil knows that one cannot innocently ask what is life. Thus he falls back on a kind of Cartesian statement that "life is life," about which he then says that if you do not find it self-evident, then you do not know what life is. He gives, however, a few dialectical examples of what life is. For example, it includes among many other things peristalsis and ideology. With this juxtaposition his ironic point is that a definition of life cannot be encapsulated in a few ideological formulas that can be brandished like flags and swords. It is the task of thought to find order in the complexity of life, he says, and then destroy that order (7:503)—which is another way of describing what Musil sees to be the artist's task of perpetual creation through the destruction of received forms, or the scientist's of perpetual doubt and questioning. Perhaps the final ironic black magic in this "unfriendly consideration" is that the mathematician in Musil comes up with some brief syllogisms expressing the relations of life, art, and kitsch. His final black magic takes the shape of logic. His play with syllogisms shows at once the distance he has from his own thought and that he knows he is pointing up some simple truths that are of great importance for a culture becoming inundated with a nationalist ideology promoted by the manipulation of kitsch.

The deflation of contemporary ideology is also central to an ill-tempered observation taking for its title a well-known line from the German romantic poet Joseph von Eichendorff, "Wer hat dich, du schöner Wald . . . ?" ("Who Made You, Oh Forest Fair . . . ?"). The kitsch image of a forest originated in the romantics and their belief that nature is a source of divine revelation. By the Weimar era a nationalism using rhetoric from romanticism had become a driving force in the ideology fueling the reactionary, illiberal mind—for which the German forest was a magical symbol. For the mind blinded by the forest, if not the trees, Musil demonstrates that, by the early twentieth century, the romantic forest had become a place of nationalist myth; whereas real German forests had largely become cultivated tree farms with a bit of decoration. He contrasts sardonically what the romantic nature seeker, or a sick person needing fresh air, wants from the woods and what the agronomist now offers in his well-managed farm. The industrial agronomist has some airy sanatoriums situated in planned and managed woods from which profits can be made at every level of exploitation. Behind the *Forstmeister* or the German forester of romantic fame stands capitalist management wanting a maximum of timber production; and after the managers, Musil points out, come the timber merchants, the sawmills, the manufacturers, the building entrepreneurs, shipyards, paper producers, and tradesmen (7:527). This list of profiteers is, to say the least, a direct answer to Eichendorff's question about who made the forest fair. It is also is a rational deflation of the romantic roots of contemporary ideology pretending to find in the well-managed rural habitat a source of "true" German values. True German values, Musil suggests, are found in a decent return on an investment in timber needing a developed system of marketing.

Several of the "Ill-Tempered Observations" deal with the function of the artist. Musil again argues in different ways that the artist's and poet's task is to bring about cultural history by changing perception. In the title "Malsteller"

("The Paintspreader"—literally somebody who puts down paint) Musil invents a neologism by analogy with the general term for writer, *Schriftsteller*. The neologism serves to point up a certain symmetry between, on the one hand, the mere painter and writer whose skills make them popular for a brief moment and, on the other hand, the *Kustler* and *Dichter*, the artist and poet who create new cultural forms. Much like Proust, Musil makes the somewhat paradoxical claim that the authentic artist and poet cannot be recognized by their immediate contemporaries because, when the artist and poet are innovative, they appear to the public to be ignorant, for they seem not to understand the aesthetic forms that the public recognizes as the acceptable conventions for art. In their innovation the authentic artist and writer belong to the future, when, at last discovered and understood, they will then appear to belong to the past during which they fixed the new conventions of today.

This paradoxical process does not apply to most writers or painters. In Musil's description of the historical process in "Kunstjubiläum" ("Art Anniversary"), it seems that with the passage of time most art simply disappears. In the case of the typical work of art, years after its disappearance the viewer or reader must wonder what it was that interested them in works that, when looked at after the passage of time, now hold no interest at all for them. In short the vast majority of past works of art and literature are dead. This view is not an expression of any belief in progress, for, as Musil remarks, progress only makes sense if it is toward a goal. Rather, the death of most artworks is a ongoing fact of history, which from this perspective is largely a history of fashions and modes. The exception is authentic art that continues to offer access to a unique realm in which living feeling and intellect continue to exist. Only this art, Musil opines, is really art, and with this statement he defends again his belief that there are two kinds of art, one that exploits received conventions and then dies and that much rarer art that destroys conventions and opens onto new cultural vistas.

As argued in "Surrounded by Poets and Thinkers," the situation of the contemporary poet is made all the more difficult, as Musil knew too well in personal terms, because contemporary society has developed armies of professors, book reviewers, and critics who live off the recognized poet. At the same time this society has signally failed to provide a way for the difficult and authentic artist to live. Moreover, looking at his own fragmented time, he returns to the theme of proliferating doctrines and ideologies. He deplores a culture in which the authentic poet must attempt to find an audience at a time of cultural confusion. Musil wonders who can hear a poet when Germany is filled with the cacophonous voices of competing doctrines ranging from the fanatics of "cherry-eating, to those of organic theater, from musical gymnastics to eubiotics, and a thousand others" (7:515). With the proliferation of sects and cults, the artist's work is submerged in the sheer number of heterogeneous and often loony cultural movements, many of them promising religious initiation. As Musil observes with bitter irony, numerous in Germany are the Romes from whose popes, unknown to the general public, thousands of the initiated expect salvation. But salvation had become a leitmotif of German culture, something Musil will satirically project back onto the Vienna of *The Man without Qualities.*[5]

Musil's satirical musings thus throw into relief the psychological dilemmas that the tensions and fragmentation of modernity have created. Modern madness can take the most unexpected shapes. For instance in "Der Riese Agoag" ("The Giant Agoag") Musil describes how a maladapted modern human can use technology to project an image of power and thus literally mechanize himself. In this short narrative, a physical fitness enthusiast without enough money to join a muscle-building club has difficulty in reaching the "triumph of morality and spirit" with which contemporary ideology endows the well-muscled body (7:531). So he works out at home, using his muscles against themselves as best he can, until one day he witnesses an accident in which a large bus knocks down a well-built young man. This near epiphany comes after the story's would-be Charles Atlas had already been beaten in the street. Since Ulrich also undergoes the same experience, it seems safe to say that Musil was convinced that one must be ready for violence at every moment. In "The Giant Agoag" the potential strongman identifies with what he sees to be real power—the bus—and gets into the bus to begin a life spent riding around in it. During his rides he celebrates imaginary victories over lesser subjects who must scurry to avoid the bus's undeniable power to flatten them. In his excellent translation of *Posthumous Papers of a Living Author* Peter Wortsman calls the organization to which the lunatic hero now belongs the Athletes-Get-on-Omnibus-Associated Group. Alas, bus-riding with Agoag is limited in its capacity to endow the hero with power. Its limits are shown when he invites a girlfriend to join him, and she is promptly appreciative of another male in the bus, one whose bulk makes the hero hesitant to attempt to inflict physical punishment upon this successful rival. Apparently one lesson is that maniac exercises in power are best done alone. In any case the satire here cuts broadly, at once portraying the unstable mind of the male subject lost in the urban environment in which the ideology of power and violence is omnipresent, but also a spoof of the individualism and faddish cult of the self to which Musil's alter ego Ulrich is, at times, addicted. Enemies of mechanization may also find grist for their mill in this tale.

The Ulrich of *The Man without Qualities* would also find an antithetical alter ego in the character described in "Ein Mensch ohne Charakter" ("A Man without Character"), one the four "Unstorylike Stories." Depicting the fragmentation brought about by modernity, this putative story sets out a contrasting study in miniature of what it means to have, or not to have, properties. To this end the narrator describes an acquaintance whose life has consisted in the acquisition of different characters, which may ultimately be a demonstration that he has no intrinsic character at all. In the course of the narration it becomes obvious that the meaning of *character* includes, in German as in English, the ideas of moral character, literary persona, and social role, so that the character that the character does not have is variable in meaning with the circumstances. When the acquaintance is a boy he is remonstrated by mother and father for having no character. They presumably believe it would be of great value later in life to have character. However, the boy thinks character really means, at least to the parents, something like the opposite of getting bad grades, skipping classes, tying tin cans to a dog's tail, killing birds with a slingshot, and other such enjoyable behavior. The narrator complicates this meaning by saying that the real opposite to having character lay in the boy's terror at the punishment he might receive for his behavior, the anguish he felt about being found out, and the torture that conscience inflicted on boys if it appeared that things might go badly for them (7:534). With this humorous juxtaposition of meanings, Musil contrasts perspectives, obligingly suggesting the way meanings are determined by circumstance and perception. Education in character demands contradictory perspectives, for the boy learns from his parent that if he lies to hide his lack of character, then having character means that he should at least lie honestly.

As an adolescent the acquaintance discovers in literature a new way to have a character. He can imitate those characters ready-made by theater and fiction. Musil offers a minicourse in poetics here. He points up that to take on a literary character is to confuse life and literature. The result is that the role conferred by the literary character usually imposes behavior that is at odds with what reality demands. This discovery leads the acquaintance as an adult to experiment by taking on various appearances from stock social characters. After he finally becomes a lawyer, his options are limited. He finds that taking on the appearance of a poet or a Christ figure would be at odds with the demands of his *Berufscharakter,* his character now defined by his profession. A lawyer's character demands, for example, that he look through his monocle differently from the way a theologian looks through his. The friend ends up, perhaps in spite of himself, acquiring the characteristics his profession imposes. This change coincides with his discovering that modern society has been waiting all along in order to endow him with a variegated character based on gender, nation, country, class, and countless other features, which compose the modern notion of identity. In confusion the acquaintance cannot decide which of these many characters he should consider his own.

Musil concludes "A Man without Character" with a satirical twist. The acquaintance acquires a definitive character through his material success, for he acquires the material traits of being rich and fat. His problems are resolved. However, he now no longer believes in the need for character, since the modern historical period, a time of warfare with its tanks and flamethrowers, obviously demands not character but discipline (7:539). With this narrative pirouette Musil brings the reader to confront the new social order in which power is signified by material excess and by demands for obedience—not by demands for moral character. The meaning of character remains ambivalent, though there is no doubt that Musil has made a marvelous satirical portrait of the German bourgeois, locked in his rolls of fat, portrayed in the end as one might find in a Weimar satirical portrait by Grosz or Dix, in which one might spy with effort some remaining features of an earlier, younger character now ensconced in the character without character. "A Man without Character" is a satirical portrait that also sheds light on how difficult is Ulrich's attempt to negotiate an ethical existence without qualities, for qualities seem to accrue to a character without his making any effort. The problem is to avoid the multiple and perhaps contradictory characters imposed by modern society.

Another nonstory, "Eine Geschichte aus Drei Jahrhunderten" ("A Story over Three Centuries"), offers another comic historical perspective on contemporary trends, namely, the question of the emancipation of women. At first glance it appears Musil deals with feminism from three arbitrarily chosen time frames, since the narrative sets out tales with three different dates, illustrating events in the past of 1729; the very distant past of 2197 B.C.; and the present moment of 1927. But it is also clear that the three dates selected are permutations on the number sequence 1279. I do not quite know what to make of these permutations, though it might appear that Musil is showing that numbers rather automatically generate history. In any case the first narration takes place during the Enlightenment, the second meditates on the third millennium before the Common Era, and the third is situated in the third decade of the twentieth century. If there is a common character in the three texts themselves, beside time existing as a permutation, it might be that the three narratives range throughout history to illustrate variations of the theme of women and their relations to men—in perhaps a kind of ahistorical historicism suggested by the recurrence of the numbers. Musil's irony here encompasses both sides of the question of women's emancipation, for he can comically entertain opposing perspectives with something like a mock-epic sense of the issues involved. Nearly all critics agree that he was unusually sensitive to women, to their needs and their rights, and it would be obtuse not to see that in this text he is trying to wrench readers out of any preconceived notions they might have about what should be the role of women. I am not certain that he is entirely successful, but I am not entirely certain as to what should be the perspective finally encompassing the three texts. The production of uncertainty may well have been Musil's goal in casting wide his historical net.

First the Enlightenment: a noted French noble is thrown for some reason to beasts of prey. He finds that the beast about to shred him up is a female. Living before the early-twentieth-century Swedish playwright August Strindberg made sexuality problematic, or so the narrator observes, the nobleman is attracted by the bestial nature of her femininity. He finds he is a male character finding himself in a female position in the act of submission. (One may recall Claudine in this regard.) Like a textbook version of a proper Victorian wife, the nobleman loses the mastery of his senses and in his happiness "no longer knew what happened to him" (7:540). This parody of male ideas about female desire is followed by a text set in the year 2197 B.C. The title's permutation arbitrarily but comically suggests continuity in change, especially the fictional precision about a distant era known mainly through speculation.

The narrator begins by asking whether there were Amazons in antiquity, presumably at the end of the third millennium. Modern biology suggests that there were not, but the narrator does not want to give up the dream of power that Amazons represent, especially the dream of being destroyed by sexual power. Relevantly, the narrator asks whether the work of the Austrian writer Leopold Sacher-Masoch (1836–1895) may or may not have had a precursor in the Greek legend of the Amazons (7:541). For his literary description of perverse sexuality, Sacher-Masoch's name is now known for its use in coining the term *masochism*. Musil is self-consciously playing with a transhistorical view of eroticism in this text, one in which men's dreams of submission to power and violence is again in the forefront. The narrator's wonder about history then brings up the ironic question as to whether those Greeks who furnish the basis for our humanistic education are to be believed at all. Reflecting on classical education based on the Greeks, he wonders if "like all Levantines" they exaggerated. With this allusion to people of the East the narrator laconically concludes, "Dark are the beginnings of civilization" (7:541). Musil's ironies are multiple in this conclusion. He refers to German education and then links it to anti-Semitic stereotypes about Jews, called Levantines and associated with dark people. The "civilization" whose origins are literally and figuratively dark evokes the stereotypical term for the inferior culture that right-wing Germans attributed to the Jews and the French, for their idea of "civilization" is inferior when compared with German *Kultur.* The satire cuts in many directions, with its idea that our Greek forebears, the models of our civilization and even of German *Kultur,* dreamed of being raped and beaten by forceful women—much like the fly that goes to be eaten by the spider. Or so suggests the narrator in his vision of the myth of the Amazons.

"A Story over Three Centuries" concludes with the third narrative showing that, if the Amazons fell in love with their conquerors, such is decidedly not the case at a meeting of the old and new cultures in 1927. It describes a factious political meeting at which the opposition to the male order is now under feminist control. A famed scientific observer, Quantus Negatus, is present at the meeting. A representative of the old order, the scientist hears the new idea, upheld by women, that the majority of men are asses. And he finds himself half convinced, despite his anguish-filled objections to the women's positions (7:543). A polemic ensues in which the two opposing parties do not allow each other to speak, though finally Negatus is comforted when a young man's voice, speaking little that is reasonable, can nonetheless sweep away twenty women's voices with its melodious power. This is the power of the senses—and perhaps a parody of Orpheus. Having had a classical education, Negatus recalls the Amazons from his school days, and his "manly curiosity" entertains the possibility of a future world turned upside down by female power. "How dark is the future of civilization," he muses, echoing the thoughts about an earlier millennium. His conclusion is that only the return of a "time of real men" can stop the triumph of the feminine (7:543). The reactionary scientist leaves the assembly, walking by women as busy powdering their faces as they were earlier busy muttering "murderous words." This sight causes Negatus to wonder why men worry their tiny heads with useless thoughts (7:544).

There is something quintessentially Weimar about this satirical series of wacky reflections that aim at blowing up conventional perceptions encoded in conservative German ideology. Musil as a student of psychology knew that fear is a great motivator of the desire for power. In "A Story over Three Centuries" he ironically portrays men who at once desire domination and are afraid of those women who want to emancipate themselves from the patriarchal domination vigorously upheld by reactionaries. It seems no hyperbole to say that he has caught the psychological climate of Weimar, in which men were willing to submit to humiliation even as they were afraid of losing power; and thus the Nazis were able to exploit these fears to take power for themselves.[6] And, to return to the issue of historicism, it seems that his whimsical play with permutations also suggests that human history, in the domain of sexual relations, has changed little, for power has been a constant factor in the way desire has been mediated. Eros is mediated by power; this is a constant theme in Musil. It may explain some of the bizarre attraction to animals that permeates his work, such as in the case of the tale of the French aristocrat who may be Musil's homage to the Marquis de Sade.

A somewhat different critique of modern ideology motivates the whimsical nonstory titled "Kindergeschichte" ("Children's Story"). Three hunters named Boom, Bang, and Pow go out, shoot at a rabbit, argue about who might have hit it, and subsequently are dressed down by the rabbit itself, who predicts a sorry end for all of them. This chastising speech may be an illusion produced by schnapps; it may be one produced by the kitsch mythology of the happy hunter that is part of folklore; or it may be a reflection of the hyperbolic kitsch of bunny rabbits. All of this seems wrapped up in the tale's final absurd image of a cat hunting rabbit eggs—despite the fact, as the narrator observes, that there are some people who maintain that bunnies lay eggs only at Easter. This wacky image, I take it, is another product of the same mindless kitsch mentality that, loving bunnies, also thinks slaughtering rabbits with guns is a jolly activity. In any case bunnies are an important part of the kitsch ideology that recycles myths that stop critical thinking, and Musil was ready to satirize any aspect of that blunted mentality. Admittedly, this tale is sufficiently opaque that one doubts that a definitive interpretation of its bunnies, hunters, and eggs is in the offing.

For a general conclusion about the first three sections of *Posthumous Papers of a Living Author,* and thus before dealing with the last tale, "The Blackbird," I offer comments on a few texts that round out our view of Musil as the ironist and sometime satirist for whom the reality of the daily world offers unending ironic readings. One of his most amusing exercises in essayistic irony is found in the ill-tempered observation called "Denkmale" ("Monuments"). Noting that our culture erects stone commemorative monuments whose official purpose is memory, the essay contends that, in fact, these monuments dedicated to the dead actually work to assure that we forget those commemorated by them. There is nothing so invisible as a public monument placed on view to keep history alive (7:506). This view of the anesthesia performed by public commemoration offers a variant on Musil's theme of the deadening of perception. Perception is readily fatigued by the daily contact with the familiar so that the familiar monument is like a stone weight placed upon the commemorated being's neck. With the monument attached, and hurled into the ocean of time, the celebrated personage disappears quickly, as it were, into a sea of oblivion (7:509). Musil thus suggests that this antithesis of intention and result is a permanent part of our modern landscape, and it is written into practically every one of the essays and parables as part of a description of the workings of modernity.

The traces of history in the present can be read when and where perception has not been blunted. In the short essay "Türen und Tore" ("Doors and Portals") Musil shows this presence of history by interpreting the significance of something as banal as the doors found in the modern city. He finds, as opposed to semantically significant doors of houses produced by yesteryear, the only original type of door produced by modern culture is the glass revolving door found in hotels and warehouses (7:505). The reduction of the door to a utilitarian function, devoid of aesthetic play, is, as Musil presents it, a metonymy for modern culture. The essential feature is reduction; ludic excess is lacking; impoverishment is the rule; and this in spite of the proliferation of cults and sects permeating the city with their hollow messages. The essay on doors and portals sets out in an exemplary way Musil's uncanny sense of the meaning of the ordinary, for no detail of the quotidian is without significance for the open eye.

The psychological significance found in everyday reality can even be garnered from a postcard, as shown in the ill-tempered observation titled "Hier ist es schön" ("It's Lovely Here"). Musil first considers how the postcards that people send are designed to make all famous places look the same through the same Technicolor glitz. In this they offer an essentially kitsch message. But selecting and sending a postcard is also part of a larger need people have to share paradoxically their experience of something special or unique by which they might endow their own existence with a certain joy, an honest joy in what is supposedly recognized to be beautiful. One wants to experience the unique, but the perception of it must be shared and mediated by others. Musil stresses that modern humans experience a contradictory need to find a special place for themselves by association with places recognized as special, or by associating themselves with a special event, usually created by the media, that anchors them in some time or place that has not been leveled by the routine of modern existence. For example, they find pleasure in saying they were on the spot when such-and-such murderer shot so-and-so in the street. Musil's essay probes the need to create a unique niche for oneself and the modern difficulty to experience something other than banality and convention. Set in opposition to the realm of the unique that makes for authentic experience, banality and convention constitute the constant negative pole of the modern world that Musil himself seems to have constantly experienced. The tension between the two poles is perhaps at the center of his work with its unceasing question: how can one experience the unique when one's experience of it is codified as reality in the kitsch of a picture postcard?

The fourth section of *Posthumous Papers of a Living Author* is a single tale, "The Blackbird." The novella has received a much more critical attention than any other text in the collection. Musil himself published it separately in a journal (and it is published in a separate edition today by the well-known publisher Reclam along with the texts that make up "Pictures"). The attention that "The Blackbird" has received is probably due to the fact that it lends itself to postmodern interpretative schemas. It can be construed to be a self-referential narration, much on the order of certain parables by Kafka. Hence it is popular among critics precisely because it proposes an undecipherable allegory that allows critics to demonstrate their hermeneutic dexterity. I say this without irony, for the tale overtly invites hermeneutics. It concludes with the second of the tale's two narrators saying that if he knew the meaning of his narration, he would not have told it to his listener. But of course he has told it, and one therefore asks, Why? Critics have given many answers, and most of them seem plausible. But precisely because of narrative's plasticity, almost any hermeneutic framework will work to generate meaning. For this reason I think it is one of Musil's most troubling texts, for it plainly attempts to destroy the possibility of grounding its meaning. It is perhaps the ultimate parable for Musil's own sense of mental fragility and lack of determination about what might make up a, if not the, modern character.

The story begins with a first-person narrator presenting two characters, Aone and Atwo, who were students together in a Catholic school. There their main activity seems to have been performing pranks. Atwo was the more agile of the two. He could do prohibited handstands on stairs, a feat that Aone could not dare to do. The unnamed narrator observes that Atwo has the natural body of an athlete that did not presage a disposition to mysticism (7:549). He then observes that the two boys later were attracted to a materialist, mechanistic philosophy, not because it is true, but for its demonic, pessimistic character (though the narrator also allows that such a philosophy might be true). Atwo studied forestry and dreamed of adventures in Russia, whereas Aone joined the workers' movement. Meeting shortly before the war, they find that they have changed in comparable ways. Atwo has had his Russian adventure and is now working for a corporation, and Aone is the editor of a journal owned by a capitalist. They have contempt for each other but remain friends. Then they encounter each other at some later time, at which point Atwo becomes the story's narrator in order to tell his friend some stories that are unusual, to say the least. What is not unusual, however, at least in the introduction narrated by an unnamed narrator, is that both are typical Germans whose life itineraries have led them to become seemingly average citizens.

Atwo's narration is thus framed by the opening first-person narration, though the reader may suspect that Musil is blurring narrative boundaries. One can easily assume that the narrator is Atwo, or Aone for that matter, since in some ways they mirror each other. And one can just as well resist this temptation by holding all possibilities in suspense. This strategy allows the reader to imagine several equally plausible axes along which the discourse unfolds, and in fact the fracturing of the axis of discourse seems to be one of the goals of the narration. This may be due to the mental illness that underlies the hysteria of modernity, as Musil saw it. This is not to say that Musil is describing a syndrome. Rather he is, as in earlier fiction, depicting a specific, unique world in which the coordinates for normal perception seem to be missing.

Atwo tells Aone about his life some years earlier in Berlin, where he lived in an urban apartment. As he describes it, it was stacked up on top of other apartments, in a city quarter in which all urban dwellers lead the same life in spaces arranged in the same manner. (Weimar painters such as Ernst Kirchner come to mind for a visualization of Berlin's *Mietskasernen,* or blocks of flats.) One night Atwo heard a nightingale singing on the roofs, or so he first thinks, and then decided it was a blackbird—a bird that mimics other birds. Interpretive possibilities are multiple here, for if the nightingale is emblematic of poetic song, the imitation of this emblem might suggest that in Berlin courtyards one can find only derivative poetry, song to the second degree. In any case this apparition of birdsong makes Atwo decide to abandon his wife in the middle of the night and to strike out on the road to the unknown. Perhaps he is imitating a hero taken from romantic literature, like a blackbird imitating a nightingale. Or perhaps he is simply unstable and hence unreliable.

Atwo tells a second story. It is a transposition of the experience Musil had on the Italian front when a flying dart dropped from an airplane struck the ground next to him. The narration casts another light on the way Musil interpreted that experience. Experiencing the closeness of death frees Atwo of the fear of death, and the uncanny experience of hearing death arriving from the air provokes a curious religious experience in him, an atheist who, as the dart approaches, feels certain that God's presence will soon be near him (7:556). And after the dart drives into the ground, he says that if somebody told him God had driven into his body, he would not have laughed, but he would not have believed it either. Musil is charting the limits of belief and disbelief. He shows that unbeliever can have an experience that momentarily negates disbelief. It is something like an empty epiphany allowing Atwo to experience a religious transformation that he does not believe in, but which he longs to experience again. From this modern, indeed modernist, perspective, religion seems reduced to a question of feeling, bereft of any transcendental dimension. Perhaps Musil is describing a form of what the literary scholar Hugo Friedrich called, with reference to the experience of modern poetry, "empty transcendence": a state of revelation that exists only in the mind, unleashed by the stimulus of the poetic word, drugs, or in this case, a deadly flying dart.[7]

And Atwo experiences the state again, he says, in narrating a third story in which he tells of his life after the death of his mother. He had not been close to his mother, but after his mother and father's death he goes to his family home and finds in his old bedroom books that he had read as a child. While reading them there one evening, he hears the blackbird come again and sing like a nightingale. The bird enters the room, and this time it can speak. The feathered visitor says that it is Atwo's blackbird and, notably, that it, the bird, is his mother (7:561). There is a strong suggestion here that Atwo's mind may be unhinged, or that he simply is fabricating a dream. Biographical critics point out that Musil himself was great affected by his mother's death, but his personal grief seems secondary to the way the text is suggesting it is narrated by a mind that is on the edge but capable of interrogating itself about what its own perceptions might mean, if anything.

To return to the idea that the narrative describes, at times, the type of empty transcendence often offered by modern poetry, it might appear that with his blackbird Musil is making an allusion to the poetry of Edgar Allan Poe. Poe was perhaps the first modern poet to theorize the possibility of achieving transcendence with nothing more than precise verbal combinations. With his blackbird visitor, it is also difficult not to think that Musil is playing, unconsciously perhaps, with reminiscences of Poe. (Young Musil ranked Poe with Heinrich Heine, Charles Baudelaire, and Paul Verlaine for their capacity to create in words the secret of music [*TB* 1:13]). Specifically the blackbird recalls Poe's laconic raven, and Musil's reader-narrator resembles greatly Poe's poet who "once upon a midnight dreary" is busy pondering weak and weary "over many a quaint and curious volume of forgotten lore," as Poe describes in the first stanza of the poem "The Raven." Comparable to the raven in function if not in size, Atwo's blackbird brings back his past that no longer exists— nevermore, as the raven famously says. Atwo's blackbird is directly related to his past, for it seems that he had tamed a blackbird in his childhood. This feathered visitor may be the same bird of yesteryear, though the reader cannot be sure since the surly creature, like the raven, speaks no more after its midnight entrance. If there is no parody in the third tale's ending, then perhaps the conclusion is also a strange homage to the mother, perhaps to Musil's mother. If not parody, it is a disjointed and nearly insane homage in which Atwo feeds worms to the bird while maintaining it is like the mother he will see nevermore (7:561).

The hermeneutic door is thrown wide open at the end when Atwo says that he tells his stories not only because he wants to find out what they mean, but also in order to learn if they are true (7:553). Atwo does not specify what order of truth he aims at with the stories: probably not literal truth, but presumably symbolic, allegorical, or perhaps even self-satirical truth. The European blackbird is a fantastic mimic, but the nature of its mimesis here is obscure, even if we call upon a raven for help in understanding him. What finally seems probable is that, not unlike Kafka, Musil's goal with this narration is to set off a quest for meaning that, in its unending proliferation, will mimic the proliferation of meanings to which the profusion of modern beliefs had given rise. In the early twentieth century the effect of competing ideologies and doctrines on the individual was to produce a narrator such as Atwo, and perhaps Aone, unhinged as they go floating freely on the surface of things, fleeing into the night. They have no sense of what the meaning of life might be, or what identity they might choose even if they wanted to. "The Blackbird" is a fitting conclusion for a demonstration of the fragmentation of self in these variegated texts, a fragmentation underscored by the constant irony with which Musil views everything.

CHAPTER 8

The Man without Qualities, Parts 1 and 2

On opening *The Man without Qualities* for the first time, the reader may well be intimidated by the novel's size and the disjointed quality of its table of contents. Its publishing history may help make sense of this appearance and explain what the reader finds available today, which is to say, one standard German edition and two English translations, as well as translations into most of the major European languages. Years of writing went into the novel's creation, and it went through several tentative versions before it became the project called *The Man without Qualities.* Musil published book 1 of the novel, containing part 1 and part 2, in 1930. These two parts will be the focal point of this chapter. They were first translated into English in 1953, and have been most recently translated again in 1995. These two parts of book 1 contain a sequence of 123 continuously numbered chapters.[1] Musil then published in late1932, shortly before Hitler took power, the first 38 chapters of book 2, which he also called part 3. Rather confusingly, however, part 3 begins numbering the chapters again with a chapter 1, "The Forgotten Sister." Book 2 was not completed. It, too, has also been twice translated into English.

Having come in 1933 to live permanently in Vienna, or so Musil thought after Hitler took power in Germany, he found himself under pressure from his publisher to get something into print. Thus Musil was about to publish another twenty sequential chapters of book 2, which is to say, twenty more chapters of part 3, in 1938. However, he took back the galleys of these chapters at the last moment. This was undoubtedly due to the futility of publishing them when the Nazis were taking over Austria. Hitler's annexation of Austria in 1938 meant that Musil had little hope of publishing further installments of the novel. Freed, in effect, from publishing pressure but without any regular financial support, he continued to imagine various endings for the novel and continued to work on it after going into exile in Switzerland. At his death in 1942 he left manuscripts in various stages of completion, testifying at once to the sometimes grandiose schema he had in mind and to the fact that his ongoing imaginative experimentation would not have allowed him to finish the novel in any near future. Perhaps he never would have finished it. In any case some of these man-uscripts, along with the withdrawn galley chapters, have been published in the standard German edition. Only the second English translation includes the gal-ley chapters and a selection of the manuscripts.[2]

The sections of the novel that Musil published in 1930 and 1932 were suf-ficient to make of him one of the premier modernist novelists in the twentieth century. This claim is as much for the novel's project to conceive the basis for a future culture as for its ironic satire of the Austro-Hungarian Empire as it was unknowingly approaching its end. Musil's is a very modernist project. He believed his novel to be a form of total cultural criticism. With it he aimed at the entire spectrum of culture, from its intellectual and moral dimension to what Emerson called the manners of everyday life. It can be argued that Musil's failure to find a conclusion to his novel demonstrates the difficulty characterizing the modernist project of transforming or, indeed, saving culture through literary discourse. On making this observation, however, we should recall that he mocks the idea of salvation and saving culture as much as any other idea circulating in Vienna before the First World War—if this is not an idea taken from Weimar and projected back on Vienna. It is not only with satirical intent in book 1 that Musil endows his character General Stumm with sufficient common sense to remark that he had never heard anyone speak of salvation before he began to frequent the modish circle gathering to plan some meaningful cultural event for the empire. At some point during Musil's writ-ing of the novel saving culture became a cliché. In this regard self-mockery is a necessary strategy in a novel whose essayistic approach to culture requires it to satirize everything, including its own intentions. From this perspective, if the novel's lack of completion illustrates a failure, it is the failure to create a discourse of salvation, a very modernist failure to create a viable myth.

Book 1 of *The Man without Qualities* is a feast for the critical intellect. The writer who wrote the essay on the mathematical man in 1913 endowed *The Man without Qualities* with a witty mathematician as the protagonist, Ulrich, a sometime Nietzschean and a perpetual skeptic. In his essay Musil portrayed the mathematician as a hero of modernity because he has not turned his back on the Enlightenment. In general this is also true of Ulrich, though he is a hero who solves few equations during the course of the novel. Having taken what he calls a year's vacation from life, he leaves his mathematical work to pursue a life devoted if not exactly to the Enlightenment, then to self-enlightenment. Readers follow the development of Ulrich's thoughts and feelings about himself and about society as he engages in much finely developed meditation on epistemology, on the relation of science to life, and on the nature of moral experience and emotion, among many other things. Large parts of the novel portray the active life of the mind, in this case, of a character with a clearly superior mind.

Ulrich undertakes meditations, and the narrator undertakes meditations on Ulrich's meditations, all of which endows the novel at times with an ironic, self-reflexive dimension in the sense that it takes itself, indirectly, for its own subject matter, often to engage in criticism of the project of developing a new ethical viewpoint. The debates about ethics are embedded in the novel's concern with the knowledge of history, or more precisely, the question as to how history can possibly be written, when it is the discouraging record of humanity's usually erroneous moral choices. *The Man without Qualities* is not exactly an historical novel, since it does not enact the fiction of seamlessly representing the past from the past's viewpoint. As we shall see, the narrator is situated in a present moment from which he views the past. But it is perhaps a new kind of historical novel in the sense that it wants to portray the perception of the past from within the past's unfolding even as the narrator is situated outside of that unfolding.

The narrative discourse begins precisely in August 1913, one year before the Austro-Hungarian Empire will declare war on Serbia and begin the chain of events that caused the First World War. Ulrich is a Viennese mathematician whose personal biography began some thirty-two years before that date. In the narrative he has begun his year's vacation, the ending of which would have coincided with the outbreak of the war had the novel been finished. His vacation from life gives him time in book 1 to frequent Viennese society and to be an observer of that city's social structure and the dynamics of the empire as seen in the capital. Satire and critical irony are hardly lacking in these observations of a culture that the narrator views after its disappearance but resurrects through Ulrich's observations.

Ulrich has not withdrawn from professional life with the explicit intent of being a social observer. First of all he wants to create a near-ascetic emptiness around himself. He wants to create a space for meditation, on epistemic issues as well as social, ethical, and psychological questions. In fact social issues largely dominate book 1. Ulrich frequents a milieu in which aristocrats and socialites look for activity, such as the novel's "Parallel Action," that can offer them the illusion of doing something meaningful for their empire. The novel's social scope narrows considerably in its third part, or book 2, after Ulrich meets a nearly forgotten sister with whom he subsequently shares his meditations on knowledge and ethics. In the two parts of book 1, however, Ulrich is engaged with society, perhaps more than he desires, and his encounters there

231

give rise to his immediate meditations. In the Vienna of 1913, as we see through Ulrich's eyes, topics such as the nature of capitalism and the readiness of the army are at least as important as contemporary epistemology, aesthetics, and ethical theory.

However, as always in Musil's work, epistemology is important, and it is not surprising that Ulrich undertakes the task of rethinking the cultural axioms that Musil himself saw undergirding modernity. These are the axioms based on oppositions as old as nature and culture, or reason and emotion, and some as new as economic reasoning and aesthetic excess. Ulrich reflects upon the various forms these oppositions take and often appears to want to elaborate an epistemological position that transcends the two cultures he finds in modern European society, to borrow the celebrated phrase of Cambridge physicist and novelist C. P. Snow.[3] It sometimes appears, indeed, that Ulrich actually wants to leave the modern world to go back to the scientific revolution of the seventeenth century and to reunite the irreconcilable epistemologies that emerged then. Ulrich resembles young Törless in more than one respect, though as an adult mathematician he, unlike Törless, knows the import of Pascal's formulations for his own thought. To recall my earlier discussion of Pascal, it can be said that Ulrich wants to overcome the two epistemologies, one based on axiomatics and the other on complexity, that the French mathematician first saw fissuring human knowledge more than three hundred years ago. Ulrich does not want to give up mathematical precision, the basis for science, which is powerful but limited in scope; nor, on the other hand, does he want to relinquish intuitive thinking, what Pascal called the *esprit de finesse,* that is broader in its uses but much more difficult because it must embrace an infinity of possible conditions. What I said earlier about Pascal thus finds application to Ulrich's conscious desire to overcome antinomies of thought. Suffice it to say here that these Pascalian distinctions underlie much of what Ulrich, a very Pascalian mathematician, often thinks, as is true in the case of the narrator and, indeed, Musil himself, a Pascalian modernist.

These comments suggest, moreover, that there is more than one mathematical epistemologist to be found thinking in the novel. To grasp this point one must see that Ulrich, the narrator, and finally Musil, the implied author, maintain a complex relationship, one complicated by the fact that the dominant rhetorical mode in the novel is irony. The rhetorical stance created by the play of irony is complex, for at times one feels that Ulrich and the narrator are one in their viewpoint. At other times one feels that Ulrich exists at some distance from, and is judged by, the narrator and, by implication, from the author who is constructing the entire work. The reader is constantly obliged to evaluate the stance of the speaking voice, be it of a character, of the narrator, or, through indirection, of the author. What is essential, then, is that Ulrich not be taken as a mouthpiece for Musil. Rather, he is part of the complex thought experiment in which Musil looks to see what might happen if a Viennese intellectual in 1913, steeped in science, philosophy, and literature, decided to question every axiom that his culture was based on. The results of this experiment may not always be positive; and it cannot be maintained that Ulrich is always correct, insightful, or even polite. The narrator knows this, even if Ulrich does not.

To make the briefest synopsis of the entire novel, one can say that it narrates, after Ulrich's withdrawal from the life of science in August 1913, first his sexual imbroglios; then his involvement in the rather absurd civic activity, the Parallel Action, undertaken by a group of well-meaning Viennese socialites, businessmen, diplomats, intellectuals, and others who want Austria to rival the German Reich in finding its place in the sun; and, finally, his meditations on epistemology, ethics, and culture. These activities take up most of book 1, with the social satire centering on the Parallel Action. The group gathered under this name undertakes the task of finding activity that will give luster to the image of the empire. The Action seeks a PR event to justify the empire's existence, as it were. To this end the participants in the Action propose to celebrate, in 1918, the forthcoming seventieth jubilee of the Austrian kaiser. They do this in part to outdo the German kaiser's forthcoming celebration of the thirtieth year of his reign during the same fated year, 1918. This was a year that was to offer neither kaiser anything to celebrate, the year in which both of their empires disappeared.

After Musil's depiction of a society unknowingly, but tenaciously, heading for its own demise, book 2 and the unpublished manuscripts focus largely on Ulrich's relation to his sister, Agathe. Book 2 will be the focal point of the following chapter, though it can be mentioned in this synopsis that in some unpublished (and unfinished) manuscripts it appears that Ulrich and Agathe achieve a mystical unity or union. In the published book 2, in conversation with Agathe, Ulrich toys with the idea that their relation might be likened to that of an Isis united with an Osiris (3:905). The idea suggested by this myth seems to be that Ulrich needs to find love to overcome his dismemberment, by which one can understand his alienation in modern culture. To achieve this impossible union with his other half, he would need to flee to a world beyond conventional morality and knowledge. Ulrich—and perhaps Musil—was tempted by the idea that, like the androgyne, he might find his double and be restored with his other half, such as Plato, our first mathematician-metaphysician, once described in his myth of the reunion of separated halves in his dialogue *The Symposium.*

In this chapter and the next, I will mainly deal with what Musil himself saw published, although the galley chapters mentioned above should also be included in this tally. These chapters are essentially completed work. Considering only the published parts of the novel, plus the twenty galley chapters, one can argue that there is an interesting unity to the novel, even in its uncompleted shape. The two parts of book 1 offer a symmetrical contrast to book 2, "Into the Millennium (The Criminals)," (in which, as stated, I include the galley chapters that almost made it into print). To illustrate this idea of symmetry based on opposition I want now to address the question of the shape of the novel as it basically exists in the two published parts.

The title of part 1 of book 1 is translated as "A Sort of Introduction" in both translations. However, translators of the title of part 2 have differed in their interpretations of the meaning of the German title, "Seinesgleichen geschieht." The first translators, Eithne Wilkins and Ernst Kaiser, translated it "The Like of It Now Happens," which is more literal than Sophie Wilkins's later version, "Pseudoreality Prevails." The later translation is perhaps more suggestive of Musil's meaning, though both translations can be defended for different reasons. For purposes of understanding the overall shape of the novel, however, I would like to point up some other possible meanings that are associated with the title "Seinesgleichen geschieht." I do this in order to show how Musil conceived this section to be in opposition to book 2 with its title proclaiming the millennium that, rather oxymoronically, conjoins paradise and criminals.

If the world of "Seinesgleichen geschieht" is understood to be set in opposition to paradise, then this world must be in some way related to the Fall into the realm of sin and perdition. The fallen world is the mundane realm of "pseudoreality," in which the repetition of the self-same characterizes the unfolding of everyday history. This reading is suggested by notes Musil jotted down in the 1930s, probably for a possible conclusion to the novel. It appears that he then saw, or continued to see, that the all-encompassing problem for the novel remained the war and its relation to the novel's unfolding. In the notes he writes that "Seinesgleichen" leads to war, which here means the repetition of the same events. This comment is followed by "All lines eventuate in the war" (5:1902). The lines of repeating events would eventuate in war, though it is of course not clear how the war would have been joined to the novel as it now stands. In any case, from Musil's perspective the plot of events constituting pseudoreality, or *Seinesgleichen,* unfolds in the realm of repetition. In this realm is found the concatenation of recurrent things that were going to end in catastrophe. The realm of the Fall, of everyday events as well as homicidal history, is made up of the simple recurrence of the ordinary that one day blows up.

In opposition, then, to the war in which pseudoreality culminates stands the millennium of book 2. This book depicts a world, nearly devoid of plot, consisting in unique events. The text unfolds narrating mainly feeling and meditation, from which a new religious dimension of life might have been the ultimate goal. It is noteworthy that Musil's notes for the novel also suggest that he conceived of war as an outbreak of madness that could be misconstrued as a form of religious activity. This is another part of the sense that pseudoreality can eventuate in hell on earth. Of course, the hard part for Musil was not to show the catastrophic results of the repetition of mundane events: the war had really happened. The hard part was to conceive of a millennium that could stand in opposition to the realm of the mundane that eventuated in the catastrophic outburst. In the form in which the novel actually exists, in the ongoing elaboration of book 2, it appears that Musil was more interested in finding an impossible millennium to oppose to *Seinesgleichen* than in wrapping the book up with a world war whose results were no mystery.

Another light is cast upon the meaning of the title "Seinesgleichen geschieht" by an unpublished but finished chapter in which Ulrich muses on the nature of social reality and the possibilities of using probability theory to explain the nature of human enterprises. Available only in Frisé's German edition, this chapter is called "Wandel unter Menschen" (roughly "Change among Humans"). In this chapter it appears that Ulrich, though scoffed at by his sister, is changing the way he thinks about everyday events. He says to Agathe that he used to consider daily occurrences as "the world of the same kind always occurring," or, in German, with clear reference to book 1, the "Welt des Seinesgleichen geschieht" (4:1210). This world was a domain of unrest without meaning, which, as Ulrich puts it, unfolded much like a brook flowing through grassless sand. Now he sees these events as constitutive of the world of the "probable human being." He wonders if the meaninglessness of the unfolding of the social world can perhaps be ordered or constrained by the application of probability theory. Using probability, one might frame laws that would show that all events conform to laws that seem missing in normal historical circumstances. Ulrich's enchantment with probability theory merely suggests another way of viewing the world of the Fall and does not introduce a new form that might affect the overall shape of the novel: like Musil, Ulrich is fascinated with the possibility of finding laws that account for the occurrence of absurd historical phenomena, but this remains simply a possibility.

And so the basic opposition of the mundane world to the millennium establishes the polarity of the novel as it exists, which would remain the case even if probabilistic laws could be found to account for the fallen world of pseudoreality. The novel starts out by affirming that some of those laws are known: the first chapter claims that the number of pedestrians smashed in the street per year is an actuarial fact. The laws of probability might even confirm that the realm of recurrent events is a world without grace, for these laws would simply reintroduce a form of general determinism—or fate, as Emerson called it—that would stand in opposition to the unique world of the other condition or the utopia of feeling Ulrich speculates about. In opposition to the unique world of the millennium, *Seinesgleichen* characterizes the world of meaningless repetition from beginning to end.

Our understanding of Ulrich as a character developing throughout this bipartite structure can be deepened if we are attentive to how he is characterized and how he changes. If pseudoreality is the realm of the Fall, then Ulrich as the central character should have some relation to myths of the Fall, and this is indeed the case. He is compared on several occasions to the devil; and in this regard he can be looked upon as the prince of negation who is the reader's guide to pseudoreality. For example, Musil ends book 1 with an ironic allusion connecting Ulrich to an image of the devil found in Schiller's work. It is significant that by the time of the conclusion of book 1, Ulrich has been engaged in a diabolically busy day. He attempts to seduce a hysterical young woman, Gerda, who has come to his house apparently for this purpose; then he views a street demonstration undertaken by fanatical pan-Germanists against the Parallel Action that besieges the house of the Action's patron, Count Leinsdorf; and finally he resists being seduced in the evening by the very Nietzschean Clarisse, the half-mad wife of his onetime friend Walter. In the midst of this flurry of activity Ulrich has a "heart to heart" talk with the novel's man of action, the German capitalist Arnheim.

Arnheim, the man with all qualities, has apparently felt threatened by Ulrich, the man without qualities, or so it appears when he tells Ulrich that he cannot believe him, especially after Ulrich tells him that modern Europe has been created by the devil (2:639). He cannot trust Ulrich, since, as Arnheim says at the end of this conversation, he is a person who would embrace the devil simply because he is a man without parallel—"weil er der Mann ohnegleichen ist" (2:646). Ulrich smells a quotation in these words, having already caught Arnheim using his prodigious memory earlier to quote Heine verbatim. And Arnheim owns up to borrowing his ideas from the playwright Schiller and the suppressed introduction to Schiller's play *The Robbers*. In this introduction Schiller writes, with reference to those who embrace evil, that there are those who would willingly embrace the devil "because he is the man without peer": "weil er der Mann ohne seinesgleichen ist" (1:482). Arnheim's memory does not quite get this quotation right, but this hardly matters. From his perspective Ulrich, the man without properties, is also a "Mann ohne seinesgleichen" who plays the role of a diabolical antagonist to Arnheim. In fact this identification ironically suggests that throughout the "Seinesgleichen geschieht" section the devil's business is taking place. Musil's intertextual play, with its allusion to Schiller as well as to biblical myth, is subtle but not abstruse; and references to Ulrich as a devil suggest, minimally, that in book 1 he is on the devil's side in undermining the aspects of the Enlightenment that the liberal capitalist Arnheim represents, especially a form of morality that Ulrich cannot abide. In fine the struggle between the two characters, between the devil and the man of reason, is a demonstration of Musil's wit, especially in that one might argue that both Arnheim qua capitalist and Ulrich qua critic play the devil's role. This play with antithesis finds a parallel in Schiller's play. In it a young aristocrat becomes a totally immoral robber in response to the evil that has been worked upon him, especially by his brother, who desires to deprive him his rightful share of property and power. From this perspective the evil worked by the injured brother could be considered to be good. Evil can be considered a good, and vice versa, which sets out a play of moral perspectives whose appeal for Musil is diabolical, so to speak.

To complete this play of perspectives, according to which the rationalist Ulrich is also of the devil's party, one can add that Musil also includes Goethe's *Faust* in his play of ironies, especially with allusions to Goethe's devil, who is the "spirit who says no to all" (*Faust,* v.1338). Ulrich is thus not only the man without qualities and without parallel, but also the master of negation and refusal. He is willing to entertain the rejection of every cultural axiom, which means that Goethe's Mephisto, the master of negation, is never long out of sight in book 1, nor is the Nietzsche who observed in *Beyond Good and Evil* that the devil is the oldest friend of knowledge (*Proverb* 129). In brief, Ulrich creates for himself a Faustian situation in which he bears the flaming torch of negation, at least before he begins to resemble a Faust in quest of some elusive absolute. Ulrich's character is illuminated by a web of allusive ironies, calling upon Nietzsche, Goethe, and Schiller, to name the greatest luminaries, all of which underline that Ulrich finds himself in the world of the Fall.

This allusive treatment of Ulrich's character finds it richest development undoubtedly in chapter 72 of book 1. Here both Goethe and Nietzsche are called upon for this chapter's essayistic interpretation of science and scientists and, by implication, the scientist hero of the novel. Both English translations translate the title of this dense chapter as "Science Smiling into Its Beard, or First Full-Dress Encounter with Evil." This is not, however, the only possible translation, since the concluding German words in the title, "mit dem Bösen," can also mean "with the evil one," which is to say, the devil. In context it seems likely that with this reference to "dem Bösen," Musil is reinforcing his web of allusions to the devil—though one may certainly interpret the term as a description of the nature of the mundane world. Chapter 72 is written essentially from the narrator's viewpoint, but the voice therein can be attributed to any scientific mind describing the scientific mind, so that it is also a description of Ulrich's mind. The text argues that science has, since Galileo in the seventeenth century, been responsible for technological progress and for ruining traditional morality. With echoes of Nietzsche, the narrator provides a genealogy for the modern scientist in which the anti-Christ and the archfiend are combined (1:302–3). Musil's narrator claims, moreover, that the old skills of the hunter and the soldier have been transmuted into the modern scientist who is honored for his seemingly civilized love of "measure and metrics," but who in reality questions everything, leaves nothing untouched, and, motivated by the desire to destroy, leaves nothing secure in his path.

Thus, according to this chapter the archfiend lives on in the modern scientist. This claim is another oblique homage to Goethe's Mephisto, the protoscientist in whom the spirit of negation finds a home, since in the character of Mephisto Goethe uses the devil as a kind of trope for all the forms of the Fall. The homage to Mephisto is even clearer when the narrator, echoing Goethe, explains that moderns avoid the term *devil* out a sense of respectability. It is evident that the devil's great triumph has been to make it disreputable to believe in him, and yet, like a well-worn metaphor, he is most present when he seems most absent. The narrator goes on to claim that even the devil may come back to God once we develop our utopian sense of exactness. Here we see an anticipation of Ulrich's utopian hope, to wit, that God and Satan may be reconciled when modernity overcomes its scissions. I will argue presently that Ulrich does, in this sense, want to stop serving the devil after he realizes that his quest for knowledge is a quest for power: at the end of book 1 he wants to renounce the *Gewalt* (violence) that he sees as intrinsic to the ravages of reason. This recognition sheds light on how the devil, as a trope characterizing power, characterizes Ulrich, a devil who wants to come back to God—another mobile trope whose nature one may have trouble defining.

In book 1 of the novel, however, Ulrich has, as the Rolling Stones famously put it, much sympathy for the devil. In the first two parts he is portrayed through a web of allusions, drawing upon multiple ironic portrayals of knowledge as the devil's work, by which Musil wants to show that, as a typical scientist, Ulrich has entered into an alliance with the forces of violence and doubt. Musil's ironies about his character are part of a modernist attempt, in the wake of Emerson and Nietzsche, to rethink values, though few writers have ranged as widely and as freely as Musil in suggesting that the devil may even be on the side of virtue (although Goethe also put that claim in Mephisto's mouth when the devil said, in verse 1335 of *Faust,* he was part of that force that constantly wants evil, but constantly creates the good). From this perspective the novel insinuates Ulrich's allegiance with the devil and his ironically Faustian compact, so as to set him against Arnheim, the capitalist rationalist who represents the dominant liberal ideology in modern Europe in 1913, if not during the Weimar era.

But Arnheim and Ulrich are also nearly brothers in that both are children of the Enlightenment: Arnheim's version of Adam Smith's rationalism justifying the ultimate role of the market owes as much to the Enlightenment, as does Ulrich's negative skepticism demanding that all axioms of thought be examined. Arnheim himself thinks of Ulrich as a brother at one point, and Ulrich comes finally to see that he is closer to Arnheim than to any of the other characters in the first part of the novel (2:547).

To complete this description of the oppositional symmetry characterizing the shape of the novel, we can speculate that the task of the novel, in book 2 or in a part never completed, would have been to overcome that aspect of the Enlightenment that eventuated in the liberal state that was about to attempt suicide through war. The millennium that the third part announces would thus foresee the end of the Fall, which is to say, the end of the devil's work and the end of pseudoreality. To be sure, in another ironic reversal, Musil's title affirms parenthetically that the millennium is the reign of criminals, by which we may perhaps understand that those who contest the philistine ideology of the dominant culture can only be branded outlaws, like Schiller's aristocratic robbers. The play of irony is heady, but Musil's strategy with irony is to use it to displace the fixed categories by which one thinks and judges. His thought experiment throughout the novel is clearly designed to oblige the reader to entertain the unacceptable: Ulrich is willing to entertain the idea that criminals are more likely to enter the new millennium than are those who have held on to the ethics of a self-satisfied capitalist culture that makes of unbridled egoism the primary virtue in life. Christ undoubtedly suggested something of the same thing, and Christian ethics are never distant in the novel's second half. However, Ulrich questions whether one can love one's neighbor as one's self, and he is loath to allow a psychopathic murderer such as the incarcerated Moosbrugger back on the streets. It is left to Clarisse to want to live out Christian idealism to the point of liberating violent criminals.

After this discussion of the oppositional shape of the two halves of the novel, let us now focus on book 1. A bit more detail about its plot is in order here. Plot is a difficult element to discuss, since part of Musil's experiment is to write a narrative contesting the seamless plot of realist fiction. Inevitably, as one reads, one pieces together an outline of narrative events in their temporal sequence, for Musil is obliged to set forth a series of events making up a chronological order, consonant with the public chronology of received history. This order of fictional events, embedded in historical chronology, is set against the discontinuous order of the novelistic discourse that one is reading. Moreover, since the history of Europe is imposed upon the narrative, the narrator supposes that the reader has this history in mind in order to make sense of allusions and details. The overall effect of this juxtaposition of history with the events of book 1 is that of a chronometer ticking off the time leading to the war that nobody in book 1 believes is going to happen. But the narrator is writing, self-consciously, on the other side of the temporal gap between 1913 and the new European society that sprang up after the war's end in 1918. The narrator knows that the war took place and that he is, in retrospect, narrating a countdown. One grand question the novel asks is precisely how in retrospect we know what it meant to have been engaged in moving forward toward historical change, and most of all toward a calamity that nobody really understands.

The events constituting the plot largely deal with Ulrich, with some narration contemporaneous with unfolding events and some narration relating events as flashbacks. For example, at some time in the past, before 1913, Ulrich wanted to be an important man, though he did not really know what that meant. Once he thought it was to be a military officer, and so he become one, and even had a love affair with a major's wife. Finding that he would never be a Napoleon, he decided to be a man of technology and studied engineering. Finally, at a later moment, he became a mathematician, a scientific profession at which he is presumably more than merely proficient. This profession did not provide answers to some fundamental questions—for example, as Ulrich ponders in a utopian mood, if life has a goal or meaning (1:246). The narrator refers with little explanation to Ulrich's recent absence from Vienna, which occurred immediately before he returns to the city to take a one-year vacation from life. Thus there is a blank spot in the narrative continuity coming before August 1913, when Ulrich begins his vacation. After this beginning of the narrative discourse, fragmentary allusions and brief flashbacks continue to offer readers information with which to construct a past narrative while they follow Ulrich in his encounters in pseudoreality. Through him the reader encounters characters attached to the Parallel Action, or old friends, or, tangentially, the imprisoned misogynist murderer Moosbrugger, whose miserable life is narrated in counterpoint to other events in the novel. He has murdered a prostitute in an act of aggression motivated only by his own fears.

The plot in book 1 also involves several recurring characters and is carried forward largely by Ulrich's interactions with them. The first such character is Leona, a nightclub singer, whose propensity to sing at any moment quickly causes Ulrich to abandon her for Bonadea. Bonadea meets Ulrich after he is beaten up in the street. She is a more tenacious lover and pursues Ulrich throughout much of the novel. Apparently she requires more erotic attention than her husband can give her, and Ulrich's position with the Parallel Action greatly enhances his charms. His attempts to spurn her seem only to excite her. Ulrich's sexual imbroglios underscore the less-than-utopian situations to which eros leads in the mundane fallen world.

Erotic temptations among other characters are set in counterpoint to Ulrich's desires. On the one hand Arnheim, the man of money and intellect, desires passionately and platonically, it seems, the woman he calls Diotima, the wife of the diplomat in whose home the meetings of the Parallel Action take place, while on the lower end of the social scale, Arnheim's servant, the African boy Soliman, desires much less platonically Diotima's Slavic maid, Rachel. The parallel established between masters and servants is as much an homage to the classical theater of eighteenth-century playwrights such as Pierre Marivaux and Pierre Beaumarchais as a comment on social mores. In the Enlightenment theater illustrated by these playwrights the rational mind is invited to evaluate critically social inequality, for maids and masters pursue each other in situations that mirror their obvious equality in eroticism and desire, if not in social status.

Ulrich is also pursued by Clarisse, the wife of an old friend, sometime enemy, named Walter. Walter is an unsuccessful pianist whose discomfiture with life reflects the fate awaiting most of those who attempt to attain something in art. His wife, to whom Ulrich gave the complete works of Nietzsche, is only marginally sane. She finds parallels between Moosbrugger, who murdered a prostitute, and Nietzsche, perhaps because the philosopher may have ended in madness from syphilis contracted from a prostitute. In any case she also dreams in book 1 of having with Ulrich a child who, as a Nietzschean superman, may achieve salvation—for whom is not altogether clear. Moosbrugger's tale, based on events that Musil documented in the Austrian newspapers of the time, sets out a narrative line in counterpoint to Ulrich and his friends' erotic games. Moosbrugger is incarcerated, awaiting sentencing, and the nature of his sentence depends on whether he is found insane. At least a borderline psychopath, he captures the attention of Clarisse. It is a measure of her own growing madness that she decides to make a cause célèbre of a case in which, if the legal authorities find the man sane, they will also execute him.

Clarisse sees a Nietzschean adventurer in this inarticulate man whose probable insanity makes him an object of scientific investigation and legal interpretation. Narrating Moosbrugger's story from the murderer's point of view, from within the character's own consciousness, Musil does a superb rendering of the inarticulate nature of the motivation that has led to the murder; and about which scientific thinking and legal thinking clash. The medical doctors think Moosbrugger is insane. However, "their reluctance as scientists to make exaggerated claims on the basis of the available evidence prevented them from challenging the verdict of the lawyers" (1:149). On the basis of legal rhetoric rather than any scientific criteria, the woman-hating Moosbrugger is declared responsible for his actions and guilty of murder.

The trial leads Ulrich to reflect that the division between psychiatrists and lawyers could be seen as merely one "example of the widespread division in daily life between, on the one hand, scientists and other workers whose activities were based on facts and empirical evidence, and, on the other hand, philosophers, lawyers and writers, whose professional sphere was that of values" (1:149). In the case of this petty criminal and psychopath, the scientists abdicate to the lawyers, a group that regards values as its professional domain. This abdication can be construed as a failure of science, which Ulrich finds emblematic of society at large in its failure to base action on knowledge. Ulrich's critical mind can only puzzle about what justifies the schism between knowing and judging, and consequently acting.

The Moosbrugger episode illustrates how Musil endows the novel with a questioning critique of social values. As seen from Ulrich's perspective, nearly every character is involved in questions relating knowledge to action. For example, that Ulrich's father is a legal scholar allows an acerbic portrayal of what makes up a career in the law. His father has made a career by defining responsibility in harsh terms, mainly through endless arguments against other legal scholars, much of which has little to do with knowledge of the nature of justice and legal responsibility. The endless ratiocinations that go into legal disputes contrast with the simple necessity of bearing the responsibility for making judgments. Decision making is the stuff of daily life, but, as Ulrich sees it, the knowledge needed for decisions is often simply lacking or derived from sources that are irrelevant. In Moosbrugger's case, most pointedly, he wonders how anyone can find scientific knowledge that allows society to decide that even a marginal being such as Moosbrugger should be legally murdered.

That Moosbrugger has not yet been executed is due to the intervention of Count Leinsdorf, the aging aristocrat who is largely responsible for the existence of the Parallel Action. The count is another key character, since much of the plot in the first half is pegged on the activities of this Viennese group that wants to outdo the Germans in their planned celebration of the German kaiser's reign. The Parallel Action is Musil's major vehicle for satirizing Austrian society. The satire turns on a sense of the absurd, using ironic dislocations based on the author's unparalleled sense of incongruity. However, his satire does not seem motivated by rage or despair, as in the type created by Swift or by Musil's French contemporary Céline, a writer who found in World War I a cause for total nihilism. Notably, Musil writes a satire that does not prevent him from portraying Count Leinsdorf with much sympathy.[4] The old man is an upholder of the empire who has no understanding as to why, on the one hand, the empire's various ethnic groups should want to leave it, or on the other hand, why Germans should indulge in nationalism and besiege his house. Like many Austrians, he thoroughly dislikes the Prussian Germans. The count thinks, moreover, that he believes in Realpolitik in his unquestioning faith in the empire and the emperor. Emblematically, the count embodies an ethos that was soon to disappear, for already in 1913 he was a living anachronism. Musil's satire shows that his existence has become pointless, but not malevolent.

Though the count is the founder of the Parallel Action, its sessions largely take place in the home of Ulrich's cousin. She is called Diotima by her admirer, Arnheim, after the priestess who initiated Socrates into wisdom. Diotima is married to a dull-witted career diplomat whose Italianate name, Tuzzi, suggests the variegated ethnic types found in the empire. The Tuzzi home is the scene of frequent encounters that lend themselves to Musil's satirical wit. For example, the diplomat husband takes little interest in his wife's Parallel Action, since his perspective from the foreign office makes him suspicious of all novelty and foreigners, and especially of the Prussian capitalist Arnheim. Arnheim is a foreign intellectual, as well as a capitalist, who, in addition to pursuing Tuzzi's wife, seemingly writes books for no particular purpose, certainly not for money. In Tuzzi's opinion, only unhappy men write books, which is to say, only Jews, since the diplomat holds the received opinion that all Jews are unhappy. Jewish he may be, but Arnheim is not especially unhappy.

The characters attached to the Parallel Action are deeply committed to finding a justification for an empire that seemingly has none, which is another source of much incongruity. In contrast to these characters' absurd quest stand out the incongruities characterizing other characters revolving around Ulrich, such as Clarisse and Walter. Notable in this regard is the Jewish banker Leo

Fischel. He is a man of liberal convictions, whose daughter, Gerda, is associating with an anti-Semite nationalist, Hans Sepp. Musil has encapsulated in this small group the contradictory tensions of Viennese society: the Jewish liberal accommodates himself, unhappily to be sure, to the anti-Semite activist who uses him as a scapegoat for all the resentment that the German nationalist minority, with their pervasive anti-Semitism, feels in an empire in which they believe they are not allowed to realize fully their natural right to rule. The critique of nationalism that Musil began in the essays comes to fruition in the portrayal of the events Sepp initiates, such as protests against the aristocratic (and almost totally German) Parallel Action that, the pan-Germanists believe, is not adequately representing Germans and their claims against the other minorities in the empire. It has even allowed a non-German to participate.

Superimposed on narrative lines involving the various characters is the narrator's perspective, from which he meditates on them and on events. In this sense the narrator is also something of a character, for he changes the temporal perspective from time to time in order to recall the then-recent war and speak of the postwar period, from which the narrator looks back on the past that has now disappeared. The narrator has a double perspective, that offered by the remembered past and that afforded by the new republican society in which he and his reader find themselves. The narrator's stance can be likened at times to that of an older person telling a younger listener, for whom Weimar is natural, about a distant culture that may seem preposterous today. From a reverse perspective the narrator knows his postwar society is of course a society about which the characters in 1913 could not have the slightest premonition. His is a new society that nothing presaged. This new society's break with the old culture of Viennese society seems to him nearly total. For example, ethnic groups now indulge freely in their nationalism, and women wear clothes that would have been a scandal merely a few years earlier. At every level of social and political analysis, then, *The Man without Qualities* is not only a retrospective meditation of the nature of history, but also a constant interrogation about what history is becoming as it unfolds, from the perspective of 1913 and from the perspective of the postwar years, informed by nationalism, kitsch, and the new fashions, both sartorial and artistic, that capitalism imposes regularly.

The double perspective provided by the narrator continues, moreover, throughout the completed parts of the novel, and it is worth jumping ahead to consider this perspective in the latter part. A kind of résumé of the narrator's ideological viewpoint occurs toward the end, in chapter 56 of the unpublished galley chapters. Here, while describing the do-gooder Professor Lindner, the narrator recalls that Europe before the war was part of a world in which there were still "colored peoples who had not yet been robbed" and there were still "millions of white people at hand who, without being able to defend themselves, had to pay for the cost of industrial and commercial progress" (4:1185). Yet, the narrator observes, it was generally believed then that someday the poor and the disinherited would be better off than they were before they were disinherited. This prewar European civilization, he observes, did offer something like a cornucopia of cultural and material goods, such that "today it is quite impossible to make it comprehensible how natural it was then to believe in the permanence of this progress and to consider prosperity and intellect [*Geist*] as something that, like grass, springs up everywhere where it is not intentionally uprooted" (4:1185). In short the belief in progress that made sense in 1913 is gone "today" at the moment the narrator is writing. The belief disappeared with the war and the economic crises of the Weimar era. And if chapter 56 can be dated to some time after 1933, sometime after Hitler had taken power, it is clear why the narrator, though not specifying the exact moment of his "today," looks back at Vienna of 1913 with nostalgia. He knows that even this now past European society, based on colonialism and class exploitation, did not preclude belief in progress that somehow seemed to justify its existence. The hope for justice that was inscribed in the horizon of that era's worldview seems now gone forever.

The gap between the narrator's world and Ulrich's embodies one form of discontinuity. There are others. From the beginning of the novel Musil also demands that the reader embrace narrative discontinuity. Discontinuity may be read as a correlate to the novel's basic axiom that modern culture has lost all semblance of unity and hence continuity. Narrative discontinuity is accentuated in this regard. For example, the novel's first nineteen chapters, constituting part 1, offer only "A Sort of Introduction," for a real introduction, the sort a realist such as Balzac, Dickens, or George Eliot might have written, would presuppose a narrator believing that he or she can grasp the unity or the pattern of the historical unfolding that encompasses the action of *Père Goriot, Great Expectations,* or *The Mill on the Floss.* Musil does not believe in this unity, nor does his narrator. The novel's first chapter, aptly called "From Which, Remarkably Enough, Nothing Develops," is a pointed demonstration of this refusal, for the chapter is at once a respectful parody of realist narration and a challenge to what we usually expect of the knowledge granted by a fictional narration. The challenge begins with the fact that the novel begins with a weather report, perhaps the first weather report in the history of literature. A weather report appears, to be sure, to be an objective piece of writing that, respecting the usual coordinates of realist fiction, precisely situates for the reader the place and time of the action—even though Musil's narrator imme-diately and paradoxically dismisses the importance of a precise location for his narrative. For his purposes, he says, every big city can illustrate the same phe-nomena, though the place is of course Vienna.

Offering a weather report about a day in August 1913, the narrator seems to be imitating, while rejecting, the journalism that has become the staple for modern knowledge of everyday events. The narrator further illustrates his point about any big city by narrating a traffic accident, another staple of jour-nalism, and the world of literally fallen reality. The arbitrary choice for inci-dent seems compounded by caprice of presentation, and the reader wonders what kind of knowledge the highlighted event can offer, except perhaps to point out that city streets are rather dangerous, though after 1913 one hardly needs a novel to know that. In ironic fact, the incident offers much, for a traf-fic accident shows that, as one observer on the scene points out, the body lying on the street proves that contemporary automobile brakes are inadequate. A female observer, to whom the first observer explains the accident, has no idea what he means by inadequate "braking range," but she is satisfied that there is in fact an explanation for this absurd event. Preempting the knowledge the observers in situ have, the narrator then explains that the accident actually illustrates the statistical laws that sociologists and newspapers use to offer knowledge of society. The two observers in the street—who, the reader learns, happen *not* to be two of the main characters in the novel—may look at one unique crushed body, but according to our scientifically informed narrator, American statistics show that the unfortunate victim is just an illustration of ironclad laws that decree that, in the modern city, so many bodies must be run over every year so we can drive our automobiles. Ulrich's "probable human being" lies stretched out on the Viennese pavement at the novel's very beginning.

The ironies are many in this opening chapter of antinarration. Most importantly, however, the reader soon realizes that the 1913 weather report also announces the countdown to August 1914, when statistics would take on the task of narrating the average body count for charging a trench defended with machine guns. History, in the sense of a narrative of unfolding events, is thus superimposed upon the arbitrary caprice of individual events that the nar-rator may or may not chose to tell. Nonetheless, the reader knows where the novel's overall plot must go if it respects historical chronology and place, and the weather report takes on the appearance of a synecdoche for scientific prog-nostication, or the kind of foreseeing that, we may recall with irony, never said a war was in the winds. From this perspective the automobile accident is a synecdoche for life in the modern city; it is one of many pointless but foresee-able daily events in the history of the city in which the man without qualities lives. Offering mock celebrations of the various forms scientific knowledge may take, the first chapter also implies that science is of dubious utility, in the modern city that also happens to be the capital of a baroque empire of medieval provenance. Contradictory impulses resonate in this introduction to "A Sort of Introduction," suggesting at once the arbitrary nature of any attempt to anchor representation in knowledge and the plethora of possibilities that any representation can indulge in—constrained only by the narrator's retrospective knowledge of the horrors of reality. And on this, I insist: the narrator does not deny the real, only absolute approaches to the real.

Of the nineteen chapters constituting this happenstance introduction, the fourth is one of the most crucial for understanding what is at stake in the rest of the novel. It is titled "If There Is a Sense of Reality, There Must Also Be a Sense of Possibility." The title announces a central theme the novel proposes to demonstrate, especially through Ulrich's refusal to embrace qualities for himself and his attempts to think out a world other than the world of pseudo-reality. It is arguable whether the novel ever really illustrates the theme, other than hypothetically. Musil is hardly unique is granting the hypothetically pos-sible as much interest as the real. After all, the quest for the possible, as an advance on the real, has been a fundamental undertaking of the European mind since at least the Enlightenment, or even earlier. Arguably, the European mind capable of conceiving the act of overcoming the status quo was born with the Renaissance; and it was the invention of utopian thought with Rabelais, Sir Thomas More, Francis Bacon, and others that then gave rise to the Enlighten-ment belief that society could and indeed should be transformed.

However, I think that the novel's sense of possibility, at least in book 1, is not predicated on the belief in utopia, which is to say, a fully cast vision of an ideal world. Initially, Ulrich's belief that reality, whatever that may be, could be something other than what it is is a form of skepticism that challenges the real through negation. One can argue that this cast of mind is the modern state of mind par excellence. In this regard the spirit of negation—Mephisto—is a modern character, and, I suggested above, he is a trope for the Fall of, or perhaps into, modernity. The skeptical mind exists by fortifying itself with a lack of belief in the necessity of what actually exists. For this mind, as Ulrich demonstrates, all is contingent. Thus, his skeptical negativity takes its shape, in part, because he accepts the Enlightenment belief that the ongoing develop-ment of reason should empower humanity to find renewed possibilities for a fuller development of human potential. In book 1, however, it may appear that

Ulrich's sense of possibility springs more from his diabolical capacity for negative critique. In book 1, before Ulrich turns to meditate upon utopian possibilities in book 2, his negative critique is centered to a large extent upon the triumph of capitalist rationality. This triumph has made it extremely difficult to believe that things might be other than what they are. Paradoxically, Ulrich finds that this is so despite the fact that capitalism radically transforms the world on a daily basis, and changes it constantly in the name of liberal capitalist principles that somehow do not change. This emerges from Ulrich's ongoing encounter with the successful Arnheim. But as a man of possibility, Ulrich contrives to look beyond the paradoxically unchanging transformations of capitalism. He looks back as well as forward, and with his mobile perspective, as the narrator says of him, he may still see the woods where the capitalist man of reality sees so many square feet of timber that pass for reality (1:17).

Ulrich himself is involved in a thought experiment to see if a character open to all possibilities can have a meaningful existence in the context of modernity. Modernity in Austria in 1913, is, however, not quite modern, as it appears in the satirical chapter 8, "Kakanien." This neologism challenges translation, since it parodies the fact that if one pronounces the initials for the combined monarchies of the Austro-Hungarian Empire, it sounds much like a child's term for excrement. The found-in-a-potty empire offers the spectacle of a society on the cusp of a modernity in which the benefits of liberalism are present in an attenuated form. The social forms and technology of the modern liberal state coexist with the curious power structure of an antiquated hodge-podge of an empire that is not quite an empire, at least when compared to modern empires such as the Reich ruled by the Austrians' Prussian cousins in the north. Austria is modern, but not too modern; liberal, but not too liberal; has automobiles, but not too many; and in general takes its distance from all the fads of the French and English, whose taste for empire is quite immoderate. It is from this satirical perspective that the narrator reports on Ulrich's consciousness as he looks at the possibilities of Austrian society and culture. At times in the satire it is true that there is little difference between the narrator's bemused viewpoint and Ulrich's.

Ulrich's and the narrator's viewpoints are not the same, however, and the reader measures Ulrich's change and development from the perspective of the narrator as well as through his inner monologues. He is a member of that upper bourgeoisie whose members often choose a career from a sense of social obligation. A successful mathematician who has dabbled in poetry, a potentially aristocratic military man, and a quintessentially modern engineer, he has had varied experience. However, from the novel's outset the narrator and Ulrich together maintain that he is a man without qualities. What the poet-mathematician means by *quality* is not entirely clear.[5] In Musil's doctoral thesis he defines qualities—or *Eigenschaften*—as precisely those properties that would accrue to a centered concept that defines a thing in itself. The young Musil earlier argued that things have qualities in the sense of nonrelativistic properties. Recall that against Mach he maintains that real properties are not relative notions defined by the measurements of functions.[6] A property or quality in the young Musil's sense is an invariant trait, part of a recurrent constellation, that can be defined in itself as a positive trait that needs no other contrasting trait for definition. In the dissertation Musil believes that Mach's relativism, defining all knowledge as knowledge of relations, is undercut if he can demonstrate there are qualities that are not necessarily defined in relation to something else. A recurrent property in this sense would offer access to the invariance that Musil wanted to be the ultimate criterion or arbiter of knowledge.

However, this kind of property is precisely what Ulrich seemingly lacks: he can find in himself no invariant trait, definable in itself, that would vouchsafe him the reality of a self that is confident about what it knows. In this sense he is a grown-up Törless who knows now that his demand for something knowable in itself with certainty is contrary to the epistemic notions of his era. He seems to accept, at times, the truth of the contention of fellow mathematician Poincaré, who, like Mach, argues that one can only know the relations between things, not things in themselves. Ulrich appears at times to be a Machean positivist whose reason does not allow him to reject the dominant epistemic axioms he has grown up with. Herein lies another importance of irony. Through irony he can disengage himself from these conventions and allow himself to experiment with various roles in the novel: neo-Machean epistemologist, but also mystical quester, Enlightenment satirist, and Nietzschean immoralist. To have no qualities, or at least to try to have no qualities, means that Ulrich can try out many roles and view the consequences. He can the turn his critique on such received polarities as feeling and reason, precision and intuition, and the other antinomies that often seem to him to block thinking rather than facilitate it.

There is great intellectual pleasure generated by Ulrich and the narrator's constant irony, satire, and wit as they alternately question and affirm the premises of post-Enlightenment culture. On the one hand Musil's constant satire of deviance from rationalist axioms underscores the intellectual demands that someone—the narrator or Ulrich—places upon the reader and upon himself. On the other hand, the rationalist in the novel—alternatively the narrator or Ulrich—is engaged in a stringent rationalist critique of the limits of reason.

This critique results in a struggle between reason and mysticism, which at times seems to be at the center of Ulrich's life. Like Musil, he is drawn to mysticism and, like Musil, views it from the exterior, as a puzzled rationalist seeking to find what is at the heart of nonrational feeling and experience.[7] Ulrich has been like the Musil who wrote in his diary, at some time when he was planning his novel, that his "task was to go into the doctrines of romanticism and mysticism" (*TB* 1:139). Musil lends to him the results of his research, but in both cases the creator and the created remain scientific observers who want very much to get inside something that is foreign to their education and their temperament. Yet the polarity is essential, for especially in book 1 does Musil use it to point out satirically the lack of commensurability between precise thinking and the kind of thinking that deals with values and judgments. From this viewpoint the unique feelings going into authentic moral experience should, somehow, open up on a unique experience that may or may not have a relation to the ecstasy of the mystics.

Ulrich's movement toward mystical awareness, if such happens, is part of a process. In the course of the novel he undergoes significant development as a character, though the discontinuous nature of the narration demands active attentiveness in order to follow the enlargement of his capacity for thought and feeling. Let us follow this process of change in the first half of the novel. Initially, Ulrich believes that he has separated thought and action. He thinks that true thought has its own nature that is different from the mental activity demanded by the active life (1:274) The novel's emblematic man of action, Arnheim, is in partial agreement with him, for he tells Ulrich that mind (*Geist*) "is a powerless spectator" to life's real processes (1:275). Ulrich thinks that Arnheim sets himself against Ulrich, because he boasts that as a man of action he realizes his pursuits through the use of political, economic, and even spiritual power relations. Ulrich, having become a representative of pure mind, rejects action, but he also knows that Arnheim is not entirely wrong. Ulrich is fascinated by what others might do, and so he joins in the Parallel Action largely to be able to observe what might happen when the society's elite joins together to find something significant to do. At first he thinks that mind must have some role in determining what is significant. However, it seems that the operations of pure thought satirically confirm Arnheim's viewpoint about the powerlessness of pure mind: as secretary Ulrich must read the myriad proposals, offering supposedly significant projects from every quarter of society, which abound in comic irrelevance and absurd incongruity. Collectively the pure mind of the Viennese produces something close to bedlam.

From this perspective the aforementioned chapter 72 about science, offering an encounter with evil, the devil, or both, is a turning point at which the reader and Ulrich begin to suspect that pure thought is always in league with the devil. Discovering that the learned participants in the Parallel Action may well be incompetent, Ulrich finds that incompetence does not preclude an inclination toward working with the devil, which the narrator characterizes by observing that, with their profusion of absurd proposals for the Action, the participants were "men in whom an inclination to evil welled up like fire under a kettle" (1:301). The scholars and thinkers, like so many versions of a nutty Faust, offer Ulrich the unending proliferation of examples of the Nietzschean will to power, all of which culminates in the narrator's overview of the history of science, referred to above, in which he finds the old savage instincts sublimated into the scientific will to truth. At this point, however, Ulrich has not yet come to his realization that his own devotion to thought is, in many respects, also a displaced way of serving power.

The fulcrum point of Ulrich's development as a character, found in his moments of meditation and self-illumination, can be pinpointed in book 1 in chapter 116, "The Two Trees of Life and a Proposal to Establish a General Secretariat for Precision and Soul." The changes Ulrich undergoes in this chapter foreshadow book 1's final chapter, "The Turning Point," with its explicitly peripatetic title. However, that final turning point is less about character and more a prelude to Ulrich's subsequent discovery of his sister and the exploration of the possibilities of life encompassing a feminine dimension. The significant turning point for Ulrich in terms of character development comes in the chapter envisaging a "General Secretariat for Precision and Soul." In this chapter Ulrich is in the company of several of the main characters who have been involved fruitlessly in the Parallel Action. Tiring of their talk, he withdraws into a meditation in which he strives to understand his growing revolt against the limitations of existence. He comes to the conclusion that when a person can just as well have every quality as no quality, or that when one feels that "only the same old thing happens" since life takes shape by always being poured out into the "same dozen cake pans," then one sees that all comes together like the "branches of a tree that hide the trunk" (2:591–92). In this context I translate "nur Seinesgleichen geschieht" as "only the same old thing," to point up that the idea of the repetition of the meaningless imagined by Ulrich is also what the title of part 2 suggests. In this context his rejection of limits is directed against the repetition of life's constant fall into banality. He refuses being molded in ever the same cake pans of pseudoreality, formed by the repetition that obliterates the unique in life.

In this moment of introspective revolt he also achieves some clarity about the shape of his own life, and about the desires and the impulses he has had. Ulrich realizes that "creation did not spring from a theory," but rather "it originated in force and love"—"Gewalt und Liebe" (2:591). A constellation of meanings attach to these two terms for Ulrich. The narrator returns to the tree metaphor to characterize how force and love have directed Ulrich's development, for his life had grown up separated into "two trees" (2:592). This metaphor strongly suggests a basic split in Ulrich's personality and perhaps a form of alienation. To the tree of force or *Gewalt* and the attendant idea of violence are attached things such as science, unambiguous meaning, reason, and the desire for mastery; whereas to the growth of love are the truth of parables, dream representations, the logic of the soul, and "the connections of things in the intuitions of art and religion" (2:593). Ulrich—soldier, engineer, scientist, sometime poet, and dreamer—sees that he has lived as if he were two beings, intellectually and emotionally split between the fundamental modes of knowledge and perception, between poetic analogy and rational clarity, to interpret the terms he uses as oppositions, namely, *Gleichnis* and *Eindeutigkeit* (2:593), parable and univocal meaning.

At this point in the novel, nearly six months or so into Ulrich's vacation from life, he, the narrator, or perhaps both realize that the single-minded desire for clear, unambiguous meanings is dangerous, for such a desire is replete with ideological and hence political dangers. Ulrich realizes that the incapacity to live with ambiguity often leads the individual who thirsts for the mastery of simple truth to join mass movements that, in their impatience and frustration with ambiguity, may explode in real violence. There is a double historical perspective on this realization, for it concerns at once the growing dangers of violence in 1913 and the gathering ideological forces wanting simple solutions to the problems of the Weimar Republic. Finally, there is an implicit condemnation of Nietzsche underlying Ulrich's realization, for Ulrich sees that he has been in the grip of the "compulsion to assault life in order to have lordship over it" (2:592). His allegiance to rationality has been an allegiance to power, which is an impulse that can lead one to embrace falsities that Ulrich knows are the antithesis of science and rationality. For instance, one may begin to lie simply because, as he says, a man who wants to master life must be able to lie; or one may embrace violence because, after long periods of fruitless talking, the demonstration of power settles things with no ambiguity. Ulrich's and the narrator's ideas are near paraphrases of Nietzsche, though they are ideas characterizing political movements for which Nietzsche had only anathema—one might argue that Ulrich uses Nietzsche to condemn him in this respect. Thus those desiring mastery and easy truth join groups and obey them in order to allow themselves a perverse freedom, since, as the narrator says, their obedience allows them the freedom to do what they would not think of doing as individuals. In this mini-essay on violence, Musil underscores that Ulrich is questioning, if not entirely rejecting, his sometime Nietzschean quest for power and mastery—a quest that defines truth as the lie in the service of power. Ulrich's realization that this is a consequence of a desire for power does not entail a rejection of science and rationality, but it does point up that the unreasoning use of reason in the service of power can lead individuals to ideological and political catastrophes. His new frame of mind motivates Ulrich's subsequent rejection of group activity and his desire to turn away from society.

In this pivotal chapter Ulrich returns to the small group discussing the Parallel Action and proposes that in 1918 they should establish, in the name of the emperor, "a world secretariat for precision and soul" (2:597). Only the old Count Leinsdorf takes seriously the project that Ulrich sees as the only way to address the most pressing of human problems: how to reconcile technological and scientific rationality with the needs of the spirit or soul. This desire is utopian, but the text implies that anything less than utopian may be catastrophic, which history would demonstrate within six months. The fact that nobody else in the room takes this proposal seriously, and perhaps not even Ulrich himself, points up the ongoing hold of pseudoreality upon the best minds.

After his realization that he has labored in the service of violence and force, Ulrich then goes through a quick series of events that finish convincing him to withdraw from the social world that does not take so-called utopian desires seriously. Gerda, the daughter of the Jewish banker Leo Fischel, comes to lose her virginity with Ulrich. Unsuccessful in that project, for she seems to end up having an hysterical fit, she does convey to Ulrich the rumor that her father has learned that Arnheim is really interested in the Parallel Action in order to facilitate his taking over Galician oil fields. Taking this rumor seriously, Ulrich goes to tell the count what he has learned and finds that nationalist pan-Germanists, believing that the Parallel Action is a plot against the Germans in the empire, have organized a street demonstration that threatens Count Leinsdorf's house. Unbeknown to Ulrich, his friend/enemy Walter is in the demonstration, which allows the narrator to meditate on the nature of the crowd. Walter feels at once excited and empty, much as he might feel at the outset of intoxication (2:627). The crowd and its relentless forward march offer him a momentary escape from anguish. The mob draws together those who have no outlet for their feelings, and in their collective existence, the narrator observes, they are capable of either violence or nobility, as they experience a new self, "half as compulsion, half as a liberation" (2:627). In this scene the crowd has, after Émile Zola's depictions, taken a new form as a character in fiction, and perhaps in history.

Errors abound in this scene as the mob besieges the count's house. As Ulrich stands in the window of the house, he realizes that the mob thinks he is the count. Contemplating the crowd surging forth, after the narrator Ulrich also recognizes that it could be a force for good as well as for evil. Moreover, much like an incipient Elias Canetti or Erich Fromm, he notes that the mass movement provides an escape and "protection from solitude [*Einsamkeit*]" (2:630). However, for once Ulrich is not in the mood to engage in a sociological analysis. He decides to tell neither Diotima nor the count what he has heard about Arnheim because, upon viewing the crowd, he feels suddenly that, in spite of their contentions, he is more closely related to Arnheim than to any of the others with whom he has been associated in the Parallel Action (2:630). More important, he feels so oppressed by his own thought experiments that, no longer desirous of going along with what he has being doing, he suddenly feels like committing a crime (2:631). He seems quite serious when he recognizes that his asocial impulse is an expression of his desire not to keep challenging society and history. Since book 2 of the novel is about criminals in the millennium—or perhaps a Christ figure as criminal—it is appropriate to underscore this moment in Ulrich's development when the idea of crime presses itself upon him as an ethical possibility.

Joyce's character Stephen Dedalus called history a nightmare from which he wished to awaken, and twentieth-century French novelist Raymond Queneau called it the science of unhappiness. In a similar vein, standing in the count's drawing room and looking at the mob that wants to make history, Ulrich views history as a series of failed undertakings, caused in part by a constant overturning of one promising spiritual leader after another. Like Stephen Dedalus, Ulrich has always felt a desire to escape the disasters called history, which for the man of possibility is the unrelenting fall into a realm always short of the possible. Seeing the crowd surging in the street, he finds that his desire reaches a strength he had not felt before. He thinks to himself that he will no longer "stand up to the world," words that are literally repeated aloud when the count declares immediately afterward to him that he must be firm in order "to stand up to the uprising"—"dieser Empörung die Stirne zu bieten" (2:633). The ironic overlap of opposing desires, expressed in the same words, underscores that Ulrich is now ready to flee the historical moment that, produced by absurd errors, may result in the mob smashing the count's windows or worse.

The nature of Ulrich's ongoing change is illuminated by his subsequent encounter with Arnheim. In a moment of impulse, he offers Ulrich a position in his corporation. Ulrich cannot imagine something for which he would be less suited (2:640). After this encounter his desire to flee takes on even greater urgency when, after his return home, Clarisse presses herself onto him and declares that she will procreate by him the "savior of the world" (2:660). The notice of his father's death is also awaiting Ulrich. The death is a fortuitous event that nonetheless is part of the turning in the plot leading into the changes of book 2. Symbolically it eliminates the source of obligation that made Ulrich feel bound to a career and conventional behavior. But even before the news of his father's death, in his meditation on his past Ulrich has come to the tentative conclusion that he is going to flee society. This notably occurs during his walk home from the count's house, when he encounters a prostitute who, reminding him by association of Moosbrugger, makes him realize that he has largely lost interest in the criminal.

The future is opening to Ulrich at this moment in the night when he decides that making sense of experience is the central challenge life is presenting him. And he returns to the idea that determination of action must be embedded in some sense of what is significant. On his walk home he thinks that finding the significant is threatened by the very means of understanding. For example, in the city so much occurs that much of the specificity of events is lost in the act of abstracting from them in order to transform them into some kind of meaningful order. This loss can occur, for example, when the fullness of life is transformed into a narration so that life's "overwhelming variety" is turned into a one-dimensional order that lines up along the "thread of the narrative" (2:650). Narration is a natural impulse, one that imposes an order on life, though by impoverishing it. As a form of narrative a novel is also embedded in life, for narrative is a life-form, one known and experienced by everybody at one time or the other, at least when a person is the narrator of his or her own life. Ulrich's reflection on narration at once affirms the inevitability of narrative as a life-form while he wonders whether it is desirable to reduce the fullness of life to the near-mathematical, but deceptive, schematic order of a narrative.

This critique of the foundations of the novel turns on more than the inevitable loss of the existential fullness of the real when one narrates. It is not clear to Ulrich whether the novel itself is even possible in his historical context. He questions whether life taking the form of a "primitive epic" can exist today when "obviously all has become intractable to narrative and no longer follows a thread, but rather spreads out in infinitely interwoven surfaces" (2:650). The "primitive epic" is undoubtedly the image of something like the linear narrative form in which a hero finds meaning in his place in a chain of events. By contrast Ulrich's image of interlocking, but nonlinear surfaces is something like an image of Musil's novel. In fine his questioning the possibility of finding the significant includes the vehicle in which he is doing the questioning.

At this moment Ulrich has caught up with his narrator in recognizing that narration, as a way of organizing experience, is deficient in many respects. Implicit in this recognition of the limits of narrative order is the appreciation of the possibility of other formal systems of representation. Musil was well aware that the history of mathematics, for example, demonstrates constantly increasing possibilities of invention; whereas in the last two thousand years rather few new forms or systems of linguistic narration have emerged to order experience. The "primitive epic" shares the same epistemic space as Euclidian geometry. Arguably, nothing close to non-Euclidian geometries exists for literature— though Musil may have had them mind when creating his own novel. In any case Ulrich, too, is now questioning the use of received "epic" forms for understanding life. This is a rather complicated form of self-referentiality in that the character's consciousness about the nature of narrative comes to coincide with the consciousness of the narrative self that informs the novel in which the character is developing.

This is not to say that Ulrich does not question narrative order before the end of the second part. In the course of book 1 he, as well as the narrator, envisage other means of organizing what might be set forth, if not exactly narrated, in a novel. This search seems clear in Ulrich's thoughts on essayism, for instance, in chapter 62, "The Earth Too, but Ulrich in Particular, Pays Homage to the Utopian Idea of Essayism." The title proposes that essayism is not just a literary form but a utopian idea. This seems to suggest that essayism is a possible form of existence, or at least an alternative to the existence of narratives and their "primitive epics," so that it is another way of ordering and knowing existence. But the idea also has existential import. Ulrich recalls having started life out with the idea that he wanted to live hypothetically, by which he means that he wanted to be able to embrace all possibilities and to weigh them as so many alternatives to reality. Nothing thus far in life has made him change his attitude; indeed he affirms that nothing he has encountered in life is certain— no order, no thing, no self, no principle—but rather that everything is caught up in an unceasing flow of change so that the future is anchored in instability and the present moment is nothing more than a hypothesis (1:250). In this sense existence seems to impose essayism on Ulrich. For the essayist, in Musil's sense, one can say that Heraclitian flux is the basis of all, with reference to the ancient Greek philosopher for whom the metaphor of the river's unceasing flow is the most apt image of the unceasing change of being.

Ulrich wants to confront the flux and to fashion his existence by recognizing that nothing has meaning except through its position in the fluctuating totality. Thus he has decided to replace the notion of the hypothetical with that of essayism. From the essayistic perspective everything in life must be envisaged from all sides to see what it is: "The value of acts or of a quality, indeed even its essence and nature, appeared to him dependent upon the circumstances that surround them, upon the goals they serve, in a word, upon the sometimes created this way, sometimes shaped that way, totality to which they belong" (1:250). Ulrich uses here another mathematical analogy to describe how he envisages the totality, for he regards moral events to be something like functional values that have meaning, like all functions, only insofar as they relate to other values. This might appear another expression of Machean relativism, though I note that a function exists only when there is a rule or equation for generating the relations. However, Ulrich is not very interested in rules, and the heady metaphor likening values to a function does not go as far as it may first appear to go. It does suggest, however, that Musil was trying to find alternatives to simple narrative for representing experience.

In any case Ulrich's embracing essayism is another aspect of his trying to live in such a way as to open himself to experience and thus to contemplate and evaluate all possibilities. This is another Nietzschean position, one Ulrich adopts before clearly realizing that in so doing he has placed himself in a position in which he is willing to endorse force and violence. But in the early part of his vacation from life, he wants to submit to no a priori judgments about values. This attitude may shed another light on his idea that values are functional variables, depending on the relation of events to contexts. Perhaps it is not quite so abstract as it sounds, at least not if we use Musil's examples to illustrate the point. We all can recognize that, say, plunging a knife into someone's abdomen is good or bad, depending on whether it is done by a surgeon or a madman. What is certain is that Ulrich's doctrine of relative contextualizing is directed specifically against Kantian ethics that evaluate experience in a priori terms, and more generally against all moral codes prescribing rules for behavior without consideration of all possibilities in a given context. Ulrich's essayism entails that he, with Mephisto-like gusto, is willing to disregard conventional morality if context and circumstance convince him that new possibilities should take him in new directions. Book 2 will more directly involve him in this quest, but in quite different terms. In book 1, in his sexual imbroglios and his attempt to find meaning in social action, Ulrich is seeking a way to maximize his possibilities. But neither Don Juan nor civic leader seem to be roles to which Ulrich, the man without qualities, can accommodate himself.

The character who most directly stands as a foil to Ulrich and thus most directly underscores his change is the novel's other self-conscious man of the Enlightenment, Arnheim. The German capitalist and prolific intellectual has come to observe the Parallel Action, perhaps to help, perhaps to further his economic empire by getting hold of oil fields lying within the Austrian Empire. What Ulrich means by the possible is derived in part from the agonic contrasts between him and Arnheim. He is tempted to deny everything the Jewish Prussian capitalist stands for, and he stands for much. Arnheim is an especially rich figure: a real historical personage, the industrialist, writer, and statesman Walter Rathenau (1867–1922), served as the model for him. Among other things Arnheim's relation to this historical figure points up that Arnheim himself is a complex character who should be judged apart from Ulrich's negative view of him.

Rathenau himself was a rich industrialist who was successful as a statesman. According to the German historian Hagen Schulze, he was a Nietzschean thinker and a man of high character who, for his attempts to guide the diplomacy of the early Weimar Republic, was assassinated in 1922 by right-wing nationalists—shades of Hans Sepp—who could not abide a Jew playing a leading role in the new republic. In his *Weimar: Deutschland 1917–1933* Schulze goes so far to say about Rathenau that in Weimar Germany "only one man could bridge over the abyss between politics and spirit [*Geist*], and he was to pay for it" (238). This judgment has such a Musil-like ring to it that one wonders if Schulze had not read Rathenau as an incarnation of Arnheim. In any event Arnheim-Rathenau is a major historical figure whom Musil has placed in the foreground precisely because his kind represents what was perhaps best in the German liberal capitalist society that nonetheless had not been able to avoid the First World War, not to mention the militant nationalism surrounding Musil as he was writing *The Man without Qualities.* It is noteworthy that as a writer Rathenau deplored the "mechanization of society" and called for the creation of a "kingdom of soul."[8] But Musil was also quite aware that in his role as industrialist Rathenau had been instrumental in organizing German industry for the war effort, and it is not by accident that Arnheim has factories that manufacture cannons (2:568).

Yet Arnheim is not simply to be equated with Rathenau. He is a fictional character who, like Rathenau, embodies the contradictions of a major industrialist who is also a humanist intellectual at the time of the triumph of liberal capitalism. Whatever may be the intellectual depth of Arnheim, it is dubious that he could change in any respect the dominant trend of capitalism, which is to submit all aspects of life to the determinations of the market. Arnheim, unlike, say, today's robber kings of American finance and energy corporations, does not entirely accept this tenet of his own enterprise. He is capable of critical thinking and at times seems to oppose his own projects. Musil uses this complex character in his confrontation with Ulrich to portray a mind that at once embraces the premises of capitalist rationality and thinks, at times, that it could be otherwise. The Enlightenment belief in the possible glimmers within Arnheim.

The relationship between Arnheim and Ulrich undergoes modification in the course of book 1. In their first encounter Ulrich cannot abide the man (1:176), a businessman who can speak with authority on everything (1:189). Book 1 ends, however, with Ulrich moved by Arnheim's attempt at friendship and even envious of the man's "unity of happiness" (1:645). Some of Arnheim's traits and beliefs are close to Ulrich's, though not his belief in the ultimate rationality of the market economy. Arnheim is a humanist thinker who, in the wake of Hegel, thinks that history is rational (1:249). Yet contradictorily, and in this much like Ulrich, he also thinks that the nature of history is to bring forth unpredictable change (1:198). At one moment he even demonstrates that he, like a Pascalian mathematician, can demonstrate the limits of calculation when he engages in a complex reasoning to show the limits of reason to General Stumm: he demonstrates the nature of the calculation that would be necessary to predict the exact movement of a billiard ball; by so doing he proves that its complexity defies the possibility of a calculus (2:570). Whether Arnheim actually believes in his own demonstration against mathematical description is an open question, since in this very moment he is courting the Austrians with open flattery of their less-than-rational way of living. He claims that they may even save the Germans from their Prussian hyperrationalism and from the death of spirit that has occurred with the loss of God (2:568–70). In other words Arnheim is trumpeting a critique of reason that is rather much at odds with his faith in the rational determination of history by market forces of which he is also a dominant representative.

The range of cultural references in the scenes between Arnheim and Ulrich reflects a kind of brilliant duel between men representing the pinnacle of German culture. This effect is enhanced when, for example, Musil engages in an intertextual play with Goethe's tragedy *Tasso* in which the prince of Ferrara is the man of action who stands opposed to the mad poet Tasso, the man of deviated feeling. In Musil's update of this confrontation, Ulrich's lack of properties may border on Tasso's madness, whereas Arnheim, literally called at times a prince of finance, is also put forth as the man of reality (1:186). Arnheim also embodies the Hegelian *Weltgeist*, the spirit of the age in its most developed form: he has mastered science, industrial technology, and is able to speak on all aspects of culture. This reference to Hegel can recall that Musil was an admirer of the Danish philosopher Søren Kierkegaard, who personally refused, with consummate irony, to be inscribed into Hegel's rational system. Not surprisingly the ironic Dane's stance is reflected in the way Ulrich uses irony to challenge Arnheim's grip on reality, which is to say, his grip on Diotima, if not on his industrial empire. The Hegelian Arnheim is shaken by Ulrich's refusal to take him quite seriously, despite the fact that he knows he has ultimate reality on his side. As an inheritor of Adam Smith and the philosophy of capitalism, Arnheim has, like all capitalists, replaced absolute spirit with the market or, in Arnheim's shorthand, with money.

The central issue for any competitive economic enterprise is profit. *Homo economicus* knows, as Arnheim puts it in a less humanistic moment, that the economic market has replaced mind, indeed, the brain. Or as the narrator says about Arnheim in a inimitable turn of phrase, "Er dachte sich das Zeitgehirn durch Angebot und Nachfrage ersatz"—roughly, he thought the forces of supply and demand have replaced the historical development of the human brain (2:409). The workings of supply and demand, as any student learns in a course in introductory economics, are automatic determinants of action that can be simply graphed to show how they determine everything: the production of guns and roses, or novels and Mercedes. And this is the reality in which the so-called great writer, as Arnheim describes him, should act like a department store owner but speak like an idealist (2:432). In Musil's satirical portrayal of Arnheim—though it is not entirely satirical—Arnheim conceives that ideas are products sold on the market like any other; so that, with advertising pushing forward one product or another, the market and the return on investment determine which books are produced.

Arnheim is contradictory in his beliefs, though perhaps not in his actions. His courting of Diotima and the Parallel Action may well have significant returns in the market. This is not to say that he is not sincerely infatuated with Tuzzi's wife, nor that he does not dream of historical changes that somehow might produce something better than the social reality of 1913. In this he is Ulrich's "brother" (2:547). As a metaphorical prince he also muses on a past that was better than the present, for he seems genuinely drawn to the aristocratic irrationalism of the past and the values that the aristocracy once produced. These were values owing nothing to a marketplace and nothing to supply and demand (2:542–43). He understands vulgarity—*Gemeinheit*—and judges it negatively, whatever market value it might have. Not unlike Ulrich, he meditates in Diotima's company on how everything might be different, though he ends his meditative pirouettes by falling back upon the capitalist vision of a world rationally determined by economic forces.

Arnheim is ultimately an apologist for his own enterprises and for what he views at times as the near-utopian success of capitalism to harness selfishness and replace violence with money. Hence his idea that money is *Verstand*—practical reason (2:509). He argues that the pursuit of profit in the market has replaced the armed conquest pursued by traditional societies, and thereby rapine has been replaced by stocks and bonds. In this he agrees with the influential sociologist Max Weber, who also thought that money was a *Kampfmittel*—a means of struggle or combat. Arnheim sounds much like Weber, who in his posthumous *Wirtschaft und Gesellschaft* (1921; "Economics and Society"), wrote that prices are the end product of struggle and compromise, hence the product of constellations of power. Thus the market represents a demand for rationality, since the act of accounting for money entails accounting for capital and by implication a rational distribution of resources rather than a distribution of goods determined by sword and plunder.[9] In short the rational capitalist with an historical sense is at one with the liberal sociologist who saw that capitalism had replaced feudalism with more than a mere change of ownership of the means of production. If prices have replaced plunder, this means that rationality has taken a new form in the capitalist era.

However, acting more like a member of a chamber of commerce indulging in hype, Arnheim goes beyond Weber, the sociologist, to make the extravagant claim that if God were to return to set up the millennium, he would advise the Lord to establish the thousand-year kingdom in accord with sound business principles. In this manner he would not need to have recourse to violence and torture—such as were presumably necessary before the advent of capitalism and the guiding laws of the market (2:508). (Musil's irony here is that in 1913 the so-called civilized capitalist nations of the world were getting ready to commit greater violence upon each other than history had ever seen before.) Arnheim's idea of a capitalist millennium should focus our attention on the fact that capitalism claims at times to represent a utopia by contrast with the past social orders. At least this is Arnheim's defensive position: from his perspective the millennium has been co-opted if not yet realized by the capitalism. Like a good Hegelian Arnheim believes that capitalism represents the most rational development of history and perhaps even the end stage of the development of history. This utopia produced by the market stands in ironic contrast with the millennium of criminals toward which Ulrich heads in the second half of the novel.

From this perspective we see that a contrast of two utopian styles, if not visions, underlies the concluding encounter of Arnheim and Ulrich in book 1.

In this encounter Arnheim tries to co-opt Ulrich by offering him a position in his organization. In contrast to his moments of utopian ebullience, however, Arnheim puts on a show for Ulrich to make clear that he is no dupe of his own rhetoric. He explicitly recognizes that the division of labor and the corporate organization resulting from that division allows those who really own capital to mask their power. Corporate organization masks both the power to destroy as well as to distribute resources. Arnheim may now be trying to show that he has read Karl Marx, who, at the outset of *The Communist Manifesto,* underscored that the modern capitalist is a destroyer of traditions, institutions, and peoples (2:638). The question is now who is the most demonic figure, Arnheim or Ulrich, for it is at this moment that Arnheim quotes Schiller from *The Robbers* and accuses Ulrich of embracing the devil. With rich irony the narrator shows that there is an element of self-description in this charge as he describes how Arnheim puts his arm around Ulrich. (The reader may well wonder who is embracing whom.) Arnheim embraces Ulrich while wondering if he had been serious with his suggestion that they should create a general secretariat for precision and soul. He wonders what this might do about the fact that modern capitalists "destroy morals and soul continuously with the latest patents" and then believe that they "can hold them together with the old household remedies offered by religion and philosophy" (2:639). Ulrich replies, with his usual irony, that he believes the devil has set up the European world and that God wants to let his competitor show what he can do (2:639). The difference between them is that Ulrich is consciously ironic in his words, whereas Arnheim does not seem aware of the irony of his situation. Thus, Musil sets his two devils against each other as ironic foils: the capitalist as destroyer looking at a Mephisto-like intellectual who cannot embrace him in return. Arnheim tries to flatter Ulrich by pointing out that some of the sharpest opponents of capitalism are among its best servants, but Ulrich is not to be purchased, probably to Arnheim's relief.

An analysis of capitalism informs Arnheim and Ulrich's confrontation, though this analysis is from an essayistic perspective. The two characters offer several contradictory perspectives on the nature of capitalism. And from this perspective the reader sees that the social world informs the characters even as the characters debate about the nature of the social world. In Arnheim's case, the industrialist, at times self-consciously, performs as both critic of and participant in the world from which Ulrich withdraws. Of course, as a social critic Arnheim may appear to be disingenuous when he tries to minimize the role that old fields have in his interest in Diotima, the Parallel Action, and Austria. Perhaps the essayism he exemplifies does not exclude hypocrisy, for this capitalist who dreams of a better world can participate knowingly in the division of labor that allows the powerful to destroy entire societies without having to touch directly or to see those who are destroyed (2:638). I stress that Arnheim is lucidly aware of the abuse of power. He even coins the term *Indirekheit* to describe the indirect exercise of power that isolates causes from their effects. In corporations, armies, and governments *Indirekheit* characterizes all modern bureaucratic structures that assure that those wielding power do not confront with full responsibility the consequences of their acts (2:638). At times Arnheim is a clear-sighted critic, as well as a Hegelian apologist, of capitalism.

Hegel was the philosopher of history who thought that the end of history had arrived with the development of the Prussian state and its system of justice. As a successful Prussian capitalist, Arnheim may be motivated to agree. Set as a foil to the Jewish, but very Prussian, Arnheim is the novel's other representative of capitalism, the Jewish but Viennese Fischel, the banker who has much less reason to be a Hegelian. However, unlike Ulrich, he still believes in the ideology of progress and has time for a few minutes of philosophy every day or so. Fischel is not a great industrialist, to be sure; in fact, he is a prototypical assimilated Viennese Jew who holds liberal values. His liberalism explains why he allows an anti-Semite into his own home, for he of course believes in tolerance—which perhaps can be taken as Musil's critique of a liberalism that does not understand the limits of tolerance. Admittedly Fischel is also catering to his daughter, Gerda, who has begun to listen to the pan-Germanist ideas of Hans Sepp, a dispassionate suitor who would be a comic character if his ideas did not directly presage the tragic fate of Jews in German culture. The critique of nationalism Musil sets out in his essays is mirrored in the confrontation between Sepp and Ulrich, in whom Sepp finds a scapegoat for the problems Germans face in the empire. Their confrontation is emblematic of the demise Viennese liberalism had undergone during the forty years or so that preceded World War I.

After this discussion of Ulrich's development and his relation to Arnheim, it is appropriate to elaborate in greater detail a point made earlier about history and knowledge. *The Man without Qualities* is at times a metahistorical novel in that it not only offers symbolic representations of historical events, but it also offers a meditation on how one might know those events even as they are unfolding, that is, before they are encompassed by or reduced to some form of narrative discourse. Ulrich (and the narrator) is well aware that his attempt to know history before it becomes the impoverished narrative called "history" demands an epistemology that does not exist, even if probability theory is highly suggestive. In spite of his belief in discontinuity Ulrich intuitively feels that all events are interrelated in some sense, in the infinite complications of individual acts and judgments that meld into social wholes that, once narrated in their temporal unfolding, are called history. In his debates with himself, and later with his sister, about how one might have knowledge of these infinite complications, Ulrich considers a series of epistemological polarities. For example, a key polarity, which underlies the crisis that he undergoes in the spring of 1914, is the fundamental problem of knowing the dichotomy created when one looks at society either as an historical totality or as a series of discrete individual facts, such as automobile accidents, muggings, and adulterous love affairs, which taken together make up the whole. The totality might be envisaged as that Hegelian realm of unfolding history and society that stands opposed to the individual *Tatsache,* or the elementary unit of scientific discourse called the empirical fact. Or alternatively the social whole can be considered as the realm of statistical necessity in which one can know with near certainty the laws of the total collectivity—how many traffic deaths, robberies, and adulteries will occur in Austria each year—and not know at all what will befall the individual Austrian on an given day. So Ulrich comes up with the idea that there are two different conceptions of mind—*Geistesverfassungen*—that coexist without conflict with each other, though they do not communicate with each other except to assure each other that each is desirable, in its own place. One cast of mind looks with precision at the individual fact, whereas the other envisages the whole—*das Ganze*—and "derives its knowledge from so-called eternal truths" (1:248). One type of mind garners success, the other type gets prestige, though, as the narrator caustically notes, the results of the first may not be worth much and those of the second may not be true.

The narrator—or is it Ulrich?—seems to oppose Hegelian historicism to Machean empiricism in his attempt to decide how one might have knowledge of society. Ulrich sees that prestige accrues to the man of action who is able to manipulate people with an eye on the totality. Such a person is the industrialist-cum-intellectual Arnheim. By contrast success can be defined as the pragmatic success of the scientist dealing with the precise mathematical relations—the Einstein or Planck who defines the coordinates describing physical reality. Prestige notwithstanding, Musil is bent on showing that the businessman, pretending to know the totality in its eternal truth, is letting Europe drift toward World War I. Ulrich's ire with Arnheim seems to reflect Musil's negative judgment on those men of prestige whose grasp of the total picture in 1914 was totally illusory.

However much the novel condemns the delusions of those who believe they understand the social totality, Musil also suggests that it is necessary to have some view of that developing totality if one is to make informed judgments about social goals. The desire to work toward goals means that one must attempt to understand whatever laws might be at work shaping the direction of history. In this sense Ulrich muses on mathematical models when he wonders, for example, if one can reconcile knowledge of the iron laws of statistics with the aleatory activities of the billions of individuals whose caprices in the aggregate obey those laws. He wonders if the problem is not unlike the problem of prediction in kinetics or particle physics. For instance one can predict with near certainty the rate of decay of an element brought about by radioactivity, without knowing which specific atom will give up a particle; analogously, statistical laws allow the prediction of how many people will be run over on the streets of Vienna each year—and we have seen that at the beginning the novel duly documents a traffic accident—but these laws are incapable of pointing out the unfortunate burgher whose life will be expended in confirmation of the laws' power to predict.

Finding himself sharing the common ignorance of social development but aware of his lack of knowledge, Ulrich thus dreams of overcoming ignorance in a utopia of exactitude where science and action are joined. This conjoining would allow him to reinvent morality, since morality demands knowledge, the difficult knowledge of what is possible as well as what should be. This utopian melding, presupposing a single epistemology, would require that Ulrich know precise facts that somehow add up to a meaningful unity or totality; but the chaos of daily experience makes him distrust the idea that a totality has any meaning. As the novel unfolds Ulrich reflects increasingly upon his utopian conjoining of knowledge and action, in a meditation on the opposition between the need to understand the totality and the exigencies of precision or exactitude. The narrator, speaking for Ulrich, as it were, narrates in an attempt to know the *Ganzheit,* the putative totality, which presupposes a consciousness capacious enough to grasp the totality necessary for judgment.

This yearning to seize the imbrication of all events determines in a sense the form of the novel. For it finally means that any event or idea that can pass the muster of plausibility can go into the novel: Ulrich's meditations, sexual affairs, conversations, a street scene in Vienna, the narrator's view of the history of science, Ulrich's writings on psychology as well as his essays about the epistemological split between exactitude and totality. At times the novel ceases to be a narrative to become something like an encyclopedia that includes a series of essays. Musil conceived of the essay as a genre offering an epistemological blending of science and poetry, and the novel resembles at time a narrated essay. The narrative project dictates that, even within the essay form, there must be narrated events that can represent, as so many synecdoches, the totality, since limited human perception dictates that the totality can only be grasped as an unfolding of disparate, single events. Facing only singular events, the anti-Hegelian narrator necessarily sees no totality, however much he may hope that from these musings might emerge the desired total picture. To be sure the Machean epistemologist lurking in Musil's narrator, as well as in Ulrich, suspects that all the little mimetic pictures in the world will never add up to any totality. Totality may be one more myth, given a patina of plausibility by the success of scientific method in making statistical predications; but it is a myth used by various ideologues in and out of the novel to bolster their private ambitions and obsessions. As such it is a myth to be reckoned with.

Hyperconscious of the epistemological polarities—or antinomies, if one prefers—that undermine his attempt to know what history, morality, or simply good judgment might be, Ulrich is obliged to think self-reflexively about the means for representation that he, the mathematician-poet, has at his disposal. If there is a commonality allowing unified knowledge, one uniting judging and knowing, the whole and the singular part, it must spring from an understanding of the common quest for representation that seemingly underlies all cultural activity. Ulrich is again rather Machean in his anthropology of knowledge, for he affirms with a Machean turn of phrase that knowledge is based on modeling or representation, as one can variously translate his term, *Darstellung*. The split between scientific and literary modes of knowing derives from the polarity between the type of propositions that the mind uses in modeling. Or as Ulrich also puts it, the split is due to the type of language used for *Darstellung*. In the aforementioned chapter "The Two Trees of Life and a Proposal to Establish a General Secretariat for Precision and Soul," he imagines one might overcome the opposition of science and values by reconciling propositions representing the dominant opposing modes of representation. He wants to unite, on the one hand, the representation achieved by figurative language and, on the other hand, the representation offered by unequivocal language, that of *Eindeutigkeit*. It is hardly clear what purport this union or reconciliation might have for the knowledge of history. True, a split characterizes those who write history, for it is often written by those who claim to use the language of univocal science and precise truth, while other historians favor *das Gleichnis,* or fictive representations and their figural truths (such as Musil himself).

Other models for history also emerge in the course of the novel. At one point in meditating on history, for example, the narrator sketches out a proto–chaos theory of history. He suggests that rather than following the linear causality suggested by the movement of a billiard ball when it is hit by another ball, history resembles the movement of clouds whose progress is unpredictable (2:361). At another moment Ulrich sees the forward progress of history motivated by the greater and greater demand for specialization. This historical development means that thinkers have now been segregated from society and placed on a type of chicken farm to lay their ideas: the end result of which will be the Bee Society in which reproduction, lust, and thinking will be separated (2:359). This image may remind one of the modern university, or it may portend an even more sinister dystopia (something of the line of what Fritz Lang imagined in his film *Metropolis).* With Walter, and perhaps simply to irritate Walter, Ulrich proposes that the history of art is the history of art denying its own forms so that the progress of culture should logically eventuate in beauty in art eliminating itself. Though momentarily pleased with this theory of the history of forms, Ulrich knows that he could just as well argue the contrary (2:367). And Arnheim does argue the contrary. In brief, in the first part of the novel the constant theorizing about and portraying of history is part of the overall countdown strategy by which Musil sets up his narrator's retrospective knowledge of history against his characters' desire to know what history will be. The cards are stacked against Ulrich, for the narrator knows that the history in which the narrator himself is immersed some years after the war was one that no one expected. It is a history that nobody could have foreseen in 1913, not even Ulrich.

To conclude these comments on book 1, history seems to disappear at the end of the novel, at least for Ulrich, when he finds that the notion of world no longer exists for him. In the final chapter, "The Turning Point," his experience of the dissolution of the world comes after the mad scene with Clarisse. Clarisse throws at Ulrich ideas that were once his own and challenges him with what he calls his "own conclusions." Her ranting has the effect upon him of a "wild music."[10] Principal among these ideas Clarisse seizes upon is the notion that we exist in a condition—*Zustand*—that has fissures through which we see another condition, an impossible condition, though Clarisse rages that she will make it through the "hole" to the other side, to which "one is bound as if to a twin with which one has grown up" (2:659). In her description she seems to anticipate what Ulrich seems later to experience, to wit, another condition, bound up with the "twin" he hardly knows—his sister, Agathe. Clarisse's sexual assault on Ulrich is the final blow needed to dissolve the world so that the world, the framework for history, ceases, for the time being, to have meaning for him (2:664). Early the next morning after this encounter, he sets out for the provincial city in which another condition, unknown to him, may be waiting on him. He is headed, criminal that he may become, toward the millennium.

CHAPTER 9

The Man without Qualities, **Book 2**

Musil published a second volume of *The Man without Qualities* in 1932. The first chapter of this book 2 is a new chapter 1, and subsequent chapters are numbered accordingly. Apparently to confuse the reader a bit more—recall that part 1 and part 2 have sequentially numbered chapters—book 2 is also called part 3. In this chapter I will deal mainly with the thirty-eight sequential chapters he published as part 3, or book 2, though I will also consider the twenty posthumous chapters that follow these sequentially as a continuation of part 3. As I mentioned earlier, these posthumous chapters are the twenty galley chapters, unpublished in Musil's lifetime, that were ready for publication in 1938. In the following discussion of what I will call, for clarity, the novel's second half, I will conclude with considerations of a few of the manuscript chapters that have been published posthumously. In doing this I do not intend to argue for any specific ending to the novel that Musil might have had in mind. However, like most readers, I can hardly refrain at times from speculating about how a particular ending might inform the novel, which is to say, I cannot help asking if some narrative telos may not guide the work's unfolding. This is a natural question, for one always assumes that a narrative has a ending that gives it final intelligibility. However, Musil may not have ever conceived how he would finish the novel, and one is probably best advised to limit one's speculation to what can be shown to be the case in what he actually published or completed. Given the quest he undertook in the novel, it may have been that it was not in the realm of possibility that he should conceive an ending for it, which, as I have argued above and elsewhere, would make of his novel an exemplary modernist failure.[1]

Critics of a more biographical bent would recall at this point that Musil's failure to finish the novel was also due to the fact that he died, after periods of poor health, in exile after the Nazis' triumph in Austria forced him to take refuge in Switzerland. The history of the novel's genesis and its publication also suggests that, as the political situation became impossible for him, Musil came, in a sense, to live the novel as he wrote it, which may mean that he did not really want to make a final decision about where to go with it and to conclude perforce with something less than a utopian ending in what had become the least utopian of times. Living the novel in exile, as it were, he did not want to take decisions that would have limited its possibilities by imposing closure. Life imposes its limits, of course, but as long as he was alive, Musil could and did experiment with imagined alternatives for the novel that may seem to have become an alternative life in a barbarous world given over to the madness whose roots he had laid bare in *Young Törless*.

It has also been argued that Musil's novel is predicated on the idea that narrative closure would be a form of imposture. An ending would be a betrayal of fidelity to experience—which notably has no endings, except the truly final one. From this perspective even the historical fact that the First World War actually occurred would at best offer an arbitrary ending. If motivated closure of narrative is impossible for a novel representing the openness of experience, then the war's outbreak would simply be a closure imposed on the narrative from without. Moreover, the narrator already finds himself living in a world for which the war is a past event, perhaps the most traumatic past event one can imagine, but past nonetheless. This means that the war is no more a stopping point for the ongoing narrative of history than the length of women's hair in the roaring twenties or the emergence of fascist political parties.[2]

If we retain something of a biographical perspective on the novel, we can also argue that Musil began work on it with the idea of experimenting with the novelistic form, if *novel* is the proper word for this mixture of narration and meditation, description and essayistic dialectic. From this perspective one can argue that he set out to write a work that did not need an ending. To be sure, in his early and in some late planning of the novel, the war's arrival was to be the conclusion; and had Musil followed this plan, the novel would probably have returned from some mythic or utopian interlude to end in the war of the trenches. Antiutopia follows utopia, perhaps. But it can also be argued that *The Man without Qualities* was never really based on the idea that a novel must have narrative closure; and as it evolved, it is not certain that Musil always wanted this ending. Thomas Mann had ended *The Magic Mountain* (1924) with his hero's descent from the clinic on a Swiss mountain to the plains, to disappear in the war's muddy trenches. Mann's example of a rather forced narrative closure, ending a novel of epistemological exploration not without similarities to Musil's novel, was more likely to irritate Musil than to attract him.

And to go a step further I add that, if the telos of the novel is to show that modern epistemology renders impossible the idea of narrative closure, then the reader may be confronting a contradictory situation. The goal of the novel would be to deny that it can have a goal. Every logician knows that a propositional contradiction will give rise to any deduction that one likes. This might seem to imply that, since no closure is possible, all are possible. I leave it up to a logician to decide if this logical dilemma really can apply to an entire novel; but at least by analogy, the contradiction may help to explain the variety of endings that critics have thought out for *The Man without Qualities,* not to mention those Musil himself suggested in the reams of manuscripts he left behind.

With this caveat in mind about contradiction, I turn to the Swiss poet and Musil's translator into French, Philippe Jaccottet, for an example of the kind of ending a gifted reader suggests. Jaccottet describes Musil's project in the third part of the novel in terms suggesting a utopian or perhaps mystical enterprise. Jaccottet says that, after Ulrich meets his forgotten sister Agathe, they retire to their house: "They have only one marvelous and dangerous concern: access to the 'other state,' that second species of reality about which Ulrich explains to his sister that one's premonition of it is anterior to every religion, that its light shines in all that's best about human life. . . . it is not only from the puppets of the Parallel Action that the brother and the sister detach themselves, and not only from European idealism, from the Vienna of 1913, from a sclerotic morality, or from a dying art; it is, progressively, from space and time."[3]

According to Jaccottet, on leaving space and time, Ulrich would, if he could, enter something like the realm of myth. Many critics follow Jaccottet's lead in this respect and, plausibly enough, often interpret Ulrich's ultimate project to be some kind of transcendence.

If this were Ulrich's goal, then Musil should have created for him a utopian discourse uniting science and ethics, rationality and creativity, or knowledge and mystical belief. The realization of a model for a discourse incorporating all these spheres, partially described at times in the novel itself, demands that the work should ideally arrive at a point beyond science and ethics. Here the work would recast or create the unity of culture that Musil sometimes seemed to believe to be the only foundation for a discourse that could meet human needs. Such a discourse would be scientific; it would be ethical; in fine it would be embodied in an epistemic *Gesamtkunstwerk*—a total artwork offering knowledge of a renewed culture and of how to achieve that knowledge. It would transcend the limitations of literature and science to create the embodied myth of total culture. From this perspective Ulrich dreamed of a literary utopia. It is not necessarily the case that Musil shared his belief in the possibility of such a utopia.

If we follow up on Jaccottet's suggestive remarks, we can entertain the idea that in the second half of the novel Musil undertakes the following thought experiment. It begins with the idea of a possible mystical union between Ulrich and his newly discovered sister, Agathe. If such a union were possible, what would be the results? It is an ethical thought experiment bordering on the forbidden, though the scientist in Musil might have argued that the imaginative enactment of near incest is not unlike combining, in the imagination, unknown chemicals and seeing what might ensue. The experiment accompanies Ulrich's yearning for some form of transcendence wherein his nascent mysticism would find the unity lacking in modern culture. This oneness might exist only in a realm of myth, suggested by the fact that the union of brother and sister reproduces an image of refound oneness for which the androgyne is the original mythic expression. In this manner Musil experiments through Ulrich's own thought experiments with mystical belief and attempts to understand the uniqueness that feelings reveal. Considering the universality of the taboo against incest, one might say Musil is also imagining through Ulrich what might be the consequences of denying the interdictions upon which culture is founded. For nothing less is at stake if the brother and sister were to deny this fundamental taboo. But it seems to be axiomatic to Ulrich that truly moral thinking must be prepared to defy convention and open to transformation—however conventional he himself may appear at times. In brief, even without a finished experiment, the reader clearly sees that Musil wants to ask what future changes could radical moral thinking force one to envisage.

In the second half of the novel, Ulrich confronts the task of finding a way to articulate his moral thinking. His world has dissolved, but for another world to exist, he must be able to express it—or express why he cannot. In this regard his wistful dreams of conjoining science and mystical experience can be illuminated by Musil's reaction to Mach. Mach laid down strict limits as to what one can meaningfully say, limits even more severe than those imposed by Kantian empiricism. By imposing reductive epistemological limits, Mach decreed, like Kant before him, that much of great human interest lay beyond these limits. Wittgenstein also arrived at a comparable conclusion in meditating on the limits of what language can say. He came to believe that if the positivists were in some sense right, then ethics and transcendental questions were better addressed by, say, a writer such as Leo Tolstoy. His fictional work could show these realms, if not "say" them, since it is not possible to formulate demonstrable propositions about them. In this sense positivism leads to mysticism. Ulrich's case is analogous to Wittgenstein's. And in the second half of novel, through Ulrich, Musil entertains the proposition that one might demonstrate,

perhaps mythically, an atheistic mysticism, with the emphasis placed on showing this mysticism in ways that get beyond the limits of empirical propositions.
Eros and ethics together demand the reconfiguration of reason, though not the
rejection of rationality. Herein lies Ulrich's constant dilemma.

This is not to say that Ulrich ever overcomes the constraints of reason.
One cannot even say that he really wants to overcome them. The respect of reason also constrains knowledge in a positive sense. Rationally skeptical Ulrich
is as much an opponent of skepticism and irrationality as he is a sometime par-
tisan of mysticism. He respects the limits imposed by reason. For example, one
cannot even imagine that he could ever use probability theory to suggest that
the acceptance of the irrational might be a good bet. In other words he would
never imitate the Pascal who figured the odds in betting on the existence of
God and decided it was a good wager. Ulrich would only bet on a mystical
union that can be experienced, can be shown, and perhaps can be articulated
and communicated. This may not be a wager one is likely to win; and, from
this perspective, one goal of the novel's conclusion might have been precisely
to show the limits of nonrational experience and the impossibility of utopia.[4]

The second half of the novel continues the countdown toward August
1914, albeit with less frequent allusive recall than in the first half. Narration
about the Parallel Action also continues, pointing up the fact that the war is
coming and that nobody has a clue about it. On the contrary, most parties in
the Parallel Action believe that in one sense or another they are preparing for
peace, even if that preparation means the Austrians must have better artillery
and military supply lines. In narrating these incongruities Musil masterfully
intertwines his portrayal of Viennese society with the ongoing debate about
ethics and ideology that Ulrich and his sister undertake in their withdrawal
from society. The link between society and Ulrich is maintained by one of
Musil's most interesting, indeed delightful characters, the General Stumm von
Bordwehr. In the novel's second half the general functions to maintain the narrative counterpoint between society and the couple's isolation. To be sure the
general is also a major character in book 1 and merits commentary to illustrate
the narrative development, minimal as it is, in the second half of *The Man
without Qualities,* as well as to place in relief the novel's one representative of
the Austrian army.

The general is not a saber-rattling militarist but, with all due allowance for
Musil's irony, another representative of those high officials who wanted to promote peace in 1914. He even affirms, late in the novel, that he is an antimili-
tarist military man who has never believed in war, especially not presently
(4:1153). He is, in short, the ideal dialectical general who embodies common

sense. Having some common sense means that he does not understand the machinations of civilian diplomats, nor the intellectual ironies that Ulrich uses, though the general finds these witticisms entertaining in the young man who once served under his command in the army. Initially the general comes to Diotima's house after receiving an unintended invitation sent as a prank by servants. He, too, falls in love with her and henceforth does his best to participate in civilian matters by initiating himself into the matters of *Geist* that Arnheim and Ulrich toss about. His initiation reaches its satirical climax in book 1 when the well-intentioned general discovers that there is nobody in the Austrian National Library who can indicate to him where might be found a book, among the two million books there, that contains the most elevated of elevated ideals. Logic as well as common sense tells him that there can be just one best thing of any category of thing, so that there must be one best idea, which he would like to bring to Diotima and the Parallel Action. Common sense tells him that this idea should be in one of the books the librarians know about. He discovers, however, that the librarians know nothing about ideas, since they do not read the books they have in their charge. They only have time for perusing the bibliographies of bibliographies with which they ply their trade as organizers of knowledge. The impatient military man finally, in questioning the librarian, calls the library an insane asylum (2:462)—a variety of institution whose organization he subsequently discovers when he is obliged to visit a madhouse with Clarisse and Ulrich.

The visit to the insane asylum stands in ironic symmetry with the general's visit to the library, for in the insane asylum he again discovers forms of organization he never suspected: in the asylum medical doctors demonstrate their mania for classification by organizing madness according to type, not unlike the librarians who employ their time creating arbitrary systems of classification. Both ideas and madmen have professional keepers with their own systems for organizing them. The general discovers continuously that the world is more complex than he ever suspected when merely drilling troops.

The general is a marvelous agent for satire. He is the outsider who stands as a foil to civilian follies, but he is not a puppet in any sense. In fact Ulrich suspects that the general may be trying to use him. In the novel's second half the general has the function of keeping Ulrich in contact with the ongoing Parallel Action and all those actions that, somehow, taken together make up the history of 1913 having become 1914. The general is an intrusive presence in the idyll developing between Ulrich and his sister, for he has no scruples about popping in whenever he wants. After Ulrich and Agathe's relationship begins on the occasion of their father's funeral in a provincial city, Ulrich returns alone to Vienna. General Stumm immediately intrudes himself. Claiming that military men have a different way of defending the peace than that of "bureaucrats," he reveals that he may also not be above cutting deals with Arnheim about oil supplies (3:777). The general, undoubtedly wanting to provoke Ulrich, informs him that in his absence Ulrich has been declared not to be the right *Tatmensch*—man of action—for finding the great deed the Parallel Action is seeking. The general's function here is to irritate Ulrich, who now finds himself relegated to the sphere of passivity. Thereupon he declares that he is withdrawing from the entire affair—from "der ganzen Geschichte," whose double meaning of "history" as well as the whole "affair" suggests an ambivalent sense of his decision to withdraw (3:779). The Parallel Action has been a trope for the course of history throughout the novel, and Ulrich's refusal aims at both.

The general will not allow his former subordinate to withdraw entirely, however. He pops in again in the springtime after Agathe has come to live with Ulrich in Vienna. General Stumm comes to tell Ulrich that he thinks a "great event" is now beginning (3:931). He also says, with some consternation, that Diotima may be about to lose the direction of the Parallel Action to another woman, perhaps because her mind has been busy studying, for personal reasons, the new science of sexology. Common sense suggests that some important changes have taken place with her, and therefore the general presses Ulrich to come to the "fateful meeting" (3:933). Before Ulrich goes to this meeting, Musil concocts another compressed day of events during which the general, Ulrich, and Clarisse visit the insane asylum in which Moosbrugger is interned—though they do not see him. This visit gives the interned madmen a chance to hail Clarisse, as one chapter title puts it, and to dampen considerably her enthusiasm for insanity. Then, on the very same day, the "great event" takes place. Though the event occupies the last five chapters of the published third part, nobody notices it, as the title of the concluding chapter title informs us—even though the general has brought Ulrich there for the purpose of seeing it.

The supposedly fateful meeting Ulrich attends with the general, coming immediately after their visit to the insane asylum, is especially rich in ideological jousting. Unfolding in the last five published chapters, it is a highpoint in the novel's second half. The first four of these chapters all have a title starting with "A Great Event Is Arising" to end with the final chapter's pointed comment that nobody noticed it taking place. These chapters show why: in the exuberance of cocktail party chatter, ideological viewpoints are exchanged with the reckless abandon characterizing all those who have no idea about what is really going on about them. In these chapters Musil grants the reader an overview of the clash of modernist worldviews on the eve of the war. For example, with his aristocratic sense of civic responsibility Count Leinsdorf wants to give men of property and education—*Bildung*—one more chance to transform society. By contrast a new participant, Diotima's rival, Melanie Drangsal, has come with her poet, Feuermaul ("fire-mouth"), to promote world peace by celebrating confidence in man's natural goodness. The official viewpoint on things is represented by the minister of war, who has come with Tuzzi to figure out what these people are really up to. Never fearful of strife, Arnheim circulates among the guests, declaring Feuermaul's ideas to be Rousseauistic images of the moment, not to mention clichés. For his part the all-knowing diplomatic Tuzzi thinks Arnheim is using the oil deal as a smokescreen to hide his real interest in promoting the pacifism wanted by the Russian tsar, which is somehow inimical to Austria's interests as Tuzzi conceives them. To Ulrich's observation that Arnheim is an arms dealer, Tuzzi shows his skill in diplomacy by contending that pacifism creates a constant market for arms, more so than war does, since actual war involves risks (3:1006). In these chapters, then, beliefs, motivations, ideas, all are subject to multiple perspectives and satirical juxtaposition. Alternating between doubt and assertion, ideas are ultimately stamped with the reminder of their uselessness to engage what actually was happening in real history.

Other participants, old and new, have other ideas, and some are not above believing in contradictory positions at the same time. However, a basic ideological polarity emerges at the meeting, pitting believers in goodness and peace against those who think a strong leader with a strong hand is the only guarantee of whatever it is they want. This polarity is perhaps a fair characterization of the first part of the twentieth century, during which, after the disappearance of emperors, Mussolini, Franco, Hitler, and Stalin were granted totalitarian power, to the repeated discomfiture of those who had held more sanguine views about how humanity might organize its political affairs. Satirically, all in the Viennese salon are for peace, more or less, and all have explanations as to how people are motivated to do what they do as they make history take place. To demonstrate these views Musil places pacifists, nationalists, aristocrats, protofascists, Marxists, and Freudians together in an elegant drawing room in which ideas ricochet about like the bullets that will be flying in a few months' time. (Only a comparison with Swift's "Battle of the Books" can suggest the scope of Musil's satire.) Meditating on what he hears, Ulrich provides one guiding thread through the ideological labyrinth and General Stumm another, as the good soldier elicits opinions and makes his comically commonsense observations.

By contrast with the general, Ulrich considers that many partial truths resonate in the meeting. It is the nature of partial truths to set up the oppositions out of which historical truth evolves into higher forms. Such is Ulrich's sense of the unending process by which truths emerge from historical development. And with a strong sense of the catastrophes this process engenders, he wonders if truth will necessarily continue to grow: "Each time humanity has taken a partial truth as the only valid one, vengeance has taken place. But from another point of view, could one have reached even this partial truth, if it had not been overvalued?" (3:1020). Blindness and hyperbolic belief have been the necessary parts of the historical process by which truth has come to be. As Ulrich construes this process, nobody can dominate the historical situation in which partial truths struggle. Perhaps this is the ultimate point in Musil's orchestration of the cocktail clash of ideologies: nobody is dominating anything except ideas. But the question is also raised as to whether this process is inevitable, or even if ideas can have as much weight as events in the demonstration of truth. And the reader may well wonder if the forthcoming war is a form of the "vengeance" about which Ulrich thinks when he envisages the way one idea attempts to conquer another.

These last five chapters of part 3 are followed by three chapters of the next twenty unpublished galley chapters that depict the general, the Parallel Action, and the political situation refracted through the events and characters associated with the Action. In these galley chapters the general continues to play his role as messenger bringing news to Ulrich of what is happening in the Action, and he keeps the reader, if not Ulrich, aware of the march of historical time. This sense of time sets off the ongoing conflict of the characters' ideological positions, which may either seem irrelevant to history or seem to be its very causes, according to perspective one takes. After the battle of ideas, the subsequent galley chapters reduce the scope of Ulrich and Agathe's engagement with the world. Their action is minimal, reduced to such events as Agathe's visiting the puritanical schoolteacher Lindner or the general's intruding again upon Ulrich. His intrusion allows him to have conversations with Ulrich, which are in turn juxtaposed with the nonevent of Agathe's reading Ulrich's diary. The juxtaposition creates a counterpoint that implicitly contrasts the world of individual thoughts with the ongoing flow of the world of history—though the flow has been reduced to a trickle by the latter part of the novel's second half. This counterpoint suggests one shape for an ending Musil envisaged in the thirties: in the two halves history and utopia are to be found on two sides of a great divide. And if the individual's thoughts and feelings are the realm of utopia, General Stumm's world of disconnected acts is the world of the gathering storms of history.

Coming with news of the Parallel Action, on one occasion the general drops a paradoxical bomb on Ulrich, as the title of chapter 49 puts it: "General von Stumm Drops a bomb. Congress for World Peace." He announces to Ulrich that there will be a world peace congress in Vienna in the fall. Significantly, this manifestation in favor of peace is scheduled to take place some weeks after the First World War had in fact begun. This congress might have given direction to the Parallel Action, at least as the general conceives it. From the perspective of Austrian diplomacy, however, the congress can be considered an attempt to co-opt the Action, perhaps by the Russian tsar, perhaps by the German Reich (4:1118). The image of the oxymoronic bomb of peace encapsulates Musil's final satirical view of the influence individuals, even organized as a lobby, may have on the inexorable and absurd unfolding of events leading to war.

Confusion reigns over history, as one absurd event is juxtaposed with another. For example, Ulrich learns that even the general is not really too sure what is going on. It turns out, in chapter 53, that the dossier concerning the Parallel Action has been taken out of the general's hands by the minister and sent to a different ministerial department, one in charge of spying. The upper ministerial levels now view the Parallel Action as a "state event," and so, Ulrich learns, Tuzzi in his capacity as a state bureaucrat may now be the key player in what may or may not happen to the group (4:1133). The satirical upshot of this portrait of state bureaucracies is that when various ministries are competing for the responsibility of overseeing the peace congress, anything can be interpreted as anything: from a ministry's perspective a peace congress may be a hostile event. Not incidentally, in the course of the debates about what a peace conference might mean, the war ministry comes up with financial support for the modernization of the army's artillery (4:1134). With satirical élan Musil depicts a process in which events consistently engender the opposite of what may have been their initially intended consequences.

The conversation between the general and Ulrich found in chapter 53, translated "The D and L Reports," offers one of the most pointed exchanges underscoring the paradoxical nature of the events and ideas that are coming together to produce the war. The general relates that, after the unnoticed "great event," he received a dressing-down from the war minister for the "philosophical" attitude he had displayed in the course of frequenting the coterie of the Parallel Action. The minister remonstrates him with the reminder that a general is not a philosopher, a general simply knows (4:1148). General Stumm's military mind emerges in this conversation, for he knows that the minister is right simply because a superior is always right (4:1149). Musil is dramatizing, with little irony, that a presupposition for war is a hierarchy of power and a system of commands. However, and this is not his least irony, Musil seems to suggest that it is not the logic of this military system that creates the conditions for war. Rather, they occur when a domineering ideology takes over the chain of command. War is also the result of *Geist,* conceived as the mixture of idea and feeling. This suggests quite strongly that the conditions of possibility for ethical action and rampant destruction both derive from the same mental state. And both Ulrich and the general, now somewhat repentant, agree that *Geist* cannot be trusted to take power and to rule (4:1151). General Stumm, philosophical perhaps in spite of himself, offers that the narrow logic favored by the military maintains order and is thus necessary for thought. He makes the pointed observation that, in contradistinction to logic, *Geist,* when imposed by civilians, is always mistrusted by military officers. The officers have learned that "it is a matter of indifference as to what kind of *Geist* it was, in the end the result has always been a war" (4:1153). Ulrich observes that the general is thus in agreement with the Prussian general Moltke—the general who defeated Austria in 1866—who said that war is a part of God's world order. But the general refuses to be taken in by Ulrich's tease and declares that he opposes such a militaristic idea, a product of *Geist,* since, he has always been antimilitaristic. Nobody today, the general says with emphasis, nobody believes in war today, in 1914.

More than a satirical depiction of the well-meant ineptitude that is leading to the war is at issue in this dialogue. It shows that Musil's understanding of history encompasses not only the possibility of describing it through statistical probability; it is also grounded in the existential sense that human beings produce but do not control absurd concatenations of events that turn against the intentions animating those events. After all, as the general and Ulrich describe it, history is produced by *Geist,* in Ulrich's sense of thought and feeling conjoined in motivating human acts. The conclusion one must draw, as the general does, is that *Geist* can produce destruction as well as in the flowering of culture. Heaven and hell spring from the same conditions, though there are no a priori conditions to spell out what may happen in this regard.

Consequently, in delving into the nature of feeling, Ulrich has no preconceived ideas about what feeling can accomplish. He is motivated by a strong ethical desire to understand how feeling enters into mind and action. He hopes this insight might lead him to understand the drives behind historical events. Feelings motivate acts far more often than does reason, and therefore understanding the nature of feeling is a prerequisite for understanding and creating an ethics that might oppose what history actually produces. In this regard Ulrich's dialogue with the general is closely linked to the treatise Ulrich is writing on the nature of feeling, a topic I will return to presently when dealing with Ulrich and Agathe.

Not all in the novel's second half is centered on Ulrich, his sister, and the general. A different perspective on the novel's world is found in the several chapters portraying Clarisse; her husband, Walter; and their guest, the philosopher Meingast. These chapters depicting Clarisse's developing mental imbalance culminate in the visit to an insane asylum and suggest another way Musil frames the work's view of history. On one hand there is the Parallel Action that, seen through the narrator's ironic perspective, is unwittingly accompanying the nation's slide toward the war. On the other hand there is the presence of individual madness throughout the novel, pointing up the deviation from norms that set out the limits of the individual's power. In the second half of the novel, when Ulrich and his sister are not the dominant focus, it is clear that the collective drive toward war and the coexistent outbreak of individual insanity are the main currents characterizing a society that does not know it is about to commit suicide. In his different roles Ulrich finds himself mediating between either collective or individual forms of deviance. And he too is moving toward deviance that some psychiatric manuals would brand with a syndrome.

Musil's fascination with madness is hardly unique to him among modernists, a fair number of whom knew mental illness with intimacy. Part of his fascination springs from the need to characterize the limits of reason. This is not just an epistemological project. Understanding the power of rationality was made necessary by the ongoing course of European history in which, by many criteria, madness replaced reason as the driving force. The burden placed upon Ulrich is that he, the rationalist utopian, must be able to recognize when the desire for the possible has passed over into the dark realm where one desires the impossible. Clarisse is an exemplary character in this regard, perhaps the most important character after Ulrich for an understanding of what is at stake in *The Man without Qualities.* She is, quite literally, a character who takes ideas seriously and, in so doing, yearns for impossible consequences. Hence, she teeters on the brink of insanity.

One may recall that at the end of book 1, at the "turning point" as Ulrich is about to depart for his father's funeral, Clarisse wants to use him to father a Nietzschean superman for humanity's salvation. When she reappears in the second half, she has changed her project, which she reveals in the letter she sends Ulrich in chapter 7. She now wants to see the incarcerated murderer Moosbrugger, awaiting adjudication of his case in a mental ward for the criminally insane. The letter itself suggests that Clarisse is mentally unbalanced, though not so much as to be unaware of what she is doing. She appears to be that kind of borderline case for which medical science, as Musil knew, has trouble finding a diagnosis, though later psychiatry came with the kind of all-embracing pigeonhole suggested by a concept such as "borderline."[5] Clarisse herself knows that the science of the mad is approximate at best, and she quotes her brother to this effect. Her brother is a doctor, significantly named Siegmund, who tells her, quoting the psychiatrist in charge of the insane asylum, that psychiatry is as much art as science. According to Siegmund, the psychiatrist is in fact a "demon circus director" (3:715). After Musil's earlier ironic play with science and the devil, the reader may well not be sure if the irony cuts against Vienna's other well-known Sigmund or in his favor, for Freud was himself a critic of psychiatry and, from another viewpoint, a discoverer of the allegorical demons who preside over the unconscious.

When, after his father's death, Ulrich goes to visit Clarisse, he finds that she has changed, and perhaps he has, too. He has lost his demonic side, and Clarisse pointedly no longer considers him to be a god or a devil. Looking at Clarisse, in contrast, Ulrich thinks that the washed-out warmth in her face is like a "little tear in the veil of life" through which nothingness, participating in nothing, looked out, a nothingness about which the narrator says that "it laid down then the grounds for much which later took place" (3:781). What this *later* refers to is enigmatic, though the description of her face is challenging. It sounds as if Ulrich and the narrator were musing on the nihilism that underlies Clarisse's frenetic attempt to find a belief system on which to base her life. Clarisse is a unique individual, but it also seems accurate to say that hers is a kind of frenzy emblematic of an entire culture. The nihilism about to engulf Europe can be read in her face, and hers is the kind of frenzy giving rise to the cults and the unbalanced beliefs found in every quarter. For a moment Clarisse puts some faith in Meingast, a philosopher redolent of the cult guru who takes in the gullible by binding them through projective emotional ties. However, he does not have a strong hold over Clarisse. In fact she revolts against his mastery as well as her husband's attempt to dominate her. She is lucid about the nature of patriarchal domination in a patchwork culture hanging on to outmoded values as it comes apart.

Though desirous of dominating her, her husband, Walter, is actually something of a pale reflection of Clarisse in that both are possessed by abstract ideas. They both believe that life should be dictated by adherence to them. By contrast, as a cult leader Meingast demands commitment to his person, preferring, however, attractive young men in the role of subordinates. He is not exactly the guru Clarisse seeks. In any case she seeks out those whose embodiment of ideas leads them to live out their logical consequences. She thinks she has found such a character in the shabby psychopath Moosbrugger, on whom she can project her own superhuman projects, such as the perverse idea that the murderer has pursued the consequences of his ideas beyond good and evil. Clarisse is, even more than Ulrich, committed to a refusal of conventions, though in her instability she has rather much lost contact with what Ulrich would take to be reality.

Ulrich's visit to Clarisse comes to an ironically tawdry conclusion when the assembled characters view, beneath Clarisse's window, an exhibitionist in the street. In this pathetic demonstration of the prevalence of everyday psychopathology, Clarisse does not find deviance. Rather she finds one more confirmation that the world is invested with meanings waiting to be revealed. She believes that signs are awaiting her everywhere, or as Walter puts it, echoing his wife, the true condition of humanity is the one in which everything is a sign (3:928). To which the brother Dr. Siegmund replies that they are both crazy; and from the point of view of medical common sense, they undoubtedly are: they want to live life as if they were in a literary text in which everything makes sense symbolically (which throws ironic light on Ulrich's desire to live as if in a novel). But an exhibitionist waiting for prey can hardly signify more than one more sign of unbalance, to which Clarisse's mania for interpretation adds another one.

The belief in the omnipresence of signs is a very literary form of madness, one also characteristic of paranoia, though paranoia does not exactly describe Clarisse's psychodynamics. In her desire to make sense of everything, to find connections everywhere, she engages in hyperbolic semiosis and ends up convincing herself that the world is full of meanings nobody else perceives.[6] This is a madness characteristic of poets, and one that Ulrich can understand but does not endorse. He understands that literature is a realm of the possible, but there are limits that separate the possible and the impossible. He may want to transform his life into a utopian text, he may want to live as if he were a character is a novel, but Clarisse's madness shows him the limits of this desire. The man of possibility recognizes in her the danger of being the woman of impossibility.

The limits of desire are concretely shown in the madness that manifests itself in the vegetable garden that Clarisse, Walter, and Siegmund cultivate in the spring of 1914. The garden is a recurrent image in utopian texts, such as the biblical garden in paradise before the Fall—and in 1914 the Fall is not distant. In Clarisse's garden there is also a reflection of Voltaire's garden at the end of the satire *Candide*. In Voltaire's garden the harried characters at last find a pedestrian paradise by peddling the vegetables they raise with the sweat of their brow. In her garden, allusively situated somewhere between the Bible and Voltaire's utilitarian Enlightenment, Clarisse manifests another aspect of insanity. She is convinced that "hallucination is grace" or that "madness is grace," to offer two readings of the word *Wahn* characterizing a state she sometimes undergoes (3:910). Madness is grace, according to Clarisse, because it is the mark that one has begun, like Christ or Nietzsche, to take ideas seriously enough to live according to them and go mad through them. This development of Clarisse's madness can be read sotto voce as Musil's own self-critique: like Clarisse, he once could conjoin, in his diaries, Christ and Nietzsche in what seems like an absurdly incongruous juxtaposition, given Nietzsche's hostility for Christianity. However, from Clarisse's perspective, each is a prophet demanding that one change one's life by living out, to the extreme consequences, the ideas they brought forward; and, hence, Christ and Nietzsche are, so to speak, brothers.

Ideas demand action, and so Clarisse declares that it is a crime to simply let things happen (3:919). She wants to take seriously the Christian imperative that one must love one's neighbor as one's self, which according to her means that one cannot passively let things simply happen. Comparably, Ulrich and his sister also spend a good bit of time trying to figure out if this fundamental Christian tenet, arguably impossible from the point of view of common sense, has any meaning. For Clarisse it has immediate meaning, because she takes *Geist* seriously, in all its multiple meanings of spirit, mind, ideas, and feeling, which make General Stumm and Ulrich rather doubt that *Geist* should be in charge of things.

A comparison with the Russian novelist Dostoyevsky imposes itself in this regard, for Clarisse greatly resembles one of those Dostoyevskian characters who are determined to live out the passion of their commitment, beyond the narrow rationalism that condemns their mind and their heart, their *Geist.* Specifically, there is a complex and rather critical intertextual relationship between Clarisse and the brothers Ivan and Alyosha of *The Brothers Karamazov.* Dostoyevsky's great skeptic, Ivan, cannot believe in a God who permits evil to exist in the world by allowing children to suffer. Ivan confronts his pious, nearly saintly brother, Alyosha, with a description of a case in which a nobleman throws a small boy to his dogs. With this horrible example of the suffering an innocent child undergoes, Ivan forces Alyosha to admit that, in spite of his strong Christian belief, he would take vengeance against the sadistic torturer. Alyosha admits, in effect, that he would give up his Christian belief in forgiveness if he were to face such evil. Dostoyevsky's example seems to reverberate negatively in Clarisse's mind when she affirms her commitment to live

out the consequences of her belief in the face of all Ivans and the demonstra-
tions they may make against her desire for the impossible. She asserts that her
Christ would never be a mine director, nor will she, by which she seems to
mean a human being who makes compromises that jeopardize the existence of
the ideal. Demanding total commitment to the ideal, she goes so far as to assert
that even Christ and Nietzsche failed in their commitment because they only
went halfway (3:915)—perhaps they failed like Alyosha—so she is determined
to go all the way, living out the logical consequences of her commitment. In
the eyes of the world this is insanity. From Clarisse's viewpoint this is grace,
which is actually a rather Pauline viewpoint, not unlike the Apostle Paul's
views on faith and madness in his epistles to the Corinthians. Not coinciden-
tally, Ulrich, too, reads Paul, and his declaration that Christians' acceptance of
faith is a form of madness before the cross.

Dostoyevsky expresses contempt for those rationalists who would limit
human passion by calling them derisively "Claude Bernard," using as an insult
the name of the French doctor who largely founded experimental physiology
(and to whom I referred earlier for his work questioning the line of demarcation between the normal and the abnormal physiological processes). Musil
seems to amuse himself in a comparable way by introducing a "Siegmund,"
Clarisse's brother, a doctor who wants to find a rational explanation for her unbalanced behavior. Proper diagnosis would mean finding a taxonomic pigeonhole with which to categorize her, though the best Siegmund can do, after
Walter says Clarisse has a sense of sin, is to categorize her with the rather lame
syndrome of "sin hallucination" (3:917). This syndrome sounds like a dated
category, a holdover from earlier nineteenth-century psychiatry—if it is not a
parody of the modern idea of the superego (or a parody of both).

I suggested earlier that Clarisse, Siegmund, Ulrich, and General Stumm
get a brief introduction to modern psychiatric taxonomy when they visit the
asylum in which Moosbrugger is interned. Their visit is organized such that
they walk through the wards and pass in review interned examples of the categories of madness. The categories dictate who is interned in which ward,
since in this asylum the mad are grouped together according to the syndrome
they exhibit. The visit offers thus a derisive image of the power of medical
reason to order the unreason it confronts as a challenge. In directly confronting those incarcerated, moreover, Clarisse views possible images of herself,
mainly negative images in which she can contemplate the sad fact that the mad
are hardly living out ideas. They are for the most part lost on the other side of
language, locked into their mania and rage, the most graphic image of which
is an inmate to whom Clarisse speaks after he declares that she is the seventh

son of the kaiser. Wondering if she could possibly agree with him, Clarisse is shocked when the inmate springs toward her and drops his blanket, revealing his penis while he masturbates "such as do apes in captivity" (3:988). This is an animal aggression that Clarisse is unable to integrate into her system of signs and revelations. Like Dostoyevsky's saintly Alyosha, she too encounters the limits to her capacity to live out an ideal. And in the most direct manner, she finds that beyond the limits of reason lies a dark world that is plainly frightening.

There are few rhetorical difficulties involved in understanding the general's intervention by which Ulrich maintains contact with the futilities of the Parallel Action. The ironic perspective on Clarisse's growing madness is also relatively unproblematic. Irony blends into the hyperbole of satire at times in both of these narrative lines. Set against these two strands of development, however, most of the second half is devoted to Ulrich's thoughts and his relations with Agathe. Here the reader encounters one of the strangest itineraries in fiction. Musil narrates the substance of two intellectuals' mental life, which also takes on the appearance of a courting ritual. The rhetorical strategy is not at all so clear when Ulrich meets his sister at his deceased father's house, has her come live with him, and withdraws from his active engagement with the Parallel Action. In one sense the narration seems to be straightforward: turning toward his sister, Ulrich's withdrawal seems to be a refusal to participate in the collective rush toward destruction, though he has no inkling of the war to come. The withdrawal can also be viewed as an extreme example of an individual commitment to self—but shared with a mirror image of himself as he makes an attempt to sort out the cultural possibilities of modernity, or that explosion of possibilities that is overwhelming Clarisse. The outcome may be psychic disequilibrium, if not insanity, or it may be the invention of a new form of existence. To understand this ongoing development the reader must negotiate a web of interlocking perspectives. They suggest that Ulrich's detachment is symbolic of a refusal of the disintegration of society that makes up the future temporal horizon of the novel; and that Clarisse's downfall reflects the plight of the individual lost in alienation. However, none of these observations about Ulrich and Clarisse make sense of the fact that it is a sister who enters into Ulrich's world. Her presence is not a component of satire, and, in itself, it is not really to be taken as an ironic trope. Her entry into the novel seems to be part of a thought experiment on which Musil meditated for a number of years.

Ulrich's meeting his sister is a strange event, not so much for its occurrence as for the fact that their coming together is used to explore themes that are not usually associated with sibling relationships, especially a brother and a sister (though a quick search of the psychological literature will show that sibling incest is a rather frequent topic). The themes emerging from their encounter are not simply love and Eros, but also, in an inextricably related way, ethics and morality, the nature of feeling, and the possibility that the individual might create a utopian mode of existence on the margins of society. These themes are interwoven in a series of interrelating essayistic texts. Ethics engages the question of one's relation to others, which in turn demands one understand the nature of feelings, for feelings motivate ethics even as they are informed by them—which I take to be one of the most original aspects of Ulrich's meditations. Feelings in turn bring up the question of the nature of love, for at times Ulrich considers love to be something like an ethical state— as the essence of Christian ethics, for example—which means it is not so much a mode of sentient being relating a human being to another, but would be a permanent condition prerequisite for all other thoughts and acts. The question of feelings is related in turn to the way one lives in society, which brings up the possibility that society might be other than it is. These interrelating thoughts branch into what might look like utopian thinking and turn again, in the circle of interlocking questions and occasional answers, back to the questions of morality and ethics, or the question of what should be, not what is.

However, these themes are concerns embodied in the context of an ongoing narration. At times they are Ulrich's concerns, but at times they are Agathe's, and occasionally they belong to other characters, and all of these are refracted through the narrator's thoughts and commentary upon the thoughts of others. Though none of these viewpoints seem devious or untrustworthy, they are subject to irony, and none of the propositions embodied in the characters' thoughts are offered with a guarantee of the veracity of what they propose, though one can certainly ponder their truth value. The thoughts in the novel are often set forth as experiments in thinking, or as essayistic assessments. Musil is not writing a philosophy manual or a psychology textbook, although much of what is written in the second half of the novel could find its place in one or the other, with enough material left over to fill up an introduction to epistemology. My main point is this regard is that ideas are espoused by characters, not professional philosophers, often in a tenuous way that stresses the open nature of the characters' commitment. There is one notable exception to this openness, and that is the schoolteacher Lindner. He is an absolute moralist who is at once a parody of himself and of the pietistic and absolute ethics that draws upon the Kantian tradition. (Musil was surely negatively impressed by Kant's rigid belief that it was always wrong to tell a lie, even if you could save a life with it.) By contrast it is the case that Agathe and Ulrich play with thoughts. We have seen that Ulrich's character and thoughts change in the course of book 1; and that this change greatly enlarges his understanding of human possibilities. In the second half of the novel he continues this process by questioning himself, though this questioning is now motivated as much by the relation he has begun with Agathe as by his withdrawal from society. The second half of the novel focuses mainly on his attempt to develop a coherent sense of what it means to be moral, and, I think, only secondarily on his interest in mystical states. It is dubious that he succeeds in formulating anything definitive, but the debates and meditations involved in Ulrich's quest are among the most engaging found in literature. For Ulrich, as for any scientist, the quest for truth means unending doubt and questioning, a process for which there are no final answers.

A brief synopsis of Ulrich and Agathe's involvement points up that their relationship turns largely on its moral meaning. If the siblings are somehow entering the millennium, as the title of part 3 puts it, they do so as "criminals," and the criminal side may be more obvious than the reign of bliss associated with the millennium. Their criminal status is moral as well as legal, and the title's irony may well be to stress that criminals from the conventional viewpoint are morally justified from the perspective of the millennium, found perhaps somewhere on the other side of history. The millennium apparently begins when, going to arrange his father's funeral, Ulrich encounters Agathe, a sister who is something like his near twin. They share the same identity but are different beings. This identity in difference is underscored by the fact that, when they first see each other, each shows up dressed as a clown in identical Pierrot attire. (Pierrot will merit more commentary presently.) The brother learns that his sister is unhappy in her second marriage, so she has decided not to return home to her husband, Professor Hagauer. Their relationship is thus immediately framed by a moral question: her possible divorce involves a serious ethical problem. For prewar society the moral problem of divorce was nearly as serious as the moral dilemma posed by the fact that Agathe also falsifies her father's last will and testament. She quite willingly commits a crime to make sure her husband gets nothing. But even these events are less heavy with ethical weight than the fact that after the funeral she comes to Vienna to set up house with Ulrich. They are becoming involved in a relationship that would be censored by society with ultimate opprobrium if the amorous attractions involved were ever known. Facing her duty, as it were, Agathe does come out in society. Her meeting the social world results in her fleeing it. Feeling herself lost, and reflecting upon her stern husband's anger, she considers suicide before meeting Lindner, the high-minded moralist. He continues the debate about ethics by trying to convince Agathe that it is her duty to stay married to the man she loathes. Agathe is intrigued by this moralizer, the antithesis of her, and he is also attracted to her in spite of the voice of morality that condemns his desires. The galley chapters suggest that Agathe's encounter with Lindner might have been developed into a significant plot line, for the antithesis set out by the two characters is replete with more possibilities for comically serious meditation on ethical choices. The galley chapters lead up to the point where Agathe has begun, without Ulrich's permission, to read his diary. In this bit of unethical prying, she learns, among other things, what he has been learning about his own feelings by living with his sister.

In the course of the second half of the novel Ulrich and his sister thus debate a number of propositions about ethics, and these propositions are set off by Lindner's ethical narrow-mindedness. The possibilities for thinking about the grounds of ethics are not unlimited, and a brief overview of the contours of Agathe and Ulrich's dialogue shows that they go through, in one sense or another, most of the major ethical doctrines available in European thought. The first source of this thought is of course the Bible, though it offers contradictory models that Musil exploits to good effect, especially in the portrayal of Agathe's dilemmas. The Judaic religious tradition with its stern ethics of the law and commandments really seems opposed the complementary Christian doctrine of love and forgiveness as the grounds for right behavior. Christian belief is central to Agathe's questions about the possibility of moral action if one must love one's neighbor as one's self. Foreign to this biblical religious tradition is the probably equally influential Aristotelian view of the good life. Ulrich meditates at length on the Greek idea that ethics is founded on virtues that lead the ethical man to happiness, the nature of which is a question central to Ulrich's meditations. These Christian and Aristotelian views by and large dominated Western thought until the Enlightenment, though a recurrent hedonist view has from antiquity to the present made pleasure in one sense or the other the justification of all actions. It is noteworthy that Ulrich and Agathe are not at all drawn to hedonism, for they find that it would devalue their relationship. Ulrich is more drawn to a modern rationalist, "emotivist" view of ethics, though he is critical of the thinkers such as Hume and Rousseau who placed a universal feeling of benevolence at the center of the desire to do good. Ulrich's view is ambivalent in this regard and probably reflects Musil's own attraction to Hume and dislike of Rousseau.

The other great ethical philosopher of the Enlightenment, Immanuel Kant, is omnipresent in the novel. His rejection of what philosophers call Rousseauistic emotivism as a basis for ethics provides fodder for the characters' meditations, as does Kant's insistence that ethics must take the shape of a rational and universal imperative grounded in reason. Ulrich fences with this idea, whereas his possible antagonist, the Kantian Lindner, shows how the modern pietistic mind has developed Kantian beliefs (or that Kantian beliefs spring from a pietistic background). He argues to Agathe that duty is duty. Against the Enlightenment views of Hume, Rousseau, and Kant, the other major modern contender for finding the grounds for morality has been the largely English utilitarian school, which proposes that the greatest utility for the greatest number is the basis for ethical behavior. Agathe scornfully dismisses utilitarianism, and presumably would reject Arnheim's defense of capitalism, drawing upon Adam Smith and Max Weber for its utilitarian justification of the market economy. Nonetheless, utilitarianism, albeit in a rather perverted form, informs Ulrich's thought when he begins to enlighten his sister about what is the dominant ethics of the time. Juxtaposed with these debates is, of course, the recurrent thought that perhaps Nietzsche was not wrong with his thought that moral belief is one more illusion produced by the will to power.[7]

The give-and-take between Ulrich and his sister dramatizes these ethical themes. At times Ulrich seems to want to be a systematic thinker, and Agathe, in her insouciance and skepticism, is the touchstone that gives the lie to his thought. Their debate transforms the essayism of the first half of the novel, for the debate about ethics, taking the form of lecture, conversation, and finally diary, is also tested by the life the two protagonists lead with each other, in short, by the possible consequences that ethics might have for them. This testing begins at the outset when Agathe, standing by the dead father's open coffin, does a quasi-striptease in taking off a garter and thrusting it into the dead father's pocket. Ulrich is shocked. It is obvious that he feels that bourgeois propriety has been offended. His reaction hardly stems from an avant-garde ethical position (3:707) By contrast, Agathe appears to be the free spirit who threatens the bourgeois moral order that Ulrich is supposedly testing. He is flabbergasted by his sister's breach in taste, not to mention disregard for the moral order that keeps daughters' garters out of their fathers' pocket and prohibits young women from showing their legs to their brothers, not to mention paternal corpses.

Agathe is a challenge to Ulrich, for he must measure his own conventionality against this sister who at times, but not always, is capable of living beyond received morality. Ulrich can be heavy-handed as, for example, in chapter 10 relating their excursion to the Swedish Rampart. During this excursion in the country, Ulrich begins making what is really a formal lecture to his sister on ethics (3:739). Making a critique of capitalist mentality and its utilitarianism, he perorates on contemporary morality based on performance ethics, the morality of the entrepreneur and the career-minded. Agathe is a sharp foil to her brother's performance, for she finally interrupts him by stating that she prefers to have no morality whatsoever rather than to be held accountable for and evaluated by what she has accomplished in life (3:740). Her challenge underscores not only Ulrich's own recognized lack of ability to accomplish much of late, but it also refuses the vulgar utilitarianism rationalizing capitalist greed. Moreover, she makes Ulrich aware that he is pronouncing a dogmatic analysis claiming some kind of finality. He acknowledges the challenge with the recognition that it is not so much deeds that one should demand today, but rather the presuppositions for those deeds—such is his "feeling" (3:741). Agathe replies with the deceptively simple but central question of the rest for the novel: "How should one do that?" (3:741). Ever ready to deflate Ulrich's heady speeches, she is something of the embodiment of the intuitive mind confronting the axiomatic thinker.

On this same excursion the notion of crime comes to the foreground. Ulrich makes the theoretical pronouncement that one might be able to be happy in crime, or that a crime could be an ethical act (3:742). Agathe challenges him again by offering him a concrete example of a crime that would make her happy: she would like to kill her husband. Undoubtedly Dostoyevsky's fictional experiments in crime are again the backdrop for their thought experiment. For example, in *Crime and Punishment* the student Raskolnikov's murder of a miserable old pawnbroker sets forth an example of an experiment in crime that the student has justified to himself intellectually, but which ends up as nothing more than a sordidly bloody ax murder. At the possibility of a real murder, Ulrich is very uncomfortable. And he knows that Agathe's freewheeling spirit is challenging him to envision the blood that will be on his theoretical happiness if she were to find out if there is happiness in crime.

The narrator also functions as a foil to Ulrich in these debates about the nature of morality. Through his presence, an essayistic dimension exists, or continues to exist, in the contrasts between the viewpoints of the narrator and Ulrich. For instance, the narrator begins chapter 11, the first of two chapters titled "Holy Conversations," by defining ethics as an order encompassing both the spirit and things. The narrator goes on to say that is it normal that young people who have not been beaten down by life should speak about morality, a term usually lacking in most people's conversation. In Ulrich's case, however, the narrator says the young man's concern with morality denotes a great disorder (3:746). The narrator's judgment of Ulrich sets out a leitmotif for much of the rest of the novel, the essayistic assessment of order and disorder. Musil approaches this theme by looking at disorder as a kind of social entropy, bringing about disintegration through increasing disorder, though disorder is also an aesthetic matter concerning the lack of harmony found in the individual's life. Ulrich has hoped that mystical thinkers may help him to find a hidden order, and following his lead, Agathe looks into Ulrich's books to see what he has found there. It is not clear if she finds much.

In any case mystical thought is of little import when Agathe confronts Ulrich with the real disorder crime may produce—even if there is supposedly purity in the crime she has actually committed (3:797). The narrative form by which her crime is revealed says much about the way Ulrich evaluates it. Her crime of tampering with the will is narrated after she commits it, after she has come to Vienna, in the flashback in chapter 15. Only then does the reader learn of her falsification of the father's last will and testament. The use of a flash-back to return to the immediate past is a curious deviation from the expected order of the unfolding narrative discourse. Placing the crime in a more distant past, with regard to the narrative order, dramatizes that Ulrich has been hesi-tant to reflect on his sister's impulses that he plainly witnessed. The indirect-ness of the flashback shows a fear on Ulrich's part to contemplate directly Agathe's criminal act. Thus, the reader only learns after the fact that he tried to counter his sister's determination by reprimanding her with a rather lame quotation from Nietzsche to the effect that even free spirits obey some rules. In the face of his reproaches Agathe throws up at Ulrich the fact that he had said that ethical decisions are often made in a dream state. However, there is nothing dreamlike about the banality to which he has recourse when he refers implicitly to the law she is violating and tells her with biblical sternness, "You shouldn't do that" (3:796). Ulrich resembles, in the flashback, the moralizing Lindner whom he holds in contempt, since the only grounds for his reproach to Agathe are simply the formal commandment that one should not do such things. Ulrich has not advanced beyond the Ten Commandments. Musil creates in such scenes an intellectual comedy in which the free spirit Ulrich is shown deviating from his own theoretical openness to experience. His recourse to ethical clichés springs not so much from respect for the law but from what appears to be the most conventional fear of consequences.

Ulrich wants to give the impression that he has recovered his equilibrium when, after psychologically confronting his sister's crime, he announces with some bravura that he and his criminal sister are entering the millennium (3:801). If so, he has been dragged into it by Agathe. Only she has shown will-ingness to transgress received norms in the name of her own freedom. Ulrich's jubilation seems forced. It suggests his difficulty in reconciling his desire to transform values with an abiding conservative outlook. Or perhaps this is a sign of his rather aristocratic viewpoint. The transformation of values he seeks depends upon finding superior ways of violating the conventional morality that he believes to be without foundation. With or without foundation, however, Ulrich continues to respect social conventions that prescribe what one should do, for which the laws governing contracts and covenants would be a prime example. Perhaps criminals do not enter easily into the millennium, even if Ulrich can argue that only criminals enter.

After the funeral Ulrich returns to Vienna without Agathe. Subsequently he tries to write a letter to her, but he cannot bring himself to mention her crime in it. His failure to write this letter takes up chapter 18, whose title about the difficulty Ulrich has in writing a letter mocks the stumbling moralist. One wonders if Ulrich's failure springs from fear of the authorities who apparently might open the letter or from self-censorship reprimanding him for his passive participation in a crime. He evades his own self-reproaches with recourse to paradox. Being good in a conventional way is not always good, or so he muses on the paradoxes inherent in the fact that he and Agathe find that good people are often boring. In his meditations here, Ulrich constructs a chiasmatic schema of moral qualities: there are good ways to be bad, bad ways to be good (3:822). Ulrich's moral paradoxes culminate, at this juncture, in an essentially Aristotelian notion that ethics is really a way of describing what consists of happiness and unhappiness (3:823).

Ulrich then historicizes his thought. He wants to move beyond Greek eudaemonism, since the belief that happiness is the goal of existence is not making him happy. Thus he reflects that at a given point in history, when the reigning masters used their power to impose their notions for happiness on society, then it followed that there were uncontested general rules determining what is moral. But contradictions unfold in the inevitable process of historical change, for the masters' rules eventually will no longer result in the happiness that the masters once knew. Historical change means that ethics becomes dysfunctional. Ulrich combines Aristotle and Nietzsche to explain to himself his own confusion about condemning and approving his sister for her criminal thoughts and criminal act. Engaging in an imaginary but very Nietzschean genealogy of morals, he wants to explain to himself why he is uncomfortable with a crime that he wants to approve. If he cannot finish the letter to his criminal sister, it may well be that however much Ulrich understands the moral contradictions generated by historical change, he has not found a way to surmount them. The master patriarchs once declared their will—in all senses—to be inviolate. Yet today Agathe's tampering with the father's will seems quite morally immoral. Ulrich would like to overcome the laws set down in history, but he can do so only in his mind, not in practice. Only Agathe seems at times to be a free spirit in this regard. But even she has doubts about her life, which lead her to consider suicide.

Ulrich's reflections on ethics take place wherever he strolls about, a sign that Musil has placed him under the sign of Socrates, the ambulatory philosopher (though Nietzsche also said he could think only when walking). One of the pivotal moments in his thought occurs during a walk before Agathe's arrival in Vienna—in chapter 22, the improbable title of which ("From Koniatowski's Critique of Danielli's Theorem to the Fall of Man. From the Fall of Man to the Emotional Riddle Posed by a Man's Sister") comically relates an imaginary math theorem to original sin and one's sister. The chapter does begin with, more or less, a critique of science. Alone, mathematician Ulrich strolls in the street and encounters a woman scientist who is about to leave for a stay in the mountains, where she claims she can sit on a rock motionless for three days. Her vacation strikes Ulrich as a form of modern Rousseauism. From his perspective the scientist's expertise in astronomy has in no way prepared her to evaluate the prepackaged nature of her moral feelings, in this case, a kind of kitsch love of nature, deriving from Rousseau's thought. Ulrich has little sympathy for Rousseauism, the original or the kitsch version. He suspects that a basic problem in moral thinking underlies her attitude. This scientist does not know how to think about feeling. Reflecting at length on what one can say about feeling, a transient thing as he later describes it, walking in the Viennese streets he is struck by the thought that ethics "is the ordering of our condition in every moment to be a permanent condition" (3:869). This street-born epiphany is followed up by the thought that "the essence of morality rests upon nothing other than the condition that important feelings remain the same" (3:871). This thought about permanence is something that Ulrich seems to hold onto, more or less permanently, for the rest of the novel.

Ulrich's view of feeling here is part of his critique of an emotivist approach to ethics of which Rousseau's thought offers a prime exemplar, though Ulrich now appears to be an anti-Rousseau Rousseauist. He admits the centrality of feeling to ethics, even if, perhaps contradictorily, he wants these feelings to be permanent. A great problem arises here if, as Ulrich also contends, all feeling is transient. Against this view he also begins to argue, problematically, that ethics must in some sense be a permanent condition. I confess I have always found it difficult to know what it means to say that ethics must be a permanent condition. If this means in a rather banal sense that ethics depends on recurrently thinking the same things, it is something of a truism, and may be nothing more than the old-fashioned virtue of constancy. If it means that one must exist in a permanently heightened state of consciousness, this is also problematic, and probably makes of ethical thinking a rare thing—

which Musil did indeed think at times. If we relate the idea that authentic ethics is rare to Ulrich's desire to find "another condition," then it appears that Musil himself probably had great doubts about whether this state could be found as a permanent condition. For one thing Ulrich would have to overcome the transience of feeling in order to find a permanent state that might be the grounds for utopia. Perhaps this is why Musil gives Ulrich the task of finding this state in a fictional text in which the essayistic probing of ideas is undertaken at the remove granted by fictional narration. Musil did not attempt to write a philosophical treatise, in his own name, demonstrating a state whose hypothetical existence can only be a matter of speculation. Ulrich does the speculating for him.

Musil continues this chapter of street-side epiphanies with Ulrich's meditation in a streetcar. From the streetcar he sees in passing a fortuitous juxtaposition of a baroque column with its modern surroundings, causing him to consider the historicity of all products of human origin—including things as abstract as "style, culture, time-bound will, or life feeling" (3:872). The historicity of everything offers another challenge to ethics and aesthetics. Moreover, Ulrich thinks that all that one calls change or progress is simply part of a strategy for covering up that humanity has never come up with a "conviction grasping the totality" that would allow the "constant development, permanent enjoyment, or the seriousness of great beauty" (3:872). At this moment Ulrich grasps the time-bound nature of human values and beliefs, in an epiphany that surely is a parody of Plato's cave, for it "befell to his mind that he'd just come from a cellar" (3:872–73). However, when he emerges into light, Ulrich sees not Plato's eternal ideas but the ever-changing, shabby ephemera called human possessions that make up normal life (the "unzähligen niedlichen Habseligkeiten")—a markedly comic antithesis to Plato's eternal ideas.[8] But lest the reader should think that this demonstration of the fragility of culture is a definitive position, Musil concludes this bravura chapter with ironically comic remarks showing the futility of historicity as a mind caste: a passing archbishop, a follower of Christ, is saluted by two jolly policemen who seem not the least concerned about the acts committed by their predecessors, those Roman centurions who once plunged a lance into the prelate's own first forebear on the cross (3:873). Street-side epiphanies seem to be part of Musil's essayistic strategy to allow ideas to contest ideas. Here, for example, historicism and ahistoricism seem equally as plausible, or as useless, for dealing with daily existence.

After meditations running through thoughts taken from figures as diverse as Rousseau, Plato, and Christ, the stage is set for Ulrich to turn once again to Nietzsche for another genealogy of morals. This one occurs at the end of the chapters that Musil actually saw published. The published chapters of part 3 move, through a series of ironic pirouettes and serious meditations, toward the great, but unnoticed, event of the last five chapters, concluding with chapter 38 in which Ulrich does his final genealogy of morals, this one set in a cocktail-party atmosphere. From the perspective of the narrative unfolding, the unnoticed great event is not so much the chatter of the members of the Parallel Action as Ulrich's meditating once again upon ethics and concluding that moral thought derives from the quest for power characterizing all history. Chapter 38 offers a nodal point for what could have been Ulrich's future development. In it he concludes that morality arises, like all forms of order, through compulsion and force. In Ulrich's history of the development of ethics, in the course of history the moral law acquires an autonomy that appears as independent as God's heaven itself (3:1024). However, this autonomy is groundless, Ulrich reasons, for there is nothing ethical founding ethics, and so he concludes with the apparent paradox that "everything is moral, only morality itself is not moral" (3:1024). It strikes me that this is only an apparent paradox, because in fact there is actually nothing paradoxical about the fact that an ethical statement does not ground itself unless one means by the concept of "ethical" a statement that contains the grounds for its own existence. I am not sure what that would resemble, but I also take it that this is the point at which Ulrich reaches his deepest doubt about the possibility of a grounded ethics.

Agathe is not convinced by Ulrich's genealogy of morals, and she makes an empirical criticism of him. She tells him that, in spite of Ulrich's unsuccessful reasoning about morality, she actually met a good man that day. On the point of killing herself, in fact, she meets Lindner, who, not unlike Ulrich, gives Agathe the occasion to challenge his ethical system. As I suggested above, Lindner's values are based on a fundamental belief in the existence of objective moral law, which is the contrary of anything Ulrich has worked out. But Agathe is not convinced by Lindner's stale moral clichés. Rather, she is brought back to life by the challenge of a male moralist with convictions. Lindner is indeed a figure of high comedy because of his convictions, both in his interaction with his thickheaded athletic son and with Agathe, a sensually alive woman who causes him to almost not respect the Kantian universal imperative and his Christian duty, both of which apparently proscribe attractive women from coming unaccompanied to a widower's home. The disparity between Lindner's moral conviction and his sexual desire creates a character whose comic equal is Agathe's husband, Hagauer, the scorned patriarch and pedagogue, who is outraged by the fact that his wife has challenged his moral authority by fleeing his custody. Both characters present variants on the classical comic situation presenting a deviance from rational norms, though

Musil's irony is that these moralists' greatest deviance is in their stern adherence to conventional ethical norms. In Lindner's case the deviance is sweetly understandable, in Hagauer's the deviance points to an indictment of the power of the patriarchal system that runs throughout the novel. The comic disparity between Agathe's husband's authoritarian desire and conjugal ineptitude do not, understandably, offer Agathe a challenge she wishes to continue to meet.

Male philosophers from Nietzsche to Derrida have embroidered on the theme that truth is a woman. Perhaps Musil had something analogous in mind in associating the feminine with the notion that truth can only emerge as a constant challenge (and his earlier short fiction might also lend support to this idea). Clarisse represents a feminine willingness to test ideas beyond limits. Somewhat comparably, Agathe is a moral challenge testing the men she meets, and somewhat differently, she does so from a kind of natural disposition independent of the exterior motivation provided by the world of ideas. For Ulrich she is an invitation to utopia, by which he seems to recognize an invitation to re-create the lost unity of being that is the condition of permanence in which morality might finally exist. By placing their relationship in this perspective Musil in turn invites us to make sense of them as criminals living in the millennium, for their union is, were it to be realized, outside the moral law and would be considered criminal in most societies. Undoubtedly in the second half it is already partly criminal, at least from the Christian perspective that makes sins of the heart the equivalent of sins of the flesh.

It is thus that Agathe, standing by Ulrich in the heat of the unknown great event, inspires him to hit upon the idea that morality is not based merely on appropriate action or on wisdom, but on "the infinite totality of the possibilities of living" (3:1028). This wine-induced epiphany seems to have erotic power, for the narrator suggests that Agathe is now in an attitude of surrender. She wants to know if one must always have a principle for what one does, to which Ulrich replies, yes, but only one. It is at this moment of ironic oneness that, according to the narrator, Agathe brings Ulrich into the "realm of the Siamese twins" and the millennium. She seems to promise to introduce Ulrich into the realm of unity, that mythic realm of total integrity, in which one principle will rule over all (3:1029). How the infinite totality of possibilities of life may be governed by one consistent or constant principle is an open question, though the task of reconciling the infinite and the one has been on philosophy's threshold at least since Parmenides and Plato. In this essayistic jousting Agathe again challenges Ulrich, for she wants to know if the utopia he envisages is a matter of ethics, and so ends the concluding published part of the novel, leaving the reader to wonder if the great unnoticed event is Ulrich's genealogy of morals, the reinvention of love, or perhaps a peace congress that is preempted by a world war.

The continuity of the galley chapters and the published part of the novel is a given, even if there may appear to be another break in narrative continuity. It is hardly the first. What is clear is that the comic incongruity produced by ethical thinking continues in the opening galley chapters portraying Lindner and then Agathe in her role as the challenger to masculine domination. In the "mighty discussion" of chapter 44, the contrast culminates in a crescendo of ethical pathos in which Lindner confronts the intentionally seductive Agathe and desperately reasons with her about duty. Agathe finds herself toying with the moral man whose flesh clearly yearns for something other than the satisfactions offered by duty done. Agathe uses Lindner as a sounding board to hear her own actions criticized, for she wants to hear if anybody really knows what duty might be in a world of pompous, power-hungry men. Her own education has taught her to be skeptical about all that men attempt to impose upon her, and Lindner is a test case for her, especially because of the purity he manifests in the disinterested moral fervor of the pious Kantian moralist. The narrator does not share her view, however, for he takes a more Nietzschean perspective and scoffs at the pretensions of disinterested reason. In this play of perspectives the satirical deflation of Lindner's high-mindedness completes the novel's ethical panorama running from the Greeks through Rousseau and Kant, Jeremy Bentham and Adam Smith, and of course Nietzsche.

The twenty galley chapters Musil that withdrew from publication in 1938 continue part 3; I propose that in their substance, if not in their numbering, they suggest a new direction. Narrative events are on the verge of disappearing in these chapters, though there are a few events upon which are pegged the ongoing meditations and dialogues. Musil has reduced narrative action to such an extent that the idea of a novel is on the verge of disappearing. Bearing in mind the experimental side of his project, one might compare the narration in these chapters to something like a musical tone poem, on the order of those created by the Viennese and French composers of the early twentieth century. With this musical metaphor in mind one can free oneself from the need to find an ongoing narrative plot and envisage the chapters with a view to their orchestration of motifs and ideas rather than events. For example, after the opening galley chapters' comic crescendo orchestrating Lindner and Agathe's moral conflict, a contrasting moment of passionate calm intervenes (4:1060). Ulrich and Agathe are together on a moonlit night during which "every prohibition would be a matter of indifference to them" (4:1083). After deciding to refuse by telephone an invitation they had received, Ulrich returns to his sister in poignant expectation. Yet he cannot accept that their relation should turn into a moon-drenched bit of kitsch, nor can Agathe, who ironically asks if the evening is going to be nothing more than some "moon-shine romanticism." With this scornful comparison, she then likens Ulrich to "Pierrot Lunaire," which recalls their mutual appearance as clowns when they met in their father's house (4:1086). Her reference to Pierrot may be to the song cycle of the Viennese composer Arnold Schoenberg, created in Berlin in 1912, or perhaps to a series of poems written by the Belgian writer Albert Giraud, whose "moon-drunk" texts were well known in German translation. And she surely has in mind the Pierrot image of Musil's favored poet Verlaine who, in poems such as "Colombine," set the stage for the clown motifs of fin-de-siècle symbolism, with their wan commedia dell'arte figures languidly seeking something like passion. Agathe herself resembles Harlequin's sweetheart, Columbine, the commedia dell'arte heroine who keeps all amorous clowns at bay.

The ironies of this series of allusions underscore that, on this night recalling the moonlit sonata and romantic rhapsody, neither Ulrich nor Agathe can imagine engaging in a sentimental comedy laid out in advance by the aesthetic conventions of their era—such as their initial encounter seemed to suggest they might when they both popped out costumed as conventional Pierrots. They question whether it is possible, in an era of kitsch, to find significance in moonlit intoxication, and wonder if they are making their emotional life conform to ready-made roles. Despairing about whether this moment of passion is mental derangement or, if not, mere sentimental debauchery, Ulrich asks if it is the fragment of another life (4:1086–87). Whatever it is, it is a nonevent; it is a state and not an act.

Ulrich's reference to "another life" points up again that one is justified in drawing a parallel between Musil and the contemporary surrealists. The surrealists, echoing Arthur Rimbaud, wanted to reinvent love as a permanent state of being. In his rejection of mere sentimental debauchery, Ulrich too desires to transform eroticism into something like a permanent other condition. This is part of his experiment, and the reader sees that his thought experiment here is approaching a limit point. That limit is reached when he retreats from "another life" that erotic bliss with his sister apparently might offer.

After this moment of near collapse, Ulrich lands on his feet, and on the day following their moonlit intoxication he returns to the essayistic attack. Or to return to our musical metaphor, he is ready to orchestrate themes illustrating his epistemological poetry. He meditates on finding access to the uniquely real that will allow him, among other things, to shake off the power of kitsch. For example, he is perturbed that the word (or universal concept) *green* will never exactly apply to the blade of grass he picks in the garden during a conversation with Agathe. There is nothing intrinsically mystical about Ulrich's concern, even if the idea that mystical illumination can offer access to the realm of the singular is a leitmotif of much mystical—and modernist—thought. One might say that it is a theme Musil wants to orchestrate in this essayistic tone poem for its mystical overtones and to suggest a critique of science. (Biologists today would probably agree with him that from a contemporary biological viewpoint, it is true that there only individuals, since a concept like that of species, for example, is simply a tool for organizing the biologist's study of similarities in breeding populations.) Though having no intention of jettisoning scientific concepts, Ulrich wants to find a way to formulate the unique aspect of every experience. His repeated concern with the failure of general concepts to espouse a unique experience serves, moreover, to underscore the limitations imposed upon inner experience when feelings are dominated by ready-made ideas; taste by received categories; and values by preformed norms. Musil is not descrying language; he is criticizing the failure to recognize that the unique is the realm of meaningful experience and value; and this theme is orchestrated throughout the later galley chapters, especially in their description of the nature of feelings. In fine Ulrich's concern with ethics now takes the shape of thoughts on the unique experience of private emotional life, a life we know when we are able to resist modeling our inner life with the cookie-cutter molds of commercial and ideological kitsch.

If Ulrich is to accept mystical revelation, it must withstand the light of day, as he puts it in chapter 46 (4:1089). After their nocturnal temptations, Agathe and Ulrich examine the nature of mystical belief, including the Pauline formulation of Christian faith. This is a moment of calm in the tone poem, in which nothing is affirmed, though much is questioned. Ulrich considers that the ungodly nature of modernity may be today's way of finding God (4:1092). He entertains a version of the *via negativa,* or the knowledge of God garnered by knowing what God is not. Discussions of theology are accompanied by their conversations on love, for from a Christian perspective these are two sides of the same coin. Like believers, Agathe and Ulrich want the millennium, not a banal love affair, though they have difficulty with the Christian belief that love is the essence of faith. This means that one should love one's neighbor, or one's *Nächsten,* as the German puts it (4:1098). In Ulrich and Agathe's case the Christian injunction to love also seems to enjoin criminality, by telling them to do what they are already too inclined to do.

After these scenes of meditation, the narrative movement of the novel then presents a counterpoint between the aforementioned scenes and those with

General Stumm. One exception is the antepenultimate galley chapter 56 that offers a flashback to Lindner. As Ulrich talks with the general, the galley chapters present Agathe's reading Ulrich's writings; and finally the reader sees Ulrich himself looking at his writing as he considers what to write. In these chapters with no events, Ulrich increasingly takes on the image of a writer, although he has sworn that he will not write a book. Musil's correspondence shows that he was not happy with the shape these final chapters had taken; or at least so his wife wrote, saying Musil wanted to transform this "difficult" material into conversations (*Briefe* 1:1449). Be that as it may, the final galley chapters represent Ulrich's diary and the notes he has written down. They are the representation of writing and suggest that Ulrich's transformation into a writer was something that Musil could not prevent. I note that this role is logically imposed by Ulrich's own desires, for his quest for permanence could find nothing except writing to give it shape. And one may feel that Ulrich's analysis of the history of psychology and his theory of emotions are not something that naturally unfolds in conversation, except perhaps in the form of the Socratic dialogue. Ulrich is often a quasi-Socratic figure, especially in dialogues with Agathe. Is it an additional Socratic irony if Musil has recourse to the Platonic strategy of using writing to assure the permanence of the spoken word in the first entries in Ulrich's diary? Notably, these entries transcribe Agathe and Ulrich's conversations on transience. Musil may well be highlighting a quasi-paradox in using Ulrich's diary for the transcription of passing talk about transience, for the act of transcription shows that not all is fleeting, even a dialogue on the ephemeral nature of all things. Inscription is permanence.

Thus Ulrich takes on the role of a writer, the narrator is shunted aside, and the reader must evaluate the direct transcription of what is Ulrich's own voice. His first diary entries turn on the historicity of everything that he and Agathe see as they walk in the ephemeral city. They are a reading of impermanence. The better part of reality, as Ulrich repeats to himself, is a product of opinion (fashions, styles, beliefs, culture itself) and the essence of opinion is to have no essence (4:1128). It is simply to change. Therefore, the world that opinion codifies for us changes, inevitably. This historicism now leads Ulrich to what may appear to be the rather astonishing conclusion that love is not a feeling, since the nature of feeling is to change. But love doesn't change, so it isn't a feeling. Love is thus a form of ecstasy, one characterizing God himself, for it must be God's nature to be in a permanent state of ecstasy so as to maintain things in existence and, through his permanent love, to embrace even what has already happened (4:1130). God exists permanently in the present moment. In conceiving God this way, Ulrich concludes that the past is denied by God's love, which means that all that has been, really is. And this conclusion neatly denies the historicism plaguing him, since he infers from it that nothing has any permanent existence and, hence, ultimately no existence. If this is a bit confusing, it is because Ulrich is drawn at once by the opposing poles of historical nihilism and a vision of ecstatic Parousia, the total plenitude of being in the present moment. He is trying to reconcile the thought of the anti-Christian Nietzsche and the vision of Plotinus, the third-century Neoplatonist who gave Christianity its metaphysical vision of permanence. Would this line of reasoning have opened up for Ulrich onto a mystical vision of ecstatic love transcending the transience of time? Perhaps, and perhaps not, for the positivist in him would surely have difficulty reconciling that with those antimetaphysicians such as Nietzsche and Mach that he carries within himself.

Ulrich also investigates in his diaries what love is not, which is to say, he examines the nature of feelings and, in the aforementioned chapter 52, writes an "historical synopsis" of emotions. To study the various opinions that make of feelings the motivator of love and ethics, he becomes a historian of theories of emotion and feeling (and starts to do consciously for the history of psychological theories what he has intuitively been doing for the history of ethics). According to Ulrich, much of classical and modern psychology derives from classical Greek thought, including what he calls the modern psychology of drives, *Triebpsychologie*. By this he designates the scientific psychology of the nineteenth century, which was replete with dozens of drives, one to explain every conceivable form of human behavior. His critical review of psychological concepts concludes with a critique of what today would be called reductionism. He sees that, after the excessive exuberance of romantic psychology, with its dozens of drives, modern psychology has been motivated by a "satanically condescending desire" for a lack of spirit—*Seelenlosigkeit*. Accordingly, modern science has eliminated spirit or mind from its purview and considers all emotions to the expression of material states (4:1144). Ulrich seems to include psychoanalysis in this critique of monistic materialism, though not by name. In any case Ulrich as historian endorses neither betting on humanity's spirituality nor reducing humanity simply to organized matter. In this historical analysis he remains a historicist looking at the ever-changing fashions in theories, which is another demonstration of the transience of all things.

There is a striking parallel between the conclusion of book 1 of the novel, when Ulrich realizes that reason can be in the service of violence, and the end of the second half, when, in chapter 52, Ulrich again considers the role of force or violence in knowledge. He examines the idea that any universally valid law compels the individual case to fit submissively into a universal category. Ulrich's observations are again part of a meditation on the ineffable nature of the unique individual, though in his work on the history of psychology his thoughts appear specifically to be directed against the psychological science in which Musil had a doctoral degree. It was, and is, easy enough to understand Ulrich's ire with the categories used in psychology and psychiatry that reduce psychic life to docile concepts. His critique of compulsion in the service of truth aims at freeing the psyche from being explained away by generalizations. In his defense of the psyche against conceptualizing, Ulrich is also contemplating how he might lay hold of the self's unique truth, perhaps in a mystical seizure lying beyond the public truths of science. However, the irony used by the scientist distrusting science makes it impossible to affirm anything definitively. Consider that he claims that love is the essence of faith, but then undermines this claim by noting that the claims of love are hard to validate empirically on the basis of love having ever played any real role in history. The ironic dialectics have no end.

To return to our musical analogy, however, we can discern a counterpoint involving some permanence when in chapter 54 Ulrich returns to the theme of feelings and ethics. He still accepts the axiom that ethics demands permanence, so he wonders how ethics can be based on something constantly changing such as feelings. At this point he sketches out a radically new position, for he observes that one cannot really know feelings since the very act of observing them changes them. He posits in effect an uncertainty principle for the psychology of feelings that is clearly analogous to the same principle put forward in the 1920s by the physicists Heisenberg and Bohr for quantum mechanics: to wit, one cannot measure both the position and the momentum of a subatomic particle such as an electron. The act of observation forces the observer to select one determinant or the other. When Ulrich attempts to decide if a feeling is a state or a process, he also says that one must opt for one determinant or the other, since a feeling can be considered to be either a state or a process, depending on the observer's perspective (4:1159–60). This idea finds a further analogy in quantum mechanics, since an electron can be described as either a wave or a particle depending on the formalism used. Ulrich's formulation is an attempt to rethink the foundations of the way one conceptualizes feelings. In a few pages it appears that he recasts the foundations of a phenomenological psychology. He also complicates considerably his task of deciding if feeling is a state or a process.

After this speculation drawing upon physics for its model, Ulrich undertakes a phenomenology of feelings and moods. His thought here has parallels with those philosophical thinkers who, in the first part of the twentieth century,

challenged the primacy accorded to the rational self as the center for philosophical thinking. Wishing to relegate reason to a secondary position in mental life, a thinker such as Martin Heidegger (1889–1976), for example,
speculated that mood and feeling can create or reveal individual worlds.[9]
Accordingly, the world of the singular subject, revealed by emotion or mood,
is as valid for finding an individual truth as is the universal world revealed by
the rational procedures of objective science with its disregard for the specificity of any single individual observer's feelings. However, Ulrich's analysis
of the world created by feelings has a agenda different from that underlying
most phenomenological analysis. In the last of the galley chapters he sets out
to describe how we might be able to find an ecstatic means to reverse perception, as he puts it, and to find another condition (4:1201). His reasoning seems
to be that, if the outer world impinges on the inner world to produce feelings,
the subject might work from feelings back out to the exterior world in order to
live in a different world. A utopian agenda again lies on the horizon of Ulrich's
writing in the final galley chapter.

The quest for utopia suggests there is more writing that Ulrich has yet to
undertake. Were there no more manuscript chapters, one would conclude that
at this point, with the last galley chapter, Musil had created a self-portrait of
the writer as utopian dreamer. One might argue that he had given a description
of the writer about to set out to portray himself on a modernist quest for a
realm of permanence. This is not an unsatisfactory conclusion for a novel, or
at least Proust thought so, for he ended *Remembrance of Things Past* with his
protagonist about to begin to write a novel based on his experiences as
described in the novel. This is not really the case with Musil, however. Ulrich
is a self-critical utopian, and it is dubious that he thought that he had found the
revelation of something that would transcend transience—even in the form of
writing. Ulrich's writing at this point is about the conditions for the quest, not
about the discovery. In fact at this point it appears that his writing will always
be about the process, not the state. There is no real end in sight.

This impression is confirmed by some of the richest complication of
Ulrich's thought as it unfolds in some of unpublished chapters that Frisé published in his edition of Musil's complete works (a number of which are available in Burton Pike's translations "From the Posthumous Papers" included in
Sophie Wilkins's translation of *The Man without Qualities*). In these meditations and in his conversations with Agathe, Ulrich ranges widely over the problems of literary epistemology and the cultural critique that literature engages,
and it seems fitting to turn to a few of these unpublished sketches. Among the
chapters Musil worked on until the end of his life is "Genialität als Frage"

("Genius as a Problem"). In it Ulrich's (and Musil's) epistemological debate with himself remains alive. He recognizes the under-determination of all phenomena—which means that no single causal chain is a complete explanation of anything—but he also entertains Musil's belief that it must be possible to find an immanent reality in phenomena. In Ulrich's case political and ethical considerations also accrue to what he sees as the position of the reductionist empirical epistemology. It inevitably results in skepticism. Mach and Nietzsche remain unnamed interlocutors when Ulrich considers, for example, Hume's skeptical empiricism and his favored example for dismissing causality, to wit, that we believe that the "sun rises in the east and sets in the west for no other reason than that up till now it always has" (4:1271). Ulrich finds empiricism to be simplistic and imagines that if he were to question Agathe about why one believes the sun does what is does, she would answer that one day it might do it differently (4:1271).

Agate would repeat Hume without knowing who he is, and so Ulrich smiles in recognition that skeptical empiricism is a natural inclination of youth, desirous of discovering all on its own. This has a ring of self-criticism, and undoubtedly it is, for Ulrich has hardly stopped being a skeptic, however much he envisions the possibility of getting beyond, without denying, empiricism.

It is as a cultural critic and ethical thinker that skeptical Ulrich is less cheerful. He sees ethical dangers that skepticism produces when the skeptic considers that the belief that the sun rises in the east is a matter of habit. This attitude can lead to the affirmation that all human knowledge is subjective, depending upon history, and consequently that from this perspective knowledge is just the "product of class or race" that has developed in the course of European history (4:1271). In attributing the grounds for truth to race and class, Musil undoubtedly has in mind, among other things, what had happened in Germany after Hitler had taken power. Musil writes Ulrich's critique from a double perspective deriving at once from his own critique of skeptical positivism and his experience of Nazi science. Nazi science wanted to replace empirical rationalism with claims to knowledge born of its racist biology and nationalist myths. Ulrich's remarks plainly reflect Musil's fear that relativist skepticism appears to corroborate Nazi ideology. His remarks reflect the problem of somebody who asks what are the criteria for truth that might allow relativism to say something against Nazi science. (The Nazis believed in racially grounded science and rejected relativity theory and quantum mechanics by branding them "Jewish science.") Musil knew that his fear was justified and that, unlike more genteel relativists, the Nazis, having defined truth through its national or racial origins, were willing to prove their superior knowledge with a bullet. And so Ulrich meditates on the necessity of grounding truth in something other than habit, for, as his creator knew by historical experience, bad habits abound.

Ulrich is also evaluating the empiricist thinker that modern liberal culture has produced. From his perspective this thinker has become the successful pragmatist—or opportunist—that he cannot abide. In hostile criticism he calls this thinker the empirical man and charges him with using his own experience to re-create always the same thing. The pragmatic thinker remains locked within his own experience, which sustains the monotonously profitable repetition of technological rationality leading to the gigantic organization of modern society. This philosophical empiricism Ulrich calls, curiously, a children's disease (4:1271).

Ulrich intends to indict Europe's technologically proficient exploitation of science, which, if it turns out an unending stream of new inventions, is incapable of creating a new culture. The Marxist will undoubtedly see in Ulrich's indictment a description of the closed logic of capitalism and its use of science in the creation of need. The Heideggarian philosopher would recognize in Ulrich's description of modernity the conditions in which science as part of metaphysics has imposed its domination upon the globe. These judgments can find a complement in an interpretation of Ulrich's description of pragmatism as a disease. With his description of the closed system of the technological age, he suggests, with the metaphor of a child's disease, the need for growth, for maturity, and for a richer culture than one founded simply on the unending renewal of needs and their elementary satisfaction through ever-larger doses of technology. Empiricism itself is not so much condemned here as is its application by a type of entrepreneur, the empirical man, the dominant type of the liberal era in which the closed logic of capitalist expansion has remained virtually unquestioned, even by socialist and fascist regimes. One recalls that in the essays Musil had deplored that the all-embracing rationalism of the Enlightenment had been reduced in scope by the transformation of reason into a tool for pragmatic achievements. In this regard Ulrich continues Musil's critique.

In many of the unpublished chapters and sketches Ulrich and the narrator turn in an epistemological circle of alternately affirming and doubting. Most of the time they are unable to overcome their ironic doubts about whether it is possible to affirm anything beyond the most limited empirical affirmations. At other times they seem committed to the possibility that one can rationally describe the world, its development in history, and perhaps a preferable alternative. Ulrich's commitment to this project is accompanied by a belief that adequate representation has to be found to bridge the gap between the rationality of science and the world of value anchored in the individual. Perhaps the most salient example of his thought concerning representation is found in chapter 62, "Das Sternbild der Geschwister oder Die Ungetrennten und Nichtvereinten" ("The Constellation of Brother and Sister; or, The Unseparated and Not United" [4:1337]. The description of the siblings as unseparated and not united is first used at the end of galley chapter 47 to describe Ulrich and Agathe's relationship.) In the unpublished chapter 62 Ulrich discusses love with Agathe, and, in so doing, tries to define the nature of the symbolic representation that he envisions as the basis for knowledge of the totality. Ulrich is in an unusually affirmative mood when he stresses the commonality of mathematics and poetry, of novels and physics, in this chapter whose title underscores his thirst for unity in difference, or the unseparated and not united. Agathe herself offers an example of unity in difference, for love of the sister can be considered love of self, which is to say, of the double that is different and the same. So love resembles, from this perspective, a type of representation.

Ulrich resorts to allegory to explain this thought. He tells Agathe a story, one recalling the tale of Martin Guerre, in which a man falsely represents himself to a woman as her husband returning from years at war (a version of which the narrator told in "Grigia"). The man gets himself accepted by the wife as the authentic husband. He is at once the same—symbolically a husband—and literally different. According to Ulrich, this sameness in difference is the nature of every sign or symbol: it is constantly what it represents while remaining different from what it signifies. Thus conceived, representation is a utopian act that erases differences while maintaining them, whether it be in love's artifices or in the symbolic calculations of a mathematician.

The epistemologist may cavil at this view of symbols, but with this view of identity within difference Ulrich can explain that by the very nature of representation, all representation is under-determined, though not arbitrary. He explains his idea to Agathe by saying that the intellectual portrayal of nature depends on an image without similarity in the sense that many different kinds of images—symbols, if one prefers—can represent something else so long as they have one specific feature that allows one to speak of depiction or representation (4:1342). The possible multiplicity of representations derives logically from the epistemological axiom that phenomena are under-determined: the only epistemic demand one can make of a representation is that, in the quite different ways that things are apprehended, one must be able to demonstrate the commonality of an original image. Invariance is found in an original image, the underlying stratum that gives rise to representation. Once one recognizes this original stratum, then Ulrich can advance the claim that, thus defined, reality exists and can be known through representation. But since knowledge is mimetic, it always privileges a specific viewpoint for the representation involved. Somewhat as in Mach and young Wittgenstein, vision may seem privileged in Ulrich's later meditations, though in what he calls a "non-sensory notion of imageability" (4:1342). However much I personally distrust any epistemological position privileging the visual, I must admit that Ulrich has a powerful argument. His view justifies the commonsense recognition that art and literature may provide as many representations as there are artists and writers; at the same time this view recognizes an underlying invariance of what is represented through the agent of representation, be it through mathematics, poetry, or painting. And with this viewpoint Ulrich hopes that under-determination and a near-mystical belief in the real are about to be reconciled. And he may have finished Musil's argument with Mach.

With this view of sameness in multiplicity Ulrich goes on to suggest how to overcome the opposition between modes of knowledge. He adumbrates a theory of pan-representation in which he claims everything can be represented by something else, by a mathematical formula or by "external sensory similarity" so that reality and theory inform each other, such as, in Ulrich's homey example, the way in which the cylinder in a music box is a portrayal of a manner of singing, or an action or plot (*Handlung*) can depict a changing feeling (4:1342). Mathematics sets the standard for precision through coordinate systems that allow mapping point by point. But Ulrich insists that the forms of mapping one thing onto another are multiple and all of equal status, be it in the form of correspondence, representability, value, exchangeability, or other forms that have their own standards. Ulrich says this includes equality and even undifferentiability as forms of correspondence in which two domains are mapped out, one on the other.

His theory is more than a way of showing that science and literature participate in the same project, for the undifferentiability that representation perforce differentiates is the name Ulrich would give to his own mythic creation of love. In this naming lies the center of his last temptation, or vision, or dream, or whatever one may call his desire to make all representations finally meld in unity. It is not easy to pin one label on his attempt to mediate between the two Pascalian epistemologies, or Snow's two cultures, or simply the division of reason and feeling, of physics and poetry, of body and soul. It may appear Ulrich wants to sublimate all into a myth of unity that would serve as a utopian grounds for thought and belief. But from his description of the multiple forms of representation, it follows that knowledge is multiple, obeying no fixed typologies, and accountable only to that which it represents. Perhaps this idea offers another way of reading *The Man without Qualities,* for Ulrich's theory of representation implies that modernist literature trades on the idea that anything can represent anything else. Joyce perhaps better than Musil knew how to organize this possibility, specifically in the catalog in *Ulysses* of everything in Dublin as so many moments in universal myth, not to mention the revels of pan-representation of *Finnegans Wake.*

Unlike Joyce, Musil also distrusted this impulse to allow anything to represent everything else, and the novel's opening tirades against pop culture show that he is irritated by the idea that a racehorse or a boxer can symbolize anything other than themselves. Ulrich comes to his theory of pan-representation late in the novel. Throughout much of the novel, Musil's own distrust of the heterogeneity of modeling and mapping reveals itself in an expressed dislike of the idea that representation is such a fluctuating, when not fickle, instrument. Kitsch representation is, for example, a form of degenerate representation that Musil cannot abide. His distrust of representation's fickleness also comes out pointedly in the portrayal of Arnheim, the capitalist who knows that in economics exchange values turn on representations that may equate anything with anything and thus allow for all types of metamorphoses. If late in the novel Ulrich himself recognizes that equal value and exchangeability are forms of representation, it is also true that at the novel's outset he does not want to participate in a society in which athletes can be represented as geniuses or vice versa. He evolves, has perhaps contradictory ideas, but he consistently dislikes a manipulator of representations like Arnheim. His cultural critique refuses to allow that all representations are really equal.

Yet the heterogeneity of representation appears to be a fact in the novel itself. From this perspective I conclude that, Joyce notwithstanding, little in the history of the novel before Musil had quite prepared readers to accept that the novel can seemingly represent anything while criticizing most of what fiction usually represents. Commenting on Musil's historical importance, another central European novelist, Milan Kundera, has pointed out with admiration that after Musil's example, one can put anything into a novel. According to Kundera, whose *Unbearable Lightness of Being* follows in Musil's path, Musil invented the novel in which everything can be a theme having the same importance. As in a cubist painting, there is no division into foreground and background: every theme can go into the foreground.[10] This means that Ulrich's considerations of the history of psychology have as much weight in the novel as the sale of oil fields to a Prussian capitalist who is getting rich by selling guns needed for peace, not to mention a love affair between a brother and a sister illustrating that criminals can enter a sacred realm. I suspect that the ironic essayist in *The Man without Qualities* would want to answer Kundera with an affirmative negative answer: yes, but of course the novel also shows that many things are not important, though their lack of importance may be important. After the scrutiny of irony, ultimately all things are not equal, but the process of finding that out which are and which are not may go on indefinitely. That is well illustrated by *The Man without Qualities,* perhaps the first novel of processes in the history of European literature.

Conclusion

Musil as Lecturer in the Nazi Period

Musil's personal involvement in the publication of *The Man without Qualities* came to an end in 1933. With few exceptions, notably with the publication of *Posthumous Papers of a Living Author,* Musil had little public presence after the Nazis took power. He devoted his life largely to trying to move forward with *The Man without Qualities.* In these concluding remarks, however, I would like to focus on three documented moments when he did step into the public arena after Hitler took power, to give lectures. These lectures are not unlike the essays: they exhibit the same complexity of thought he develops in writing, and like the essays they present thoughts developed in response to the ongoing historical crisis of European culture. However, in them Musil made his voice literally present to make an ethical statement in a time of great danger. As such, the lectures represent a kind of unintentional final testament of the writer. Musil undoubtedly would have appreciated the unintentional irony that they are a last testimony given by a writer who found himself reflecting on history even as history was preparing to push him from the public stage.

As a preface to these three lectures, I return to an unpublished essay Musil worked on after the Nazis took power, "The Ruminations of a Slow-witted Mind." In this essay he worked out a tentative version of his response to the Nazis. He sought to understand the Nazis by trying to take seriously the premises of their "movement" (8:1413). For example he undertakes to examine, with scientific objectivity, the Nazi claim that the Jews had perverted German culture. In a thought experiment Musil asks himself if he had been so blinded by the Jews that he did not perceive their universal presence corrupting everything. Making short shrift of this absurd claim, Musil goes on to defend the thesis that, at a time when politics aims to regulate the mind, the writer must maintain autonomy of mind—or *Geist* (8:1425). As we have seen, *Geist* is a key concept for Musil, referring to mind, soul, and spirit, and at times it means something like culture. In Musil's usage *Geist* includes both the affective and moral qualities of mental life as well as the intellect. In this unpublished essay he ponders the fact that he was always against activism, by which he means the direct mixing together of *Geist* with politics and practical activities. This is because, he tells himself, one cannot be good at everything; rather, one must use judgment as to whether one can accomplish anything by what one does—or as he ironically notes, you do not write with your foot; you do not stand on your hand (8:1426–27). Here as throughout his work Musil comes to the conclusion that the mind, for its proper functioning to create culture, demands autonomy. Given the brutal onslaught of the Nazis, Musil's essay was not likely to be published. Yet it shows that Musil felt it incumbent upon himself to formulate a position vis-à-vis National Socialism. Musil's is an ethical position, though not one that necessary equates ethics with direct acts. His insistence on the necessity of the writer's disengagement is a difficult position, since the Nazis, as Musil lucidly recognized, would gladly consign his version of *Geist* and all its products to fire and ashes (8:1416).

"The Ruminations of a Slow-witted Mind" is the esssayistic working out of thoughts that Musil then reformulated for a public lecture, "Der Dichter in dieser Zeit" (translated as "The Serious Writer in Our Time"). This lecture on the writer and politics was presented to a rather special and concerned public. Musil addressed it in 1934 to the Schutzverband deutscher Schriftsteller in Österreich on the occasion of the twentieth anniversary of the association. Having fled Nazi Germany the year before, in late 1934 Musil found himself a German-language author in Austria, whether he wanted to be or not. Moreover, he was now in an Austrian Republic in which writers had seen that the government had socialist workers shot down in the streets and in which the Chancellor Dollfuss had been subsequently assassinated in an attempted Nazi coup. Musil and his colleagues had to reconcile themselves with the fact that, to prevent a Nazi takeover, Dollfuss had been establishing an Austrian form of fascism modeled on the Italian total state. The state was being elevated into the position of the supreme authority in all quarters of life, though without the totalitarian scope of Hitler's regime. Law still held sway, more or less, and writers such as Musil could hope to lead something like a normal life, though the future was far from certain. In this distressing context Musil wanted to talk about what writers might expect in an historical time in which society had turned its back on all the values the European writer embodied. And specifically he wanted to talk about this historical moment in which Austria had become, as he put it, the Noah's ark for German culture (8:1252).

In this lecture on the writer Musil undertook analysis that aimed at defending the rights of the individual creative artist while it offered a lucid analysis of the era of violence in which Europeans now found themselves. According to Musil, an era of unending violence had begun in 1914. This new era was also one of anti-individualism. In the lecture Musil took a broad view of European history in declaring that Russia, Italy, and Germany were all engaged in creating what Mussolini had first called the collectivism of the total state (8:1245). With typical wit and insight Musil remarked, however, that even in these states individualism had not totally disappeared, since each collective form was tied to a great individual in a pyramidal relation in which the führer was on the top (8:1249). Musil concludes from this paradox of the so-called collectivist state that, if humans are not ants, then the individual remains the "Träger der Kollektivität"—the bearer or carrier of the collectivity (8:1250).

And with this demonstration that the individual is still alive, Musil returns to his favored themes of the transhistorical nature of culture. In effect, in this lecture in Vienna in 1934 he makes a manifesto for the independence of culture and a fortiori art from the narrow determinations of nation, race, and class. The cultural tradition an artist recognizes is a tradition thousands of years old. It is a tradition outlasting all political transformations (and sotto voce all Reichs intending to last a thousand year). Thus, Musil declares that in "an Egyptian sculpture is found expressed something deeper about the German soul than in all German art expositions" (8:1250). In an era in which the Germans were obliged to view expositions of so-called degenerate art and the rise of Nazi kitsch, Musil's statement is a ringing challenge for his audience to remember their historical roots in the universal human culture that begins centuries before the modern nation state. The time scales by which one weighs culture are for the individual artist not years, but centuries, indeed, millennia. And no state, only the individual, can transform this tradition into living culture.

Musil regrets that in the immediate moment it has become nearly impossible to separate politics and *Geist,* though this represents a confusion of domains. Yet, since a "separation of the domains of literature and politics can hardly be carried out today and exists even potentially not at all," then one must work to inculcate in everyone a feeling about the difference of their functions (8:1254). With lucidity about the conditions of possibility that history has imposed on the writer, Musil calls for an historical perspective to enable the ongoing creation of a culture. It is a perspective that may defend the individual against what history seems in the present moment to decree against the individual. German-language writers in Vienna were apparently quite receptive to Musil's defense of the writer against the growth of collectivism that they were witnessing at that moment.

Musil's second occasion to make a public lecture came in 1935 when he was invited to Paris to participate in Le Congrès international des écrivains pour la défense de la culture. Though directly and personally threatened by the Nazis, Musil publicly refused to embrace any position that made politics and

311

culture synonymous. Repeating with even greater irony what he had written in his essay for himself in 1933, he stated that he did not feel he should write on politics any more than he should write on other important topics, such as hygiene, quite simply because he was not a specialist in the area. Implying that hygiene is as important as politics—indeed, perhaps implying that there might be hygiene for politics—Musil thought that, for the writer, the important question is what is culture, the writer's special domain.

To this question he gave a difficult answer, one far too subtle for an oral presentation to a congress of militants. The answer sheds much light on why Musil conducted himself as he did from 1933 until his death. The response he elaborated in Paris in 1935 separated culture from politics, even as it separated culture from the nation-state or the ministry of patriotic propaganda. Culture is, Musil said, bound to no transitory political form. In this sense he again declared that culture is transhistorical, for it is larger than any historical entity, such as the transient individual nation-state, and larger even than transient national languages, for cultural forms live on after the demise of the national states and languages that were instrumental in giving rise to them. (For example, tragedy needs neither Athens nor Attic Greek to continue to exist.) Confronting the collectivisms that seemed to be the victorious political ideologies in Europe in 1935, Musil insisted that the "bearer" of culture is not the collective but the individual writer or thinker, since it is through the individual that tradition is renewed and continued: tradition is "reborn" in the present in each individual's creative act. And by this act of renewing tradition Musil had in mind science as well as writing, philosophy as well as art. Literature, no more than physics, did not belong to any one country or political movement. Yet one can be a writer or scientist only by learning and then developing the tradition in which the cultural forms called science and poetry exist. The implications of Musil's speech are extremely wide-ranging, for they were as much a critique of the Nazi condemnation of "Jewish science" as the Soviet attack on "bourgeois art." This did not escape his left-wing audience, who did not like what they heard.

In Paris Musil was, I think, overtly provocative in refusing to recognize any a priori conditions for the historical development of culture, except the recognition that it is international in its scope and dependent upon tradition for its ongoing existence. Neither communists nor fascists could be happy with Musil's underscoring the importance of the individual in the genesis of culture, and in fact some participants in the congress were outraged. Setting the individual against the collective, Musil defended, in effect, the autonomy of culture against the Nazi and Communist bureaucracies that wanted to transform all forms of culture into expressions of the total political state. The individual, he said with biting irony, could even create under an enlightened despot—provided of course that the despot was enlightened. Stalinists in the crowd may have felt the irony, as perhaps would have supporters of Hitler, if any had been present.

Moreover there is another side of Musil's lecture that probably escaped all but the Germans present in Paris. They knew that Musil, in setting forth his argument in terms of culture and politics, was alluding to an old debate that had animated Germans about the failure of Germany and Germans to have a political existence that was equal to their cultural existence. The argument about the supposed disparity between cultural importance and political weakness was prevalent in the German world at least until Bismarck and the creation of the German Reich; and it continued to echo in German minds long afterward. In fact, after the debacle of the First World War, Germans began debates about their cultural "superiority" while wondering how to justify their political vicissitudes after they had been defeated on the battlefield and humiliated by the Versailles treaty. Musil's defense of culture against politics was a refusal of the political side of the debate. Implicit in his argument is the suggestion that the belief in the desirability of Germany's having political power commensurate with its cultural importance had eventuated in the First World War; and implicit, too, was the suggestion that this belief was now responsible for the rise of the Nationalist Socialist movement. Musil's antinationalism was consistent and coherent.

Musil apparently gave his lecture on the "serious writer" again in Basel in late 1935. Then he gave his last new public lecture in 1937, just a year before the Nazis annexed Austria. It is another marvelous but difficult public lecture that can be taken as his public statement about the Nazis. Published later as a small book, it is laconically called *Über die Dummheit* (*On Stupidity*), a title whose concision suggests Musil's affinities with classical moral analysis. In his lecture Musil analyzes language usage to come to ethical understanding. To wit, he points out that stupidity is not a univocal concept simply designating a lack of intellectual capacity. On the contrary, it is as much a problem of feeling as intellect—and as a form of feeling, Musil implies, it is related to ethics, for feeling motivates much of what we do. Musil first uses Kantian-type antimonies (or seemingly mutually exclusive concepts) to show that, on the one hand, it appears we cannot talk about stupidity since it is not a simple concept; and, one the other hand, since we do argue about what stupidity is, it must have some conceptual basis in language allowing discussion. In fact, more like the later Wittgenstein than Kant, Musil goes on to show that the concept of stupidity plays many roles in language and that these various usages are part of a fundamental way of dealing with experience. In the lecture he examines the overlapping meanings of words that are implied by stupidity. Notions such as brutality, perversion, kitsch, and various affective or emotive defects are inter-related in our understanding of the experience of stupidity. Stupidity is implied, for example, when we speak of vanity, for that implies that the vain fall short of their capabilities. And brutality is a way of describing how stupid-ity acts: brutality is the praxis of *Dummheit* (8:1275). Insults are another form of stupidity. Musil never spells it out, but it is obvious that all of these terms, though they deal with everyday experience, also describe the behavior and attitudes of the Nazis. The "banality of evil," as Hannah Arendt phrased it in describing the Nazi bureaucrat Adolf Eichmann, is also described by Musil in the form of an intellectual and emotive stupidity that applies as much to a street ruffian as to an SS officer (which, I note, Eichmann notably was, having helped organize the SS in Austria).

Musil is aware that only in a historical context does stupidity become problematic. The historical context, he implies, has allowed stupidity at the current moment to take on a form of collective existence. He thus finds him-self living at a moment in history when the values of the Enlightenment, specifically truth and freedom, have ceased to be "the markers of human-worth" (8:1284). In the place of these values, which allowed the liberal Ger-man bourgeoisie to face the future with confidence, a crisis resulting from the loss of values has spread panic. Musil uses the norms of statistical reasoning to show that action born of panic is another form of stupidity. Panic induces multiple blind attempts at escaping entrapment through repeated instinctual reactions. These attempts correspond to statistical patterns that can be ex-plained by the blindness motivating them. With this recourse to the statistics of stupidity Musil suggests a way of understanding the political behavior of a large percentage of the German population during the Weimar era and later.

Moreover Musil says that when a fundamental concept such as under-standing is no longer stable (8:1284), then the attempt to understand the lack of understanding—stupidity—is perhaps impossible. That was the challenge for the writer at that historical moment. The lecture thus portrays Musil trying to understand how the impossible became possible. It is something of a cliché to note that with the advent of the Nazis one of the most civilized countries became the most barbarous. Musil wants to go beyond the horror of this tru-ism, as he was directly experiencing it, to understand how, if the concepts describing understanding lose their validity, then the standards for rationality are undermined and the irrational can appear to be a norm. And with this de-velopment, any proposition can plausibly claim truth value.

Musil concludes his lecture by returning to the idea that there are different types of stupidity. He believed that it was singularly important to make a distinction between ordinary stupidity—one associated with jolly red cheeks and even virtuous action—and a stupidity born of a willed refusal of intelligence. Stupidity due to lack of education is perpetual, but stupidity of the educated is quite different. I think that we may assume that in this regard Musil has in mind the extraordinarily high percentage of German doctors, lawyers, professors, and intellectuals who were active Nazi supporters. The "higher stupidity" characterizing these educated professionals "is the true sickness of education"—or what Musil calls *Bildungskrankheit* (8:1287). He coins this term, playing upon words *Geist* and *Krankheit* (sickness), since these two terms are put together to mean mental illness. The type of stupidity he calls *Bildungskrankheit* cannot technically be called a mental illness, at least in the then-current context, though there is a strong suggestion that it should be. For, as Musil says, *Bildungskrankheit* endangers life itself (8:1288). Musil insists that the opposite of this "intelligent" stupidity is not so much pure understanding, for the professors have put their intelligence in the service of their feelings. Understanding can serve any goal, even the worst. As Musil would have it, the opposite of intelligent stupidity would be *Geist,* the mind moved appropriately by a combination of thought and feeling (8:1289). Here the ethical quest of *The Man without Qualities* is brought forth in the public arena: Musil wants to find a way to define and perhaps develop a *Geist* that would point to new modes of existence, or at least a renewed sense of the integrity of mind. His defense of mind is again part of his program for finding the wholeness of mind that will not only overcome the collective stupidity around him, but also advance the goal of mind functioning in accord with its own nature.

If the lecture on stupidity reflects in many ways ideas developed in his published essays as well as in *The Man without Qualities,* we are not surprised to read that Musil concludes his lecture by admitting that he has utopian yearnings. It is utopian, he says, to want to find access to what is really significant—*das Bedeutende*—that would allow stupidity to be criticized by both intellect and feeling (8:1290). Both feeling and intellect must be united if one is to be capable of finding the significant, which is to say the proper, activity for mind, and what is significant must be found before one undertakes action. In the meanwhile Musil concedes that the only sure way to combat stupidity is to recognize our limitations, for we are all at times somewhat stupid in our actions. We are often half-blind. Musil's final suggestion is that we oppose *Bescheidung,* by which he means something like modesty, to stupidity (8:1290). This is a notion that recalls Aristotle's definition of virtue, as indeed does his view that the mind has an activity that is proper to it. As a modern ethical notion for politics, Musil's call for modesty also parallels what the French writer Albert Camus wrote some twenty years later, that a democrat's first virtue must be modesty if the hubris of totalitarian politics is to be resisted. Lived from within, as well as viewed from without, the experience of the spread of Nazi ideology could only be seen as a collapse of modesty or the disappearance of reasoned temperance and the feeling of the limitations that characterize moral desires. The Nazi superman, like the communist utopian, saw no limits to his desire. Standing before history, Musil, the *Dichter*, could only modestly deplore the rise of stupidity. He knew, of course, that no single act by a poet, however insightful, could stem the wave of irrationality that had eventuated in the Nazi phenomenon. But his final lecture, *On Stupidity*, shows that he knew well what changes must occur if the conditions for the rise of the Nazi and other fanatics were to be eliminated. Musil's lectures remain as relevant today as they did in those dark times when he took time away from *The Man without Qualities* to be himself a man with ethical qualities.

Notes

Chapter 1. Life and Career

1. The reader who wants to know virtually everything that has been compiled about Musil's life can turn to the massive *Robert Musil: Eine Biographie* (Reinbek: Rowohlt, 2003) by Karl Corino, who has written several other books and articles about Musil. Everything in my account of Musil's life has been checked against Corino's definitive biography. I have also used, among other sources, Musil's diaries and letters. In the concluding bibliography of this book, the reader will find some other suggestions for understanding Musil's life, but Corino's biography is now the standard source for biographical information.

2. There is some question about dates in this period of Musil's life. I follow the dates set forth in Corino's biography.

3. An interesting study of this not-well-known group is to be found in Klaus Petersen, *Die "Gruppe 1925": Geschichte und Soziologie einer Schriftstellervereinigung* (Heidelberg: Winter, 1981).

4. Annette Daigger, "Musils Vortrag in Paris," in *Musil anders: Neue Erkundungen eines Autores zwischen den Diskursen,* ed. Gunther Martens, Clemens Ruthner, and Jaak de Vos (Bern: Lang, 2005), 77–78.

5. Wilfried Berghahn, *Robert Musil in Selbstzeugnissen und Bilddokumenten* (Reinbek: Rowohlt, 1986), 127.

6. A complete CD-ROM of Musil's manuscripts is now available from the Center for Musil Studies at the University of Klagenfurt. In personal correspondence about this CD-ROM, Walter Fanta, the director of the center, wrote to me in November 2007 that the "Klagenfurter Ausgabe Robert Musils" will not be available on the Internet, nor, because of copyright, would it be available in any other format.

7. This was the opinion of Helmut R. Boeninger in 1952, though he recognized that an anonymous *TLS* review in October 28, 1949, may also be considered as the moment when Musil was "rediscovered" in the Anglo-Saxon world. The review, "Empire in Space and Time," is believed to have been written by Ernst Kaiser and Eithne Wilkins. See "The Rediscovery of Robert Musil," *Modern Languages Forum* 37 (1952): 109–19.

Chapter 2. Early Diaries and Doctoral Dissertation

1. Ralph Waldo Emerson, "On Behavior," in *Essays and Lectures* (New York: Library of America, 1983), pp. 1037–39. All page citations in the text are to this edition.

2. Patrizia C. McBride, *The Void of Ethics: Robert Musil and the Experience of Modernity* (Evanston, Ill: Northwestern University Press, 2006).

3. Friedrich Nietzsche, *Zur Genealogie der Moral,* in *Werke III,* ed. Karl Schlechta (Frankfurt: Ullstein, 1969), 889.

4. Hannah Hickman, *Robert Musil and the Culture of Vienna* (LaSalle, Ill: Open Court, 1984), 150–63.

5. Dagmar Barnouw, "Skepticism as a Literary Mode: David Hume and Robert Musil," *Modern Language Notes* 93 (1978): 852–70.

6. For this translation I have drawn upon Robert Musil, *On Mach's Theories,* intro. G. H. von Wright, trans. Kevin Mulligan (Munich: Philosophia, 1980), 75.

7. Guillaume Gorretta, "Ernst Mach," in *Les philosophes et la science,* ed. Pierre Wagner (Paris: Gallimard, 2002), 634.

8. Ernst Mach, *Beiträge zur Analyse der Empfindungen* (1886), quoted in Franz Kuna, *Modernism 1890–1930,* ed. Malcolm Bradbury and James MacFarlane (Atlantic Highlands, N.J.: Humanities Press, 1976), 122.

Chapter 3. *Young Törless*

1. Clinton Shaffer offers a rich analysis of the rhetoric of fiction used in *Young Törless,* as well as an overview of critical opinion in this regard. See "*In loco parentis:* Narrating Control and Rebellion in Robert Musil's *Die Verwirrungen des Zöglings Törleß,*" *Modern Austrian Literature* 35, nos. 3–4 (2002): 27–51.

2. The doyen of Musil studies, Burton Pike, says quite reasonably that Törless makes a flight from circumstances and problems that have become too much for him (*Robert Musil: An Introduction to His Work* [Ithaca: Cornell University Press, 1961], 54). Commenting on Pike, Harry Goldgar, a Freudian critic, says the real explanation is offered by the psychoanalytical insight that such a fugue occurs when unconscious conflicts are overwhelming, typically, as here, after the patient imagines his problems are solved, but the conflict is such that he may even suffer amnesia, as Törless seems to do. Freudians always have the last word ("The Square Root of Minus One: Freud and Musil's Törless," *Comparative Literature* 7 [Spring 1965]: 129).

3. The discussion about the crisis of language in *Young Törless* began with the much-cited article by Lothar Huber, "Robert Musils *Törless* und die Krise der Sprache," *Sprachkunst: Beiträge zur Literaturwissenschaft* 4 (1973): 91–99. Cf. Jerry A. Varsava, "Törless at the Limits of Language: A Revised Reading," *Seminary: A Journal of Germanic Studies* 20 (September 1984): 188–204, as well as Hannah Hickman for an account of Törless's relation to language in her *Robert Musil and the Culture of Vienna.*

4. I am drawing upon Shaughan Lavine for a paraphrase about the infinite, that ever-troublesome concept that he calls "mathematics' persistent suitor." This is the title of the second chapter of Lavine's elegant *Understanding the Infinite* (Cambridge, Mass.: Harvard University Press, 1994). See also Rudolf Taschner's lecture, *Musil, Gödel, Wittgenstein und das Unendliche* (Vienna: Picus, 2002).

5. Robert Smith stresses that in 1902 Musil began reading Mach, specifically Mach's *Populär-wissenschaftliche Vorlesungen* (1896), at the same time he began to write *Young Törless* ("The Scientist as Spectator: Musil's *Törless* and the Challenge to Mach's Neo-Positivism," *German Review* 75 [Winter 2000]: 41).

6. In his study of the Viennese intellectual background of Karl Popper's philosophy, historian Malachi Haim Hacohen has observed about nineteenth- and twentieth-century Austrian philosophy that "generation after generation, Austrian philosophers argued against Kant, sought to assure themselves that they were not Kantians, and competed in explaining why. The spectacle of a culture constantly endeavoring to exorcise a dead philosopher provides the best testimony to his influence" (*Karl Popper, the Formative Years, 1902–1945: Politics and Philosophy in Interwar Vienna* [Cambridge: Cambridge University Press, 2000], 58).

Chapter 4. Experiments in Narrative and Theater

1. Fred Lönker, "'Die Landschaft nicht im Wagen suchen.' Der frühe Musil und die Psychologie," *Scientia Poetica* 1 (1997): 183–205.

2. David Midgley, "Writing against Theory: Musil's Dialogue with Psychoanalysis in the 'Vereinigungen,'" in *Robert Musil and the Literary Landscape of His Time,* ed. Hannah Hickman (Salford, U.K.: Department of Modern Languages, University of Salford, 1991), 72–93

3. I pursue this topic at much greater length in my *Revels in Madness* (Ann Arbor: University of Michigan Press, 1999).

4. Recordings of excerpts of Alexander Moissi's performance are available on the Internet. A CD of other performances accompanies an invaluable volume of essays, *Max Reinhardt und das deutsche Theater,* ed. Roland Koberg, Bernd Stegemann, and Henrike Thomsen (Berlin: Henschel, 2005).

5. Agatha Schwartz, "Robert Musil als Dramatiker," *Fidibus* 19 (1991): 2.

6. Wilhelm Braun, "Musil's *Die Schwärmer,*" *PMLA* 80 (June 1965): 298.

7. The classic study of this question is George Canguilhem's *Le normal et le pathologique* (Paris: Presses Universitaires françaises, 1961).

8. See in this regard Egon Naganowski, "'Vinzenz' oder der Sinn des sinnvollen Unsinns," *Musil Studien* 4 (1973): 89–122. He ties Musil's play into theater history and explicates its relation to the Dada movement.

Chapter 5. *Three Women*

1. For further background and reception of this collection of stories, see Peter Henninger, "Robert Musil's Novellas in the Collection *Drei Frauen,*" in *A Companion to the Works of Robert Musil,* ed. Philip Payne, Graham Bartram, and Galin Tihanov (Rochester, N.Y.: Camden House, 2007), 223–50.

2. Ritchie Robertson deals with Musil's use of Lucien Levy-Bruel and anthropology in his essay "Musil and the 'Primitive Mentality,'" in *Robert Musil and the Literary Landscape of His Time,* ed. Hannah Hickman (Salford, U.K.: Department of Modern Languages, University of Salford, 1991), 13–33.

3. The intertextual play in "The Lady from Portugal" is rich. For example, Joachim von der Thüsen points out relations to Gottfried Keller, Maeterlinck, and Richard Beer-Hofmann in "'Die Portugiesen': Zur Frage der Literarischen Tradition bei Robert Musil," *Neophilologus* 81 (1997): 433–44.

4. Mikhail Bakhtin develops his ideas about carnival in *Rabelais and His World*, trans. Helene Iswolsky (Cambridge, Mass.: MIT Press, 1968). Alina C. Hunt has studied analogies with Musil in "Toward an Unfinalizable Dialogue: Robert Musil's Essayism and Bakhtinian Dialogism," *College Literature* 95 (June 1995): 116–25.

5. See Walter H. Sokel, "Kleist's 'Marquise of O.,' Kierkegaard's 'Abraham,' and Musil's 'Tonka': Three Stages of the Absurd as the Touchstone of Faith," *Wisconsin Studies in Contemporary Literature* 8 (1987): 505–16.

Chapter 6. Epistemology and Politics in the Essays

1. Klaus Amann has written a substantial introduction to the political side of Musil's essay writing in his edition of some of Musil's writing from the *Nachlass: Robert Musil, Literatur und Politik: Mit einer Neuedition ausgewählter politischer Schriften aus dem Nachlass* (Reinbek: Rowohlt, 2007).

2. An overview of Musil's so-called conservatism can be found in Galin Tihanov, "Robert Musil in the Garden of Conservatism," in *A Companion to the Works of Robert Musil*, ed. Philip Payne, Graham Bartram, and Galin Tihanov (Rochester, N.Y.: Camden House, 2007), 117–50.

3. Steven Beller, *A Concise History of Austria* (Cambridge: Cambridge University Press, 2006), 9.

4. My point about Pascal is confirmed by Karl Corino, in personal correspondence in which he points out allusions to Pascal in Musil and regrets that Allied bombing destroyed Musil's library so that we do not know which editions of Pascal he used. See *TB 1:*389, for example.

5. The classic study of this question is Morris Kline, *Mathematics: The Loss of Certainty* (New York: Oxford University Press, 1980).

6. Jeffrey Herf, *Reactionary Modernism: Technology, Culture, and Politics in Weimar and the Third Reich* (Cambridge: Cambridge University Press, 1984), 53.

7. Ibid., 57.

8. Barnouw, "Skepticism as a Literary Mode," 855.

9. Guntram Vogt, "Robert Musils ambivalentes Verhältnis zur Demokratie," *Exilforschung, Text+Kritik* 2 (1984): 319.

10. Carl E. Schorske has written what many take to be the definitive book on Viennese culture in his *Fin-de-siècle Vienna: Politics and Culture* (New York: Knopf, 1981). In his *Concise History of Austria,* Beller takes a revisionist position with his criticism of Schorske's idea that it was the crisis of liberalism that led Vienna's bourgeoisie to "retreat in the temple of art and the psyche, and hence to the great cultural flowering that made *fin de siècle* Vienna so famous" (169).

11. French philosopher Jacques Bouveresse of the Collège de France argues in fact that Musil opposed Hegel on nearly every major point of Hegelian philosophy. See his

Robert Musil: L'homme probable, le hasard, la moyenne et l'escargot de l'histoire (Paris: L'Eclat, 1980).

12. This point is argued in I. B. Cohen, *The Triumph of Numbers: How Counting Shaped Modern Life* (New York: Norton, 2005).

13. Paul Valéry, "La crise de l'esprit," in *Oeuvres complètes,* vol. 1 (Paris: Gallimard, 1957), 992.

Chapter 7. Ethics and Aesthetics

1. "The 'Demise' of the Theater" remained on Musil's mind. This is spelled out in a diary entry from the thirties in which he also spells out what he means by classical theater: the ancients, Jean Racine, Molière, Shakespeare, Johann Gottfried von Herder, Goethe (*TB* 1:818).

2. I would point out that Musil neglects the education he derived from the critical realism developed in France in the fictional work of Honoré de Balzac, Stendhal, and Flaubert—all writers for whom science is an unquestioned authority and value and for whom fiction is a form of rational critique. In critical realism one sees the transmutation of the Enlightenment idea of philosophical critique into the idea of cultural criticism, which in nonfiction writers then came to fruition in Emerson and Nietzsche (and in England in Matthew Arnold and John Ruskin), thinkers for whom the function of literature is a education in, and a critique of, all aspects of life, from the most personal to the most collective. From this historical perspective Nietzsche stands out as the culmination of all the preceding currents of cultural and ethical criticism. He was the philosopher-educator of two generations of modernists for whom the educational function of art is a critique of values.

3. For much of my discussion of ideology I draw upon the original work of Jeffrey Herf, *Reactionary Modernism.* Other insights come from Sebastian Haffner, *Von Bismarck zu Hitler: Ein Rückblick* (Munich: Kindler, 1987); Hagen Schulze, *Weimar: Deutschland 1917–1933* (Berlin: Severin & Siedler, 1982); and Gordon Craig, *Germany, 1866–1945* (New York: Oxford University Press, 1978).

4. In his *Robert Musil und das Projekt der Moderne* (Frankfurt: Lang, 1988), 83, the Italian critic Aldo Venturelli suggests that, for his ethnology, Musil drew upon studies in animal psychology done by his mentor, Carl Stumpf.

5. I make this comment about "salvation" in light of Sebastian Haffner's comments on his youth spent in Berlin in the Weimar era. In his remarkable posthumously published memoirs, written in 1940, he recalls that at the time, especially in northern and eastern Germany, people experienced the "horror vacui and the desire for 'salvation': salvation through alcohol, through superstition, or even better through a great, totally overwhelming, cheap mass intoxication—*Massenrausch.*" My translation from *Geschichte eines Deutschen: Die Erinnerungen, 1914–1933* (Stuttgart & Munich: Deutsche Verlags-Anstalt, 2000), 71.

6. I paraphrase here the argument about the origins of Nazism from Erich Fromm's classic work *Escape from Freedom* (New York: Holt, Rinehart & Winston, 1941).

7. Hugo Friedrich's concept of the "empty transcendence" sought in much modernist poetry could find application to Musil in some important ways. See his *Die Struktur der modernen Lyrik* (1958), available in several editions, and translated as *The Structure of Modern Poetry: From the Mid-Nineteenth to the Mid-Twentieth Century*, trans. Joachim Neugroschel (Evanston, Ill.: Northwestern University Press, 1974).

Chapter 8. *The Man without Qualities,* Parts 1 and 2

1. The first translation of the novel into English in 1953 by Eithne Wilkins and Ernst Kaiser does not include any previously unpublished manuscript material, since they based their translation on what was then available in German. Subsequently, Adolf Frisé offered a large selection of these manuscripts in his 1978 edition of *Der Mann ohne Eigenschaften*. Included in Sophie Wilkins's admirable translation of the novel, published by Alfred A. Knopf in 1995, Burton Pike has translated a selection "From the Posthumous Papers." All of my references to the novel are to the Frisé edition. Translations are my own, though I have looked at both translations in English and Philippe Jaccottet's excellent translation into French.

2. For the definitive history of the genesis of the novel, see Walter Fanta, *Die Entstehungsgeschichte des "Mann ohne Eigenschaften" von Robert Musil* (Vienna: Böhlau, 2000).

3. In the Rede Lecture of 1959 at Cambridge University C. P. Snow coined the idea of "two cultures." With this the Cambridge physicist and novelist Snow designated the opposition of, and lack of communication between, scientific and humanistic thinking that he found at work throughout the modern world. The lecture was published as *The Two Cultures and the Scientific Revolution* (Cambridge: Cambridge University Press, 1959). This extremely influential, and often contested, work has been reprinted many times since.

4. In deflating some of the pretensions of postmodern readings of Musil, David Midgley has updated the criticism of Musil's satire in his "Looking beyond Satire in Musil's *Der Mann ohne Eigenschaften,*" *Austrian Studies* 15 (2007): 96–111.

5. For a view of the mystical meaning of being without qualities, see Jochen Schmidt's book on Musil's relation to the mystic Meister Eckhart, *Ohne Eigenschaften: Eine Erläuterung zu Musils Grundbegriff* (Tübingen: Niemeyer, 1975).

6. Or to quote the thesis, the property of "having the mass X is more closely connected with a body in which it is constantly found than with any comparative bodies, referred to in an arbitrary way, so that by appealing to an individual example, there is found in experience, to which Mach appeals, at least the beginning for the formation of a concept of property" (*BzM* 64).

7. The distinction of *ratio* and *Mystik* are notions at the center of many critical discussions of Musil. I paraphrase here Wolfdietrich Rasch, in *Robert Musil,* ed. Renate von Heydebrand (Darmstadt: Wissenschafliche Buchgesellschaft, 1982), 72; cf. throughout Elisabeth Albertsen, *Ratio und 'Mystique' im Werk Robert Musils* (Munich: Nymphenburger, 1968). Albertsen, in beginning her book with a quote from the 1955

edition of the diaries to the effect that rationality and mysticism are the poles of the time, goes on to compare this polarity with a magnetic field (237).

8. A reader desirous of acquaintance with Rathenau's ideas can find his essays and letters available on Internet sites—and find that Musil knew Rathenau's ideas quite well.

9. Max Weber, *Wirtschaft und Gesellschaft* (Tübingen: Mohr, 1972), 58.

10. Nietzscheans will find, and have found, here Musil's dissolution of self to be a reflection of what Nietzsche described as the surrender to Dionysian forces conveyed by music. If so, Apollonian Ulrich seems now ready to give himself over to the forces of the irrational. But Musil did not need to read *The Birth of Tragedy* to find in Ulrich's development away from Nietzsche that he is ready for an experience less constrained by the rationality that has been his professional credo; no more than did Jim Morrison of the Doors when he sang, some years after Clarisse expounded the same idea, that he wanted to "break on through to the other side." (Morrison, like Musil, probably did read *The Birth of Tragedy,* however.)

Chapter 9. *The Man without Qualities,* Book 2

1. I make this argument at greater length in the chapter on Musil in my *Fiction Refracts Science* (Columbia: University of Missouri Press, 2005).

2. This at least is what Burton Pike thinks. In his latest work on the novel he argues that no ending is possible, for in both its structure and underlying philosophy the novel can only propose a deferral of meaning, a quest for an open-ended future that Musil could never have concluded in any meaningful way. See *"Der Man ohne Eigenschaften:* Unfinished or without End?" in A *Companion to the Works of Robert Musil,* ed. Philip Payne, Graham Bartram, and Galin Tihanov (Rochester, N.Y.: Camden House, 2007), 371–94.

3. Philippe Jaccottet, *Eléments d'un songe* (Paris: Gallimard, 1961), 24–25.

4. This argument that Musil wanted to demonstrate the failure of utopia is well argued by McBride in her *Void of Ethics.*

5. This category, now a syndrome of the diagnostic manuals for psychiatrists, is usually attributed to the work of neo-Freudians such as the Viennese psychoanalyst Heinz Kohut (1913–1981) or the Viennese American doctor Otto Kernberg (1928–). The concept was formulated some time after Musil had written his novel, but its roots lay in the Viennese psychoanalytic milieu.

6. I develop this argument at length in my study of literature and madness, *Revels in Madness,* especially in the chapter on madness and modernism.

7. I have found Alasdair MacIntyre very useful in working out the ideas in this section on ethics. See his polemical *After Virtue,* 3rd ed. (Notre Dame: University of Notre Dame Press, 2007). For those who are uncomfortable with philosophical argument, I also recommend they consult the classic *Encyclopedia of Philosophy* (New York: Macmillan, 1972). This multivolume work remains unsurpassed for the quality of its contributors. Shorter aids are to be found in either the Oxford or the Cambridge dictionaries of philosophy. Unfortunately most specialized works on Musil and the philosophers presuppose too much background for the uninitiated reader.

8. The allegory of the cave comes from Plato's dialogue *The Republic,* in which the philosopher's education is compared to that of a prisoner who, having been locked in a cave in which he has seen nothing but shadows cast by the light there, emerges into daylight, sees the sun, and can return to the cave to understand truly what he has seen in the darkness. In other words the philosopher sees the form, or Eidos, of the Good and understands that what he takes for the good on earth is but a reflection of that eternal form. I add that I do not find much of the substance of Plato's theory of justice and the good directly reflected in Musil's work. However, it must be added that nobody has paid more homage to the form of the Platonic dialogue than Musil.

9. I am not suggesting Musil is directly drawing on Heidegger, whose influential work *Time and Being* was published in 1927. There is only one reference to Heidegger in the diaries, and it is not flattering. I am suggesting a parallel, which to say a common critique of the investigation of self that takes only the intellect as the starting point for understanding the nature of mind.

10. Milan Kundera, *Les testaments trahis* (Paris: Gallimard, 1993), 198.

Selected Bibliography

Selected Works in German by Musil

Beitrag zur Beurteilung der Lehren Machs. Reinbek: Rowohlt, 1980.
Briefe, Nachlese: Dialogue mit dem Kritiker Walther Petry. Ed. Adolf Frisé. Saarbrücken: Internationale Robert-Musil-Gesellschaft, 1994.
Briefe Nach Prag. Ed. Barbara Köpplová and Kurt Krolop. Reinbek: Rowohlt, 1971.
Briefe, 1901–1942. 2 vols. Ed. Adolf Frisé. Reinbek: Rowohlt, 1981.
Gesammelte Werke. 9 vols. Ed. Adolf Frisé. Reinbek: Rowohlt, 1978–1981. (Later editions of *Der Mann ohne Eigenschaften* repeat the pagination of this edition.)
Tagebücher. 2 vols. Ed. Adolf Frisé. Reinbek: Rowohlt, 1983.

Translations of Musil into English

The Confusions of Young Törless. Trans. Shaun Whiteside. New York: Penguin, 2001.
Diaries, 1899–1941. Trans. Philip Payne. New York: Basic Books, 1998.
The Enthusiasts. Trans. Andrea Simon. New York: Performing Arts Journal Publications, 1983.
The Man without Qualities. 3 vols. Trans. Eithne Wilkins and Ernst Kaiser. London: Secker & Warburg; New York: Coward-McCann, 1953–1955.
The Man without Qualities. 2 vols. Trans. Sophie Wilkins and Burton Pike. New York: Knopf, 1995.
On Mach's Theories. Trans. Kevin Mulligan. Washington, D.C.: Catholic University of American Press; Munich: Philosophia, 1982.
Posthumous Papers of a Living Author. Trans. Peter Wortsman. Hygiene, Colo.: Eridanos, 1987.
Precision and Soul: Essays and Addresses. Trans. Burton Pike and David S. Luft. Chicago: University of Chicago Press, 1990.
Selected Writings. Trans. Burton Pike. New York: Continuum, 1986.
Tonka and Other Stories. Trans. Eithne Wilkins and Ernst Kaiser. London: Secker & Warburg, 1965. Republished as *Five Women.* Boston: Godine, 1986.
Young Törless. Trans. Eithne Wilkins and Ernst Kaiser. London: Secker & Warburg; New York: Pantheon, 1955.

Bibliographies of Works about Musil

The starting points for the study of Musil are these volumes.

Mehigan, Tim. *The Critical Response to Robert Musil's Man without Qualities.* Columbia, S.C.: Camden House, 2003. This work includes two pages of bibliographies of Musil criticism as well as overview of criticism of the novel.

Payne, Philip, Graham Bartram, and Galin Tihanov, eds. *A Companion to the Works of Robert Musil.* Rochester, N.Y.: Camden House, 2007. This updates other bibliographies.

Rogowski, Christian. *Distinguished Outsider: Robert Musil and His Critics.* Columbia, S.C.: Camden House, 1994. Useful overview of Musil criticism through the early nineties.

Selected Critical Works

Books

Albertsen, Elisabeth. *Ratio und "Mystik" im Werk Robert Musils.* Munich: Nymphenburger, 1968. Fundamental study of reason and mysticism in Musil.

Althaus, Horst. *Zwischen Monarchie und Republik: Schnitzler, Hofmannsthal, Kafka, Musil.* Munich: Fink, 1976. Useful for historical contextualizing.

Amann, Klaus. *Robert Musil, Literatur und Politik: Mit einer Neuedition ausgewählter politischer Schriften aus dem Nachlass.* Reinbek: Rowohlt, 2007. A very good introduction to Musil's political thinking prefaces some of his posthumous writing.

Appignanesi, Lisa. *Femininity and the Creative Imagination: A Study of Henry James, Robert Musil and Marcel Proust.* New York: Harper & Row, 1973. Study of the debate about the nature of femininity.

Arntzen, Helmut. *Musil-Kommentar sämtlicher zu Lebzeiten erschienener Schriften ausser dem Roman "Der Mann ohne Eigenschaften."* Munich: Winkler, 1980. This and the next book are very useful commentaries, especially on expressive categories of language.

———. *Musil-Kommentar zu dem Roman "Der Mann ohne Eigenschaften."* Munich: Winkler, 1982.

———. *Satirischer Stil in Robert Musils "Der Mann ohne Eigenschaften."* Bonn: Bouvier, 1960. 2nd ed., 1970; 3rd ed., 1982. A rather mechanical study of satire that has been starting point for everything since.

Bangerter, Lowell A. *Robert Musil.* New York: Continuum, 1988. A general introduction that believes Musil had an ending for *The Man without Qualities.*

Bauer, Sibylle, and Ingrid Drevermann. *Studien zu Robert Musil.* Cologne & Graz: Böhlau, 1966. Underscoring the importance of ethics in Musil.

Baumann, Gerhart. *Robert Musil: Zur Erkenntnis der Dichtung.* Bern: Francke, 1965. An important early critic for a positive evaluation of Musil.

Baur, Uwe, and Elisabeth Castex, eds. *Robert Musil: Untersuchungen.* Königstein: Athenäum, 1980. Critical essays.

Baur, Uwe, and Dietmar Goltschnigg, eds. *Vom Törless zum Mann ohne Eigenschaften.* Munich: Fink, 1973. Interesting collection of critical essays.

Bausinger, Wilhelm. *Robert Musil: "Der Mann ohne Eigenschaften." Studien zu einer historisch-kritischen Ausgabe.* Hamburg: Rowohlt, 1964. Early study of the genesis of the novel.

Berghahn, Wilfried. *Robert Musil in Selbstzeugnissen und Bilddokumenten.* Reinbek: Rowohlt, 1963. Reprinted several times. Still perhaps the best introduction available.

Bernstein, Michael André. *Five Portraits: Modernity and the Imagination in Twentieth-Century German Writing.* Evanston, Ill.: Northwestern University Press, 2000. Musil in company with Celan, Rilke, Heidegger, and Benjamin in confronting the crisis of European culture.

Blasberg, Cornelia. *Krise und Utopie der Intellektuellen: Kulturkritische Aspekte in Robert Musils Roman "Der Mann ohne Eigenschaften."* Stuttgart: Heinz, 1984. Defense of Musil's utopia through cultural analysis.

Böhme, Hartmut. *Anomie und Entfremdung: Literatursoziologische Untersuchungen zu den Essays Robert Musils und seinem Roman "Der Mann ohne Eigenschaften."* Skripten Literaturwissenschaft, no. 9. Kronberg: Scriptor, 1974. An influential study of social categories in Musil.

Böhn, Andreas. *Vollendende Mimesis: Wirklichkeitsdarstellung und Selbstbezuglichkeit in Theorie und literarischer Praxis.* Berlin & New York: De Gruyter, 1992. Musil, Benjamin, and Jean Paul and a theory of mimesis.

Bouveresse, Jacques. *Robert Musil: L'homme probable, le hasard, la moyenne et l'escargot de l'histoire.* Paris: L'Eclat,1980. A splendid study of Musil and probability by a philosopher and specialist in Wittgenstein.

Bringazi, Friedrich. *Robert Musil und die Mythen der Nation: Nationalismus als Ausdruck subjectiver Identitätsdefekte.* Frankfurt: Lang, 1998. Deals with the critique of nationalism.

Brokoph-Mauch, Gudrun, ed. *Robert Musil: Essayismus und Ironie.* Edition Orpheus, no. 6. Tübingen: Francke, 1992. Essays on a key topic for understanding Musil.

Brokoph-Mauch, Gudrun. *Robert Musils "Nachlass zu Lebzeiten."* New York & Frankfurt: Lang, 1985. Thematic study that gives this work a major place in Musil's opus.

Burckhardt, Judith. *Der Mann ohne Eigenschaften von Robert Musil: oder, Das Wagnis der Selbstverwirklichung.* Bern: Francke, 1973. An existentialist approach emphasizing the quest for authenticity in the novel.

Büren, Erfhard von. *Zur Bedeutung der Psychologie im Werk Robert Musils.* Zurich: Atlantis, 1970. A comprehensive study from the perspective of psychology.

Cantoni, Remo. *Robert Musil e la crisi dell'huomo europeo.* Milan: Cisalpino-Goliardica, 1972. The Italian perspective on the crisis of culture.

Chardin, Philippe. *Musil et la littérature européenne.* Paris: Presses Universitaires de France, 1998. Excellent comparative literature study with essays relating Musil to a wide range of European writers.

327

Checconi, Sergio. *Musil.* Florence: La nuova Italia, 1969. Good introduction for the Italian reader.

Corino, Karl. *Robert Musil: Eine Biographie.* Reinbek. Rowohlt, 2003. The definitive biography.

———. *Robert Musils "Vereinigungen": Studien zu einer historisch-kritischen Ausgabe.* Munich: Fink, 1974. For the Freudian viewpoint.

Cornetti, Jean-Pierre. *Robert Musil, ou L'alternative romanesque.* Paris: Presses Universitaires de France, 1985.

Dawidowski, Christian. *Die geschwächte Moderne: Robert Musils episches Frühwerk in Spiegel der Epochendebatte.* Frankfurt: Lang, 2000. New attention to the early work.

Dinklage, Karl, ed. *Robert Musil: Leben, Werk, Wirkung.* Hamburg: Rowohlt, 1960. An essential early volume of assorted essays on Musil.

Döring, Sabine A. *Ästhetische Erfahrung als Erkenntnis des Ethischen: die Kunsttheorie Robert Musils und die analytische Philosophie.* Paderborn, Germany: Mentis, 1999. Musil's rapport with the Vienna Circle.

Dowden, Stephen D. *Sympathy for the Abyss: A Study in the Novel of German Modernism: Kafka, Broch, Musil, and Thomas Mann.* Tübingen: Niemeyer, 1986. A study of their cultural critique.

Dresler-Brumme, Charotte. *Nietzsches Philosophie in Musils Roman "Man ohne Eigenschaften."* Frankfurt: Athenäum, 1987. Literature as history, and vice versa.

Düsing, Wolfgang. *Erinnerung and Identität: Untersuchungen zu einem Erzählproblem bei Musil, Döblin und Doderer.* Munich: Fink, 1982. Discusses the problem of identity through memory in Musil and two other authors.

Fanta, Walter. *Die Entstehungsgeschichte des "Mann ohne Eigenschaften" von Robert Musil.* Vienna: Böhlau, 2000. Definitive study of how Musil composed his novel.

Finlay, Marike. *The Potential of Modern Discourse: Musil, Peirce, and Perturbation.* Bloomington: Indiana University Press, 1990. On the overturning of the classical episteme's idea of hermeneutics.

Frier, Wolfgang. *Die Sprache der Emotionalität in den "Verwirrungen des Zöglings Törless" von Robert Musil: Ein Beitrag zur angewandten Textlinguistik.* Bonn: Bouvier, 1976. An attempt to use applied linguistics to explain literary language.

Frisé, Adolf. *Plädoyer für Robert Musil.* Reinbek: Rowohlt, 1980. An essential book for those who want to understand what Musil's devoted editor was about.

García Ponce, Juan. *La errancia sin fin: Musil, Borges, Klossowski.* Barcelona: Anagrama, 1981. Musil among the postmodernists in Argentina and France.

Gilla, Thomas. *Versuche der Auflösung-Andeutungen von Synthesen.* Würzburg: Königshausen & Neumann, 2004. Study of myth.

Gnam, Andrea. *Die Bewältigung der Geschwindigkeit: Robert Musils Roman "Der Mann ohne Eigenschaften" und Walter Benjamins Spätwerk.* Munich: Fink, 1999. Interesting study of scientific theories of space and their relation to Musil in the first half of the book.

Goltschnigg, Dietmar. *Mystische Tradition im Romans Robert Musil: Martin Bubers "Ekstatische Konfessionen" im "Der Mann ohne Eigenschaften."* Heidelberg: Stiehm,

1974. Study of Musil's use of the work of the Jewish theologian Martin Buber and his views on mysticism.

Gradischnig, Hertwig. *Das Bild des Dichters bei Robert Musil.* Munich: Fink, 1976.

Gunia, Jürgen. *Die Sphäre des Ästhetischen bei Robert Musil: Untersuchung zum Werk am Leitfaden der Membran.* Würzburg: Königshausen & Neumann, 2000.

Gunther, Martens. *Ein Text ohne Ende für den Denkende: Zum Verhältnis von Literatur und Philosophie in Robert Musils "Der Mann ohne Eigenschaften."* Frankfurt & New York: Lang, 1999. For those interested in interdiscursive analysis of philosophical texts.

Harrison, Thomas. *Essayism: Conrad, Musil, and Pirandello.* Baltimore: Johns Hopkins University Press, 1992. Reading of Musil's view of the plurality of truths.

Henninger, Peter. *Der Buchstabe und der Geist: Unbewusste Determinierung im Schreiben Robert Musils.* Frankfurt: Lang, 1981. An aggressively Lacanian reading.

Herwig, Dagmar. *Der Mensch in der Entfremdung: Studien zur Entfremdungsproblematik anhand des Werkes von Robert Musil.* Munich: List, 1972. An existentialist approach to the question of alienation.

Heydebrand, Renate von. *Die Reflexionen Ulrichs in Robert Musils Roman "Der Mann ohne Eigenschaften": Ihr Zusammenhang mit dem zeitgenössischen Denken.* Münster: Aschendorff, 1966. One of the first important studies of the influences at work in Musil.

Heydebrand, Renate von, ed., *Robert Musil.* Darmstadt: Wissenschaftliche Buchgesellschaft, 1982. Several interesting critical essays.

Hickman, Hannah. *Robert Musil and the Culture of Vienna.* La Salle, Ill.: Open Court, 1984. One of the best books on Musil for understanding his cultural context.

Hochstätter, Dietrich. *Sprache des Möglichen: Stilistischer Perspectivismus in Robert Musils "Der Mann ohne Eigenschaften."* Frankfurt: Athenäum, 1972. Study of the formal qualities of Musil's language.

Hoffmann, Christoph. *Der Dichter am Apparat: Medientechnik, Experimentalpsychologie und Texte Robert Musils 1899–1942.* Munich: Fink, 1997. Discourse analysis from a nearly structuralist viewpoint.

Hoffmeister, Werner. *Studien zur erlebten Rede bei Thomas Mann und Robert Musil.* The Hague: Mouton, 1965. Study of monologues with considerations of self-reflexivity.

Hogen, Hildegard. *Die Modernisierung des Ich: Individualitätkonzepte bei Siegfried Kracauer, Robert Musil, und Elias Canetti.* Würzburg: Königshausen & Neumann, 2000. Sociology of the self in the film theorist, Musil, and the Nobel laureate.

Holmes, Alan. *Robert Musil "Der Mann ohne Eigenschaften": An Examination of the Relationship between the Author, Narrator and Protagonist.* Bonn: Bouvier, 1978. Despite solecism in title, a fundamental study of narrative perspectives.

Howald, Stefan. *Ästhetizismus and ästhetische Ideologiekritik.* Munich: Fink, 1984. Asks some interesting questions about aesthetics and ideology.

Hüppauf, Bernd-Rüdiger. *Von sozialer Utopie zur Mystik: Zu Robert Musils "Der Mann ohne Eigenschaften."* Munich: Fink, 1971. An influential study of mysticism in the novel.

Huszai, Villö. *Ekel am Erzählen: Metafictionalität in Werk Musils, gewonnen am Kriminalfall Tonka.* Munich: Fink, 2002. The title says it all.

Jaccottet, Philippe. *Eléments d'un songe.* Paris: Gallimard, 1961. Very good critical essays by a well-known poet and Musil's French translator.

Jonsson, Stefan. *Subject without Nation: Robert Musil and the History of Modern Identity.* Durham, N.C.: Duke University Press, 2000. A cultural critique with an interesting postcolonialist slant.

Kaiser, Ernst, and Eithne Wilkins. *Robert Musil: Eine Einfuhrung in das Werk.* Stuttgart: Kohlhammer, 1962. A groundbreaking study that unfortunately is very dated both for its psychological methodology and its lack of sensitivity.

Karthaus, Ulrich. *Der andere Zustand: Zeitstrukturen im Werk Robert Musils.* Berlin: Schmidt, 1965. Another fundamental study for determining later Musil criticism on the other condition.

Kraft, Herbert. *Robert Musil.* Vienna: Palu Zsolnay, 2003. Well-written study of Musil's life and its interface with the novel.

Kraft, Thomas. *Musils Mann ohne Eigenschaften.* Munich: Piper, 2000. Good introduction to the novel with keys for a roman à clef.

Kühn, Dieter. *Analogien und Variation: Zur Analyse von Robert Musils Roman "Der Mann ohne Eigenschaften."* Bonn: Bouvier, 1965. A study of allegory and systematic ambiguity.

Kühne, Jörg. *Das Gleichnis; Studien zur inneren Form von Robert Musils Roman "Der Mann ohne Eigenschaften."* Tübingen: Niemeyer, 1968. Ingenious reading of the novel's inner form to show it excludes closure.

Longuet-Marx, Anne. *Proust, Musil, partage d'écritures.* Paris: Presses Universitaires de France, 1986.

Laermann, Klaus. *Eigenschaftslosichkeit: Reflexionen zu Musils Roman "Der Mann ohne Eigenschaften."* Stuttgart: Metzler, 1970. A lively post-1968 polemic illustrating criticism as social critique.

Lönker, Fred, *Poetische Anthropologie.* Munich: Fink, 2002. One of Musil's most interesting recent critics.

Luserke, Matthias. *Wirklichkeit und Möglichkeit: Modaltheoretische Untersuchungen zum Werk Robert Musils.* Frankfurt: Lang, 1987. Complicated but challenging study of ethical modes in Musil.

Luserke, Matthias, *Robert Musil.* Stuttgart: Metzler, 1995.

Luft, Davis S. *Robert Musil and the Crisis of European Culture.* Berkeley: University of California Press, 1980. Excellent study of one of the fundamental themes in Musil.

Magris, Claudia. *Der habsburgische Mythos.* Salzburg: Müller, 1966. Fundamental book for all later arguments about Musil's historical context: the myth of the Hapsburgs.

Marini, Loredana. *Der Dichter als Fragmentist: Geschichte und Geschichten in Robert Musils Roman "Der Mann ohne Eigenschaften."* Bern: Lang, 2001. On a key aspect of the narration.

Martens, Gunther, Clemens Ruthner, and Jaak de Vos, eds. *Musil anders: Neue Erkundungen eines Autors zwischen den Diskursen.* Bern: Lang, 2005. For those interested in interdiscursive narratology.

Mauthner, Margarete. *Das zerzauberte Hause.* Berlin: Transit, 2004. A book about Musil's wife, Martha.

McBride, Patrizia C. *The Void of Ethics: Robert Musil and the Experience of Modernity.* Evanston, Ill: Northwestern University Press, 2006. Excellent study of modernity, ethics, and the form of Musil's novel.

Mehigan, Tim. *Robert Musil.* Stuttgart: Reclam, 2001. Introductory overview with the student in mind.

Monti, Claudia. *Musil, la metaforica della scienza.* Naples: Pironti, 1983. A good study of Musil and science.

Moore, Gene M. *Proust and Musil: The Novel as Research Instrument.* New York: Garland, 1985. Competent comparative literature study.

Müller, Gotz. *Ideologiekritik und Metasprache in Robert Musils Roman "Der Mann ohne Eigenschaften."* Munich: Fink, 1972. A neo-Marxist study of parodistic work of intertextuality in the novel.

Mulot, Sibylle. *Der junge Musil: Seine Beziehung zu Literatur und Kunst der Jahrhundertwende.* Stuttgart: Heinz, 1977. Fundamental study of what the young Musil studied and knew.

Nusser, Peter. *Musils Romantheorie.* The Hague: Mouton, 1967. A study focusing on the sense of possibility in the novel.

Osses, José Emilio. *Robert Musil en tres obras sin cualidades.* Santiago: Editorial Universitaria, 1963. Good introduction for the Spanish-language public.

Paulson, Ronald M. *Robert Musil and the Ineffable: Hieroglyphe, Myth, Fairy Tale and Sign.* Stuttgart: Heinz, 1982.

Payne, Philip. *Robert Musil's "The Man without Qualities": A Critical Study.* Cambridge: Cambridge University Press, 1988. A study of Ulrich's existential condition: the discovery of freedom.

Payne, Philip, Graham Bartram, and Galin Tihanov, eds. *A Companion to the Works of Robert Musil.* Rochester, N.Y.: Camden House, 2007. Latest update of Musil studies by a group of the leading specialists.

Pekar, Thomas. *Musil zur Einführung,* Hamburg: Junius, 1997.

———. *Die Sprache der Liebe bei Robert Musil.* Munich: Fink, 1989. The contradictory models of love found in Musil.

Peters, Frederick. *Robert Musil, Master of the Hovering Life.* New York: Columbia University Press, 1978. An interesting introduction to Musil through a psychological study.

Pfeiffer, Peter C. *Aphorismus und Romanstrucktur: Zu Robert Musil's "Der Mann ohne Eigenschaften."* Bonn: Bouvier, 1990. Relates the novel's development to Musil's historical situation.

Pieper, Hans-Joachim. *Musils Philosophie: Essayismus und Dichtung im Spannungsfeld der Theorien Nietzsches und Maches.* Würzburg: Königshausen & Neumann, 2002. Solid study of relationship to Mach and Nietzsche.

Pike, Burton. *Robert Musil: An Introduction to His Work.* Ithaca: Cornell University Press, 1961. The starting point for Musil studies in English.

331

Pott, Hans-Georg. *Robert Musil.* Munich: Fink, 1984. Eclectic study of relation of science to reality.

Pott, Hans-Georg, ed., *Robert Musil: Dichter, Essayist, Wissenschaftler.* Munich: Fink, 1993. Essays dealing with essayism and science.

Rasch, Wolfdietrich. *Über Robert Musils Roman "Der Mann ohne Eigenschaften."* Göttingen: Vandenhoeck & Ruprecht, 1967. Propounded view that utopia could not stand up in the novel to the forces of dissolution. Very influential critic.

Reich-Ranicki, Marcel. *Sieben Wegbereiter: Schriftsteller des zwanzigsten Jahrhunderts; Arthur Schnitzler, Thomas Mann, Alfred Döblin, Robert Musil, Franz Kafka, Kurt Tucholsky, Bertolt Brecht.* Stuttgart: Deutsche Verlags-Anstalt, 2002. Germany's best-known and most influential critic (and he doesn't really like Musil).

Reinhardt, Stephan. *Studien zur Antinomie von Intellekt und Gefuhl in Musils Roman "Der Mann ohne Eigenschaften."* Bonn: Bouvier, 1969. A study of mind and feeling using concepts of the Frankfurt School.

Reis, Gilbert. *Musils Frage nach der Wirklichkeit.* Königstein: Haine, 1983. A defense of the specificity of literary discourse.

Rendi, Aloisio. *Robert Musil.* Milan: Di Comunità, 1963. Good introduction for the Italian-language reader.

Reniers-Servranckx, Annie. *Robert Musil: Konstanz und Entwicklung von Themen, Motiven und Strukturen in den Dichtungen.* Bonn: Bouvier, 1972. Sees the search for a new, future concept of humanity as Musil's starting point.

Rogowski, Christian. *Implied Dramaturgy: Robert Musil and the Crisis of Modern Drama.* Riverside: Ariadne, 1993. Some of the best work on Musil's theater.

Roth, Marie-Louise. *Robert Musil, Ethik und Ästhetik.* Munich: List, 1972. One of the basic works on ethics and the influence of science by one of Musil's most influential critics.

Roth, Marie-Louise, and Pierre Béhar, eds. *Musil an der Schwelle zum 21. Jahrhundert: Internationales Kolloquium Saarbrücken 2001.* Bern: Lang, 2005. Recent papers given by contemporary Musil scholars.

Rottger, Brigitte. *Erzählexperimente: Studien zu Robert Musils "Drei Frauen" und "Vereinigungen."* Bonn: Bouvier, 1973. Musil as experimentalist.

Ryan, Judith. *The Vanishing Subject: Early Psychology and Literary Modernism.* Chicago: University of Chicago Press, 1991. Very insightful study of the relation of psychology and literature in the early twentieth century.

Schaffnit, Hans Wolfgang. *Mimesis als Problem. Studien zu einem ästhetischen Begriff der Dichtung aus Anlass Robert Musils.* Berlin: De Gruyter, 1971. Using reader-response theory to show that Musil conceptualized a new reader.

Schelling, Ulrich. *Identität und Wirklichkeit bei Robert Musil.* Zurich: Atlantis, 1968. Solid historical study.

Schmidt, Jochen. *Ohne Eigenschaften: Eine Erlaüterung zu Musils Grundbegriff.* Tübingen: Niemeyer, 1975. Fundamental study of mysticism in Musil.

Schmitter, Sebastian. *Basis, Wahrnehmung und Konsequenz: Zur literarischen Präsenz des Melancholischen in den Schriften von Hugo von Hofmannsthal und Robert Musil.* Würzburg: Königshausen & Neumann, 2000.

Schneider, Günther. *Untersuchungen zum dramatischen Werk Robert Musils.* Bern & Frankfurt: Lang, 1973. One of the first works on Musil's theater.

Schrader, Monika. *Mimesis und Poiesis: Poetologische Studien zum Bildungsroman.* Berlin & New York: De Gruyter, 1975. Also deals with mysticism.

Schramm, Ulf. *Fiction und Reflexion: Überlegungen zu Musil und Beckett.* Frankfurt: Suhrkamp, 1967. A study of satire with regard to science and technology.

Sebastian, Thomas. *The Intersection of Science and Literature in Musil's "The Man without Qualities."* Rochester, N.Y.: Camden House, 2005. Very readable and lucid book on the question of science.

Seeger, Lothar Georg. *Die Demaskierung der Lebenslüge.* Bern & Munich: Francke, 1969. Study of the novel's denunciation of the corruption of Austrian society.

Sera, Manfred. *Utopie und Parodie bei Musil, Broch und Thomas Mann.* Bonn: Bouvier, 1969. Musil and the critique of the Enlightenment.

Siegel, Martin. *Identitätskrise als Beziehungskonflickt: Robert Musils Erzählungen vor dem Problem gefährdeter Intersubjectivität.* St. Ingebert: Röhrig Universitätsverlag, 1997. Interesting psychological study.

Stern, J. P. *The Dear Purchase: A Theme in German Modernism.* New York: Cambridge University Press, 1995. Essay on Musil dealing with the intersection of history and fiction.

Strelka, Joseph. *Kafka, Musil, Broch und die Entwicklung des modernen Romans.* Vienna: Forum, 1957. Still very interesting, fundamental work for establishing a basic understanding of Musil's modernism.

Strutz, Joseph, and Johann Strutz, eds. *Kunst, Wissenschaft und Politik von Robert Musil bis Ingeborg Bachmann.* Munich: Fink, 1986.

———, eds. *Robert Musil, Literature, Philosophie, Psychologie.* Munich: Fink, 1984.

———, eds. *Robert Musil, Theater, Bildung, Kritik.* Munich: Fink, 1985.

———, eds. *Robert Musil und die kulturellen Tendenzen seiner Zeit.* Munich: Fink, 1983. These and the preceding four volumes contain essays by various Musil specialists.

Strutz, Joseph, and Endre Kiss, eds. *Genauigkeit und Seele: Zur österreichischen Literatur seit dem Fin de siècle.* Munich: Fink, 1990. Essays on the turn of the turn of the century.

Sussman, Henry. *Psyche and Text: The Sublime and the Grandiose in Literature, Psychopathology, and Culture.* Albany: State University of New York Press, 1993. Studies of Musil from the viewpoint of a disciple of philosopher Jacques Derrida.

Swales, Martin. *Studies of German Fiction in the Age of European Realism.* Lewiston, Penn.: Mellen, 1995. Chapter on satire and utopia in Musil.

Taschner, Rudolf. *Musil, Gödel, Wittgenstein und das Unendliche.* Vienna: Picus, 2002. Witty and comprehensible lecture on three versions of the infinite by an Austrian mathematician.

Thiher, Allen. *Fiction Refracts Science: Modernist Writers from Proust to Borges.* Columbia: University of Missouri Press, 2005. A chapter on Musil's use of science.

Thöming, Jürgen C. *Zur Reception von Musil- und Goethe-Texten: Historizität der ästhetischen Vermittlung von sinnlicher Erkenntnis und Gefühlserlebnissen.*

Munich: Fink, 1974. Using reader-response theory to discuss the creation of the readers' expectations.

Vatan, Florence. *Robert Musil et la question anthropologique.* Paris: Presses Universitaires de France, 2000. Insightful work that underscores the importance of anthropology in Musil.

Venturelli, Aldo. *Robert Musil und das Projekt der Moderne.* Frankfurt: Lang, 1988. Good study for situating Musil in modern culture.

Webber, Andrew. *Sexuality and the Sense of Self in the Works of Georg Trakl and Robert Musil.* London: University of London, 1990. Neo-Freudian work on the role of the gaze.

Wicht, Gérard. *Gott meint die Welt keineswegs wörtlich: Zum Gleichnisbegriff in Robert Musils Roman "Mann ohne Eigenschaften."* Bern & New York: Lang, 1984. Study of the possibilities of allegory in Musil.

Willemsen, Roger. *Das Existenzrecht der Dichtung: Zur Rekonstruction einer systematischen Literaturtheorie im Werk Robert Musils.* Munich: Fink, 1984.

Willemsen, Roger. *Robert Musil: Vom intellectuellen Eros.* Munich: Piper, 1985. The two studies by Willemsen represent the explosion of postmodern poetics in Musil criticism.

Zima, P. V. *L'ambivalence romanesque: Proust, Kafka, Musil.* Paris: Le Sycamore, 1980. Studies Musil's critique of language.

Selected Essays and Articles

Allemann, Beda. "Robert Musil und die Zeitgeschichte." In *Literatur Und Germanistik nach der Machtübernahme: Colloquium zur 50.Wiederkehr des 30. Januar 1933,* edited by Beda Allemann, 90–117. Bonn: Bouvier, 1983. By the leading literary Heideggerian of the preceding generation: Musil and history.

Bachmann, Dieter, "Robert Musil. 1880–1942." In *Essay und Essayismus,* 157–92. Sprache und Literatur, no. 55. Stuttgart: Kohlhammer, 1969.

Bachmann, Ingeborg. "Ins tausendjährige Reich." *Akzente* 1 (1954): 50–53. Important essay for the rediscovery of Musil by one of the most important Austrian writers after the war. This issue of *Akzente* is highly recommended.

Barnouw, Dagmar. "Skepticism as a Literary Mode: David Hume and Robert Musil," *Modern Language Notes* 93 (1978): 852–70. Stimulating study of the relation between skeptics of two different centuries, with a good introduction to Hume.

Bauder, Mauthias. "Musil und das Dispositiv der Moderne." In *Moderne/Postmoderne.* edited by Monika Fludernick, 83–99. Trier: Wissenschaftlicher, 2003. For the postmodern approach.

Baumann, Gerhart. "Robert Musil: Die Struktur des Geistes und der Geist der Struktur." *Germanische-Romantische Monatsschrift* 41 (1960): 420–42. An important early essay dealing with Musil's problematic *Geist.*

———. "Robert Musil: Eine Vorstudie." *Germanisch-Romanische Monatsschrift* 34 (1953): 292–316. Influential beginning of Musil criticism after the war.

Bausinger, Wilhelm. "Robert Musil und die Ablehnung des Expressionismus." *Studi Germanici* 3 (1965): 383–89. Deals with the vexing question of Musil's relation to expressionism.

Boehlich, Walter. "Untergang und Erlösung." *Akzente* 1 (1954): 35–50.

Boeninger, Helmut R. "The Rediscovery of Robert Musil." *Modern Language Forum* 37 (1952): 109–19. Beginning of Musil criticism in English.

Braun, Wilhelm. "Musil's *Die Schwärmer,*" *PMLA* 80 (1965): 292–98. One of the first studies to show the ethical meaning of Musil's play.

Carr, Gilbert J. "The 'Hapsburg Myth' Ornament and Metaphor: Adolf Loos, Karl Kraus, and Robert Musil." *Austria Studies* 15 (2007): 65–79. Recent study of cultural history.

Castex, Elisabeth. "Probleme und Ziele der Forschung am Nachlass Robert Musils." *Colloquia Germanica* 10 (1976/77): 267–79. Marks a moment when Musil's studies have taken on a definite shape.

Coetzee, J. M. "Robert Musil's *Diaries.*" In *Stranger Shores: Literary Essays, 1986–1999,* 104–22. London: Secker & Warburg, 2001. The nuanced opinions of a Nobel Prize–winner who takes his distance.

Cohn, Dorrit. "Psyche and Space in Musil's 'Vollendung der Liebe." *Germanic Review* 49 (1974): 154–68.

———. "Psycho-Analogies: A Means for Rendering Consciousness in Fiction." In *Probleme des Erzählens in der Weltliteratur: Festschrift für Käte Hamburger,* edited by Fritz Martini, 291–302. Stuttgart: Klett, 1971. Fundamental study by one of the best critics of the rhetoric of fiction.

Desportes, Yvon. "Etude comparative d'un style et d'une philosophie: Une oeuvre de Musil à la lumière de Mach." *Revue d'Allemagne* 6 (1974): 79–90. More on Mach.

Dipert, Randall R. "Mathematics in Musil." In *Writing the Austrian Traditions,* edited by Wolfgang Huemer and Marc-Oliver Schuster, 143–59. Edmonton: Wirth-Institute for Austrian and Central European Studies, 2003. Very useful for those whose grasp of mathematics is not on a par with Musil's.

Erickson, Susan J. "Essay/body/fiction: The Repression of an Interpretive Context in an Essay of Robert Musil." *German Quarterly* 56 (1983): 580–93. Interesting postmodern reading of repression in the work of the text.

Erkhart, Claus. "Le poids de la mémoire: Quelques réflexions sur la nouvelle 'Tonka' de Robert Musil." *Germanica* 33 (2003): 57–75.

Feger, Hans. "Die Moral des nächsten Schritts: Von der Lüge im aussermoralischen Sinn bei Robert Musil." *Monatshefte für Deutschsprachige Literatur und Kultur* 97 (2005): 78–100. Ethical criticism returns in the new millennium.

Fischer, Ernst. "Das Werk Robert Musils: Versuch einer Würdigung." *Sinn und Form* 9 (1957): 851–901. Long study by the most influential Marxist of the time.

Frank, Manfred. "Auf der Suche nach einen Grund: Über den Umschlag von Erkenntiskritik in Mythologie bei Musil." In *Mythos und Moderne,* edited by Karl Heinz Bohrer, 318–62. Frankfurt: Suhrkamp, 1983. One of the best modern critics on the question of epistemology in Musil.

Freese, Wolfgang. "Robert Musil als Realist: Ein Beitrag zur Realismus-Diskussion." *Literatur und Kritik* 9 (1974): 514–44.

———. "Zur neueren Musil-Forschung: Ausgaben and Gesamtdarstellungen." *Text + Kritik* 21/22 (1983): 86–144. Includes a lively evaluation of the preceding years of Musil research.

Goldgar, Harry. "The Square Root of Minus One: Freud and Musil's Törless." *Comparative Literature* 7 (Spring 1965): 126–30.

Harrington, Austin. "Robert Musil and Classical Sociology." *Journal of Classical Sociology* 2 (2003): 59–76. From a sociologist's viewpoint.

Hickman, Hannah. "Freud, Musil and Gestalt Psychology." *Austrian Studies* 3 (1992): 95–108. Very good study for an understanding of Musil's relation to psychoanalysis and psychology.

Huber, Lothar. "Robert Musils *Törless* und die Krise der Sprache." *Sprachkunst: Beiträge zur Literaturwissenschaft* 4 (1973): 91–99. One of the most cited articles in the discussion of Musil's view of language.

Hunt, Alina C. "Toward an Unfinalizable Dialogue: Robert Musil's Essayism and Bakhtinian Dialogism." *College Literature* 95 (1995): 116–25. Study of Musil's commonalities with the great Russian literary theorist.

Hüppauf, Bernd. "Musil in Paris: Robert Musils Rede auf dem Kongress zur Verteidigung der Kultur (1935) im Zusammenhang seines Werkes." *Zeitschrift für Germanistik (neue Folge)* 1 (1991): 55–69. On Musil's defense of individualism.

Kermode, Frank. "A Short View of Musil." In *Puzzles and Epiphanies,* 91–107. London: Routledge & Kegan Paul, 1962. One of the best critics in English thinks Musil failed to respect the conventions of closure the novel demands.

Lönker, Fred. "'Die Landschaft nicht im Wagen suchen': Der Frühe Musil und die Psychologie." *Scientia Poetica* 1 (1997): 183–205. A good explanation of why Musil rejected the use of psychology to explain his work.

Margris, Claudio. "Die Odyssee des Robert Musil." *Merkur* 33 (1989): 139–55. The thoughts of perhaps the best Italian Germanist.

Mehigan, Tim. "Moral und Verbrechen: Einige Gedanken über Robert Musils intellektuelle Position." *Wirkendes Wort* 45 (1995): 227–40. Insightful study especially with regard to Nietzsche.

———. "Robert Musil, Ernst Mach und das Problem der Kausalität." *Deutsche Vierteljahrsschrift für Literaturwissenschaft und Geistesgeschichte* 71 (1997): 264–87. Good explanation of the centrality of Mach to Musil's worldview.

Menges, Karl. "Robert Musil und Edmund Husserl: Über phänomenologische Strukturen im *Mann ohne Eigenschaften*." *Modern Austrian Literature* 9 (1976): 200–209. Sheds light on how Musil used Husserl's phenomenology.

Michel, Karl Markus. "Die Utopie der Sprache." *Akzente* 1 (1954): 23–35. Begins the debate on Musil's position on language.

Midgley, David. "Experiments of a Free Spirit: Musil's Explorations of Creative Morality in *Der Mann ohne Eigenschaften*." In *Ecce Opus: Nietzsche-Revisionen im 20. Jahrhundert,* edited by Rudiger Görner and Duncan Large, 111–24. Göttingen:

Vandenhoeck & Ruprecht. 2003. Musil's relation to Nietzsche by one of Musil's best readers.

———. "'Das Hilflose Europa': Eine Aufforderung, die politischen Essays von Robert Musil neu zu lessen." *German Quarterly* 67 (1994): 16–26. On the importance of Musil's essays.

———. "Looking beyond Satire in Musil's *Der Mann ohne Eigenschaften,*" *Austrian Studies* 15 (2007): 96–111. An update of the criticism of Musil's satire and a timely response to postmodern criticism of Musil.

———. "Writing against Theory: Musil's Dialogue with Psychoanalysis in the 'Vereinigungen.'" In *Robert Musil and the Literary Landscape of His Time,* edited by Hannah Hickman, 72–93. Salford, U.K.: Department of Modern Languages, University of Salford, 1991. Excellent reading of Musil showing why psychoanalytic interpretation is a distortion.

Moser, Walter. "The Factual Fiction: The Case of Robert Musil." *Poetics Today* 5 (1984): 411–28.

Muller, Götz. "Isis und Osiris: Die Mythen in Robert Musils Roman *Der Mann ohne Eigenschaften.*" *Zeitschrift für deutsche Philologie* 102 (1983): 583–602. On the question of what Musil attempted to accomplish with Ulrich's relationship to his sister.

Naganowski, Egon. "'Vinzenz' oder der Sinn des sinnvollen Unsinns." *Musil Studien* 4 (1973): 89–122. Relates the farce to theater history and to the Dada movement.

Otten, Karl. "Robert Musil, Schwärmer und Rationalist." *Das neue Forum* 4 (1955): 273–75. Musil's polarities.

Renner, Rolf Günter. "Postmoderne Perspektiven im Text der klassichen Moderne: Robert Musil." In *Die postmoderne Konstellation: Theorie, Text und Kunst im Ausgang der Moderne,* 124–44. Freiburg: Rombach, 1988.

———. "Transformatives Erzählen: Musils Grenzgang im *Mann ohne Eigenschaften.*" *Germanic Review* 66 (1991): 70–80. This and the preceding essay offer postmodern readings.

Robertson, Ritchie. "Musil and the 'Primitive Mentality.'" In *Robert Musil and the Literary Landscape of His Time,* edited by Hannah Hickman, 13–33. Salford, U.K.: Department of Modern Languages, University of Salford, 1991. Excellent reading dealing with Musil, Levy-Bruel, and anthropology.

Roth, Marie-Louise. "Essay und Essayismus bei Robert Musil." In *Probleme der Moderne: Studien zur deutschen Literatur von Nietzche bis Brecht. Festschrift für Walter Sokel,* edited by Benjamin Bennett, Anton Kaes, and William J. Lillyman, 117–31. Tübingen: Niemeyer, 1983. Essayism seen by one of Musil's best critics.

Ryan, Judith. "Validating the Possible: Thoughts and Things in James, Rilke and Musil." *Comparative Literature* 40 (1988): 305–17. This and the following essay are very insightful about the nature of perception in Musil.

———. "The Vanishing Subject: Empirical Psychology and the Modern Novel." *PMLA* 95 (1980): 857–69.

Schwartz, Agatha. "Robert Musil als Dramatiker." *Fidibus* 19 (1991): 1–65. This hard-to-find article is one of the best overviews of Musil's theatrical work.

Shaffer, Clinton. "*In loco parentis:* Narrating Control and Rebellion in Robert Musil's *Die Verwirrungen des Zöglings Törless.*" *Modern Austrian Literature* 35 (2002): 27–51. Very good reading of the rhetoric of fiction in the novel.

Sokel, Walter H. "Kleist's 'Marquise of O.,' Kierkegaard's 'Abraham,' and Musil's 'Tonka': Three Stages of the Absurd as the Touchstone of Faith." *Wisconsin Studies in Contemporary Literature* 8 (1987): 505–16. Background for understanding Musil's interest in Kierkegaard.

———. "Robert Musil und die Existenzphilosophie Jean-Paul Sartres: Zum 'existenz-philosophischen Bildungsroman' Musils und Sartres." In *Literaturwissenschaft und Geistesgeschichte: Festschrift für Richard Brinkmann,* edited by Jürgen Brummack et al. Tübingen: Niemeyer, 1981. An influential reading from an existentialist viewpoint.

———. "Robert Musils Narrenspiegel." *Neue deutsche Hefte* 7 (1960/61): 199–214. Reprinted in *Wort in der Zeit* 9 (1963): 51–64. Early call to recognize the complexity of Musil's writing.

Strelka, Joseph. "'Seinesgleichen geschieht' oder Wie lange noch 'erfindet' man Musil-Kritik? Bemerkungen zum gegenwärtigen Stand der Nachlass-bearbeitung und der Editionsarbeiten am Werk Robert Musils." *Modern Austrian Literature* 9 (1976): 200–209. The unending problem of a proper edition of Musil's work.

Thüsen, Joachim von der. "'Die Portugiesin': Zur Frage der Literarischen Tradition bei Robert Musil," *Neophilologus* 81 (1997): 433–44. Intertextual relationships with Keller, Maeterlinck, and Beer-Hofmann.

Varsava, Jerry A. "Törless at the Limits of Language: A Revised Reading." *Seminary: A Journal of Germanic Studies* 20 (1984): 188–204. A reply to and critique of Lönker's view of the crisis of language.

Venturelli, Aldo. "Die Kunst als fröhliche Wissenchaft: Zum Verhältnis Musils zu Nietzsche." *Nietzsche-Studien* 9 (1980): 302–37. One of Musil's best philosophical critics on Musil's relation to Nietzsche.

Vogt, Guntram. "Robert Musils ambivalentes Verhältnis zur Demokratie." *Exilforschung, Text + Kritik* 2 (1984): 310–38. An excellent response to those who fail to see the complexity of Musil's attitude toward politics.

Weissberg, Liliane. "Versuch einer Sprache des Möglichen: Zum Problem des Erzählens bei Robert Musil." *Deutsche Vierteljahrsschrift und Geistesgeschichte* 54 (1980): 464–84. Uses poststructuralist narrative theory.

Willemsen, Roger. "Dionysisches Sprechen: Zur Theorie einer Sprache der Erregung bei Musil and Nietzsche." *Deutsche Vierteljahrsschrift für Literaturwissenschaft und Geistesgeschichte* 60 (1986): 104–35. Poststructuralist reading of Nietzsche for a reading of Musil.

Williams, Cedric Ellis. "Robert Musil: Vanity Fair." In *The Broken Eagle: The Politics of Austrian Literature from Empire to Anschluss,* 146–86. London: Elek, 1974. Good study of the historical background for understanding Musil.

Ziolkowski, Theodore. "James Joyces Epiphanie und die Überwindung der empirischen Welt in der modernen deutschen Prosa." *Deutsche Vierteljahrsschrift für Literaturwissenschaft und Geistesgeschichte* 35 (1961): 594–616. An attempt to relate Musil to another major modernist writer.

Index

absolutism, aristocratic, 2
activism, political, 13, 309–10
Adorno, Theodor, 15, 214
aesthetics: as comparative model, 163; and ethics, 43, 196–202; modernist, 200–201
algorithms, axiomatic, 162
allegory, rhetoric of, 208
Amazons, Greek legend of, 221–22
ambiguity, 68
"Amsel, Die" (Musil). See *Posthumous Papers of a Living Author* (Musil): "The Blackbird"
androgyne, Platonic myth of, 86
animal imagery: in *The Enthusiasts,* 104; in essays, 208–9, 225–28; in *Three Women,* 132–35; in *Unions,* 89, 90, 91
anthropology, 135, 183
anti-average man, 22
anti-Christ, 238
anti-individualism, 310–11
anti-intellectualism, 161–62, 196
antiliberalism, 158
antimonies, 313
anti-Semitism, 158, 182, 221–22
Apollinaire, Guillaume, 118
Aragon, Louis, 13
Arendt, Hannah, 314
aristocracy, 2, 55
Aristotle, 23, 287, 291
Arnold, Matthew, 321n2
art: death, 217; degenerate, 311; educational role, 189–92; goals, 198–200,

216–18; science versus, 202–3; types, 217. *See also* kitsch
"Art as Technique" (Shklovsky), 200
Artaud, Antonin, 118, 201
artist, function of, 216–18
atoms, 32, 48
Austrian Republic, 158, 173, 310
Austro-Hungarian Empire: *Anschluss* with Germany, 176–80; authentic versus average culture in, 178; fall, 1, 21, 158, 172–73; German culture versus, 173; multicultural nature, 2, 56; Musil's essays on, 172–73; Musil's support of, 7; political regimes, 157–58; post–World War I division, 180; provincialism, 4; scientific practice in, 30
average man, 22, 25, 177
axiomatics, 232

Bacon, Francis, 247
Bakhtin, Mikhail, 136–37, 201
Balázs, Béla, 196
Balzac, Honoré, 51, 245, 321n2
banality, 224–25
Barbusse, Henri, 13
Barnouw, Dagmar, 36, 168
Basel, Switzerland, 313
Baudelaire, Charles, 227
Beaumarchais, Pierre, 241
Beauvoir, Simone de, 69
Becher, Johannes, 10
Beckett, Samuel, 116

Freudian psychology, satires of, 213–14
Friedrich, Hugo, 227, 322n7 (ch. 7)
Friedrich-Wilhelm University (Berlin, Germany), 3
Frisé, Adolf, 43, 302, 322n1

garden imagery, 281–82
Garreta, Guillaume, 40–41
Geist (mind/spirit): and Austria-German union, 176–80; and culture, 28, 174–76; and essay form, 157; experience versus, 166–69; and nation-state, 176–80, 184; and poet, 13; and politics, 309–10, 311; stupidity versus, 315; use of term, 175–76; and war, 278
Gemeinde, 179
Geneva, Switzerland, 15–16
geometry, 161, 162
German culture: Austrian culture versus, 173; and Enlightenment, 155; Musil satires of, 221–22; post–World War I debates over, 313; salvation as leitmotif of, 218
German Empire, 158, 180, 183
Germany, 17: Austrian *Anschluss* with, 176–80; educational decline, 190–92; Nietzschean influence in, 209; political regimes, 157–58; post–World War I publishing in, 214; racism, 183; right-wing ideology, 214–16, 311; scientific practice, 30; sects/cults, 217–18. *See also* National Socialism
"Gesang des Todes, Der" (Musil), 8
"Gesang zur Nacht" (Trakl), 78
Gesellschaft, 179
Gestalt psychology, 5, 45
Gide, André, 52
Giraud, Albert, 297
Gobineau, Arthur de, 181
godlessness, 8
Goethe, Johann Wolfgang, 77, 96, 190, 192, 205, 237–39, 259–60, 321n1

Goethe Prize, 12
Goldgar, Harry, 318n2 (ch. 3)
Gorky, Maksim, 117
Great Expectations (Dickens), 245
"Grigia" (Musil), 305; animal imagery, 206–7, 209; cave death scene, 127; European modernity satirized, 124–27; historical context, 119; ironic distance, 126–27; name symbolism, 120–21; Nietzschean influence on, 120–21, 125–26; religious imagery, 127–28; romantic allusions, 120–22, 126–27; setting, 119, 122, 127; time as employed in, 123–24; title, 120; World War I influence on, 122
Grosz, George, 8, 116, 220
Gruppe 1925, 9–10

Haas, Willy, 10
Habermas, Jürgen, 170
Hašek, Jaroslav, 130
Hacohen, Malachi Haim, 319n6 (ch. 3)
Haffner, Sebastian, 321n5
Hamlet (Shakespeare), 96, 106–8, 115
Hamsun, Knut, 3
Hasenclever, Walter, 10
Hegel, G. W. F., 20, 174, 175, 178, 184, 193, 259–60, 263, 320–21n11
Heidegger, Martin, 127–28, 302, 304, 324n9
Heimat (military journal), 6
Heimatliteratur, 174
Heine, Heinrich, 227
Heisenberg, Werner, 34, 301
Helmholtz, H. L., 41, 44
Hemingway, Ernest, 6, 130
Heraclitus, 256
Herder, Johann Gottfried von, 178, 191, 192, 321n1
Herf, Jeffrey, 167
historicism, 119–20, 223, 264
Hitler, Adolf, 12, 15, 204, 229, 275, 313. *See also* National Socialism

"Temptation of Quiet Veronica, The" (Musil) *(continued)*
93–94; narrative voices, 91; as psychiatric case study, 95–96; theatrical devices employed in, 91
Tertullian, 151–52
Thales, 175
theater, classical, 191, 321n1
Theatre in der Kommandantenstrasse (Berlin, Germany), 12
Théorie physique, La (Duhem), 32
theosophy, 72
Thomson, J. J., 32
Three Women (Musil), 10; *The Enthusiasts* compared to, 120; romantic allusions, 119–20; *Unions* compared to, 119; World War I influence on, 119, 122. *See also* "Grigia" (Musil); "Lady from Portugal, The" (Musil); "Tonka" (Musil)
Thüsen, Joachim von der, 320n3 (ch. 5)
Tieck, Ludwig, 120
Time and Being (Heidegger), 324n9
Tiroler Soldaten-Zeitung (military journal), 6
Tolstoy, Leo, 271
"Tonka" (Musil): criticism of, 137; Dostoyevsky's "Krotkaya" compared to, 137–39, 140, 146–47; dream imagery, 144–46; epiphany, 152–53; epistemological quest, 38, 141, 142–44; ethics and truth in, 149–53; faith in, 151–53; memory images, 139–41; narration, 138–42, 144, 146–47, 153; narrative order, 142; Nietzschean influence on, 150; perspectivism, 146–49; reality principle in, 146; reverse perspective needed for, 137; science and complexity in, 163; setting, 119; thread metaphor, 149; time adverbs as used in, 141
totalitarianism, 158

Tractatus (Wittgenstein), 10, 29–30, 41–42
Trakl, Georg, 78, 80
transcendence, 88, 270, 322n7 (ch. 7)
Traumnovelle (Schnitzler), 64
Treatise of Human Nature, A (Hume), 36–37
Triebpsychologie, 300
Twilight of the Idols, The (Nietzsche), 20

Über die Dummheit (Musil), 14, 313–16
"Über Robert Musils Bücher" (Musil), 87
Übermensch (superman), 26, 27, 29
Ubu roi (Jarry), 118
Ulysses (Joyce), 307
Unbearable Lightness of Being (Kundera), 307
Unions: Two Stories (Musil), 6, 83–96; *The Enthusiasts* compared to, 99, 108; as experimental fiction, 83–84; irony, 108; science/humanism integrated in, 84; *Three Women* compared to, 119; title, 85; *Young Törless* compared to, 83, 85. *See also* "Perfecting of Love, The" (Musil); "Temptation of Quiet Veronica, The" (Musil)
University of Vienna, 29
Untimely Meditations (Nietzsche), 205
utilitarianism, 288–89
utopianism, 21, 198, 270, 281–82, 285, 302, 315–16

Valéry, Paul, 187–88
Vereinigungen: Zwei Erzählungen (Musil). See *Unions: Two Stories* (Musil)
Verlaine, Paul, 227, 297
Versailles, Treaty of, 313
"Versuchung der stillen Veronika, Die" (Musil). See "Temptation of Quiet Veronica, The" (Musil)